HANDBOOK OF
MENTALIZATION-BASED
TREATMENT

HANDBOOK OF MENTALIZATION-BASED TREATMENT

Edited by

Jon G. Allen and Peter Fonagy

John Wiley & Sons, Ltd

Email (for orders and customer service enquiries): cs-books@wiley.co.uk
Visit our Home Page on www.wiley.com

Reprinted November 2006, January 2007, July 2007

Other Wiley Editorial Offices

John Wiley & Sons Inc., 111 River Street, Hoboken, NJ 07030, USA

Jossey-Bass, 989 Market Street, San Francisco, CA 94103-1741, USA

Wiley-VCH Verlag GmbH, Boschstr. 12, D-69469 Weinheim, Germany

John Wiley & Sons Australia Ltd, 42 McDougall Street, Milton, Queensland 4064, Australia

John Wiley & Sons (Asia) Pte Ltd, 2 Clementi Loop #02-01, Jin Xing Distripark, Singapore 129809

John Wiley & Sons Canada Ltd, 6045 Freemont Blvd, Mississauga, ONT, L5R 4J3, Canada

Wiley also publishes its books in a variety of electronic formats. Some content that appears
in print may not be available in electronic books.

Library of Congress Cataloging-in-Publication Data:

Handbook of mentalization-based treatment / edited by Jon G. Allen
and Peter Fonagy.
        p. cm.
    Includes bibliographical references and index.
    ISBN-13: 978-0-470-01560-5 (cloth : alk. paper)
    ISBN-10: 0-470-01560-8 (cloth : alk. paper)
    ISBN-13: 978-0-470-01561-2 (pbk. : alk. paper)
    ISBN-10: 0-470-01561-6 (pbk. : alk. paper)
    1. Psychotherapy.   2. Mental healing.   I. Allen, Jon G.   II.
Fonagy, Peter, 1952-   .
        [DNLM: 1. Psychotherapy – methods.   2. Mental Healing.   3. Men-
tal Processes.   4. Psychoanalytic Theory.   5. Self Concept.
    WM 420 H23173 2006]
    RC480.5.H36 2006
    616.89′14 – dc22

2006012598

British Library Cataloguing in Publication Data

A catalogue record for this book is available from the British Library

ISBN-13: 978-0-470-01560-5 (HB)   978-0-470-01561-2 (PB)

Typeset in 10/12pt Times by Laserwords Private Limited, Chennai, India

To Yvonne

–J. G. A.

To Fran and Nina

–P. F.

CONTENTS

ABOUT THE EDITORS

Jon G. Allen is Senior Staff Psychologist at The Menninger Clinic in Houston, Texas, holds the Helen Malsin Palley Chair in Mental Health Research and is Professor of Psychiatry in the Menninger Department of Psychiatry and Behavioral Sciences at the Baylor College of Medicine in Houston, Texas. He is author of *Traumatic Relationships and Serious Mental Disorders* (Wiley) and *Coping with Trauma: Hope through Understanding* and *Coping with Depression: From Catch-22 to Hope* (American Psychiatric Publishing) and co-author of *Borderline Personality Disorder: Tailoring the Treatment to the Patient* (American Psychiatric Publishing) and *Restoring Hope and Trust: An Illustrated Guide to Mastering Trauma* (Sidran Institute). He is Past Editor of the *Bulletin of The Menninger Clinic*, Associate Editor of the *Journal of Trauma and Dissociation*, and member of the editorial board of *Psychiatry*.

Peter Fonagy PhD FBA is Freud Memorial Professor of Psychoanalysis and Director of the Sub-Department of Clinical Health Psychology at University College London. He is Chief Executive of the Anna Freud Centre, London. He is Consultant to the Child and Family Program at the Menninger Department of Psychiatry and Behavioral Sciences at Baylor College of Medicine. He is a clinical psychologist and a training and supervising analyst in the British Psycho-Analytical Society in child and adult analysis. His clinical interests centre around issues of borderline psychopathology, violence and early attachment relationships. His work attempts to integrate empirical research with psychoanalytic theory. He holds a number of important positions, which include Co-Chairing the Research Committee of the International Psychoanalytic Association, and Fellowship of the British Academy. He has published over 300 chapters and articles and has authored or edited several books. His most recent books include *Psychoanalytic Theories: Perspectives from Developmental Psychopathology* (with M. Target – published 2003 by Whurr Publications), *Psychotherapy for Borderline Personality Disorder: Mentalization Based Treatment* (with A. Bateman – published 2004 by Oxford University Press) and *What Works For Whom? A Critical Review of Psychotherapy Research* (with A. D. Roth – published 2005 by Guilford).

LIST OF CONTRIBUTORS

Jon G. Allen, PhD Helen Malsin Palley Chair in Mental Health Research; Professor of Psychiatry, Menninger Department of Psychiatry and Behavioral Sciences at the Baylor College of Medicine; Senior Staff Psychologist at The Menninger Clinic, Houston, Texas.

Anthony W. Bateman, MD Consultant Psychiatrist in Psychotherapy, Halliwick Unit, St Ann's Hospital, Barnet, Enfield and Haringey Mental Health Trust; Visiting Professor, University College London, UK.

Thröstur Björgvinsson, PhD Associate Professor of Psychiatry, Menninger Department of Psychiatry and Behavioral Sciences at the Baylor College of Medicine; Program Director, Obsessive-Compulsive Disorder Program, The Menninger Clinic, Houston, Texas.

Efrain Bleiberg, MD Alicia Townsend Friedman Professor of Psychiatry and Developmental Psychopathology, Vice Chairman, and Director of the Division of Child and Adolescent Psychiatry, Menninger Department of Psychiatry and Behavioral Sciences at the Baylor College of Medicine; Training and Supervising Psychoanalyst, Houston-Galveston Psychoanalytic Institute; Medical Director, Professionals in Crisis Program, The Menninger Clinic, Houston, Texas.

Susan W. Coates, PhD Clinical Professor of Psychology in Psychiatry, College of Physicians and Surgeons, Columbia University; Member of the Teaching Faculty, Columbia Center for Psychoanalytic Training and Research, New York, New York.

Pasco Fearon, PhD, DClinPsy Senior Lecturer in Psychology, University College London, UK.

Peter Fonagy, PhD Freud Memorial Professor of Psychoanalysis, University College London; Chief Executive, The Anna Freud Centre; Director, Child and Family Program, Menninger Department of Psychiatry and Behavioral Sciences at the Baylor College of Medicine; London, UK.

Glen O. Gabbard, MD   Brown Foundation Chair of Psychoanalysis and Professor of Psychiatry, Menninger Department of Psychiatry and Behavioral Sciences at the Baylor College of Medicine; Joint Editor-in-Chief, International Journal of Psychoanalysis; Training and Supervising Psychoanalyst, Houston-Galveston Psychoanalytic Institute; Houston, Texas.

John Hart, LCPC   Senior Behavior Therapist, Obsessive-Compulsive Disorder Program, The Menninger Clinic, Houston, Texas.

G. Tobias G. Haslam-Hopwood, PsyD   Assistant Professor of Psychiatry, Menninger Department of Psychiatry and Behavioral Sciences at the Baylor College of Medicine; Staff Psychologist and Director of Professional Assessment Services at The Menninger Clinic; Houston, Texas.

Jeremy Holmes, MD, FRCPsych   Consultant Psychiatrist/Psychotherapist, Visiting Professor of Psychotherapy, University of Exeter, UK.

Lisa Lewis, PhD   Associate Professor of Psychiatry, Menninger Department of Psychiatry and Behavioral Sciences at the Baylor College of Medicine; Director of Psychology and Director of Psychotherapy Services, The Menninger Clinic, Houston, Texas.

Melissa Martinez, MD   Instructor, Mood Disorders Center, Menninger Department of Psychiatry and Behavioral Sciences at the Baylor College of Medicine, Houston, Texas.

Linda C. Mayes, MD   Arnold Gesell Professor, Child Psychiatry, Pediatrics and Psychology, Yale Child Study Center; Chairman, Directorial Team, Anna Freud Centre; New Haven, Connecticut.

Jacqueline C. McGregor, MD   Assistant Professor of Psychiatry, Menninger Department of Psychiatry and Behavioral Sciences at the Baylor College of Medicine; Private Practice, Houston, Texas.

Robert Michels, MD   Walsh McDermott University Professor of Medicine and Psychiatry, Cornell University; Training and Supervising Analyst, Center for Psychoanalytic Training and Research, Columbia University, New York, New York.

Lisa A. Miller, MD   Clinical Instructor, Coordinator of Neuroscience Education, Menninger Department of Psychiatry and Behavioral Sciences at the Baylor College of Medicine; Neuroimaging Research Fellow, Mental Illness Research and Clinical Care Program, Veterans Affairs Medical Center; Candidate, Houston-Galveston Psychoanalytic Institute; Houston, Texas.

Richard L. Munich, MD   Bessie Callaway Professor and Vice-Chairman, Menninger Department of Psychiatry and Behavioral Sciences at the Baylor College of Medicine; Vice President and Chief of Staff, The Menninger Clinic; Training and Supervising Psychoanalyst, Houston-Galveston Psychoanalytic Institute; Houston, Texas.

Lois S. Sadler PhD, APRN, BC, PNP   Associate Professor of Nursing, Yale University School of Nursing, New Haven, Connecticut.

John Sargent, MD   Professor of Psychiatry and Pediatrics, Menninger Department of Psychiatry and Behavioral Sciences at the Baylor College of Medicine; Director of Child and Adolescent Psychiatry, Ben Taub General Hospital, Houston, Texas.

Carla Sharp, PhD   Assistant professor, Child and Family Program, Menninger Department of Psychiatry and Behavioral Sciences at the Baylor College of Medicine, Houston, Texas.

Arietta Slade, PhD   Professor of Clinical and Developmental Psychology, The City College and Graduate Center of the City University of New York; Associate Research Scientist, Yale Child Study Center; Roxbury, Connecticut.

April Stein, PhD   Assistant Professor of Psychiatry, Menninger Department of Psychiatry and Behavioral Sciences at the Baylor College of Medicine; Program Director, COMPAS Program, The Menninger Clinic, Houston, Texas.

Helen Stein, PhD   Consultant, New York State Psychiatric Institute, Center for the Study of Trauma and Resilience; Private Practice, New York, New York.

Mary Target, PhD   University Reader, Psychoanalysis Unit, University College London; Professional Director, The Anna Freud Centre, London, UK.

Stuart W. Twemlow, MD   Professor of Psychiatry, Menninger Department of Psychiatry and Behavioral Sciences at the Baylor College of Medicine; Editor-in-Chief, International Journal of Applied Psychoanalytic Studies; Medical Director, HOPE Program, The Menninger Clinic, Houston, Texas.

Laurel L. Williams, DO   Assistant Professor of Psychiatry, Menninger Department of Psychiatry and Behavioral Sciences at the Baylor College of Medicine; Assistant Director of Residency training, Child and Adolescent Psychiatry; Director of the Baylor Child, Adolescent and Family Clinic; Houston, Texas.

FOREWORD

Susan W. Coates

What do the following anecdotes have in common?

A boy, observed by Kanner, is enjoying a summer day at the beach. He spots something in the distance that captures his interest. Off he goes, straight toward the goal. But on the way he steps over everything in his path: blankets, news-papers, hands, feet, torsos.

A mother observing a videotape of her son crying is asked what she thinks is going on. She replies, "He always does that, he's OK."

A boy, age 8, notices a scowl on his mother's face and asks, "Mommy are you angry at me or are you just in a bad mood or upset about something else?"

A mother observes a videotape of her daughter at school having a temper tantrum and reflects that she thought her daughter was upset that day because she was getting a cold and was feeling exhausted and sick.

These four disparate anecdotes can be examined from the vantage point provided by the comparatively new concept of "mentalization." The first and second are examples of the absence of mentalization, and the third and fourth indicate high levels of mentalization. Mentalization can be defined as keeping one's own state, desires, and goals in mind as one addresses one's own experience; and keeping another's state, desires, and goals in mind as one interprets his or her behavior. Simply put, each of us has the capacity to be a simple self, a self that experiences the world directly – for example, feels cold, happy, angry, and so forth. But we also can access a more complex self: a self that looks at itself, a self that takes itself as an object of thought and reflection – for example, I see that I was depressed or excited when I said or did such and such a thing. In Jon Allen's apt phrase, mentalization can be thought of as having empathy for oneself.

In the first anecdote, the boy is autistic. His behavior, which utterly though not maliciously disregards the feelings, indeed even the existence, of his fellow beach-goers, is a classic example of what traditionally has been called "mindblindness." Mindblindness has long been considered a hallmark of autistic functioning, though perhaps this view may need some amending. In any event, mindblindness can be thought of as the opposite of mentalization. In the second anecdote, the mother sees that her son is upset but she negates the meaning of the upset and makes no effort to understand what he is experiencing.

The third anecdote shows that the child understands that his mother's behavior is determined by her state of mind. He recognizes that he cannot know by just looking at her what she is actually feeling. He is concerned that she may be angry at him, but he realizes that her expression may be about something else. In the fourth anecdote, the mother sees that her daughter is upset and works to understand why her daughter's equilibrium might have been undermined by feeling sick that day.

It may be held a virtue of the concept of mentalization that it lends itself to such diverse applications and that in each instance the concept provides an incisive way of looking into the heart of the matter. What additionally makes the new concept so exciting in my view is that it comes to us on the basis of solid, replicable research into fundamental issues in development. I refer here to the broad program of research carried out by Peter Fonagy and his collaborators.

As most prospective readers of this volume undoubtedly know, the origin of the new concept is to be found in the study of attachment. Let me briefly recap the development of modern attachment theory. John Bowlby provided the original theoretical statement of attachment as the fundament for human relatedness. Mary Ainsworth, in turn, invented a novel procedure whereby the status of attachment could be reliably measured in one-year-old toddlers, with the result correlated with maternal behaviors during infancy. Mary Main, in her turn, devised a research instrument, the Adult Attachment Interview, which could predict the quality of the child's attachment on the basis of the parents' individual responses to questions about their parents. Between the contributions of these three seminal figures, it has become possible – indeed necessary – to think of the development of object relations in the child in a multi-generational context that includes the parents and their own remembered experiences. Remarkably, this new body of thought was reliably anchored in empirical studies of great robustness. Thinkers and observers were out of the armchair and into the psychology laboratory and the clinic.

It was in this general context that Peter Fonagy and his collaborators made a startling new discovery. It turns out that mentalization, defined as the capacity to be specifically aware of mental states as such and to use this awareness in regulating affect and negotiating interpersonal relationships, provides a critical link in the transmission of attachment security across generations. That is to say, mothers and fathers who scored high on this dimension on the Adult Attachment Interview tended to have children who were secure. And, importantly, this was true even though the parents might themselves have had a history of past trauma or current unresolved grief, factors which were otherwise likely to impact negatively on the security of their children. Insight is not only good for you but it is even better for your children.

But there was more. Fonagy and his collaborators had tumbled to something not only important, but generative. It rapidly emerged that secure children in their turn tended to develop the rudiments of the capacity for mentalization faster than did their insecurely attached peers. Quite separately, it also emerged that in adult borderline patients the capacity for mentalization appeared to be severely compromised, and that this deficit could be meaningfully linked to their own history of abuse and neglect as children. Finally, it appeared that the concept of mentalization could be utilized to provide a unique lens for interpreting the data from a large outcome study of the treatment of children conducted at the Anna Freud Centre.

In summary, mentalization has been empirically linked to important findings in development, in the understanding of psychopathology, and in the conceptualization of treatment efficacy for both children and adults – and here I have only mentioned the very first findings of what has become a vast research effort on multiple fronts. What we have here is something of a conceptual revolution, one that is still underway. The prospects for further research and exploration are truly exciting. In this volume distinguished clinicians take the next step to explore the usefulness of the concept of mentalization to clinical work in a broad spectrum of settings and in relation to varieties of clinical challenges. I expect the reader of this volume will be as tantalized as I have been by the important new vistas that their contributions open up.

PREFACE

Jon G. Allen and Peter Fonagy

In advocating mentalization-based treatment we claim no innovation. On the contrary, mentalization-based treatment is the least novel therapeutic approach imaginable: it addresses the bedrock human capacity to apprehend mind as such. Holding mind in mind is as ancient as human relatedness and self-awareness. Nonetheless, fostering the capacity to mentalize might be our most profound therapeutic endeavor: cultivating a fully functioning mind is a high aspiration indeed.

Might we claim that *all* psychotherapy is mentalization-based treatment? Hardly. This would be akin to the claim that all therapy that influences behavior is behavior therapy, that all therapy that influences thinking is cognitive therapy, or that all therapy that influences intrapsychic conflict is psychodynamic psychotherapy. All therapy requires mentalizing on the part of the patient and the therapist; mentalization-based *treatment* entails explicit attention to mentalizing in the therapeutic process; and mentalization-based *therapy* structures attention to mentalizing through specific therapist training and treatment manuals. This volume aims to interest clinicians of diverse theoretical orientations in mentalization-based treatment and to acquaint them with mentalization-based therapy.

The concept of mentalization emerged in the psychoanalytic literature in the late 1960s but diversified in the early 1990s when Simon Baron-Cohen, Chris Frith, and others applied it to neurobiologically based deficits in autism and schizophrenia and, concomitantly, Peter Fonagy and his colleagues applied it to developmental psychopathology in the context of attachment relationships gone awry. This volume reviews work in the latter tradition, wherein mentalizing is construed as a dynamic skill, the performance of which is compromised, for example, in the context of intense affects associated with conflicts in attachment relationships.

Following the principle that psychotherapeutic interventions be tailored directly to psychopathological processes, mentalization-based therapy was first developed and researched in the treatment of individuals with borderline personality disorder, a condition that often develops in conjunction with trauma in attachment relationships. More recently, befitting its developmental origins, mentalization-based therapy is being applied to families and mother-infant dyads. Currently, we are expanding the realm of mentalization-based treatment, exemplified by programs at The Menninger Clinic, which specializes in time-limited inpatient treatment for patients with heterogeneous treatment-resistant psychopathology. We are promoting a cohesive conceptual framework throughout the clinical services by employing attachment theory and the concept of mentalizing. In the process, we are educating staff members, patients, and their family members about mentalizing such that the word is becoming part of everyday parlance. But this aspiration for conceptual cohesiveness faces the challenge of integrating mentalizing with what is perforce an eclectic treatment program that includes psychopharmacology, a therapeutic milieu, individual and group psychotherapy, as well as cognitive behavior therapy and dialectical behavior therapy, all implemented by a multi-professional team with the patient at the center. Thus this volume evolved from the authors' collective experience in employing the concept of mentalizing to assist in understanding diverse forms of psychopathology as well as our experience in conducting a range of mentalization-based interventions and our ever-expanding experience in educating mental health professionals and consumers alike.

While mentalizing is a basic human capacity that we generally take for granted, the concept is surprisingly hard to pin down. Thus, in Part I, "Conceptual and Clinical Foundations," Jon Allen's chapter launches the volume by explicating the concept and its distinctiveness from related terms. Jeremy Holmes continues this clarification in a chapter articulating the place of mentalizing in psychoanalytic theory where it remains rooted.

In launching Part II, "Developmental Psychopathology," Peter Fonagy's chapter establishes the scientific foundation for mentalization-based treatment. Fonagy ensconces an integrative neurobiological theory of mentalizing in an evolutionary framework as a prelude to reviewing research on the development of mentalizing in the attachment context and in social relationships more generally. Carla Sharp's chapter follows naturally, reviewing contemporary research to show how childhood psychopathology can be understood through the lens of mentalizing deficits, in the course of which she delineates different forms of mentalizing impairments. Glen Gabbard's chapter concludes this section by explaining how neurobiological research enhances our understanding of mentalizing deficits in the development and treatment of borderline personality disorder.

Part III, "Incorporating Mentalizing in Established Treatments," illustrates how explicit attention to mentalizing can be integrated into different therapeutic approaches. Richard Munich shows how a focus on mentalizing can be incorporated into psychodynamic psychotherapy, poignantly illustrated by a particularly challenging interaction with a treatment-resistant patient. Thröstur Björgvinsson and John Hart systematically address a common question: how does mentalization relate to cognitive therapy? Continuing in this vein, Lisa Lewis's chapter forges links between mentalizing and dialectical behavior therapy skills training as enhanced by interventions from positive psychology.

Part IV, "Mentalization-based Therapy," presents a range of applications wherein mentalizing is a relatively exclusive focus of treatment. The section fittingly begins with the developmental roots of mentalization-based therapy, Anthony Bateman and Peter Fonagy's evidence-based treatment program for persons with borderline personality disorder. The section continues with the next developmental step, Short-term Mentalization and Relational Therapy (SMART), an integrative approach to family therapy for children and adolescents. Pasco Fearon and colleagues' chapter summarizing the treatment approach is followed by Laurel Williams and colleagues' discussion of the challenges in training therapists to conduct mentalization-based therapy. Next, Efrain Bleiberg's chapter conveys the benefits of employing mentalizing as a conceptual framework for a specialized inpatient program for professionals in crisis. The section concludes with Toby Haslam-Hopwood and colleagues' chapter describing their psycho-educational program designed to foster a therapeutic alliance in mentalization-based treatment by explaining the concept to patients and their family members – an endeavor that is having the unanticipated benefit of clarifying the concept for the authors.

The concluding section, "Prevention," illustrates the broader social implications of problems in mentalizing. Lois Sadler and colleagues summarize their pioneering work in helping mothers engage in mentalizing interactions with their at-risk infants to provide a foundation in attachment that will initiate a more positive developmental trajectory. Stuart Twemlow and Peter Fonagy describe a school-based program that effectively decreased bullying by enhancing mentalizing at a social-system level. The volume concludes with Helen Stein's chapter employing a research-based case study to illustrate the whole point of mentalization-based treatment: promoting resilience.

We are in the fortunate position to present these clinical applications of mentalization-based treatment by virtue of more than a decade-long international collaboration of colleagues in the Child and Family Program, the brain child of Efrain Bleiberg which Peter Fonagy and Jon Allen were privileged to lead in its formative years when The Menninger Clinic remained in Topeka, Kansas. Now, in the context of the clinic's relocation to Houston, Texas, the Child and Family Program is flourishing in the context of a consortium of extraordinarily supportive and intellectually stimulating institutions: the Anna Freud Centre, University College London, the Yale Child Study Center, the Menninger Department of Psychiatry and Behavioral Sciences at the Baylor College of Medicine, and The Menninger Clinic. This work would not have been possible without the administrative support of these institutions and innumerable collaborators whom the contributors to this volume are proud to represent.

PART I

CONCEPTUAL AND CLINICAL FOUNDATIONS

1

MENTALIZING IN PRACTICE

Jon G. Allen

I will need this entire chapter to explicate the concept of mentalizing (Fonagy, 1991), but we can get started with the idea of attending to states of mind in oneself and others – in Peter Fonagy's apt phrase, holding mind in mind. I had been working intellectually with this concept for many months before I noticed how it was influencing the way I was conducting psychotherapy with traumatized patients. I remember the session in which theory and practice came together in my mind:

> The patient, a man in his mid-forties, had been hospitalized for treatment of depression and panic attacks associated with intrusive posttraumatic memories stemming from sexual assaults in his childhood. A much older neighborhood boy had tormented and terrorized him. The patient characterized this older boy as being "wild-eyed and crazy," and the patient had been utterly convinced that his tormentor would follow through on his threat to set the family's house on fire if he were to tell his parents about the abuse.

> Profoundly ashamed, the patient had not told anyone about the experience, and he had largely succeeded in putting it out of mind. Although he had struggled with depression episodically throughout his adult life, he had maintained loving relationships with his wife and three children, and he had become a partner in a highly successful medical practice. All went well until he was blindsided by what he perceived to be a frivolous lawsuit, which turned out to be a nightmare. The aggressive legal scrutiny of his practice that ensued led him to feel as if he were being "raped." Only after weeks of a downhill slide did he associate this intrusive psychological assault in adulthood with his childhood trauma.

> Naturally, the patient had been doing everything possible to block the traumatic images and associated body sensations from his mind – including abusing alcohol

Handbook of Mentalization-Based Treatment. Edited by J. G. Allen and P. Fonagy.
© 2006 John Wiley & Sons, Ltd.

and sleeping medicine, which only exacerbated his growing depression. As his avoidant defenses gradually eroded, the intrusive childhood memories came to the fore. But these memories had an unreal quality that made them even more disturbing. The patient wanted my help in getting rid of these memories. How was I to proceed?

As trauma therapists of many theoretical persuasions would have done, I asked him to talk through the particular childhood assault he remembered most clearly; he did so without undue anxiety, but he was dissociatively detached from the memory. As many therapists might have done, I asked him to tell it again as if it were happening to him at the moment. He recounted the event far more emotionally and, afterward, indicated that the experience had taken on a greater sense of reality. Remembering was painful, but not overwhelming. He was able to calm himself by imagining that he was sitting on a boulder overlooking a mountain range.

At this juncture, the point of mentalizing became clearer to me: rather than putting the traumatic memories *out* of mind, the patient would be better served by being able to have the memories *in* mind – as emotionally bearable and meaningful experience, albeit unpleasant and painful. Hence, I suggested that he change strategies: rather than endeavoring to avoid thinking about the traumatic event, he could practice bringing it to mind deliberately without becoming too immersed in it, and then he could use his comforting imagery to relax and put the memory out of mind. He was able to do so and, in the process, developed a sense of control over his mind. Thereafter, rather than being blindsided and panicked by the intrusion of the memory, when the inevitable happened and something reminded him of the trauma, he was able to tolerate the images, work with them, and put them out of mind. He no longer feared his own mind, as patients with posttraumatic stress disorder invariably do; rather, he developed a sense of confidence that he could cope with whatever came to mind.

I would characterize my therapeutic intervention as an exposure-based procedure (Foa & Kozak, 1986), but I now prefer to conceptualize the process as assisting the patient to mentalize rather than merely "desensitizing" him, an unduly passive concept. Desensitization entails new learning: the patient becomes desensitized by virtue of engaging in the active work of mastery through mentalizing.

Another example typical of trauma treatment:

A woman in her early thirties was hospitalized in the aftermath of a suicide attempt precipitated by her husband's announcing his intention to file for divorce after he ultimately became fed up with her abusive rages. Her parents had divorced when she was eight years old. She lived with her mother for several months afterwards, but her father fought for custody after her mother's depression and alcohol abuse escalated to the point that the patient was seriously neglected. For the patient, the situation went from bad to worse. Her father had remarried quickly after the divorce; the patient's stepmother was resentful of her presence; and the stepmother became increasingly abusive psychologically and physically. As her father's new marriage deteriorated, he spent more time away from the home. As resentful as she had become of her mother, the patient berated her for being "palmed off" on her father while simultaneously pleading with her mother to take her back. Her mother consistently refused.

The patient was talented and engaging and, despite this history of attachment trauma, she did not give up on seeking attachments. She was able to maintain solid friendships and supportive relationships with teachers and coaches. She earned a university scholarship, enabling her to leave home at the first opportunity. She married soon after graduation, indicating in the psychotherapy that her husband had appealed to her as a "strong, silent type" – a protector. The "silent" facet proved to be the bane of her marriage; she came to experience her husband as emotionally unavailable, and she felt emotionally neglected. Predictably, the more antagonistically she voiced her resentment, the more her husband withdrew. The patient's behavior became increasingly regressive – downright childlike in her tearful tantrums. Her husband ultimately had enough and planned to end the marriage.

Before I began working with her in the inpatient context, the patient had been in an outpatient psychotherapy process in which she became immersed in reviewing traumatic memories. Unfortunately, this process only seemed to escalate her distress, and her functioning continued to deteriorate. I began working with her in psychotherapy soon after she was hospitalized, and it was apparent that, in light of her regressed functioning, the whole treatment should focus on containment – developing emotion-regulation skills and supportive relationships – rather than further processing traumatic memories. Initially, the patient agreed wholeheartedly with this approach; she was overwrought and exhausted, in part from the previous expressive therapy. Unsurprisingly, her enthusiasm for the process waned as I gently encouraged her to contain her emotions and to focus on coping in the present. Instead, she wanted the consolation she had not received in childhood; indeed, she angrily demanded it.

Plainly, rather than working on the trauma therapeutically, the patient had been re-enacting her traumatic past in her current relationships, with her husband and in the therapy as I, too, seemed emotionally unavailable. The hospital treatment provided an opportunity not only for individual psychotherapy but also for family work to address ongoing problems with her husband and her parents. All this work was sustained by nursing care that supported more adaptive functioning. Confronting her pattern of re-enactment both in the family work and in the individual psychotherapy enabled her to perceive and understand how, unwittingly, she had been undermining the attachments she so desperately needed. Concomitantly, a small shift on both her parents' part enabled the patient to feel "heard" for the first time in her memory. Gradually, the patient learned to express her feelings and assert her needs more effectively, and she moved toward reconciliation with her husband.

Again, there is nothing unusual in this therapeutic approach. I was guided by my belief that symptoms of posttraumatic stress disorder are evoked and maintained by re-enactments of traumatic relationship patterns: these re-enactments evoke the reminders that trigger posttraumatic intrusive memories (Allen, 2005a). The alternative to re-enactment is mentalizing, that is, developing awareness of the connections between triggering events in current attachment relationships and previous traumatic experiences. No less important is the other side of mentalizing: cultivating awareness of the impact of one's behavior on attachment figures.

Of course Freud (1914–1958) could have explained all this to me about a century ago; in promoting mentalizing, I was striving to help my patient remember rather than repeat. Engaging in some amalgam of exposure therapy and psychodynamic psychotherapy, I have not introduced any novel techniques or interventions. Nonetheless, employing the concept of mentalizing has clarified my thinking about what I am doing, bolstered my sense of conviction in the process, and perhaps thereby contributed to my effectiveness in subtle ways.

On the face of it, enjoining mental health professionals to attend to the mental seems absurdly unnecessary. Yet, in light of the increasing hegemony of biological psychiatry with the associated increase in reliance on medication and the concomitant decline in use of psychotherapy (Olfson et al., 2002), we should not underestimate the value of reiterating the obvious: we must keep mind in mind. But we must do more than re-invigorate a waning tradition. On closer inspection, the ostensibly plain concept of mentalizing turns out to be highly complex and invariably confusing, as we continually rediscover in striving to explain it to patients – our best critics (see Haslam-Hopwood and colleagues, Chapter 13). The conundrum, as Dennett (1987) rightly mused: "[H]ow could anything be more familiar, and at the same time more weird, than a mind?" (p. 2). Undaunted, we proceed in the spirit Searle (2004) advocated: "Philosophy begins with a sense of mystery and wonder at what any sane person regards as too obvious to worry about" (p. 160).

This chapter first defines mentalizing and explicates its daunting conceptual heterogeneity; second, sharpens the concept of mentalizing by contrasting it with several related terms; third, highlights the conditions that facilitate mentalizing in clinical practice; fourth, having placed the cart squarely before the horse, makes the case for the value of mentalizing; and, lastly, defends the word.

MENTALIZING IN ACTION

Familiar yet slippery, our concept of mentalizing tends to become all-encompassing, potentially extending beyond manageable bounds. Mentalizing pertains to a vast array of mental states: desires, needs, feelings, thoughts, beliefs, reasons, hallucinations, and dreams, to name just a few. Mentalizing pertains to such states not only in oneself but also in other persons – as well as nonhuman animals, for that matter. And, as a mental activity, mentalizing includes a wide range of cognitive operations pertaining to mental states, including attending, perceiving, recognizing, describing, interpreting, inferring, imagining, simulating, remembering, reflecting, and anticipating.

To recapitulate: assimilating the word, mentalizing, entails grappling with a somewhat paradoxical entangling of the familiar and the unfamiliar, the ordinary and the mysterious. This seems just right: so it is with understanding other persons and oneself. Having got us deep into the thicket, I will now attempt to do some clearing by making a few key distinctions. First, I will contrast "mentalizing" with "mentalization," pleading the case for the active verb. I will also emphasize that mentalizing is suffused with emotion. Then I will grapple with the most vexing form of heterogeneity in the concept: the distinction between mentalizing explicitly (reflectively) and mentalizing implicitly (intuitively).

Mentalizing is Action

Dewey (McDermott, 1981) characterized the distinction between the suffixes "-ing" and "-tion" as "one of the most fundamental of philosophic distinctions, and one of the most neglected" (p. 244). In accord with Dewey and in the spirit of Schafer's (1976) action language, I advocate using the participle (or gerund), "mentalizing," instead of the noun, "mentalization," so as to keep the emphasis on mental *activity* (Allen, 2003). Mentalizing is something we *do* – or fail to do as well as we might. We clinicians aspire to mentalize and we encourage our patients to mentalize.

In the fine print, the *Shorter Oxford English Dictionary* gives two senses to the transitive verb, mentalize: "to give a mental quality to" and "to develop or cultivate mentally." Clinically, we use the word most often in the first sense, to refer to the process of ascribing mental states to the actions of others and oneself. To the extent that our therapeutic efforts are successful, we are mentalizing in the second sense, cultivating our patients' mental capacities. Somewhat more precisely, we can define mentalizing as *imaginatively perceiving and interpreting behavior as conjoined with intentional mental states*. The term, intentional, boils down to this: mental states like thoughts and feelings are *about* something (Searle, 1998); in contrast, a material object is not about anything – a brick just *is*.

Mentalizing is action, and much of mentalizing is something we do interactively. Ideally, while interacting, each person remains attentive to mental states, holding the other person's mind in mind as well as their own. I use the cartoon depicted in Figure 1.1 in educational groups to illustrate simplistically what is in fact, a mind-bogglingly complex dynamic process. And mentalizing interactively in dyads is simple compared to mentalizing interactively in groups – family groups not least.

To reiterate, mentalizing is not only something we do; it is also something we can fail to do. Interacting in the mentalizing mode, we aspire to understand each other as autonomous persons and to influence each other on the basis of our understanding. In the nonmentalizing mode, we can dehumanize and treat each other as objects, becoming coercive and controlling. Mentalizing, we can

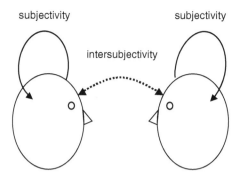

Figure 1.1 Mentalizing interactively

persuade another person to step aside; failing to mentalize, we can nudge him or her aside.

Emotion in Mentalizing

The word, mentalizing, can be misleading to the extent that "mental" connotes coldly intellectual or rational as opposed to "emotional." On the contrary, at its most meaningful, mentalizing is suffused with emotion. Many of the mental states that we are most keen to mentalize are emotional states – in ourselves as well as others. The process of mentalizing emotional states is itself emotional; empathizing is a prime example. Much of the clinical work we do boils down to mentalizing in this ordinary sense: thinking about feelings in oneself and others. And we do not think unemotionally about feelings; we feel about feelings, for example, feeling anxious or ashamed about feeling angry. As one patient in a psychoeducational group wisely put it, in mentalizing, we aspire to *feel clearly*.

Hence we must not pit reason against emotion; rather, I construe mentalizing as a form of emotional knowing (Nussbaum, 2001b). Scientifically minded, we are prone to separate the world of facts from our subjective responses to these facts. Yet we regularly ascribe emotional properties to the world, for example, seeing decayed food as disgusting or an angry face as frightening. Often enough, our emotional perceptions are reasonable and justified:

> Our emotional dispositions can, so to speak, *attune* us to the world around us, enabling us quickly and reliably to see things as they really are, and thus to respond as we should. In short, emotions enable us to *get things right*. (Goldie, 2004, p. 255; emphasis in original)

To underscore this point, one of the earliest forms of mentalizing is social referencing: prior to acquiring language, infants check their caregiver's emotional take on objects and events to see how they should respond. Infants and their caregivers routinely engage in pre-linguistic emotional commentary about the world, and these emotional expressions can be construed as primitive predications (Eilan, 2005), efforts to "get things right." As Damasio (2003) has explicated best, we rely on the informativeness of our feelings far more than we realize, and nowhere is this more true than in mentalizing interactively with other persons.

Mentalizing Explicitly

The easy facet to understand, if not always to do, is mentalizing explicitly, that is, thinking and talking about mental states. As clinicians, we continually mentalize explicitly, for example, thinking and talking (emotionally) about our patients' thoughts, beliefs, emotions, desires, and motives. And we continually engage our patients in this process of mentalizing explicitly, encouraging them to think and talk (emotionally) along with us. We engage our patients in mentalizing explicitly not just about themselves but also about important persons in their life – sometimes including us. Mentalizing explicitly covers a large domain, and I will stake out some of this territory next.

Most fundamentally, as I have already noted repeatedly, mentalizing explicitly pertains to self and others. The processes by which we mentalize explicitly about ourselves and other persons are substantially different (Moran, 2001). Suffice it to say that knowing one's own mind is no less daunting than knowing the mind of another; if self-knowledge were infallible, psychotherapists would be out of business.

We mentalize in different time frames. We often mentalize about current mental states (e.g., thinking about what someone feels at the moment). Yet we also think about past mental states (e.g., wondering why someone else did something). And we can anticipate future mental states (e.g., wondering how someone might feel if we say something). This capacity to shift time frames is crucial to much of our clinical work inasmuch as we endeavor to translate hindsight into foresight. Much of the explicit mentalizing we facilitate is after the fact; we encourage our patients to reflect on reasons for their past actions and to sort out how problematic interactions unfolded. We hope that hindsight will facilitate more effective online mentalizing in similar situations in the future.

Related to differing time frames are variations in scope: we can focus narrowly on a mental state at the moment (e.g., wondering what someone feels) and expand our concern to include recent events (e.g., wondering what happened recently that led her to feel that way). We can further broaden our purview to include past history (e.g., wondering what childhood experience might relate to her proclivity to feel that way in response to a recent event).

Much of our explicit mentalizing takes the form of *narrative* – we are continually creating stories about mental states. Any feeling calls for a story: What was the situation? What happened? How did you interpret it? What did you do? And any feeling calls for a story about other feelings. In psychotherapy, we can always inquire appropriately, "And *what else* did you feel?" Ultimately, the full story behind any mental state – its widest scope – is the whole autobiography. As Wittgenstein appreciated, knowing everything about any given state of mind tells us little:

> Even if I were now to hear everything that he is saying to himself, I would know as little what his words were referring to as if I read *one* sentence in the middle of a story. Even if I knew everything now going on within him, I still wouldn't know, for example, to whom the names and images in his thoughts related. (Quoted in Monk, 2005, p. 105, emphasis in original)

Mentalizing Implicitly

Mentalizing implicitly – being implicit – is more elusive than mentalizing explicitly. To draw attention to the implicit, which is beyond words, we must be explicit, pointing with words. This distinction marks the difference between implicitly knowing how to do something and explicitly knowing that something is the case. When we mentalize explicitly, we do so consciously and deliberately; when we mentalize implicitly, we do so intuitively, procedurally, automatically, and non-consciously. Yet we cannot draw a bright line between mentalizing implicitly and mentalizing explicitly; rather, in Karmiloff-Smith's (1992) terms, we are distinguishing the poles of a gradual process of representational redescription from implicit to explicit, which takes place over the course of development – and over the course of psychotherapy.

As with mentalizing explicitly, we mentalize implicitly with respect to self and others. We mentalize others implicitly, for example, in conversations: we take turns and consider the other person's point of view, to a large extent – when all goes smoothly – without needing to think explicitly about it. We also mentalize others implicitly when perceiving and responding to their emotional states: we automatically mirror them to some degree, adjusting our posture, facial expression, and vocal tone in the process. Were we to attempt all this explicitly, we would come across as stiff and wooden rather than naturally empathic.

If mentalizing others implicitly is elusive, the phenomenon of mentalizing oneself implicitly – unreflectively – is even more so. Here goes: we have an intrinsically ineffable *sense of self* (Stern, 2004). As Searle (2004) put it, "there is something that it feels like to be me" (pp. 298–299). Most fundamentally, our sense of self is intertwined with agency (Marcel, 2003) – a feeling of doing. Our sense of self is also anchored in emotional states (Damasio, 1999). Fonagy and colleagues (Fonagy, Gergely, Jurist & Target, 2002; Jurist, 2005) proposed the concept of *mentalized affectivity* to characterize this emotional sense of self. Mentalized affectivity entails being "conscious of one's affects, while remaining in the affective state" (Fonagy et al., 2002, p. 96) as well as apprehending one's emotional states as meaningful. This form of mentalizing is essential for emotion regulation, which entails identifying, modulating, and expressing affects – the latter not just outwardly to others but also inwardly, to oneself (Fonagy et al., 2002). Not all emotional states entail mentalizing implicitly; on the contrary, we work clinically with patients who are prone to being swept away by emotion, carried along into impulsive action, without any felt sense of self. We encourage such patients to push a metaphorical pause button by mentalizing (Allen, 2005a); that is, we urge them to attend to their emotional state and to sit with their feelings, thereby enriching their sense of self.

Mentalizing implicitly in relation to oneself, then, entails an emotional state connected to the self – a pre-reflective, felt sense of self that is inextricable from the agentive sense of self, the initiator of purposeful action. Mentalizing implicitly, one has a sense of self as an emotionally engaged agent – "what it feels like to be me" in the process of thinking, feeling, and acting.

CONCEPTUAL COUSINS

A slew of terms occupies portions of the territory of mentalizing, for example, self-awareness, introspection, reflectiveness, observing ego, metacognition, and theory of mind. Short of attempting an encyclopedic rendering, I will provide some guidance through a tangled web of concepts: mindblindness, empathy, emotional intelligence, psychological mindedness, insight, mindfulness, rationality, agency, and imagination. I have little interest in making obsessive distinctions; rather, because considerable instructive theoretical and empirical work has been done under the banner of these other rubrics, I hope to shed additional light on mentalizing and especially its adaptive aspects.

Mindblindness

We can begin clarifying mentalizing by considering its antithesis, mindblindness, a term that Baron-Cohen (1995) introduced as follows:

> Imagine what your world would be like if you were aware of physical things but were blind to the existence of mental things. I mean, of course, blind to things like thoughts, beliefs, knowledge, desires, and intentions, which for most of us self-evidently underlie behavior. Stretch your imagination to consider what sense you could make of human action (or, for that matter, any animate action whatsoever) if, as for a behaviorist, a mentalistic explanation was forever beyond your limits. (p. 1)

Baron-Cohen employed mindblindness to characterize the core deficit in autism; in this usage, mindblindness is based on stable neurobiological impairment. Loosening the boundaries of the term, I think mindblindness aptly captures failures in mentalizing more generally. That is, we might think of *dynamic mindblindness* in relation to transient or partial failures of mentalizing, for example, as they arise in conjunction with intense emotional conflicts in attachment relationships. Thus, to a greater or lesser extent, all of us behave mindblindly at times to varying degrees; those with psychopathology are liable to be mindblind more often and to greater degrees.

Empathy

Defined narrowly, empathy entails awareness of emotional states of distress in others – a good swath of mentalizing's territory. Rogers (1951, 1992) brought empathy into prominence in the practice of psychotherapy, and empathy has been the focus of extensive developmental research, especially insofar as it is conducive to pro-social behavior (Eisenberg, Losoya & Spinrad, 2003).

Preston and de Waal (2002) articulated a particularly instructive theory of empathy that illustrates its convergence with mentalizing. These authors proposed a perception–action model, which "specifically states that attended perception of the object's state automatically activates the subject's representations of the state" (p. 4). Preston and de Waal noted the relevance to empathy of the intriguing discovery of *mirror neurons* (in motor and parietal cortexes); these neurons are activated not only when performing actions but also when observing them (Rizzolatti & Craighero, 2004). For example, the same mirror neurons are active when you reach for a cup and when you watch another person reaching for a cup. Hence our mirror neurons afford a kind of automatic motor resonance when we observe others' actions. Analogously, Gallese (2001) summarized indirect evidence suggesting that we simulate not only observed actions but also observed sensations and emotions.

Although the discovery of mirror neurons provides a tantalizing lead to the neural basis of what we experience automatically and implicitly as resonance with others, Preston and de Waal (2002) emphasize that mirror neurons alone cannot provide empathy. Indeed, like mentalizing more broadly, empathy spans a broad range of responsiveness, from more implicit to more explicit. Preston and de Waal proposed a hierarchy of empathic responses, all of which involve subject–object state matching. A precursor to empathy is *emotional contagion*, wherein subject–object emotional matching occurs without self–other differentiation. *Empathy* proper also entails subject–object emotional matching but additionally requires self–other differentiation and emotion regulation, a combination of self-awareness and other-awareness – in effect, awareness of the other in the self. Such empathy can be implicit, intuitive, and automatic. More advanced *cognitive empathy* requires explicit imaginative capacity, actively working with representations of shared experience (including deliberately generating these representations on the basis of one's own memories).

Although empathy is but one facet of mentalizing, it might be the most important. Sometimes when attempting quickly to convey the gist of mentalizing, I point out that if we extended the concept of empathy to include empathy for oneself, the terms would be nearly synonymous.

Emotional Intelligence

Countering two millennia of philosophy that has generally advocated the taming of passion by reason, current work in psychology and philosophy is converging in an about-face, construing passion as reason's ally (Evans & Cruse, 2004; Nussbaum, 2001b). We must leave room for reasonable passion and passionate reasoning. Yet passion remains the *potential* ally of reason, and individuals differ in their capacity to employ passion adaptively – the focus of theory and research on emotional intelligence.

Mayer, Solovey, and their colleagues (Mayer & Salovey, 1997; Mayer, Salovey & Caruso, 2000) characterize emotional intelligence as the ability to reason with emotions, and they carve out four broad domains:

(1) *perceiving and expressing emotion* includes identifying emotions in oneself in relation to physical sensations, thoughts, and feelings as well as identifying emotion in other persons and cultural products;
(2) *accessing and assimilating emotion* in thought entails using emotions to prioritize thinking, judgment, and memory;
(3) *understanding and analyzing emotion* includes labelling emotions, including complex amalgams of emotion and shifts in emotional states; and
(4) *regulating emotion* includes being able to stay open to feelings as well as monitoring and regulating emotions reflectively and adaptively.

Although the idea of emotional intelligence was quickly popularized (Mayer, 2001), the development of well-designed measures akin to IQ tests (Mayer, Caruso & Salovey, 2000) has spurred a wealth of theory and research (Barrett & Salovey, 2002), including sophisticated work on emotion regulation that has particular clinical relevance (Goss & John, 2002; Parrott, 2002). Conceptually, emotional intelligence overlaps not only with empathy but also with Linehan's concept of *wise mind* (Robins, Ivanoff & Linehan, 2001), Ekman's (2003) advocacy of *attentiveness* to feelings, and mentalized affectivity as discussed earlier.

Psychological Mindedness and Insight

The concept of psychological mindedness was originally developed to capture a prospective patient's amenability to psychoanalytic treatment; hence psychological mindedness has been defined in the narrowest sense as "the ability to identify dynamic (intrapsychic) components and to relate them to a person's difficulties" (McCallum & Piper, 1996, p. 52). Albeit with the same intent, Appelbaum (1973) defined psychological mindedness somewhat more broadly: "A person's ability to see relationships among thoughts, feelings, and actions, with the goal of learning the meanings and causes of his experiences and behavior" (p. 36). Thus expanded, the import of psychological mindedness extends far beyond amenability to psychotherapy.

In its initial sense, psychological mindedness would pertain to what we construe as mentalizing explicitly with respect to the self. Yet Farber broadened the concept to apply also to others: "Essentially, psychological-mindedness may be considered a trait, which has as its core the disposition to reflect upon the meaning and motivation of behavior, thoughts, and feelings in oneself and others" (Farber, 1985, p. 170). Moreover, whereas the earlier concepts of psychological mindedness imply a relatively cognitive and intellectual orientation – a capacity for insight – Farber broadened the concept to include an experiential-affective mode, the latter pertaining to persons who demonstrate "an intuitive sensitivity to interpersonal and intrapsychic dynamics and . . . the capacity to use their own feelings to understand and help others" (p. 174). Thus, broadened to include not only awareness of self and others but also explicit and implicit facets, psychological mindedness occupies much of the territory of mentalizing as we have defined it.

Yet a widely used self-report scale developed to assess individual differences in psychological mindedness (Conte et al., 1990; Conte, Ratto & Karasu, 1996; Shill & Lumley, 2002) expands the concept beyond mentalizing. The scale's structure includes not only factors related to psychological awareness (i.e., access to feelings, interest in what motivates behavior, and interest in understanding oneself and others) but also factors directly related to making use of psychotherapy (i.e., an inclination to talk about problems and a capacity for change). Thus operationalized, the psychological-mindedness scale has shown some relation to the capacity to engage in psychotherapy and to benefit from it (Conte et al., 1990, 1996). Yet, consistent with the expanding breadth of the concept, research on the psychological-mindedness scale has gone far beyond the psychotherapy context. Psychological mindedness is positively correlated with a wide range of psychological constructs associated with mental health, including assertiveness and sociability (Conte, Buckley, Picard & Karasu, 1995), openness to experience (Beitel & Cecero, 2003), tolerance for ambiguity (Beitel, Ferrer & Cecero, 2004), mindfulness, empathy, and emotion regulation (Beitel, Ferrer & Cecero, 2005), as well as secure attachment (Beitel & Cecero, 2003). Psychological mindedness also has been shown to correlate inversely with measures of impaired functioning, including alexithymia (Shill & Lumley, 2002), neuroticism (Beitel & Cecero, 2003), depression (Conte et al., 1995), anxiety (Beitel et al., 2005), and magical thinking (Beitel et al., 2004).

Especially in light of its originally close tie to amenability to psychoanalysis, the concept of psychological mindedness has been closely linked to that of insight.

Appelbaum (1973) advocated, however, "distinguishing between psychological-mindedness as a process, and insight as a product of the process" (p. 37). Employing the verb, mentalizing, highlights the process by focusing on mental activity; we place more emphasis on process than content, being more interested in fostering skill in mentalizing than in the specific mental content resulting from exercising the skill explicitly (i.e., particular insights).

Mindfulness

Mindfulness has been defined in the Buddhist literature as "keeping one's consciousness alive to the present reality" (Hahn, 1975, p. 11). With an eye toward empirical investigation, Brown and Ryan (2003) construed mindfulness as "an enhanced attention to and awareness of current experience or present reality" characterized by "especially *open* or *receptive* awareness and attention" (p. 822, emphasis in original). Mindfulness refers to a quality of consciousness irrespective of the objects of consciousness; thus mindfulness overlaps mentalizing to the extent that it entails attentiveness to mental states in particular. Hence, Brown and Ryan's work on mindfulness encompasses some facets of mentalizing, for example, including "receptive attention to psychological states" and "sensitivity to ongoing psychological processes" (p. 823). The time frame of mentalizing is broader, however, inasmuch as one can mentalize about the past or the future, whereas mindfulness is present-centered. Moreover, whereas mentalizing (explicitly) is a reflective process, mindfulness is construed as "pre-reflective . . . perceptual and non-evaluative . . . openly experiencing what is there" (p. 843).

Brown and Ryan developed a brief self-report measure of mindfulness, which is positively correlated with emotional intelligence and a wide range of indices of mental health and general well-being (i.e., higher positive emotionality and lower negative emotionality along with greater vitality, autonomy, competence and relatedness). The authors summarized,

> high scorers . . . tend to be more aware of and receptive to inner experiences and are more mindful of their overt behavior. They are more "in tune" with their emotional states and able to alter them, and they are more likely to fulfill basic psychological needs. (p. 832)

The relation of mindfulness to emotion regulation bears underscoring. As stated earlier, we have used the metaphor of employing mentalizing to push the pause button so as to regulate impulsive emotional behavior (Allen, 2001, 2005a). Similarly, Brown and Ryan (2003) proposed that:

> as a form of receptive awareness, mindfulness may facilitate the creation of an interval of time or a gap wherein one is able to view one's mental landscape, including one's behavioral options, rather than simply react to interpersonal events. (p. 844)

I construe mentalizing with respect to present mental states in self and others as *mindfulness of mind*. I do not believe that the term mindfulness is redundant; on the contrary, emphasizing mindfulness – or in Ekman's (2003) terms, attentiveness – is a good way to cultivate mentalizing. In a sense, our psychoeducational intervention (see Haslam-Hopwood and colleagues, Chapter 13) could be construed primarily as an effort to clarify the territory of mentalizing for the purpose of promoting mindfulness or attentiveness to it.

Rationality and Agency

Explicit mentalizing is a substantial domain of our rationality, that is, our capacity to act on the basis of reasons (Scanlon, 1998; Searle, 2001). Fully rational action is based on attending to an appropriate range of considerations, deliberating among alternatives, and making optimal choices. Clinically, we aspire to promote rationality whenever we urge our patients to think before they act.

Patients sometimes erroneously equate mentalizing with thinking, that is, "using your mind." Plainly, thinking is far broader; we think about much more than mind (Arendt, 1971). Ditto rationality: not all reasoning pertains to mental states. To illustrate, one is behaving rationally, thinking before acting but not necessarily mentalizing, when refraining from drinking and driving to avoid a wreck; one is mentalizing when refraining from drinking and driving to avoid infuriating one's spouse. Conversely, mentalizing goes beyond rationality insofar as it is not limited to reasoning (i.e., to the extent that mentalizing remains implicit and not deliberative).

To the extent that it entails rationality, mentalizing enhances *agency*, that is, the capacity to initiate action for a purpose (Allen, 2006; Allen, Munich & Rogan, 2004). Mentalizing exemplifies agency in promoting self-determination and enhancing our capacity to influence others (Bandura, 2001). By encouraging attentiveness to mental states, we are endeavoring to capitalize on the executive functions of consciousness in general (Dehaene & Naccache, 2001; Jack & Shallice, 2001) and the benefit of effortful control in particular, namely, increased response flexibility (Posner & Rothbart, 1998; see also Fonagy, Chapter 3 of this book).

Imagination

The mind is fundamentally imaginative (McGinn, 2004; Sartre, 2004), and mentalizing is a form of imaginative activity. Mentalizing implicitly, we do not merely see, we *see as*: we do not just see a furrowed brow on the face; we see the furrowing as a scowl, and we see the person scowling as being irritated or downright menacing. Mentalizing explicitly, we find meaning in behavior, generating explanations in the form of creative stories. Much of the imaginativeness involves metaphorical thinking; our language is rife with it (Lakoff & Johnson, 2003). But mentalizing explicitly and creatively is not limited to language; striving to empathize, we imaginatively conjure up visual and other sensory images as we strive to see, feel, and think from others' perspectives; we engage in co-reasoning and same thinking (Heal, 2003).

Intriguingly, mentalizing puts us in a realm between objective reality and fantasy; hence mentalizing's links to Winnicott's (1971) betwixt and between concept of potential space (Bram & Gabbard, 2001). As Ogden (1985) put it, potential space refers to a "frame of mind in which playing might take place" (p. 139). In a similar vein, Fonagy and colleagues (Fonagy, 1995; Fonagy et al., 2002; Target & Fonagy, 1996; Fonagy, Chapter 3) place mentalizing between two modes of experiencing. The *psychic equivalence* mode collapses the differentiation between inner and outer, fantasy and reality, symbol and symbolized: mind = world. Psychic equivalence is evident in dreaming (i.e., the dream is real) and in posttraumatic flashbacks (i.e., remembering is reliving). The *pretend mode* cuts loose from reality; no longer tethered, the pretender is in an imaginary world. By contrast, the *mentalizing mode* implicitly or explicitly entails awareness of the mind's intentionality or aboutness: a mental state – a thought with feeling – is a particular perspective or take on a given reality. In short, being imaginative, mind is *decoupled* from reality while remaining *anchored* to it (Leslie, 1987).

Consistent with the imaginativeness of mind, in our work with patients, we explicitly promote a *pro-mentalizing attitude of inquisitiveness*, coupled with tentativeness and open-mindedness. As Figure 1.2 depicts, effective mentalizing entails restrained or *grounded imagination*, being imaginative without entering into the imaginary. Thus, mentalizing occupies the middle of a continuum: nonmentalizing and failure to decouple is at one end (e.g., being concrete or stimulus bound), whereas distorted mentalizing and failure to anchor is at the other end (e.g., imagination losing touch with reality as in paranoid thinking). The mentalizing attitude of inquisitive curiosity – including asking instead of assuming what someone thinks and feels – grounds imagination. A final twist: because the object of mentalizing is a person – oneself or others – mentalizing entails imagining the imaginative. Capturing the converse of mindblindness, it is no accident that McGinn (2004) gave his instructive book on imagination the title, *Mindsight*.

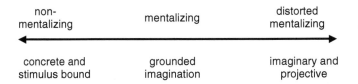

Figure 1.2 Failures of imagination in mindblindness

PRACTICING MENTALIZING

Mentalizing is a skill with substantial individual variations (Fonagy, Steele, Steele & Target, 1997). A host of developmental factors contribute to skill in mentalizing, and adverse childhood experiences – especially trauma in attachment relationships – can undermine its development (Allen, 2001; Fonagy et al., 2002; Fonagy & Target, 1997). Moreover, psychopathology of various sorts at any time in life, such as major depressive episodes, can undermine mentalizing. Yet we contend clinically not only with stable deficits but also with intra-individual variations, the latter consistent with viewing mentalizing capacity as a *dynamic skill* (Fonagy & Target, 1997), the converse of which is dynamic mind-blindness. Moreover, as Sharp highlights (see Chapter 4), impaired mentalizing includes not only *failures* to mentalize (mindblindness in the sense of obliviousness to mental states) but also *distortions* in mentalizing (mind *mis*reading or unrestrained imagination).

Given the potential obstacles to mentalizing, we often need help from others – including psychotherapists – to do so effectively. Often enough, we do not know our own mind. In the process of dialogue with another person, we are able to clarify what we think and feel; that is, we come to feel more clearly. Anticipating Winnicott's (1971) interest in mirroring by two millennia, Aristotle argued this point:

> It is a most difficult thing, as some of the sages have also said, to know oneself ... moreover, we cannot ourselves study ourselves from ourselves, as is clear from the reproaches we bring against others without being aware that we do the same things ourselves ... when we ourselves wish to see our own face we see it by looking into a mirror, similarly too, when we ourselves wish to know ourselves, we would know ourselves by looking to the (other). (Quoted in Nussbaum, 2001a, p. 364)

Mentalization-based treatment is designed to promote positive attitudes toward mentalizing (e.g., a spirit of inquisitiveness) and to enhance skill in mentalizing (e.g., by increasing attentiveness to it and providing practice). To reiterate, focusing on process rather than specific content, mentalization-based therapy is not intended to create specific insights, for example, through discovering the developmental origins of internal conflicts or relationship problems. This is not to deny that insight is important; on the contrary, insight is part and parcel of self-understanding. Rather, the point of mentalization-based therapy is to enhance the patient's capacity to *generate insight* on the fly. An autobiography is not the proper product of psychotherapy; rather, psychotherapy promotes the capacity to construct and reconstruct an autobiographical narrative as suits one's present purposes. As Holmes (1999) aptly put it, "psychological health (closely linked to secure attachment) depends on a dialectic between story-making and story-breaking, between the capacity to form narrative, and to disperse it in the light of new experience" (p. 59). Arendt (2003) perspicaciously recognized that the capacity to think in an open-minded dialogue with oneself depends on the quality of the relationship one has with oneself: "if you want to think you must see to it that the two who carry on the thinking dialogue be in good shape, that the partners be friends" (p. 185).

Any reasonable and effective psychotherapy is likely to enhance mentalizing capacity. Indeed, by facilitating affect modulation and promoting organized thinking, effective psychotropic medication will do so as well. As this volume attests, for example, psychodynamic psychotherapy (Chapters 2 and 6), cognitive therapy (Chapter 7), and dialectical behavior therapy (Chapter 8), all promote mentalizing – if not with the precision of mentalization-based therapy. But the effectiveness of any brand of therapy depends on the therapeutic relationship climate and, just as secure attachment is conducive to the development of mentalizing capacity in childhood, a secure attachment climate promotes mentalizing in psychotherapy. As Bowlby (1988) construed it, the psychotherapist's role

> is to provide the patient with a secure base from which he can explore the various unhappy and painful aspects of his life, past and present, many of which he finds it difficult or perhaps impossible to think about and reconsider without a trusted companion to provide support, encouragement, sympathy, and, on occasion, guidance. (p. 138)

With this quotation in mind, I once made the comment in a psychoeducational group that the mind can be a scary place. A patient presciently responded: "Yes, and you wouldn't want to go in there alone!" Bowlby could not have put it better.

Psychotherapy promotes mentalizing by virtue of providing opportunities for practice, inside sessions and out. Thus conducting psychotherapy is akin to giving piano lessons, perhaps with particular emphasis on playing duets. Piano teachers do not tell their students how to play; they show them and play along with them. Thus piano teachers must have at least a modicum of skill – ideally, a considerable degree.

Of course, all the developmental factors that enhance or undermine mentalizing capacity in patients pertain equally to therapists. Unsurprisingly, being human, psychotherapists' mentalizing capacity varies from patient to patient and from time to time with a given patient (Diamond, Stovall-McClough, Clarkin & Levy, 2003). Munich's experience (Chapter 6) provides an illuminating example of momentary mindblindness illuminated by mentalizing in hindsight. Particularly crucial for patient and therapist are a history of secure attachment and, thoroughly entangled with this, a capacity for affect regulation that affords an optimal level of emotional arousal. Psychotherapists and their patients are in the same boat. To play mentalizing duets effectively, they must rely on whatever developmental competence they have achieved. At any given moment, their performance will depend on the same factors: the extent of secure attachment (i.e., mutual trust in the relationship) and an optimal level of arousal (see Figure 1.3). Thus,

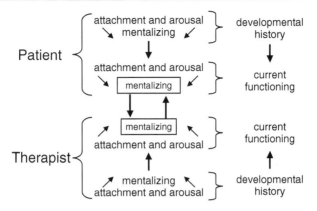

Figure 1.3 Meeting of minds in therapy

much psychotherapeutic effectiveness consists in fostering a safe and a secure climate – a largely implicit mentalizing skill.

WHY MENTALIZE?

I have left relatively implicit in this chapter the conviction that we should promote mentalizing in clinical practice because mentalizing is adaptive. I believe that, ironically, we have tended to underestimate the significance of mentalizing by neglecting its intrinsic value in favor of its instrumental value and by construing its instrumental value too narrowly.

Instrumental Value

We are a social species, and mentalizing lies at the heart of our sociality (see Fonagy, Chapter 3). Awareness of others' mental states enables us to interact effectively, and explicit mentalizing in particular is essential for interpersonal problem solving. Similarly, explicit mentalizing (self-awareness) promotes intrapersonal problem solving, most notably, the capacity for emotion regulation.

What I have said thus far is consistent with the theory-of-mind slant on mentalizing: just as we need to learn "folk physics" to predict and control the inanimate world, we need to adopt the intentional stance as Dennett (1987) characterized it and learn "folk psychology" to predict and control the interpersonal (and intrapersonal) world (Carruthers, 1996; Gopnik & Meltzoff, 1997). No doubt we all mentalize in this sense some of the time, and perhaps some of us mentalize in this sense much of the time. Yet Heal (2003, 2005) cogently challenges the view that we typically use psychological concepts to infer inner states for the sake of predicting and influencing the behaviors such states bring about. She considers this science-minded view to be a serious distortion of what we are generally doing when interacting with others:

Our relations with other people do not have the same structure as our relations with inanimate objects, plants, or machines. We do not deal with our family members, friends, colleagues, or fellow citizens as we do with volcanoes, fields of wheat, or kitchen mixers, namely, by trying to figure out the nature and layout of their innards so that we can predict and perhaps control them. (Heal, 2003, pp. 42–43)

Instead, Heal argues that we employ our psychological understanding to influence others and anticipate their responses only in a loose sense. Generally, we aim not for prediction and control but rather for reciprocal communication and collaboration in joint projects:

What we hope of another with whom we interact is not that he or she will go through some gyrations, which we have already planned in detail, but that he or she will make some contributions to *moving forward* the joint and cooperative enterprise in which we are both, more or less explicitly, engaged. (p. 43; emphasis added)

Well put: *moving forward* together is precisely what we aspire to do in psychotherapy; this is a far cry from theorizing for the sake of prediction and control. Indeed, it is the very unpredictability and uncontrollability of others that renders interactions and joint endeavors worthwhile; without this open-endedness, relationships and projects would go nowhere.

Moving from the quasi-scientific prediction-control model to a focus on mutuality opens the door to a glaringly underemphasized value of mentalizing: the capacity to *be influenced* by others. Mentalizing enables us to be open to the minds of others, amenable to their influence, able to take in other perspectives, and thereby able to be guided into or persuaded of better ways of thinking, feeling, and acting. In short, receptive mentalizing enables us to learn and grow through relationships, including psychotherapy relationships. Hence failure to mentalize might be the basis of much resistance to psychotherapeutic influence. Gergely and Csibra (2005) captured this adaptive facet of mentalizing in elucidating our species-specific capacity for *pedagogy*, which enables us to engage in an extraordinarily rapid and accurate process of teaching and learning.

Intrinsic Value

Mentalizing has many adaptive benefits, but we also do it for its own sake: we thrive on *meeting of minds* from the beginning of life. Reddy (2005) reviewed evidence that, in the first few months of life, infants respond emotionally to attention directed to them, and she proposed that "the awareness of attention to the self may be the most direct and powerful form of attention that is possible" (p. 86). Toward the end of the first year, infants move from dyadic (self–other and self–world) to triadic (self–other–world) relationships, a move that radically transforms the sense of self (Tomasello, 1999). Then they not only follow their mother's gaze to attend to the object of her attention but also begin actively drawing their mother's gaze to objects, for example, by pointing (Franco, 2005). Around the middle of their second year, infants strategically establish what Gomez (2005) calls *attention contact*, for example, actively checking to ensure that they capture their mother's gaze before pointing to the object toward which they desire to direct her attention (Franco, 2005). Attention contact bears intrinsic value: infants not only engage in joint attention for instrumental purposes (e.g., to obtain a desired object) but also for the sheer pleasure of sharing attention with their mother (Heal, 2005). Joint attention also provides the occasion for reciprocal emotional "commenting" as described earlier; as development proceeds, emotional exchanges are often accompanied and refined (but not supplanted) by linguistic communication.

Joint attention is the foundation of mentalizing (Tomasello, 1999); is it a form of mentalizing? Plainly, to be actively engaged in attention contact, infants do not need an explicit psychological concept of attention as an inner mental state. But neither do adults. We psychologically minded mental health professionals are liable to over-mentalize attention, falling prey to mind–behavior dualism (i.e., attention = behavior + mental state). Throughout life, we *perceive* others' attention as a gestalt, embodied in action; we do not *infer* it behind action (Gomez, 2005; Hobson, 2005; Reddy, 2005). Excepting autistic persons, we all become folk psychologists, capable of inferring mental states and explaining actions accordingly; yet we do not thereby transcend our non-inferential (implicit) capacities for attention contact and emotional "commentary," and these remain the basis of our sense of connection with each other in the world.

Over the course of development, as mentalizing capacity becomes increasingly refined, meeting of minds entails increasing levels of intimacy – with the implicit sense of connection established in joint attention potentially enhanced by knowledge gained through conversation (explicit mentalizing). I would characterize mentalizing at its best by two features: accuracy and richness. Interpersonally, mentalizing entails fully grasping the reality of another person. We cannot take this capacity for granted. Keenly aware of our proclivity to distort reality through the lens of our projections, Murdoch (1971) proposed, "We are not used to looking at the real-world at all" (p. 63). I believe further that, mentalizing accurately and richly is most likely to occur in the context of a benevolent and accepting attitude, a proposal that is consistent with the well-established relationship between secure attachment and mentalizing capacity (Fonagy et al., 1991; Meins, Fernyhough, Russell & Clark-Carter, 1998; see also Fonagy, Chapter 3). Murdoch (1971) took this point to the limit in asserting that, when it comes to seeing others accurately, reality is "that which is revealed to the patient eye of love" (p. 39). In the context of psychotherapy, Lear (2003) made the same point (quoting Loewald):

> In our work it can be truly said that in our best moments of dispassionate and objective analyzing we love our object, the patient, more than at any other time

and are compassionate with his whole being. In our field, scientific spirit and care for the object certainly are not opposites; they flow from the same source. (p. 51)

In the same spirit, Kandel (2005) cited an inspiring quotation from the 1769 commencement address at the Columbia University College of Physicians and Surgeons given by Samuel Bard, who was awarded the first MD degree in America for his service to the college:

> In your Behavior to the Sick, remember always that your Patient is the Object of the tenderest Affection to some one, or perhaps to many about him; it is therefore your Duty, not only to endeavor to preserve his Life; but to avoid wounding the Sensibility of a tender Parent, a distressed Wife, or an affectionate Child. Let your Carriage be humane and attentive, be interested in his Welfare, and shew your Apprehension of his Danger. (p. 383)

A tall order: in its ideal form, mentalizing enables intimacy, a loving sense of connection with the reality of another person. Achieving this intersubjective connection in psychotherapy involves what Stern and his colleagues call *moments of meeting* (Stern, 2004). These moments are the rare exception rather than the rule – even in a psychotherapeutic relationship established for the purpose of an open and honest meeting of minds. Viewed in this way, mentalizing is more than a skill; it is a virtue, a loving act (Allen, in press). This is not to say that, in the loving effort to see, we will love all we see. On the contrary, mentalizing at its best reveals the full scope of our humanity and inhumanity.

I have emphasized the intrinsic value of mentalizing in conjunction with inter-subjectivity, ranging from joint attention in infancy to intimacy in adulthood, occasionally evident in moments of meeting in psychotherapy. I also believe that we might extend the intrinsic value of mentalizing into the relationship one has with oneself. In the spirit of Murdoch (1971), we might construe ideal mentalizing also as entailing a loving and compassionate view of oneself as one really is. We could think of self-love in this optimal sense as *bonding* with oneself (Swanton, 2003), an idea that suggests the possibility of establishing a secure attachment relationship with oneself (Allen, 2005a, 2006). To repeat the point just made, I am not suggesting that we love all we see in ourselves either; if secure attachments required it, there would be none.

Misuse and Overuse

A caveat: virtue as it might be, like many other skills, mentalizing can be employed for ill as well as for good. Psychopaths are highly skilled at decipher-ing mental states, a skill they employ manipulatively and exploitatively. Sadists derive pleasure from tormenting others, which also requires some attunement to mental states. Ditto terrorists' terrorizing. Nonetheless, psychopathy, sadism, and terrorism entail a profound but *partial failure* of mentalizing, namely, a failure of empathy in the sense of being able to *identify* with the distress of other persons (Allen, 2005b).

Like many other skills, mentalizing can be employed not only wrongly but also to excess, in a hypervigilant way. A child raised in a violent or abusive household, for example, might become exceedingly attentive to others' mental states so as to anticipate and avoid danger. Or a child may be highly attuned to a parent's depressed mood in aspiring to ameliorate it. Characteristic preoccupation with others' mental states – especially dysphoric states – is likely to be associated with chronic distress. Similarly, excessive preoccupation with one's own mental states could be distressing and counterproductive, for example, leading away from flexible mentalizing into becoming mired in anxious and depressive rumination. In short, as much as we praise it, there is much more to life than mentalizing, and more to do in the world than relating to ourselves and other persons.

WHY "MENTALIZE"?

We have taken a bold step at The Menninger Clinic in transporting the technical psychological construct, mentalizing, into the everyday clinical lexicon. We are using the word not just with our colleagues but also with patients and their family members. But our experience in explaining the idea of mentalizing to colleagues and patients has provided us with a glaring example of the fact that assimilating such unfamiliar words is not necessarily easy, especially when we use an unfamiliar word for a familiar concept. As Mikhail Bakhtin explained:

> The word in language is half someone else's. It becomes "one's own" only when the speaker populates it with his own intention, his own accent, when he appropriates the word, adapting it to his own semantic and expressive intention ... many words stubbornly resist, others remain alien, sound foreign in the mouth of the one who appropriated them and who now speaks them ... Language is not a neutral medium that passes freely and easily into the private property of the speaker's intentions; it is populated – overpopulated – with the intentions of others. Expropriating it, forcing it to submit to one's own intentions and accents, is a difficult and complicated process. (Quoted in Wertsch, 1998, p. 54)

In this chapter, I have raised some reservations about mentalizing that have arisen in the course of our educational efforts. To reiterate, employing an unfamiliar word for a set of familiar phenomena leaves us open to the charge of fobbing off old wine in new bottles. Two retorts: first, the new word has the advantage of spotlighting attention on the concept's territory; second, there is new wine in the bottles. What concerns me more, mentalizing needs humanizing in two senses: first, to the degree that mentalizing connotes an intellectually mental process, we need to emotionalize the concept; second, to the extent that mentalizing connotes a manipulatively instrumental orientation toward relationships, we need to keep its receptive and intersubjective aspects in view. At its best, mentalizing is probably the most loving thing we can do.

In promoting mentalizing, we are not advocating linguistic imperialism; we have no reason to co-opt other terms. Empathy, emotional intelligence, psychological mindedness, mindfulness, and a host of others are perfectly good words in their proper context. But I do believe that mentalizing carves out unique territory. As my review of mentalizing's conceptual cousins illustrates, there is no equivalent concept. Here, the richness of the concept proves to be a double-edged sword. Of all the distinctions I have made among facets of mentalizing, two are most fundamental: self versus other and explicit versus implicit. In light of the considerable differences among the permutations of these two distinctions, one might argue that we need four concepts, not just one. But that would be a mistake; clinically, we strive for integration. We encourage patients to be attentive to similarities and differences in perspectives between self and others. And we encourage explicit mentalizing to direct patients' attention to implicit processes. While we encourage problem solving and conflict resolution through mentalizing explicitly, our ultimate goal is to foster the natural process of mentalizing implicitly for the sake of a greater sense of connection in relationships and with oneself.

We clinicians are impatient; notwithstanding the conceptual thicket I have plunged into here, we are advocating the immediate clinical utility of the concept of mentalizing, not just for us therapists but also for our patients and their family members. But we are not content with our current understanding. Mentalizing is not like scientific reasoning, but a much-needed science of mentalizing is evolving. As this whole volume attests, of all the conceptual cousins, mentalizing is most thoroughly anchored in multiple overlapping domains of scholarly literature, psychological theory, and scientific research: philosophy (i.e., philosophy of mind and ethics, as I have hinted here), psychoanalysis, attachment theory, developmental psychology (e.g., theory of mind), developmental psychopathology, neuroscience, and evolutionary biology (see Figure 1.4). In short, the breadth of mentalizing's emerging scientific foundation promises to be its greatest strength (see Fonagy, Chapter 3): through

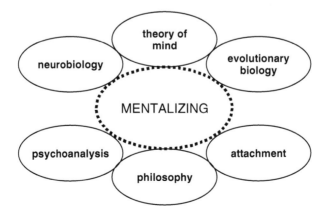

Figure 1.4 Links to other domains of knowledge

research, we will refine the concept, learn better how to promote the process in the service of prevention and treatment, and evaluate the effectiveness of our increasingly refined clinical interventions. This volume presents progress to date. Read on.

REFERENCES

Allen, J. G. (2001). *Traumatic Relationships and Serious Mental Disorders*. Chichester, UK: Wiley.

Allen, J. G. (2003). Mentalizing. *Bulletin of The Menninger Clinic*, *67*, 87–108.

Allen, J. G. (2005a). *Coping with Trauma: Hope through Understanding* (2nd edn). Washington, DC: American Psychiatric Publishing.

Allen, J. G. (2005b). Evil, mindblindness, and trauma: challenges to hope. Presented at the *Psychotherapy and Faith Conference of the Institute for Religion and Health*, Houston, TX.

Allen, J. G. (2006). *Coping with Depression: From Catch-22 to Hope*. Washington, DC: American Psychiatric Publishing.

Allen, J. G. (in press). Psychotherapy: the artful use of science. *Smith College Studies in Social Work*.

Allen, J. G., Munich, R. L. & Rogan, A. (2004). *Agency in Illness and Recovery*. Houston, TX: The Menninger Clinic.

Appelbaum, S. A. (1973). Psychological-mindedness: word, concept and essence. *International Journal of Psycho-Analysis*, *54*, 35–46.

Arendt, H. (1971). *The Life of the Mind*. New York: Harcourt.

Arendt, H. (2003). *Responsibility and Judgment*. New York: Schocken.

Bandura, A. (2001). Social cognitive theory: an agentic perspective. *Annual Review of Psychology*, *52*, 1–26.

Baron-Cohen, S. (1995). *Mindblindness: An Essay on Autism and Theory of Mind*. Cambridge, MA: MIT Press.

Barrett, L. F. & Salovey, P. (eds) (2002). *The Wisdom in Feeling: Psychological Processes in Emotional Intelligence*. New York: Guilford.

Beitel, M. & Cecero, J. J. (2003). Predicting psychological mindedness from personality style and attachment security. *Journal of Clinical Psychology*, *59*, 163–172.

Beitel, M., Ferrer, E. & Cecero, J. J. (2004). Psychological mindedness and cognitive style. *Journal of Clinical Psychology*, *60*, 567–582.

Beitel, M., Ferrer, E. & Cecero, J. J. (2005). Psychological mindedness and awareness of self and others. *Journal of Clinical Psychology*, *61*, 739–750.

Bowlby, J. (1988). *A Secure Base: Parent-child Attachment and Healthy Human Development*. New York: Basic Books.

Bram, A. D. & Gabbard, G. O. (2001). Potential space and reflective functioning: towards conceptual clarification and preliminary clinical implications. *International Journal of Psycho-Analysis*, *82*, 685–699.

Brown, K. W. & Ryan, R. M. (2003). The benefits of being present: mindfulness and its role in psychological well-being. *Journal of Personality and Social Psychology*, *84*, 822–848.

Carruthers, P. (1996). Simulation and self-knowledge: a defence of theory-theory. In P. Carruthers & P. K. Smith (eds), *Theories of Theories of Mind* (pp. 22–38). Cambridge, MA: Cambridge University Press.

Conte, H. R., Buckley, P., Picard, S. & Karasu, T. B. (1995). Relationship between psychological mindedness and personality traits and ego functioning: Validity studies. *Comprehensive Psychiatry*, *36*, 11–17.

Conte, H. R., Plutchick, R., Jung, B. B., Picard, S., Karasu, T. B. & Lotterman, A. (1990). Psychological mindedness as a predictor of psychotherapy outcome: a preliminary report. *Comprehensive Psychiatry*, *31*, 426–431.

Conte, H. R., Ratto, R. & Karasu, T. B. (1996). The psychological mindedness scale: factor structure and relationship to outcome of psychotherapy. *Journal of Psychotherapy Practice and Research*, *5*, 250–259.

Damasio, A. (1999). *The Feeling of What Happens: Body and Emotion in the Making of Consciousness*. New York: Harcourt Brace.

Damasio, A. (2003). *Looking for Spinoza: Joy, Sorrow, and the Feeling Brain*. New York: Harcourt.

Dehaene, S. & Naccache, L. (2001). Towards a cognitive neuroscience of consciousness: basic evidence and a workspace framework. In S. Dehaene (ed.), *The Cognitive Neuroscience of Consciousness* (pp. 1–37). Cambridge, MA: MIT Press.

Dennett, D. C. (1987). *The Intentional Stance*. Cambridge, MA: MIT Press.

Diamond, D., Stovall-McClough, C., Clarkin, J. F. & Levy, K. N. (2003). Patient-therapist attachment in the treatment of borderline personality disorder. *Bulletin of The Menninger Clinic*, *67*, 227–259.

Eilan, N. (2005). Joint attention, communication, and mind. In N. Eilan, C. Hoerl, T. McCormack & J. Roessler (eds), *Joint Attention: Communication and Other Minds* (pp. 1–33). New York: Oxford University Press.

Eisenberg, N., Losoya, S. & Spinrad, T. (2003). Affect and prosocial responding. In R. J. Davidson, K. R. Scherer & H. H. Goldsmith (eds), *Handbook of Affective Science* (pp. 787–803). New York: Oxford University Press.

Ekman, P. (2003). *Emotions Revealed*. New York: Holt.

Evans, D. & Cruse, P. (eds). (2004). *Emotion, Evolution, and Rationality*. New York: Oxford University Press.

Farber, B. A. (1985). The genesis, development and implications of psychological-mindedness in psychotherapists. *Psychotherapy*, *22*, 170–177.

Foa, E. B. & Kozak, M. J. (1986). Emotional processing of fear: exposure to corrective information. *Psychological Bulletin*, *99*, 20–35.

Fonagy, P. (1991). Thinking about thinking: some clinical and theoretical considerations in the treatment of a borderline patient. *International Journal of Psycho-Analysis*, *72*, 639–656.

Fonagy, P. (1995). Playing with reality: the development of psychic reality and its malfunction in borderline personalities. *International Journal of Psycho-Analysis*, *76*, 39–44.

Fonagy, P. & Target, M. (1997). Attachment and reflective function: their role in self-organization. *Development and Psychopathology*, *9*, 679–700.

Fonagy, P., Gergely, G., Jurist, E. L. & Target, M. (2002). *Affect Regulation, Mentalization, and the Development of the Self*. New York: Other Press.

Fonagy, P., Steele, H. & Steele, M. (1991). Maternal representations of attachment during pregnancy predict the organization of infant-mother attachment at one year of age. *Child Development*, *62*, 891–905.

Fonagy, P., Steele, M., Steele, H. & Target, M. (1997). *Reflective-Functioning Manual for Application to Adult Attachment Interviews, Version 4.1*. London: Psychoanalysis Unit, Sub-department of Clinical Health Psychology, University College London.

Franco, F. (2005). Infant pointing: Harlequin, servant of two masters. In N. Eilan, C. Hoerl, T. McCormack & J. Roessler (eds), *Joint Attention: Communication and Other Minds* (pp. 129–164). New York: Oxford University Press.

Freud, S. (1914–1958). Remembering, repeating, and working-through. In J. Strachey (ed.), *The Standard Edition of the Complete Psychological Works of Sigmund Freud* (Vol. 12, pp. 147–156). London: Hogarth Press.

Gallese, V. (2001). The "shared manifold" hypothesis: from mirror neurons to empathy. *Journal of Consciousness Studies*, *8*, 33–50.

Gergely, G. & Csibra, G. (2005). The social construction of the cultural mind: Imitation learning as a mechanism of human pedagogy. *Interaction Studies*, 6, 463–481.

Goldie, P. (2004). Emotion, reason, and virtue. In D. Evans & P. Cruse (eds), *Emotion, Evolution, and Rationality* (pp. 249–267). New York: Oxford University Press.

Gomez, J.-C. (2005). Joint attention and the notion of subject: insights from apes, normal children, and children with autism. In N. Eilan, C. Hoerl, T. McCormack & J. Roessler (eds), *Joint Attention: Communication and Other Minds* (pp. 65–84). New York: Oxford University Press.

Gopnik, A. & Meltzoff, A. N. (1997). *Words, Thoughts, and Theories*. Cambridge, MA: MIT Press.

Goss, J. J. & John, O. P. (2002). Wise emotion regulation. In L. F. Barrett & P. Salovey (eds), *The Wisdom in Feeling: Psychological Processes in Emotional Intelligence* (pp. 297–318). New York: Guilford.

Hahn, T. N. (1975). *The Miracle of Mindfulness: A Manual on Meditation*. Boston, MA: Beacon Press.

Heal, J. (2003). *Mind, Reason and Imagination*. New York: Cambridge University Press.

Heal, J. (2005). Joint attention and understanding the mind. In N. Eilan, C. Hoerl, T. McCormack & J. Roessler (eds), *Joint Attention: Communication and Other Minds* (pp. 34–44). New York: Oxford University Press.

Hobson, R. P. (2005). What puts the jointness into joint attention? In N. Eilan, C. Hoerl, T. McCormack & J. Roessler (eds), *Joint Attention: Communication and Other Minds* (pp. 185–204). New York: Oxford University Press.

Holmes, J. (1999). Defensive and creative uses of narrative in psychotherapy: an attachment perspective. In G. Roberts & J. Holmes (eds), *Healing Stories: Narrative in Psychiatry and Psychotherapy* (pp. 49–66). London: Oxford University Press.

Jack, A. I. & Shallice, T. (2001). Introspective physicalism as an approach to the science of consciousness. In S. Dehaene (ed.), *The Cognitive Neuroscience of Consciousness* (pp. 161–196). Cambridge, MA: MIT Press.

Jurist, E. L. (2005). Mentalized affectivity. *Psychoanalytic Psychology*, 22, 426–444.

Kandel, E. R. (2005). *Psychiatry, Psychoanalysis, and the New Biology of Mind*. Washington, DC: American Psychiatric Publishing.

Karmiloff-Smith, A. (1992). *Beyond Modularity: A Developmental Perspective on Cognitive Science*. Cambridge, MA: MIT Press.

Lakoff, G. & Johnson, M. (2003). *Metaphors We Live By*. Chicago, IL: University of Chicago Press.

Lear, J. (2003). *Therapeutic Action: An Earnest Plea for Irony*. New York: Other Press.

Leslie, A. M. (1987). Pretense and representation: the origins of "theory of mind". *Psychological Review*, 94, 412–426.

Marcel, A. (2003). The sense of agency: awareness and ownership of action. In J. Roessler & N. Eilan (eds), *Agency and Self-awareness* (pp. 48–93). New York: Oxford University Press.

Mayer, J. D. (2001). A field guide to emotional intelligence. In J. Ciarrochi, J. P. Forgas & J. D. Mayer (eds), *Emotional Intelligence in Everyday Life* (pp. 3–24). Philadelphia, PA: Psychology Press.

Mayer, J. D. & Salovey, P. (1997). What is emotional intelligence? In P. Salovey & D. J. Sluyter (eds), *Emotional Development and Emotional Intelligence* (pp. 3–31). New York: Basic Books.

Mayer, J. D., Caruso, D. R. & Salovey, P. (2000). Emotional intelligence meets traditional standards for intelligence. *Intelligence*, 27, 267–298.

Mayer, J. D., Salovey, P. & Caruso, D. R. (2000). Models of emotional intelligence. In R. Sternberg (ed.), *Handbook of Intelligence* (pp. 396–420). Cambridge, UK: Cambridge University Press.

McCallum, M. & Piper, W. E. (1996). Psychological mindedness. *Psychiatry*, 59, 48–63.

McDermott, J. J. (ed.) (1981). *The Philosophy of John Dewey*. Chicago: University of Chicago Press.

McGinn, C. (2004). *Mindsight: Image, Dream, Meaning*. Cambridge, MA: Harvard University Press.

Meins, E., Fernyhough, C., Russell, J. & Clark-Carter, D. (1998). Security of attachment as a predictor of symbolic and mentalizing abilities: a longitudinal study. *Social Development*, 7, 1–24.

Monk, R. (2005). *How to Read Wittgenstein*. New York: Norton.

Moran, R. (2001). *Authority and Estrangement: An Essay on Self-Knowledge*. Princeton, NJ: Princeton University Press.

Murdoch, I. (1971). *The Sovereignty of Good*. London: Routledge.

Nussbaum, M. C. (2001a). *The Fragility of Goodness: Luck and Ethics in Greek Tragedy and Philosophy* (rev. edn). New York: Cambridge University Press.

Nussbaum, M. C. (2001b). *Upheavals of Thought: The Intelligence of the Emotions*. Cambridge, MA: Cambridge University Press.

Ogden, T. H. (1985). On potential space. *International Journal of Psycho-Analysis*, 66, 129–141.

Olfson, M., Marcus, S. C., Druss, B., Elinson, L., Tanielian, T. & Pincus, H. A. (2002). National trends in the outpatient treatment of depression. *Journal of the American Medical Association*, 287, 203–209.

Parrott, W. G. (2002). The functional utility of negative emotions. In L. Feldman Barrett & P. Salovey (eds), *The Wisdom in Feeling: Psychological Processes in Emotional Intelligence* (pp. 341–359). New York: Guilford.

Posner, M. I. & Rothbart, M. K. (1998). Attention, self-regulation and consciousness. *Philosophical Transactions of the Royal Society of London, Series B, Biological Sciences*, 353, 1915–1927.

Preston, S. D. & de Waal, F. B. M. (2002). Empathy: its ultimate and proximate bases. *Behavioral and Brain Sciences*, 25, 1–20.

Reddy, V. (2005). Before the "third element": understanding attention to the self. In N. Eilan, C. Hoerl, T. McCormack & J. Roessler (eds), *Joint Attention: Communication and Other Minds* (pp. 85–109). New York: Oxford University Press.

Rizzolatti, G. & Craighero, L. (2004). The mirror-neuron system. *Annual Review of Neuroscience*, 27, 169–192.

Robins, C. J., Ivanoff, A. M. & Linehan, M. (2001). Dialectical behavior therapy. In W. J. Livesley (ed.), *Handbook of Personality Disorders* (pp. 437–459). New York: Guilford.

Rogers, C. R. (1951). *Client-Centered Therapy: Its Current Practice, Implications, and Theory*. Boston, MA: Houghton Mifflin.

Rogers, C. R. (1992). The necessary and sufficient conditions of therapeutic personality change. *Journal of Consulting and Clinical Psychology*, 60, 827–832.

Sartre, J. P. (2004). *The Imaginary* (J. Webber, Trans.). New York: Routledge.

Scanlon, T. M. (1998). *What We Owe to Each Other*. Cambridge, MA: Harvard University Press.

Schafer, R. (1976). *A New Language for Psychoanalysis*. New Haven, CT: Yale University Press.

Searle, J. R. (1998). *Mind, Language and Society*. New York: Basic Books.

Searle, J. R. (2001). *Rationality in Action*. Cambridge, MA: MIT Press.

Searle, J. R. (2004). *Mind: A Brief Introduction*. New York: Oxford University Press.

Shill, M. A. & Lumley, M. A. (2002). The psychological mindedness scale: factor structure, convergent validity and gender in a non-psychiatric sample. *Psychology and Psychotherapy: Theory, Research and Practice*, 75, 131–150.

Stern, D. N. (2004). *The Present Moment in Psychotherapy and Everyday Life*. New York: Norton.

Swanton, C. (2003). *Virtue Ethics: A Pluralistic View*. New York: Oxford University Press.

Target, M. & Fonagy, P. (1996). Playing with reality: II. The development of psychic reality from a theoretical perspective. *International Journal of Psycho-analysis, 77,* 459–479.

Tomasello, M. (1999). *The Cultural Origins of Human Cognition*. Cambridge, MA: Harvard University Press.

Wertsch, J. V. (1998). *Mind as Action*. New York: Oxford University Press.

Winnicott, D. W. (1971). *Playing and Reality*. London: Routledge.

2

MENTALIZING FROM A PSYCHOANALYTIC PERSPECTIVE: WHAT'S NEW?

Jeremy Holmes

A new verb has entered the Anglo-Saxon psychoanalytic lexicon. *Mentalizing*, and its related noun *mentalization*, were introduced by Fonagy, Target, Gergely, Bateman, Jurist (Bateman & Fonagy, 2004; Fonagy, Gergely, Jurist & Target, 2002), and Allen (2003) as part of a project delineating a framework for the effective treatment of people suffering from borderline personality disorder. The question behind this chapter is whether this new and – to this author's ears – rather ungainly word, with its abstract and latinate connotations, adds substantially to our existing conceptual armamentarium. My aim – initially for my own benefit – is to clarify its definition, phenomenology, intellectual roots, and possible clinical applications.

Bion (1962) states that "Psycho-analytic virtue lies not in the number of theories the psychoanalyst can command but the minimum number with which he can meet any contingency" (p. 88). The question therefore is whether mentalizing lies above or below this Bionic Ockham's razor line.

DEFINITION

Neither mentalizing nor mentalization are to be found in the *Oxford English Dictionary* (as main entries) or *Chambers*; nor do they appear in Rycroft (1982), or Laplanche and Pontalis' (1973) psychoanalytic thesauruses. They derive from the adjective "mental", defined in the Oxford English Dictionary as "of, or pertaining to, the mind". Bateman and Fonagy (2004, p. 21) define it as "the

Handbook of Mentalization-Based Treatment. Edited by J. G. Allen and P. Fonagy.
© 2006 John Wiley & Sons, Ltd.

mental process by which an individual implicitly and explicitly *interprets* the actions of himself and others as *meaningful* on the basis of *intentional mental states* such as personal desires, needs, feelings, beliefs and reasons" (my italics).

This definition suggests four inter-related aspects of the concept:

- Mentalizing as a "meta-cognitive" phenomenon, in the sense that it refers to the capacity for interpretation of thoughts and actions – to think about thinking or, to use Meins' phrase, to be "mind-minded" (Meins, Fernyhough, Russell & Clark-Carter, 1998).
- Mentalizing is concerned with the meanings which we attribute to our own and others' actions – that is, to the implicit or explicit hypotheses we use to understand why we, or another, might have thought or done such and such a thing.
- This links with a third aspect, which picks up on mentalizing as a key attribute of persons, as opposed to the inanimate world. Implicit in mentalizing is Dennett's (1987) intentional stance – the capacity to have projects, desires and wishes.
- Finally, mentalizing is not a fixed property of mind, but is a process, a capacity or skill, which may be present or absent to greater or lesser degree.

PHENOMENOLOGY: WHAT DOES IT *FEEL* LIKE TO MENTALIZE – OR NOT TO?

The Fonagy–Target model of mentalization arises out of research using the Adult Attachment Interview (Fonagy, Steele, Steele & Target, 1997). Their "reflective function" subscale provides an operationalized quantitative measure of the capacity for mentalization. Transcripts of Adult Attachment Interviews are rated using the following criteria:

- awareness of the nature of mental states, for example, *"Sometimes I wonder if I'm just making all this up"*;
- explicit efforts to tease out the mental states underlying behaviour, for example, *"I suppose my mother was pretty stressed at the time and didn't have much room to think about us kids"*;
- recognition of the developmental aspects of mental states, for example, *"I was so young at the time I didn't realize that the things my step-dad asked me to do weren't quite normal"*; and
- showing awareness of mental states in relation to the interviewer, for example, *"Being here means I'm on my best behaviour, but inside I feel pretty churned up and confused"* (Bateman & Fonagy, 2004, p. 75; author's examples interpolated).

The following non-clinical example illustrates the vicissitudes of mentalization in everyday life.

Example 1: The Emergence of Mentalization in the Face of Traumatic Loss

Mary, aged 85, had been married to John, 90, for 65 years. Following a fall and hip fracture, John became bedridden. He was admitted to hospital and was very ill. Mary lived alone but was in close contact with her daughter, Elizabeth, by telephone. When Elizabeth phoned about her father's progress, Mary said: "Dad's not himself today. It must be those tablets the doctors are giving him." The next day the phone message was: "The doctors seem to think that John is not at all well." Elizabeth, who lived some distance away, decided she needed to be at her mother's side. When she arrived, Mary was able to say: "Do you know, I think I may be finding it difficult to face the fact that Dad might not get better."

Mary's initial response to the possibility of losing her husband was denial and projection; the problem was attributed to the doctors and their tablets. She continued to keep her feelings at bay, focusing on what were the doctors' views, rather than what she felt. Only when her daughter arrived was she able to mentalize, that is, to look at her own feelings in relation to John's likely demise, and how difficult she had been finding it to face the situation.

This example illustrates the interpersonal aspect of mentalizing and its link to secure attachment. Overcoming denial became possible when the presence of Elizabeth provided Mary with the secure base she needed to explore her feelings. She could then look at how her perception of reality had been distorted by her need to ward off painful affect.

In addition this example suggests that degrees of mentalizing are possible, depending on the attachment context. As the painful truth began to sink in, Mary moved from absent mentalizing, through partial awareness of other's states of mind ("The doctors seem to think . . ."), to fuller self-mentalizing ("I seem to be having trouble . . .").

Mary gradually became able to self-mentalize. The next example introduces the developmental aspect of mentalizing and illustrates the relationship between self-mentalizing and mentalizing in relation to others.

Example 2: Mentalizing and Motherhood

A six-month-old baby cries in the night, waking her parents. Her mother, still in bed, turns to her partner. She says: "Oh, the little fiend, she *knows* I've got to get up really early tomorrow to go work. I'll be really washed out. She's just doing it to punish me." She then goes to her child, saying to herself, or even out loud to the baby: "You poor little thing . . . I wonder what it can be this time . . . Are you too hot? Is your nappy wet? Have you had a bad dream?" She picks the child up and soothes her, does what is necessary, and in a few minutes the whole family is asleep again.

Contrast this with a similar situation but where the caregiver might be alone and/or stressed or intoxicated. She will still, eventually, go to the crying baby, but now she might shout at her, saying, "You little devil ... You're just doing this to annoy me ... How *dare* you wake me up like that ... now *get back to sleep*."

In the first case, the mother starts with a lapse of mentalizing – in her sleep-deprived state she cannot differentiate between her feelings and those of the baby (equivalence mode; see below). Her experience of her child's crying is seen only from the perspective of her own feelings of panic and paranoia. But with the help of her partner she is able to retrieve a mentalizing stance and is able to reflect both about her own mental state and that of her child. She is now able to contain her irritation and resistance to being woken, to bracket them off, seeing them for what they are – her feelings, not those of the baby. This clears the way for her to offer a secure attachment response to the distressed child, based on responsiveness and the capacity to put herself into the child's shoes.

In the second case, the mother's capacity to mentalize is severely compromised. She is distressed and either highly aroused or drugged, both of which are inimical to mentalizing (Bateman & Fonagy, 2004). She is slow to respond and, when eventually she does, she sees the baby's distress only in terms of her own feelings rather than those of the child.

This type of self-referential response is similar to that described by Lyons-Ruth (Lyons-Ruth & Jacobvitz, 1999) as hostile/intrusive, and is typical of one group of parents whose children's attachment status is classified as "disorganized". The other main grouping is parents described as "fearful", who, in this hypothetical example, might simply lie in bed in a terrified and helpless state themselves, unable to respond to their child's distress. Disorganized attachment – via either route – is a putative precursor of, or vulnerability factor for, borderline personality disorder in adulthood (Holmes, 2003) and, parenthetically, these responses are reminiscent of the reactions of mental health professionals when confronted by disturbed behaviour in such patients. Like the first mother, the initial reaction is often one dominated by overwhelming counter-transference, high anxiety levels and compromised mentalizing. The patient is seen as deliberately "winding us up", malevolent or dangerous. This in turn can drive nonmentalized responses such as instant discharge from hospital or overprotective use of compulsory detainment. With the help of staff support and supervision, however, these reactions, like those of the sleepy mother and her partner, can be defused, and a mentalizing attitude regained. Many such patients have had adverse developmental experiences. The following example illustrates such a case, reconstructed in psychotherapy.

Example 3: Sexual Abuse and Mentalization

While her mother was doing an evening shift at the local supermarket, 10-year-old Abigail was left with an apparently helpful neighbour who regularly sexually abused her. When Abigail refused to go to the babysitter, her mother flew into a rage and threatened to put her into care. Abigail said that the man was "not very nice", but this again provoked a furious response, and she was told that she had no right to say such things about such a kind man.

Linehan (1993) suggests that people suffering from borderline personality disorder have grown up in an "invalidating" environment. Thus Abigail is twice invalidated, first by her abuser, and second by her mother who failed to respond to her distress cues. The mentalization response is inherently validating. Had her mother been able to mentalize, she would have interpreted Abigail's refusal to go to the babysitter as meaningful and motivated by the need to protect herself. She would perhaps also have been stimulated to self-mentalize, and consider the feelings *she* had about this man – that there was something "creepy" about him – feelings she might hitherto have pushed to one side in view of her need to survive economically. As mentioned above, like mothers of children classified as disorganized with respect to attachment (Lyons-Ruth & Jacobvitz, 1999; Holmes, 2003), and rhesus monkeys faced with variable foraging conditions (Suomi, 1999), her mothering skills were impaired by the severe psychological and environmental stress to which she was subjected. Stress is the enemy of mentalization; when anxiety reaches a certain level the mentalizing brain goes offline and moves into survival-mode (Allen, 2003).

Summarizing the phenomenology of mentalizing we can say that it: involves the capacity to empathize, that is, to be able to put oneself in another's shoes; encompasses the ability to see and evaluate oneself and one's feelings from the outside; denotes a capacity to differentiate feelings *about* reality from reality itself; is a graded rather than all-or-nothing phenomenon; is related to arousal; and is enhanced by the presence of a secure soothing partner or other intimate.

CONCEPTUAL ORIGINS OF MENTALIZING

The notion of mentalizing has four distinct grandparental roots: cognitive psychology; psychoanalytic object relations theory, especially the work of Bion; francophone psychoanalysis; and attachment-theory-influenced developmental psychopathology.

Cognitive Psychology

Cognitive psychologists have adopted the philosophical notion of theory of mind to explain some of the difficulties experienced by people suffering from autism as well as the formal and developmental differences between autistic and normal modes of thought (Baron-Cohen, 1995; Hobson, 1993). In order to operate in the intensely social world of human interaction, it is necessary to understand that others have minds – similar, but never identical, to one's own. We need to know "where someone is coming from" in order to meet our own needs and pursue our projects.

It has been suggested that the social difficulties experienced by autistic individuals arise from their inability to conceptualize others as having minds and therefore viewpoints different from their own (see Sharp, Chapter 4). People are therefore viewed as no different from things, and cannot be understood to have projects, desires and plans, which may or may not intersect with those of the autistic subject. As a result the interpersonal world is inexplicable and unpredictable, resulting in defensive withdrawal and self-preoccupation.

In normal development, theory of mind, rather than being inborn, has been elegantly demonstrated to arise in children in the first five years of life. In false-belief tasks, children are asked to predict where adults might search for a missing object, which unbeknown to them has been moved from one container to another. Around the age of three, children assume that others' view of the world is necessarily identical to their own and that therefore the deceived subject will still correctly retrieve the missing object. By the age of five, the children can see that deception is possible and therefore that one person's mind will view the world differently from another, depending on information available to him – and that therefore the searching adult is capable of getting things wrong. It is only a small step from this to mentalization, that is, the view that the world is always filtered through a perspectival mind, which may be more or less accurate in its appreciation of reality.

Bion and Object Relations

The Kleinian psychoanalyst W. R. Bion (1962, 1967) proposed a highly abstract schematized theory of the origins of thinking. Bion was concerned with the general origins of thought itself, rather than the specific and rather sophisticated cognitive-affective ability that mentalizing represents. Nevertheless, his ideas help us look more deeply into what is involved in mentalizing.

Bion starts from Freud's idea that thinking – which we could also call imagination – arises in response to an absence: no breast, therefore imagine a breast. Absence is akin to loss and is, in Bion's Kleinian world-view, experienced by the infant as inherently "bad" and frustrating, and therefore in need of expulsion/ projection from the paradisal inner world of "goodness".

Next, Bion differentiates between thoughts and the apparatus (his word), which thinks the thoughts, namely, thinking. Thoughts must be contained by a thinker who can think them. He calls the capacity to think thoughts, alpha function. Alpha function transforms beta elements (thoughts without a thinker) into alpha elements, which are then available for being thought about, that is, mentalization.

Bion then postulates a conflict between the desire to rid oneself via projection of those "bad" thoughts which, because they arise from loss, are inherently disturbing, and the capacity to modify them so that they can be indeed be thought. He sees the outcome of this conflict as depending in part on the capacity of the infant to tolerate frustration (which, in his model, is needed for thinking rather than evacuation), and in part on the ability of the "breast" (i.e., the mother to whom the "breast" is attached) to help the infant with his frustrations, to accept the projections and gently to return them in a form in which they can now be "thought". This process is closely linked with the *naming* of feelings (e.g., "Mummy's going away to the toilet for a minute, but you don't need to worry too much because she will be back soon").

In the absence of a containing mother, or where there is little ability to tolerate frustration (i.e., a genetic factor), the outcome will be excessive projective identification, which sows the seeds of psychopathology in later life, including a deficit in the capacity for mentalizing. Thus, in the example in the previous section, the stressed mother projectively identifies her infant as her persecutor, rather than being able to mentalize herself into a receptive state of mind. This in turn may interfere with the infant's developing capacity to mentalize, since his feelings will not have been recognized and "realized" (Bion's word) by the mother, and, instead, the mother's feelings ("You just want to wake me up to wind me up") will have invaded the infant self as an alien nidus (Fonagy et al., 2002; Fonagy, Chapter 3).

In Bion's account, successful transformation of beta into alpha elements leads to the establishment of a "contact barrier", as originally proposed by Freud, between unconscious and conscious thinking. This means that an individual can differentiate between the somatic sensations, unnamed desires and proto-feelings, which comprise preconceptions, on the one hand (beta elements), and thoughts or conceptions (alpha elements), which form the stuff of rational thought on the other hand. This differentiation enables an individual confidently to distinguish reality from fantasy, a key component of the ability to mentalize.

Francophone Psychoanalysis

Bion starts from Freud's idea that, ultimately, thinking – the mind itself – is a response to, and a bulwark against, frustration. Thinking maintains equilibrium in the inevitable gaps in attachment continuity: the five-year-old child can go happily to school because he carries with him a thought/memory/imaginative picture of a loving parent in his mind to whom he can turn in times of stress or danger.

Francophone psychoanalysis can be differentiated from the Anglo-Saxon variety in a number of ways, including a much greater adherence to Freud's early ideas, and to psychoanalysis as an inclusive self-sufficient theory. In approaching mentalizing they start from Freud's idea – contained in his unpublished Project (Freud, 1895) – that thought arises out of the binding of otherwise untrammelled drive-energies. In the absence of such binding, psychic energy is either discharged through action or diverted into somatic processes – emerging clinically as acting out or somatization.

Thus Luquet (1981) and Marty (1991) start from the clinical phenomenon of somatization disorders conceived in terms of *pensée operatoire* – operational or robot-like thinking, devoid of affect, which they see as characteristic of this group of patients. *Pensée operatoire* is the French equivalent of the Anglo-Saxon notion of alexithymia, that is, the inability to put feelings into words. Mentalization from this perspective is the antithesis of *pensée operatoire* or, as Lecours and Bouchard (1997) put it, disruptive impulsion (i.e., acting out). It encapsulates the capacity to transform drives into feelings, and to represent, symbolize, sublimate, abstract, reflect on and make meaning out of them. Without mentalizing, repeating (acting out) is inevitable; with reminiscence goes freedom.

Thus while mentalization is in English semi-neologistic, the term has been current in francophone psychoanalysis for a quarter of a century. Lecours and Bouchard (1997) put forward a sophisticated hierarchical classification of *degrees* of mentalization. At one extreme lie unmentalized libidinal excitations, which emerge chaotically as "somatisations, crude violent behaviour and self mutilation that force defantasised conflicts into the interpersonal arena" (Lecours & Bouchard, 1997, p. 862); at the other extreme is an abstract reflexive stage which, in a psychoanalytic context, might enable a patient to say to his analyst: "I know that whenever I feel this tired-exhausted feeling, I have left something aside, that I am angry but cannot somehow feel it" (Lecours & Bouchard, 1997, p. 865).

To summarize so far: Bion implicitly, and the francophones explicitly, have used the idea of mentalization long before its advent into the world of empirical clinical and developmental psychoanalysis. As I shall argue, the new Anglo-Saxon slant brings a narrowing of meaning and more specific, testable and limited application in contrast to the philosophical preoccupations of its earlier users.

Developmental Psychopathology

In introducing ideas about mentalizing to the Anglo-Saxon community, Fonagy and his colleagues bring a British empiricist and Winnicottian interpersonalist slant to the notion of mentalizing (Winnicott, 1971). In Winnicott's notion of transitional space, the conscious/unconscious contact barrier is expanded into a buffer *zone* – a *two-man's land* – in which reality and fantasy overlap. In this *speilraum* there is suspension of disbelief: thoughts and feelings can be played with as though they were real, while reality can be safely deconstructed as though it were fantasy.

The introduction of the Winnicottian model is seen most explicitly in Fonagy and Target's (1997) distinction between pretend and equivalence modes of thinking, which also owes a debt to Segal (1991). They see children who are unable to differentiate pretend from equivalence as handicapped in two distinct ways.

- In equivalence mode, the world as it is will be mistaken for – seen as equivalent to – the world coloured by feelings. Thus, for example, a child unable to differentiate pretend from equivalence would be *un*able to ask: "Mummy, are you really cross with me today, or just pretending?"
- A child trapped in pretend mode may withdraw into a world of fantasy or become over-controlling, for example, insisting that an imaginary friend be fed or dressed in parallel with himself or herself ("controllingness" is a common developmental sequel to disorganized attachment in infancy; Lyons-Ruth & Jacobvitz, 1999).

In both cases, children cannot see that the way the world is *perceived* – by themselves or others – must be taken into account when considering what is or is not the case. Mentalization implies the capacity to differentiate between pretend and equivalence modes, to keep them separate, and to allow traffic between them, along the lines already referred to in Bion's image of the semi-permeable contact barrier between conscious and unconscious thought.

Borderline personality disorder sufferers suffer from the lack of a robust sense of self: at a profound level they do not know who they are or how they impact others. This lack of awareness inevitably restricts or destabilizes their capacity to form intimate relationships, and to operate effectively in the interpersonal world. The capacity to make this distinction arises, in Fonagy et al.'s view, from intense interactive processes between caregiver and child in the early years of life (Fonagy et al., 2002; Fonagy, Chapter 3). In normal development, transitional phenomena – especially *mirroring* interactions between caregiver and child – provide the basis for this sense of self. The child learns who he is and what his feelings are through the capacity of the caregiver to reflect back his gestures via playful mirroring responses. As development proceeds, playing alone or with others, his imaginative development, and sense of what the world is really like develop *pari passu*. He begins to build up a picture of where internal and external reality begin and end. This enables him to factor in the contribution of his own feelings to his appreciation of the world – in other words, to mentalize. In parallel with this emergence of self-mentalizing abilities, or possibly prior to them, he begins to be able to take into account others' mentalizing as an explanation for their actions and reactions.

A key notion underlying the concept of mentalization is the empirical finding that, when parents' attachment status was assessed before the birth of a child, high reflective function in the parent predicted secure attachment in the child – especially where mothers reported that they themselves had been deprived or harmed in childhood (Fonagy et al., 1997). This suggests that the capacity for mentalizing is protective against the psychologically damaging impact of childhood deprivation or harm. Potential borderline personality disorder sufferers may have had developmental experiences which compromise mentalizing; conversely, those who are resilient have the mitigating capacity for mentalizing which counteracts the psychological harm done by trauma.

The general premise underlying this approach is that secure attachment leads to the emergence of mentalizing and, reciprocally, that the capacity for mentalizing is a marker of secure attachment. An impressive array of evidence supports the view that a mother's capacity to mentalize in relation to her offspring, and to be playful with them, is strongly associated with secure attachment measures in those children (e.g., Slade, 1999; Meins et al., 1998). Conversely, there is increasing evidence that extreme forms of insecure attachment, especially disorganized attachment, compromise mentalizing abilities in later life (Grossman, Grossman & Waters, 2005). This insecurity, in turn, may act as a vulnerability factor for the emergence of borderline personality disorder (Holmes, 2003).

Recapitulation

Thinking about mentalizing has arisen out of the clinicians' needs to understand and work effectively with difficult patients. Each of the four groups of theorists just discussed takes a particular clinical/diagnostic phenomenon as its starting point. Cognitive psychologists are searching for ways of thinking about the social and interpersonal deficits associated with autism. Bion was preoccupied with thought disorder as seen in psychosis (using the term psychoanalytically rather than psychiatrically); in the consulting room, patients are unable to make connections between their own thoughts or their analyst's interpretations. The francophone psychoanalysts started from somatization disorders as seen in persons who, in their view, tend to express emotion somatically rather than verbally. Fonagy and his colleagues focus on the painful relationships with self and others characteristic of borderline personality disorder.

CLINICAL APPLICATIONS

Three examples taken from psychotherapeutic work will illustrate how the concept of mentalizing can help in clinical practice.

Example 4: The Momentary Emergence of Mentalization in a Borderline Patient

Peter was an in-patient on an acute psychiatric admission ward. The ward staff were at their wits' end about how to help him. Some saw him as manipulative and destructively dependent and believed that he should be discharged immediately; others believed that he needed a lot of help but did not know how to get through to him. He had been detained in hospital for several months thanks to his tendency to cut himself repeatedly, especially when he was drunk. He was 26 and had been in and out of hospital for at least eight years. His main "career" had been as a psychiatric patient, diagnosed as suffering from alcoholism, depression and borderline personality disorder.

Peter was referred to a specialist personality disorder clinic to see if anything could be done to break the cycle of self-harm and prolonged hospital admissions, and no real sense of progress. He was a rather engaging young man with a nice smile, who, it turned out, was a pretty good guitarist and in his teens had his own band. But he conveyed a sense of defeatedness and despair as well. He couldn't see a way forward, and was acutely aware of the difference between his state and that of the average 26-year-old man. He seemed rather proud in a macho way of his ability to drink vast amounts of cider, and to tolerate the pain he inflicted on himself when he punched walls and cut his arms.

Peter described a typical episode. He was on the ward wanting some medication. He asked a staff member for some "as required" medication, but his request was refused. He felt an upsurge of rage, got into an altercation, and stormed off the ward and out of the hospital. As he walked down the road he found himself crying and feeling utterly miserable and desolate. Then an idea formed in his mind. He went to the nearest shop, bought some razor blades, and made for public toilets where he locked himself in and cut his wrists. Eventually the police, who had been alerted to his disappearance, found him; he was returned to hospital.

I reflected his story back to him as follows:

> "You *want* something badly, relief from tension; you can't get it; you fly into a *rage* with your depriver; beneath the rage you feel *utterly alone* and abandoned; then your anger focuses in on yourself and your body, the only thing that seems to be within your *control*; you go somewhere where you are alone, a place of *primitive bodily needs*; finally your plight is recognized, at least partially, and you are *rescued*." (I try to emphasize the key words, since I sense he may not absorb the whole speech, which contradicts the dictum that interventions, especially with borderline patients, should be short and to the point.)

A faint, semi-triumphant smile flickered across Peter's face, almost as though he had been "found out", caught red-handed putting his hand in the till of his own life. "Yep, that just about sums it up," he replies. He had told us earlier about his parent's dreadful rows throughout his childhood and how he used to steal away up to his room, and cover his ears with the pillow in order to block out the screams.

I went on: "Perhaps that lonely public toilet is reminiscent of you alone in your bedroom with the rows going on all around you. Cutting yourself is an attempt to block out the mental pain and helplessness by inflicting physical pain on yourself."

I asked Peter if he felt anyone on the ward understood him.

No one, he insisted.

I asked, what about his key-worker (whom I knew to be an excellent nurse)?

"Oh, she just thinks I'm a waste of space like everyone else," he replied.

"Do you really mean that?"

"Well, I don't suppose she *really* does. It's just the way I feel about it most of the time."

Here, at last, is Peter mentalizing: the nurse doesn't really reject him, but that is his *perception* of her attitude. This case illustrates the combination of empathy and challenge, which is needed to foster mentalization in borderline patients. Neither alone is sufficient. The patient needs to feel secure – that he is being listened to and understood, not judged. Only then is he in a position to reflect on his affective experience. But to turn his attention to this reflection may require a degree of mild verbal coercion, that is, challenge. Challenge in therapy implies close involvement with patients, not letting them evade painful topics, "forcing" them to face the implications of their behaviour. None of this effort is likely to be successful in the absence of secure attachment, which lowers physiological arousal and so paves the way for the possibility of mentalization. Put another way, mentalization requires tolerance of vulnerability – feeling safe enough to risk the possibility that one might get things wrong, recognizing that emotion can drive out reason.

Example 5: Transference versus Mentalization

Naomi was a 30-year-old unmarried secondary-school biology teacher. She found intimate relationships very difficult. Whenever she formed the beginnings of a relationship with a man, she felt used, taken over or misunderstood, and that she was losing her sense of self – at which point she would bring things to an abrupt halt.

Naomi came into therapy after several episodes of suicidal depression. She had had a previous period of psychotherapy, which came to a sudden end when she revealed her intense romantic feelings towards her therapist, and he promptly terminated the treatment.

The child of a single parent, Naomi had and continued to have a very close relationship with her mother, whom she felt she had to protect and look after. In the course of therapy she was critical of her therapist in minor ways: complaining about his dusty room, the un-artistic arrangement of his pictures, and his insistence on commenting on her late arrival for sessions, when, in her view, it was "none of your business – it is entirely up to me when I decide to turn up".

On one occasion she informed her therapist that he was clearly bored with her, since he kept yawning throughout the session and, what was more, he obviously had to drink strong black coffee before her session in order to stay awake – and there was the proof (pointing to an empty cup on the desk).

The therapist's own construction of the relationship was very different. True, she was a difficult patient, with a fragile sense of self, who found his interpretations as intrusive as the advances of her occasional male admirers. He felt that she was simultaneously trying to please him – as she did her mother – while surreptitiously resenting and undermining this effort. He worried a lot about her depression and suicidality. The coffee cup was adventitious and unrelated to whatever feelings he did or did not have about Naomi – at least to the limits of his own mentalized self-scrutiny.

Thus, her conviction that the cup symbolized his boredom represented a probable failure of mentalization. The threat and anxiety associated with being in the intimacy of the therapeutic situation meant that for Naomi only one view was possible: that the therapist couldn't tolerate being with the "boredom" of her depression. She could not entertain the possibility that this view – even to view it as a "view" implies a degree of mentalization – might be a manifestation of her depression and self-loathing. The lack of what Bion (1962) calls the contact barrier between the unconscious and conscious mind meant that she took what was a product of her depressive imaginings to be the real thing.

In an attempt to enhance mentalization, the therapist said: "You sometimes get into a muddle between what is going on in your mind and what is going on in the world, including other people's minds. Perhaps the coffee cup stands for your feelings of despair about yourself, and the idea that you must be intolerable to be with. While it is not impossible that I might be bored with you (although I don't believe that I am), it is difficult for you to consider that that cup might just be there, or that I might be tired because I had a bad night or for some other reason – or simply like the taste of coffee."

Focusing on the capacity for, or absence of, mentalization is a necessary precursor to interpreting the content of communications. He did *not* say, for example, in Bionic mode: "I think that my absence (this session followed close on the heels of a break) has aroused such black and bleak feelings of emptiness and envy in you that they have had to be got rid of into the cup filled with dark liquid, which you now fear taking back into yourself for fear of destroying me and the therapy in the process." If the patient cannot mentalize, such statements appear at best incomprehensible and, at worst, persecutory.

Thus, transference – the perception of the therapist as bored with her in the same way that her abandoning father and previous therapist had been is antithetical to mentalization. Therapy can be seen as an attempt gradually to help the patient see her transferential feelings for what they are.

The therapist employed a mentalization-influenced approach, attempting to strengthen the boundary between fantasy and reality, to suggest that there is a difference between what is, and what merely might be, the case. It was also tentative in its use of metaphor. At one level metaphor is inherently mentalizing, since an image, while containing an important psychological truth, is by definition in the mind rather than out there in reality. The idea of the cup as a metaphor for her bad feelings about herself had the potential to strengthen Naomi's mentalizing capacities, since metaphor-making enhances playfulness and the use of transitional space as the participants can add to and creatively modify each other's imagery. But for the unmentalizing, metaphors can be confusing, merely adding to the breakdown of reality testing rather than strengthening it.

POSSIBLE PSYCHOANALYTIC OBJECTIONS TO MENTALIZATION

Mentalizing as a concept has three distinct intellectual roots. Bion and the cognitive psychologists draw on a philosophical tradition going back at least to Kant's distinction between the thing-in-itself (known only to God) and our appreciation of it. The francophone psychoanalysts remain true to Freud, linking present-day clinical experience with his unpublished Project and early drive-based formulations. Fonagy and his colleagues represent the tradition of Anglo-Saxon empiricism and link clinical experience with the findings of developmental psychopathology. What makes Fonagy and his colleagues' use of the term distinctive is its precision and restrictedness. The francophones and Bion aim for a *total* explanation of the process of thought itself, whereas Fonagy and colleagues concentrate on a specific aspect of thinking: the ability to understand others and oneself as intentional agents. Paradoxically, this more modest aim may provide more potency than attempts to use psychoanalytic ideas to explain the entire workings of the human mind.

Comparing Fonagy's notion of mentalizing with Bion's formulations, there are striking similarities and significant differences. Bion sees the capacity for "thinking" as dependent on the mother's (and by implication the analyst's) capacity for "reverie", that is, her capacity to love her infant in a way that enables her to tolerate his projections, contain them, metabolize them, and return them for re-introjection when the moment is right.

Bion's view can be compared with the Fonagy model in which the infant's sense of self, his security and ultimately his capacity for reflexive function depends on the mother's capacity to put her own feelings to one side, and to mirror accurately his states of mind within the context of a secure base. This process leads in time to a child who has an internal image of himself, introjected from his mother's responsive and accurate reflections of his moods, feelings and desires. The Fonagy model is thus essentially visual, in comparison with Bion's alimentary metaphor; Bion writes almost exclusively in terms of "breast/nipple" and mouth, while much of the research underlying the Fonagy model focuses on facial and eye contact between mother and child.

A key feature of both models is the notion of affect regulation. In Bion's terminology, this is frustration tolerance. In the Fonagy model, secure attachment means modulation and down-regulation of painful affect, aided by the caregiver who is not unduly upset by infant's distress and who knows not to "take it personally". This relative calmness in the face of distress fosters mentalizing, since clinical, developmental and neurophysiological studies all show that excessive arousal and mentalizing are mutually incompatible (Bateman & Fonagy, 2004; Fonagy, Chapter 3). There is a clear link with borderline personality disorder here: failure of self-soothing and affective disturbance is a crucial diagnostic feature of this condition.

There are also at least two important differences between Bion's alpha function/containment theory and mentalization. First, as mentioned, Bion was concerned with the origins of thought itself, and he attempted to devise a theory that would encompass psychotic thought disorders. But it seems unhelpful to view everything that is not mentalizing as "beta elements", since people with compromised mentalizing skills can still get along fairly well in many aspects of their lives. Not all of them are in any meaningful sense psychotic, even though there may be psychotic islands within an otherwise normally functioning personality.

Second, there is an interesting contrast in the emphasis each theorist places on where the activity and responsibility for health or pathology lies. In the Bion model the mother's role is relatively passive, as the term "reverie" implies. Her job is to "dream" her infant. The child by contrast is the instigator: his inability to tolerate frustration and to evacuate unwanted feelings underlies the inability to think productively and to know what is real and what is not. In the Fonagy model the reverse is the case. The mentalizing, secure-base-providing mother is active, fluidly moving into her infant's mental space and providing the "marking" (i.e., exaggerated mirroring responses) and contingent responses (i.e., arising out of the child's gestures, not her own needs), which the child requires. While Bion's model is more interpersonal than classical drive theory as drawn on by the francophone analysts, it is not fully interpersonal in the way that the Winnicott–Fonagy approach is. For the latter there are two interacting subjectivities in interplay with one another, while for Bion the "(m)other" is mainly a receptacle for the infant's projections, and there is no interpersonal mutually mentalizing space between.

Third, for all its mathematical pretensions, the Bion model is essentially a metaphor, explicitly derived from alimentation. A model, as opposed to a metaphor, can be operationalized and subject to experimental confirmation or disconfirmation; a metaphor is more akin to a poetic image, which can be felt intuitively to be more or less true. Thus, the two approaches come from different worlds of discourse.

A number of other possible objections to the concept of mentalizing flow from this discussion. The Fonagy view is essentially an environmental/deficit model; the child is deprived of the capacity for mentalizing by deficient or malevolent parenting. Overcoming this deficit in therapy might be thought of as akin to Alexander and French's (1946) questionable "corrective emotional experience". Psychoanalysts such as Caper (1999) have argued strongly against this approach, both theoretically and technically, seeing it as essentially anti-analytic and leading to collusive and ultimately unhelpful support, rather than promoting radical psychic change.

By contrast, Bateman and Fonagy (2004) argue that the inability to mentalize is indeed a structural deficit, and that until it is instated, "normal" psychoanalytic interpretations and reconstructions are unlikely to be effective. Their set-up for effective therapy for people suffering from borderline personality disorder is specifically designed to foster mentalizing, for example, through the use of groups as well as individual therapy so that patients can regularly see themselves and their actions reflected through the eyes of their fellow sufferers. Therapy is necessarily supportive, in the sense of providing and continually aiming to repair a secure base, because psychological and physiological security are preconditions for mentalizing.

As mentioned, effective therapy for people with borderline conditions is also necessarily challenging, especially of the patient's potential for self-directed aggression and destruction, and because close engagement is essential for effective mirroring. Just as a mother will deliberately and humorously exaggerate her baby's distress in order, paradoxically, to lessen it, so therapy needs to home in on the borderline patient's potential for aggression and highlight it if the patient is to be able to manage, own and ultimately to mentalize it (Kernberg, 1992). Therapists who thrust themselves to the fore with premature transference interpretations (which may be experienced by their patients as hostile and self-referential) or, conversely, those that practise extreme reticence and opacity (who may be felt as withdrawn and frightened) are in danger of repeating, or at least activating, the borderline patient's developmental experience of intrusiveness or withdrawal; in so doing, they may simply reinforce pathology rather than helping to overcome it.

A further objection comes from the view that mentalizing is just another word for the familiar psychoanalytic concept of insight. Bateman and Fonagy (2004) explicitly characterize mentalizing as a new word for old concepts. However, there is an essential difference in that insight usually refers to specific nuggets of self-understanding (e.g., that someone tends to become aggressive when confronted by older men, or compulsively seductive with married women, and to understand these tendencies in Oedipal terms); in contrast, mentalizing refers to a *process* or function. But all psychoanalytic psychotherapy, it might be said, aims to promote mentalizing. So, again, what's new? The counter-argument here is that Fonagy postulates a specific defect in the *apparatus* of thought (to use Bion's word), and therapy is designed to help establish reflective capacity – before the traditional aim of insight-promotion can be pursued.

Finally, mentalization might be accused (if abstract nouns can stand accused) of being too cognitive for psychoanalytic taste. What, it might be argued, is the difference between psychoanalytic-fostered mentalizing and cognitive behavioural therapy (CBT), where the patient is encouraged to examine his erroneous thoughts and how they might be modified? One answer to this might to argue that there are indeed overlaps between psychoanalytic mentalization-based therapy and cognitively influenced treatment such as CBT and dialectical behaviour therapy (Linehan, 1993), and that integrative approaches represent the future of psychotherapies generally (Holmes & Bateman, 2001; Gabbard, Beck & Holmes, 2005; see also Björgvinsson and Hart, Chapter 7; Lewis, Chapter 8). However, the main point is that CBT approaches to borderline personality disorder are likely to be as relatively ineffective as traditional psychoanalytic ones if they fail to address first the need to establish the *capacity* for mentalizing, before moving on to examining specific instances where it succeeds or fails.

CONCLUSION

This chapter argues for a cautious welcome to mentalizing as a useful addition to psychoanalytic thinking and, in its operationalized form, to research. As a form of meta-ratiocination, mentalization encourages therapists as well as patients to subject their ideas and feelings to constant scrutiny in order to arrive at a greater approximation to the truth. Thus counter-transference in its modern garb is but a specific prompt to mentalize: the therapist must always be asking herself, "Why am I thinking and feeling in this particular way at this specific moment?" That stricture applies to our theoretical predilections as much as it does to our responses to our patients. If taken seriously, such mentalization-informed use of counter-transference is de-centring, an aspect of postmodernism. This means that there are no fixed theoretical reference points for the fully mentalizing therapist, no certainty other than that there is no certainty. Living with that challenge is a pedagogic, practical and moral task that any therapist wishing to work effectively with borderline patients must meet face to face. The message of this chapter is that the notion of mentalizing as developed by Fonagy and his colleagues is an invaluable aid in that enterprise.

REFERENCES

Alexander, F. & French, T. (1946). *Psychoanalytic Therapy: Principles and Applications.* New York: Ronald Press.

Allen, J. G. (2003). Mentalizing. *Bulletin of The Menninger Clinic, 67,* 87–108.

Baron-Cohen, S. (1995). *Mindblindness: An Essay on Autism and Theory of Mind.* Cambridge, MA: MIT Press.

Bateman, A. & Fonagy, P. (2004). *Psychotherapy for Borderline Personality Disorder: Mentalization Based Treatment.* Oxford: Oxford University Press.

Bion, W. (1962). *Learning from Experience.* London: Heineman.

Bion, W. (1967). *Second Thoughts.* New York: Jason Aronson.

Caper, R. (1999). *A Mind of One's Own.* London: Routledge.

Dennett, D. C. (1987). *The Intentional Stance.* Cambridge, MA: MIT Press.

Fonagy, P. & Target, M. (1997). Attachment and reflective function: Their role in self-organization. *Development and Psychopathology, 9,* 679–700.

Fonagy, P., Gergely, G., Jurist, E. L. & Target, M. (2002). *Affect Regulation, Mentalization, and the Development of the Self.* New York: Other Press.

Fonagy, P., Steele, M., Steele, H. & Target, M. (1997). *Reflective-Functioning Manual for Application to Adult Attachment Interviews, Version 4.1.* London: Psychoanalysis Unit, Sub-department of Clinical Health Psychology, University College London.

Freud, S. (1895). *Project for a Scientific Psychology* (standard edn), Vol. 1, pp. 295–397. London: Hogarth Press.

Gabbard, G., Beck, J. & Holmes, J. (2005). *Oxford Textbook of Psychotherapy.* Oxford: Oxford University Press.

Grossman, K., Grossman, K. & Waters, E. (2005). *Attachment from Infancy to Adulthood: The Major Longitudinal Studies.* New York: Guilford.

Hobson, P. (1993). *Autism and the Development of Mind.* London: Lawrence Erlbaum.

Holmes, J. (2003). Borderline personality disorder and the search for meaning – an attachment perspective. *Australian and New Zealand Journal of Psychiatry, 37,* 524–532.

Holmes, J. & Bateman, A. (2001). *Psychotherapy Integration: Models and Methods.* Oxford: Oxford University Press.

Kernberg, O. (1992). *Aggression in Personality Disorders and Perversions.* New Haven: Yale University Press.

Laplanche, J. & Pontalis, J.-B. (1973). *The Language of Psychoanalysis.* London: Hogarth.

Lecours, S. & Bouchard, M.-A. (1997). Dimensions of mentalization: outlining levels of psychic transformation. *International Journal of Psycho-Analysis, 78,* 855–875.

Linehan, M. (1993). *Cognitive Behavioural Treatment of Borderline Personality Disorder.* New York: Guilford.

Luquet, P. (1981). Le changement dans la mentalization. *Revue Française de Psychoanalyse, 45,* 1023–1028.

Lyons-Ruth, K. & Jacobvitz, D. (1999). Attachment disorganisation: unresolved loss, relational violence, and lapses in behavioural and attentional strategies. In J. Cassidy & P. Shaver (eds), *Handbook of Attachment*. New York: Guilford.

Marty, P. (1991). *Mentalization et psychosomatique*. Paris: Laboratoire Delagrange.

Meins, E., Fernyhough, C., Russell, J. & Clark-Carter, D. (1998). Security of attachment as a predictor of symbolic and mentalizing abilities: a longitudinal study. *Social Development, 7*, 1–24.

Rycroft, C. (1982). *Critical Dictionary of Psychoanalysis* (2nd edn). London: Penguin.

Segal, H. (1991). *Dream, Phantasy, Art*. London: Routledge.

Slade, A. (1999). Attachment theory and research: implications for the theory and practice of individual psychotherapy with adults. In J. Cassidy & P. Shaver (eds), *Handbook of Attachment*. New York: Guilford.

Suomi, S. (1999). Attachment in rhesus monkeys. In J. Cassidy & P. Shaver (eds), *Handbook of Attachment*. New York: Guilford.

Winnicott, D. W. (1971). *Playing and Reality*. London: Routledge.

PART II

DEVELOPMENTAL PSYCHOPATHOLOGY

3

THE MENTALIZATION-FOCUSED APPROACH TO SOCIAL DEVELOPMENT

Peter Fonagy

The emergence of the capacity to conceive of mental states as explanations of behaviour in oneself and in others is the organizing construct of the mentalization-focused approach to social development (Fonagy, Gergely, Jurist & Target, 2002; Fonagy & Target, 1997a). Unusually, for what is fundamentally a psychoanalytic approach, we have elaborated our model on the basis of empirical observations as well as clinical work. In research studies, we have used the term *reflective function* to refer to a quantified index of attachment-related mentalization. We assume that the capacity to mentalize is a key determinant of self-organization and that, along with contributory capacities of affect regulation and attention control mechanisms, mentalizing capacity is acquired in the context of early attachment relationships. Disturbances of attachment relationships will therefore disrupt the normal emergence of these key social-cognitive capacities and create profound vulnerabilities in the context of social relationships.

Mentalization is a term originally introduced by French psychoanalysts (e.g., Luquet, 1987; Marty, 1990), but the concept evolved in a different direction in the 1980s when an extremely active research programme in developmental psychology elucidated the timing of the acquisition of the capacity to understand that people are capable of having false beliefs about the world (Wellman, 1990). Yet a number of researchers consider the resulting construct of *theory of mind* and its false-belief paradigm to be too narrow as it fails to encapsulate the relational and affect regulative aspects of interpreting behaviour in mental state terms (Carpendale & Chandler, 1996). Developmentalists also have started to use the term *mentalizing* as an alternative, because it is not limited either to

Handbook of Mentalization-Based Treatment. Edited by J. G. Allen and P. Fonagy.
© 2006 John Wiley & Sons, Ltd.

specific tasks or particular age groups (Morton & Frith, 1995; O'Connor & Hirsch, 1999).

We define mentalization following a tradition in philosophy of mind established by Brentano (1973/1874), Dennett (1978) and others as a form of mostly preconscious imaginative mental activity, namely, perceiving and interpreting human behaviour in terms of intentional mental states (e.g., needs, desires, feelings, beliefs, goals, purposes, and reasons). Mentalizing is imaginative because we have to imagine what other people might be thinking or feeling; an important indicator of high quality of mentalization is the awareness that we do not and cannot know absolutely what is in someone else's mind. We suggest that a similar kind of imaginative leap is required to understand one's own mental experience, particularly in relation to emotionally charged issues. In order to conceive of others as having a mind, the individual needs a symbolic representational system for mental states and also must be able to selectively activate states of mind in line with particular intentions, which requires attentional control.

As this whole chapter will explicate, we have mapped the process by which the understanding of the self as a mental agent grows out of interpersonal experience, particularly primary object relationships (Fonagy, 2003). The baby's experience of himself as having a mind or psychological self is not a genetic given; it evolves from infancy through childhood, and its development critically depends upon interaction with more mature minds, assuming these are benign, reflective and sufficiently attuned. Mentalization involves both a self-reflective and an interpersonal component and is underpinned by a large number of specific cognitive skills that include an understanding of emotional states, attention and effortful control, and the capacity to make judgments about subjective states as well as thinking explicitly about states of mind – what we might call mentalization proper. In combination, these functions provide the child with a capacity to distinguish inner from outer reality and internal mental and emotional processes from interpersonal events.

Providing the broad scientific foundation for the clinical approaches articulated throughout this volume, this chapter provides an overview of the mentalization-focused approach to social development from a thoroughly bio-psycho-social framework. In the spirit of Bowlby's pioneering work, the chapter begins by addressing the cardinal role of mentalizing in the evolution of attachment and then summarizes contemporary neurobiological research bearing on the cognitive, affective and relational aspects of mentalizing. This biological perspective provides the backdrop for a discussion of the role of mentalizing in the development of the agentive sense of self, followed by a broader consideration of the role of interpersonal relationships in the maturation of mentalizing capacities. The chapter concludes by discussing how attachment trauma contributes to the development of psychopathology by virtue of undermining mentalizing capacity.

EVOLUTIONARY AND NEUROBIOLOGICAL LINKS BETWEEN ATTACHMENT AND MENTALIZATION

The Selective Advantages of Attachment

More than most psychologists – let alone psychoanalysts – John Bowlby (1969) had cast attachment theory into the mould of a fledgling sociobiological approach. The prolonged vulnerability of the mammalian infant clearly necessitates biological preparedness of the infant's penchant to seek protection from conspecifics (older members of the same species) coupled with the attachment figures' disposition to provide caretaking. The biological preparedness to encode the nature of the interaction between infant and caregiver as a template or working model may carry particular selective advantages in orienting the individual to the most adaptive strategies in a particular risk environment (Belsky, 1999a).

As our understanding of the interface of brain development and early psychosocial experience increases, we can see that the evolutionary role of the attachment relationship goes far beyond giving physical protection to the human infant. Attachment ensures that the brain processes that come to subserve social cognition are appropriately organized and prepared to equip the individual for the collaborative and cooperative existence with others for which the brain was designed (Fonagy, 2003).

In our view the major selective advantage conferred by attachment to humans is the opportunity that nearness to concerned adults affords for the development of social intelligence and meaning-making (Fonagy, 2003). Alan Sroufe (1996) and Myron Hofer (2004) were the key instigators in extending attachment theory from a concern with the developmental emergence of a complex set of social expectancies to a far broader conception of attachment as an organizer of physiological and brain regulation. More recent work has begun to articulate the associated biological pathways (e.g., Plotsky et al., 2005; Zhang, Chretien, Meaney & Gratton, 2005). This body of work illustrates how processes as fundamental as gene expression or changes in receptor densities are influenced by the infant's environment. The brain is experience-expectant (Siegel, 1999).

The Selective Advantages of Mentalization

Mentalization is arguably the evolutionary pinnacle of human intellectual achievement. But what has driven the selection processes of the two million or so years of human evolution towards a consciousness of mental states in self and others? Was it to meet the periodic challenges the physical environment presented to our ancestors who were presumably only somewhat more agile and strong than we are? Surprisingly, leaps forward in human brain size in the course of evolution do not correspond to what we know about ecological demands on our hominid ancestors (e.g., climatic variability, threat of predation, and availability of prey).

The evolutionary biologist Richard Alexander (1989) proposed a widely accepted model of how humans evolved their minds. He suggested that our exceptional intelligence evolved not to deal with the hostile forces of nature but rather to deal with competition from other people. This further evolution occurred only *after* our species had already achieved relative dominance over their environment. At that point we became our "own principal hostile forces of nature" (Alexander, 1989, p. 469). And to meet this challenge to the survival of our genes, those with common genetic material had to cooperate.

All species face competition from conspecifics but humans are special in the role that social groups play in achieving success in this regard. A kind of evolutionary arms race probably took place among ever more effective social groups (Flinn, Geary & Ward, 2005). The successes of one's coalition depended on competency in social cognition, the key part of which is the symbolic representation of mental states, what we call mentalizing. Competition with intelligent conspecifics requires skill in understanding and outsmarting other people. As the intelligence of the opposition increased so too did the requirement for ever-greater ability for communication, imaginative social understanding, the anticipation of counter strategies, and the evaluation of strategies for meeting these imaginative mental simulations. The construction and manipulation of mental scenarios (of thoughts about thoughts and feelings) thus acquired a major reproductive advantage. The assumption that the mind governs actions and the possibility of interpreting and anticipating behaviour permits cooperation, offers competitive advantage, and continually selects for increasingly higher levels of social interpretive capacity.

The Interpersonal Interpretive Function

The capacity to interpret human behaviour (Bogdan, 1997) requires the intentional stance: "treating the object whose behaviour you want to predict as a rational agent with beliefs and desires" (Dennett, 1987, p. 15). We label this capacity the *interpersonal interpretive function* (IIF), an evolutionary-developmental function of attachment. Unlike Bowlby's internal working model concept, its function is not to encode representations of attachment experiences, nor is it a repository of personal encounters as in Stern et al.'s (1998) concept of schemata-of-ways-of-being-with. Rather, the IIF is a cluster of mental functions for processing and interpreting new interpersonal experiences that includes mentalization and the cluster of psychological processes on which effective mentalizing depends (Fonagy, 2003).

The emphasis on interpretation is helpful because we are particularly concerned with the possibility of the *mis*interpretations and *mis*perceptions of others' thoughts, feelings and intentions. Interpretive function also underscores the perspective-taking facet of mentalization that equips us to recognize how individuals can come to different conclusions with the same set of facts at their disposal (Carpendale & Chandler, 1996). Following Baron-Cohen's (2003) distinction between theory of mind and empathy, we have suggested that a cognition-oriented interpersonal interpretive function (IIF-C) is complemented by an emotion- or affect-oriented set of processes (IIF-A). Earlier, Henry Wellman proposed a related developmental transition from a desire psychology of toddlers to a belief-desire psychology of three- to four-year-olds (Bartsch & Wellman, 1995). We also include in IIF-A the notion of *mentalized affectivity*, which refers to the simultaneous experiencing and knowing of a feeling.

Three Neural Systems of Social Cognition

We have considered four emotional processing and control mechanisms that contribute to the developmental unfolding of interpretative function: labelling and understanding affect, arousal regulation, effortful control, and specific mentalizing capacities (Fonagy & Target, 2002). We propose that these interpretive functions are subserved by three separate but interconnected and interacting nodes within the brain that are related to social-detection, affect regulation and cognitive regulation (Adolphs, 2003; Nelson, Leibenluft, McClure & Pine, 2005).

The first node consists of a hard-wired set of structures that categorizes stimuli as social and deciphers or detects their social purpose. The brain regions that make up this social-detection node include the fusiform face area, the superior temporal sulcus, and the anterior temporal cortex. These regions have been shown to be involved in carrying out basic perceptual processes on social stimuli.

The second node is concerned with affect and encompasses regions of the brain engaged by reward and punishment. The generation of affect imbues social stimuli with emotional significance and modulates emotional arousal. The system has a significant role in mediating attachment experience and is activated by attachment-related stimuli. Brain regions that make up the affect-regulation node include the amygdala, hypothalamus, nucleus accumbens, and bed nucleus of the stria terminalis. These regions interact with the social-detection node, giving social stimuli emotional significance.

Our primary concern, the third node, is devoted to cognitive regulation. Its key functions include inhibiting pre-potent responses (effortful control), mediating goal-directed behaviour, and mentalizing (as exemplified in perspective taking and theory-of-mind tasks). The brain regions that make up the cognitive-regulation node include the dorsomedial pre-frontal cortex and the ventral pre-frontal cortex. There are several systems within these structures that mediate different aspects of regulation and control, including integrating emotion with cognitive processing and making accurate social judgments. Each of these aspects of social intelligence subserves different aspects of interpersonal interpretation.

Of greatest concern for mentalizing are evolutionary changes in human brain structure concerned with cognitive mediation of social intelligence in conjunction with a 10% expansion in parts of the pre-frontal cortex (Semendeferi & Damasio, 2000) along with an increased richness of interconnections between neurons (Miller & Cohen, 2001). These structures underpin awareness of social dynamics and the capacity to imagine responses to changes in these dynamics (Geary, 2005). The brain structures involved appear to be manifold yet reasonably specific to aspects and components of the task of understanding mental states. Developmental and neuropsychological observations help identify the likely components of mentalization.

The foundations of mentalization are present in non-human species. Recent work on the *mirror-neuron system* (Gallese, Keysers & Rizzolatti, 2004; Rizzolatti & Craighero, 2004) claims that understanding others' actions requires the activation of the mirror-neuron system, and understanding others' emotions requires the activation of viscero-motor centres. Motor neurons, originally found in the ventral premotor cortex of the macaque monkey, respond both when the monkey *performs* a particular goal-directed act and when it *observes* another individual performing a similar action (Gallese, Fadiga, Fogassi & Rizzolatti, 1996). Action observation automatically activates the same neural mechanism triggered by action execution or even by the sound produced by the same action (Kohler et al., 2002). The mirror-neuron system also encompasses communicative actions, both in monkeys (Ferrari, Gallese, Rizzolatti & Fogassi, 2003) and in humans (Rizzolatti & Craighero, 2004). In a recent functional magnetic resonance imaging (fMRI) study, participants observed communicative mouth actions in humans, monkeys and dogs, which led to the activation of different cortical foci corresponding to the different observed species; actions in the motor repertoire of the observer (e.g., biting and speech reading) were mapped accordingly onto the observer's motor system (Buccino et al., 2004).

Extrapolating from mirror-neuron research, we might conceive of a two-level system underpinning mentalization: a frontal-cortical system that invokes declarative representations and a mirror-neuron system subserving a more immediate and direct understanding of the other. In the anterior insula, visual information concerning the emotions of others is directly mapped onto the same visceromotor neural structures that determine the experience of that emotion in the observer (Wicker et al., 2003). This direct mapping can occur even when the emotion of others is merely imagined (Singer et al., 2004). Gallese and Goldman hypothesize a shared sub-personal neural mapping between what is enacted and what is perceived that can be used to predict the actions of others (Gallese, 2003; Goldman & Sripada, 2005). This automatically established link between agent and observer may not be the only way in which the emotions of others can be understood, but the simulation of actions by means of the activation of parietal and premotor cortical networks may constitute a basic level of experiential understanding that does not entail the explicit use of any theory or declarative representation.

Mentalization also entails *inhibitory controls* necessary for the child to suppress the pre-potent assumption that everyone else shares the same knowledge and beliefs; these controls thereby enable the child to recognize the existence of separate minds (Moses, Baldwin, Rosicky & Tidball, 2001). Studies of response conflict unequivocally indicate that inhibitory controls require the activation of the anterior cingulate cortex (ACC) along with the dorsolateral pre-frontal cortex and superior parietal lobe (e.g., Braver, Barch, Gray, Molfese & Snyder, 2001; Sylvester et al., 2003).

Accumulating evidence indicates that some structures responsible for *understanding affect* in others are independent from systems that mediate belief attribution. Neural systems associated with the perception and experience of emotions include the extrastriate cortex, right parietal cortex, right fusiform gyrus, orbitofrontal cortices, amygdala, insula, and basal ganglia (Adolphs, 2002; Hamann, 2003).

Belief attribution – reasoning about false beliefs or making judgments about someone's knowledge or ignorance about a topic – increases brain activity in the medial pre-frontal cortex (anterior to the ACC), temporal poles bilaterally, anterior superior temporal sulcus, and bilateral temporo-parietal junction extending into posterior temporal sulcus (Ferstl & von Cramon, 2002; Vogeley et al., 2001). These areas appear to be specific to belief attribution rather than general reasoning about people or reasoning about non-mental false representations or hidden cues, in general. The medial pre-frontal cortex shows significant increases in activation during false-belief stories but not stories about true beliefs that could be action-based and that require no representational component (Fletcher et al., 1995; Gallagher et al., 2000). From such observations some reviews limit the uniquely theory-of-mind area to the medial pre-frontal region of the cortex (Gallagher & Frith, 2003).

The cortical systems associated with the *attributions of desires and goals* have been investigated using vignettes, cartoons and animations that depict or suggest a character's intentions. Looking at these stimuli tends to be associated with moderately enhanced activity in the brain regions linked to belief attributions, including the medial pre-frontal cortex and posterior superior temporal sulcus (e.g., Saxe & Kanwisher, 2003; Schultz et al., 2003). When subjects engage in simple games with an unseen agent as contrasted with playing a computer, the activation of the medial pre-frontal cortex is increased (Gallagher, Jack, Roepstorff & Frith, 2002). This part of the brain appears to respond more to any story that contains a person than to stories that do not involve humans (Saxe & Kanwisher, 2003).

Given that mentalization is a solely human capacity, a broad-brush approach to its localization might be to identify brain aspects unique to humans. There is a class of large and clustered spindle cells unique to humans in the ACC (Nimchinsky et al., 1999), and there are other unique features of human neuroanatomy, such as increased lateralization, that underpin social interpretation. There was a disproportionate expansion in humans of the right pre-frontal cortex and the frontal pole (Holloway, 1996; Zilles et al., 1996), areas of the brain that have been shown by imaging studies to be involved in self-awareness as well as the ability to remember personal experiences and to project oneself into the future (Tulving, 2002).

Mentalizing pertains to interpreting mental states in both self and others. Representing the contents of one's own mind taps into the same meta-representational capacity required for representing the contents of another's mind (Frith & Frith, 2003). Self-awareness and awareness of the mental states of others are closely linked in terms of the brain areas involved. Mentalization does not just facilitate collaboration and positive relationships but also facilitates social survival through competition. Self-awareness enables us to modify the way we present ourselves to others and to mislead them. The right pre-frontal cortex may "allow us to see ourselves as others see us so that we may cause competitive others to see us as we wish them to" (Alexander, 1990, p. 7).

The Evolutionary Psychology of Mentalization

The evolutionary leap in human intelligence over the past four hundred thousand years or so was partly driven by a self-perpetuating need to understand how the minds of our competitors work. As the mind needs to adapt to ever more challenging competitive conditions, the capacity cannot be fixed by genetics or constitution; it must be optimized through a prolonged period of development by a group of kin, that is, attachment figures. Mentalization exists not only to permit superior adaptation to the physical environment through facilitating social collaboration and well-functioning kinship groups but also to support competition for survival when social groups are at odds. Thus, the social brain must continuously reach higher and higher levels of sophistication to stay on top. Evolution could not leave it to genes alone.

Evolution has charged attachment relationships with ensuring the full development of the social brain. The capacity for mentalization, along with many other social-cognitive capacities, evolves out of the experience of social interaction with caregivers. Increased sophistication in social cognition evolved hand in hand with apparently unrelated aspects of development, such as increased helplessness in infancy, a prolongation of childhood, and the emergence of intensive parenting.

We have proposed a mechanism for this process rooted in dialectic models of self-development (Cavell, 1991; Davidson, 1983). Children discover minds in their objects as they try to find themselves in their actions. This approach explicitly rejects the classical Cartesian assumption that mental states are apprehended by introspection; on the contrary, mental states are discovered through contingent mirroring interactions with the caregiver (Gergely & Watson, 1999). Psychoanalysts have long assumed that the child's capacity to represent mental states symbolically is acquired within the primary object relationship. Therefore, early disruption of affectional bonds not only will set up maladaptive attachment patterns but also will undermine a range of capacities vital to normal social development. Understanding minds is difficult if one has not had the experience of being understood as a person with a mind.

Are we placing an excessive burden upon the caregiver–infant relationship? Would nature have created a system fundamental to the development of social cognition if it were so vulnerable to the vicissitudes of the relationship of the mother and her infant? We must remember that placing the social development of a human infant in the hands of one adult is a recent phenomenon compared to the previous average of four relatives who had a genetic stake in the child's survival (Hrdy, 2000). Recent neurobiological evidence discussed next buttresses the ecological view of attachment relationships as pivotally linked to mentalizing capacities.

The Neurobiology of Attachment

Paradoxically, although secure attachment relationships promote the development of mentalizing capacities, recent neuroimaging studies demonstrate that some attachment phenomena also *deactivate* mentalizing. This research helpfully underscores the sheer complexity of the relations between attachment and mentalizing. Secure attachment probably enhances mentalizing; yet being in an attachment relationship, which activates the attachment system, probably makes people less acutely aware of and judgmental about the mental states of others. As suggested earlier, this configuration creates flexibility and an opportunity to practise in a safe context that makes attachment the ideal vehicle for the development of social cognition. Thus, whether attachment inhibits or enhances mentalizing depends on the general quality of the attachment relationship as well as dynamic variations in the emotional state of the relationship.

The neurobiology of attachment is now linked to the mesocorticolimbic dopaminergic reward circuit, which also plays a key role in mediating the process of addiction (Insel, 1997; Panksepp, 1998). Nature hardly created a brain system specifically to subserve cocaine and alcohol abuse; addictions are the accidental by-product of the activation of a biological system that underpins the crucial evolutionary function of attachment (Insel, 1997; Panksepp, 1998). Iron-ically, attachment can be construed as an addictive disorder (Insel, 2003) in the sense that falling in love, which is stimulated by social/sexual activity, entails the activation of an oxytocin- and vasopressin-sensitive circuit within the anterior hypothalamus (MPOA) linked to the ventral tegmental area and the nucleus accumbens (Insel, 2003). fMRI studies indicate specific activation of these reward-sensitive pathways in the brain of somebody seeing their own baby or partner as compared to another familiar baby or other persons' partners (Nitschke et al., 2004).

In two separate imaging studies, Bartels and Zeki (2000, 2004) reported that the activation of areas mediating maternal and/or romantic attachments appeared simultaneously to suppress brain activity in several brain regions mediating different aspects of cognitive regulation and control and including those asso-ciated with making social judgments and mentalizing. Bartels and Zeki (2004) suggest grouping these reciprocally active areas into two functional regions, which we designate system A and system B. *System A* includes the middle pre-frontal, inferior parietal, and middle temporal cortices mainly in the right hemisphere, as well as the posterior cingulate cortex. These areas are specialized for attention and long-term memory (Cabeza & Nyberg, 2000), and they have variable involvement in both positive (Maddock, 1999) and negative (Mayberg et al., 1999) emotions. These areas may be specifically responsible for integrating emotion and cognition, for example, in emotional encoding of episodic memories (e.g., Maddock, 1999). In addition, lesion studies suggest a role in judgments involving negative emotions (Adolphs, Damasio, Tranel, Cooper & Damasio, 2000). It is possible that, as projections from the affect-oriented limbic/paralimbic regions modulate the activity of these areas, they could subserve mood-mediated inhibition or enhancement of cognitive processing (Mayberg et al., 1999). These areas also may play a role in recalling emotion-related material and generating emotion-related imagery (Maddock, 1999) that may be relevant to understanding the typology of attachment.

The second set of areas deactivated by the activation of the attachment system, *system B*, includes the temporal poles, parietotemporal junction, amygdala, and mesial pre-frontal cortex. Activation of these areas is consistently linked to nega-tive affect, judgments of social trustworthiness, moral judgments, theory-of-mind tasks, and attention to one's own emotions. System B constitutes the primary neural network underlying the ability to identify and interpret mental states (both thoughts and feelings) in other people (Frith & Frith, 2003; Gallagher & Frith, 2003) as well as in the self (Gusnard, Akbudak, Shulman & Raichle, 2001). The structures in system B are also associated with intuitive judgments of moral appropriateness (Greene & Haidt, 2002) and of social trustworthiness based on facial expressions (Winston, Strange, O'Doherty & Dolan, 2002).

The pattern of activation of the attachment system and the two overlapping cognitive information processing control systems has important implications for our understanding of the nature of individual differences in attachment, the relationship of attachment and mentalization and, consequently, our understanding of dysfunctions associated with mentalizing deficits. Broadly, three conditions in attachment relationships inhibit or suppress aspects of social cognition associated with mentalizing the attachment figure. First, the love-related activation of the attachment system, mediated by dopaminergic structures of the reward system in the presence of oxytocin and vasopressin, inhibits neural systems that underpin the generation of negative affect and that sometimes prompt mentalizing. This is to be expected: a key function of the attachment system is moderating negative emotions in infancy and, indeed, throughout life (Sroufe, 1996). Second, threat-related activation of the attachment system (e.g., triggered by loss or harm) deactivates mentalizing by virtue of evoking overwhelming negative affect. Third, a stable secure attachment relationship obviates the need for mentalizing insofar as the need to make judgments of social trustworthiness that distance us from others becomes less relevant and indeed may impede relationships with those to whom we are strongly attached.

These findings are extremely important. From the evolutionary perspective, competition requires thinking about motives, but attachment involves trust. To be attached to others is to trust them implicitly, to assume that their motivation is known and benign; indeed, love is blind and the mental states of the attachment figures will perhaps always remain somewhat enigmatic. Psychotherapy might provide a much-needed opportunity for clarification and elaboration of the thoughts and feelings of attachment figures in the past and present in part because the "heat" has moved from them to the analyst in the transference.

To recapitulate, intense emotional states in attachment relationships – be they related to passionate love or threat – deactivate mentalizing capacities. In contrast, stable security presents little need to mentalize. Yet we know that secure attachment also *facilitates* mentalizing. We explain this seeming paradox by proposing that three general qualities of secure attachment relationships are conducive to mentalizing. First, *moderate* levels of negative affect associated with inevitable conflicts and fears in the attachment relationship will evoke the need to mentalize; yet the security and soothing provided by the generally benevolent relationship will afford the needed emotional containment to support mentalizing. Second, while not consistently *necessitating* mentalizing, a secure attachment relationship provides a level of positive emotional arousal conducive to *interest* in mentalizing. Closely related to this second point is the third and crucial point: in a secure attachment relationship, the attachment figure is continually mentalizing the infant or child (in the context of ordinary stressors and otherwise) and thus actively stimulating mentalizing.

To elaborate this third point, acquiring the capacity to think about mental states is likely to be facilitated by attachment because it is safe to make mistakes. Attachment has been selected by evolution as the principal training ground for the acquisition of mentalization because attachment is a marker for shared genetic material, reciprocal relationships and altruism. Attachment is a generally non-competitive relationship in which the aim is not to outsmart others; thus learning about minds can be safely practised. Conversely, extreme neglect – the absence of mentalizing on the part of attachment figures – profoundly undermines the development of mentalizing. As observations of the Romanian orphans attest, missing out on early attachment experience creates a long-term vulnerability from which the child may never recover; the capacity for mentalization is never fully established, leaving the child vulnerable to later trauma and unable to cope fully with attachment relationships (e.g., Rutter & O'Connor, 2004). More importantly, trauma – especially attachment trauma – constitutes the extreme of threat-related activation of attachment, which decouples the capacity for mentalization.

Implications of Attachment–Mentalization Reciprocity

Under a range of conditions just enumerated, there is a reciprocal relation between the activation of the attachment system and mentalizing activity. The neural association between attachment and mentalization confirms the link we have identified between the two systems at a behavioural level, and the reciprocal activation of attachment and mentalization is also consistent with the assumption of an evolutionary learning function that we assigned to the primary attachment relationships as the context for the acquisition of some of the basics of social cognition.

Yet we also have emphasized the dynamic and variable nature of the attachment–mentalizing relation. We have demonstrated how the parent's capacity to mentalize in the context of an attachment relationship facilitates the development of secure attachment in the infant (Fonagy, Steele, Moran, Steele & Higgitt, 1991). Taking an evolutionary perspective, the parent's capacity to mentalize reduces the child's need to monitor the parent for trustworthiness. Relaxing the need to know the intentional state of the other facilitates the emergence of a strong attachment bond. The caregiver's high level of contingency with the infant's behaviour enhances a sense of being known. In this way secure attachment establishes a robust sense of an agentive self which can later be used as the basis for an understanding of others' mental states through a process that has been described as one of simulation, projecting oneself into the mental state of the other. We also have seen that theory of mind emerges precociously in children who were securely attached in infancy (e.g., Meins, 1997), a finding to be expected when there are fewer calls for the kind of threat-related activation of the attachment system that suppresses mentalizing. Accordingly, mentalization in the parent engenders secure attachment, which in turn is the context for the precocious development of mentalization in the child.

Furthermore, the capacity to mentalize in the context of attachment is likely to be somewhat independent of the capacity to mentalize in non-attachment relationships (Fonagy & Target, 1997a). Our specific measure of mentalization in the attachment context (Fonagy, Target, Steele & Steele, 1998) predicts behavioural outcomes that other measures of mentalization do not. For example, in a quasi-longitudinal study of young adults, we found that the impact of trauma on mentalization in attachment contexts mediated the quality of adult romantic relationships, but mentalization measured independently of the attachment context did not (Fonagy, Stein, Allen & Fultz, 2003a).

In sum, the key consideration explaining the positive general association between secure attachment and mentalizing capacities is this: securely attached children need not activate their attachment system as often and thus have greater opportunity to practise mentalizing in the context of the child–caregiver relationship. Further, Belsky's (1999b) evolutionary model of attachment classification suggests that, when resources are scarce, insecure attachment strategies are most adaptive insofar as children must monitor carefully the unpredictable caregivers' mental states, and they are forced to find alternative social contexts to acquire social-cognitive capacities. Thus, insecurely attached children are deprived of some developmental learning opportunities for understanding minds in relatively non-conflictual and exploratory ways – at least in the context of attachment relationships.

Mentalization and Attachment Classification

From an evolutionary perspective, mentalization may be less relevant in the attachment context than in competitive social contexts; nevertheless, mentalizing accurately in attachment relationships also is highly desirable. Individuals who are able to mentalize while thinking about romantic partners or offspring will manage these relationships better; they may have less turbulent attachment relationships; and they may be particularly effective in resolving inevitable conflicts and arguments. Hence secure attachment is marked by a relatively good capacity to generate coherent narratives of turbulent interpersonal episodes (Main, 2000). From a neurobiological perspective, we would predict that individuals who are able to retain a relatively high activation of the parieto-temporal junction together with the mesial pre-frontal cortex in the presence of the activation of the reward-sensitive dopaminergic mesolimbic pathways are most likely to be classified as secure in their attachment.

We speculate that the two principal insecure attachment strategies also may be interpretable in terms of the relative state of activation of attachment-related brain systems. Insecure-dismissing individuals are those who, because of their adverse past attachment experiences, become particularly effective in inhibiting both reciprocal systems outlined above. This deactivation would then be expected to lead to a reduced availability of long-term memories imbued with either positive or negative emotion, giving rise to the typical narrative pattern of an inability to recall attachment experiences and to recover emotion-laden memories in interviews aimed at activating the attachment system. Dismissing individuals also might manifest an unthinking or inconsiderate approach to intimate interpersonal relations (Main, 2000). By contrast, in insecure-preoccupied individuals, the attachment system may be less effective in suppressing the activity of the two reciprocal systems, resulting in greater negativity in attachment narratives and unusually good access to past attachment experience, giving the impression of current preoccupation with past events (Main, 2000).

In sum, insecurity may entail either too little or too much deactivation of emotional memory, negative affect, moral and social judgments, and mentalizing. Plainly, this model also allows for variations and degrees: different attachment relationships may achieve different degrees of deactivation of the two reciprocally activated structures.

THE DEVELOPMENT OF AN AGENTIVE SELF

The Model of Contingent Mirroring

William James (1890) distinguished two facets of the self, the "I" – self as agent – and the "me" – the self-representation. The agentive self, the self that acts and experiences continuity and control, is in essence the awareness of mind in the self as the driver of behaviour and as distinct from mind of others in interaction with the self. Our evolutionary neurobiological speculations imply that children's caregiving environments play a key role in the development of their acquisition of an understanding of increasingly complex levels of self-agency: the physical and social stance progresses to teleological, intentional and representational stances in turn (Fonagy et al., 2002).

In the first months the baby senses that he is a *physical agent* whose actions can bring about changes in bodies with which he has immediate physical contact (Leslie, 1994). Concomitantly, from birth, the baby senses himself as a *social agent*: through interactions with the caregiver, the baby learns that his communicative displays produce effects at a distance on his caregiver's behaviour and emotions (Neisser, 1988). The sense of self as a physical and social agent probably evolves through an innate contingency-detection mechanism that enables the infant to analyse the probability of causal links between his actions and stimulus events (Watson, 1995).

Prior to the age of about three to four months, infants show a preference for perfect action-stimulus contingencies; at that age, they switch to preferring nearly, but clearly not perfect contingencies (Bahrick & Watson, 1985). The initial preoccupation with perfectly response-contingent stimulation (provided by the proprioceptive sensory feedback that the self's actions always generate) allows the infant to differentiate his agentive self as a separate entity in the environment and to construct a primary representation of the bodily self.

The switch that takes place in the contingency-detection module at about three months predisposes infants to turn their attention to high-but-imperfect contingencies – the kind of contingent reactivity that is characteristic of the interactions of infant-attuned caregivers, exemplified by their empathic mirroring reactions to the infant's affective displays. Repeated experience with such affect-reflective caregiver reactions is essential for infants to become sensitized to, and to construct differentiated representations of, their internal self-states, a process we termed *social bio-feedback* (Gergely & Watson, 1996). Through providing such a state-reflective scaffolding environment, a congenial and secure attachment relationship can vitally contribute to the emergence of early mentalizing capacities, allowing infants to discover or find their psychological self in the social world (Gergely, 2001). The discovery of the representational or psychological (fully mentalized) self is probably based in the same mechanism. Children with autism do not make the three- to four-months switch from perfect to imperfect contingency seeking and consequently show little interest in the social world (Gergely & Watson, 1999; Koós & Gergely, 2001).

Regulating Emotion and Secure Attachment

The development of an understanding of affects illustrates the significance of highly contingent responsiveness. At first, infants are not introspectively aware of different emotion states. Rather, their representations of emotions are primarily based on stimuli received from the external world. Babies learn to differentiate the internal patterns of physiological and visceral stimulation that accompany different emotions through observing their caregivers' facial or vocal mirroring responses (e.g., Legerstee & Varghese, 2001; Mitchell, 1993). First, the baby learns to associate his influence over his parents' mirroring displays with improvement in his emotional state: he feels better simply by virtue of eliciting a mirroring response. Eventually, this leads to an experience of the self as a regulating agent. Second, the establishment of a second-order representation of affect states creates the basis for affect regulation and impulse control: affects can be manipulated and discharged internally as well as through action; they also can be experienced as something recognizable and hence shared. Affect expressions by the parent that are not contingent on the infant's affect will undermine the appropriate labelling of internal states which may, in turn, remain confusing, experienced as unsymbolized and hard to regulate.

Two conditions must be met if the capacity to understand and regulate emotion is to develop: first, reasonable congruency of mirroring whereby the caregiver accurately matches the infant's mental state and, second, *markedness* of the mirroring whereby the caregiver is able to express an affect while indicating that she is not expressing her own feelings (Gergely & Watson, 1999). For affect mirroring to serve as the basis of the development of a representational framework, the parent must indicate that her display is not for real; it is not an indication of how she *herself* feels. Consequently, two difficulties may arise. First, in the case of incongruent mirroring, the infant's mirroring-based representation will not correspond to the internal constitutional state, repeated experience of which might predispose to a narcissistic structure analogous to Winnicott's false-self (Winnicott, 1965). Second, in cases of unmarked mirroring, the caregiver's expression may be seen as externalization of the infant's experience; this might establish a predisposition to experiencing emotion through other people as in a borderline personality structure (Fonagy et al., 2002). An expression congruent with the baby's state, but lacking markedness (i.e., the parent's own real emotion), may overwhelm the infant, making his experience seem contagious or universal and thus more dangerous. The baby's perception of a corresponding but realistic negative emotion is likely to escalate rather than regulate the emotional state, leading to cumulative traumatization rather than containment.

The distressed child looks for a representation of his mental state in the response of the parent; then he may internalize the response and use it as part of a higher-order strategy of affect regulation. The secure caregiver soothes by combining mirroring with a display that is incompatible with the child's feelings, for example, expressing distress coupled with loving tenderness or anger coupled with surprise. These marked emotional responses demonstrate contact coupled with some detachment and affect mastery on the part of the parent. This formulation of sensitivity has much in common with Bion's (1962) notion of the role of the mother's capacity to mentally *contain* the affect state that feels intolerable to the baby, and to respond in a manner that acknowledges the child's mental state yet serves to modulate unmanageable feelings (see Holmes, Chapter 2). Well-regulated affect in the infant–parent dyad is internalized by the child to form the basis of a secure attachment bond and a corresponding internal working model (Sroufe, 1996). This formulation is supported by research showing that measures of each parent's mentalizing capacity during pregnancy independently predict the child's later security of attachment (Fonagy, Steele, Moran, Steele & Higgitt, 1992). If the quality of affect regulation is the key to the infant's being securely attached, then the mother's capacity to mentalize should increase the chance of secure attachment in the infant through establishing better affect regulation. However, this inference must be tested more directly, because the parents' capacity to mentalize was measured in relation to their own childhood and their capacity to do likewise with their child was assumed rather than observed.

Parental Mentalization, Affect Regulation, and Secure Attachment

Three programmes of work have examined interactional narratives between parents and children (Grienenberger, Kelly & Slade, 2005; Koren-Karie, Oppenheim,

Dolev, Sher & Etzion-Carasso, 2002; Meins, Ferryhough, Fradley & Tuckey, 2001; Oppenheim & Koren-Karie, 2002; Schechter et al., 2005; Slade, 2005; Slade, Grienenberger, Bernbach, Levy & Locker, 2005). Meins and colleagues assessed mentalizing from mothers' verbalizations to a six-month-old infant. For example, mothers were asked, "Can you describe [child] for me?" and their responses were categorized as being mental, behavioural, physical or general (Meins & Fernyhough, 1999). This is an offline measure of mentalizing, but Meins and colleagues also developed a more online measure based on 20 minutes of free play coded for appropriate mind-related comments. Mind-related comments were shown to be predictive of attachment security at 12 months (Meins et al., 2001), mentalizing capacity at 45 and 48 months (Meins et al., 2002), and stream of consciousness performance at 55 months (Meins et al., 2003). In Oppenheim and colleagues' studies, the mothers provided commentaries on their own previously recorded playful interaction with their child. Both studies found that high levels of mentalization of the child in the mothers' narratives were associated with secure infant–mother attachment. Both studies also demonstrated that mentalizing of the child in the context of the mother–child relationship, rather than global sensitivity, predicted security of attachment. Yet the studies assessed mentalization differently: Meins assessed the quality of the parents' thinking about the child in real time in the course of an interaction, whereas Oppenheim employed a more reflective, offline measure. Both measures yielded an indication of the parent's quality of mentalization of a particular moment of interaction; neither measured the extent to which mothers generally mentalize their relationship with their child.

Slade and colleagues' (Slade et al., 2005) study extends previous observations by using an autobiographical memory measure, the Parent Development Interview (PDI), rather than an episode of observed interaction. These researchers found strong relationships between attachment in the infant and the quality of mentalizing in the parent about the child. The PDI aggregates mentalizing across many episodes of interaction, yielding a prototype from the mother's autobiographical memory (Conway, 1996). In a structural model of autobiographical memory, Conway (1992) proposed that two types of autobiographical memories exist within a hierarchical autobiographical memory system: unique, specific events and repeated, general memories. The PDI accesses general memories assumed to have a preferred level of entry to the autobiographical memory system (Addis, McIntosh, Moscovitch, Crawley & McAndrews, 2004).

The PDI permits scrutiny of the extent of mentalizing in the commentary on remembered events and thus reveals the mother's offline reflective mentalizing capacity and her predominant stance towards the child as an intentional being, perhaps reflecting many hundreds of interactions and thus providing greater accuracy of prediction. Thus, the PDI indexes more than simple mind-mindedness (Meins et al., 2001), measured as the complexity of mental state terms and concepts used. High scorers on the PDI mentalizing scale are aware of the characteristics of mental functioning in their infant and grasp the complex interplay between their own mental states and the child's inner experience.

Informative as it may be, this research does not take us far enough; we need to know what mothers who have problems mentalizing are actually *doing* in their interactions with their infants. Helpfully, Slade and colleagues' (Slade et al., 2005) study included 10 infants with disorganized attachment whose mothers' mentalizing scores are a standard deviation below those who are secure. Grienenberger and colleagues' (Grienenberger et al., 2005) meticulous study of the mother–infant interactions in this sample showed that mothers of infants with disorganized attachment showed such nonmentalizing behaviours as demanding a show of affection from the infant, fearful behaviour, or intrusive negative behaviours such as mocking or criticizing, along with narratives that show little appreciation that the infant's mind cannot be directly read or that depict her as having no feelings, thoughts or wishes. A strong correlation between the mentalizing narratives and interactive behaviour suggests that the same control mechanism may be responsible for both, and a common neural basis also might underpin both tasks. Hence the mentalizing system might provide input for the organization of both social interaction and person-centred autobiographical narrative.

Through this research, Slade and her colleagues might have closed the transmission gap between parent and infant attachment that Marinus van Ijzendoorn (1995) identified over a decade ago. As we currently formulate it, the mother's secure attachment history permits and enhances her capacity to explore her own mind and promotes a similar enquiring stance towards the mental state of the new human being who has just joined her social world. This stance of open, respectful exploration makes use of her awareness of her own mental state to understand her infant – but not to a point where her understanding would obscure a genuine awareness of her child as an autonomous being. The awareness of the infant, in turn, reduces the frequency of behaviours that would undermine the infant's natural progression towards evolving its own sense of mental self through the dialectic of interactions with the mother. In this context, then, Slade and her group implicitly see disorganization of attachment as the consequence of an undermining of a mental self, or disorganizing the self.

Affect regulation, the capacity to modulate emotional states, is closely related to mentalization, which plays a fundamental role in the unfolding of a sense of self and agency. In this account, affect regulation is a prelude to mentalization; yet, once mentalization occurs, the nature of affect regulation is transformed: not only does mentalizing allow adjustment of emotional states but also, more fundamentally, mentalizing is used to regulate the self. This is an instance of the general principle that the child's capacity to create a coherent image of mind depends on an experience of being perceived as a minded being by the attachment figure.

Mentalized affectivity (Fonagy et al., 2002) marks a mature capacity for affect regulation and denotes discovery of the subjective meanings of one's own feelings. Mentalized affectivity lies at the core of many psychosocial treatments, representing the experiential understanding of one's feelings in a way that extends well beyond intellectual understanding. Here we encounter resistances and defences, not just against specific emotional experiences but also against entire modes of psychological functioning – not just distortions of mental representations standing in the way of therapeutic progress but also inhibitions of mental capacities or processes (Fonagy, Edgcumbe, Moran, Kennedy & Target, 1993). Thus we can misunderstand what we feel, thinking that we feel one thing while truly feeling something else. More seriously, we can deprive ourselves of the entire experiential world of emotional richness. For example, the inability to imagine psychological and psycho-social causation may be the result of the pervasive inhibition and/or developmental malformation of the psychological processes that underpin these capacities.

Establishing Attentional Control

Posner and Rothbart (2000) refer to the ability to inhibit a dominant response to perform a subdominant response as *effortful control by attention*. Early attachment promotes attentional control as the child internalizes the mother's ability to divert the child's attention from one thing to another (Fonagy, 2001). The capacity for effortful control is strongly related to a child's observed willingness to comply with maternal wishes and, indeed, to embrace the maternal agenda (Kochanska, Coy & Murray, 2001). Withholding an impulsive response is a prerequisite for mentalizing, which requires the foregrounding of a distal second-order non-visible stimulus (mental state) in preference to what immediately impinges on the child (physical reality). Theory-of-mind tasks likewise require the child to inhibit pre-potent responses to directly perceived aspects of current reality in favour of generating a response on the basis of less salient representations of reality attributed to other minds. Alan Leslie considers theory of mind to be "a mechanism of selective attention. Mental state concepts simply allow the brain to attend selectively to corresponding mental state properties of agents and thus permit learning about these properties" (Leslie, 2000, p. 1245).

The major function of attachment is the control of distress, and attentional processes must play a key role if the attachment system is to achieve this objective (Harman, Rothbart & Posner, 1997). The interaction between infant and caregiver trains the infant to control distress by orienting the infant away from the source of distress through soothing and involving him in distracting activities. Self-regulation is modelled by the caregiver's regulatory activity. Joint attention with a caregiver serves a self-organizing function in early development (Mundy & Neal, 2001), and intelligence is related to early attachment security (Cicchetti, Rogosch & Toth, 2000; Jacobsen & Hofmann, 1997; van Ijzendoorn &

van Vliet-Visser, 1988). Several studies are consistent with our suggestion that early attachment relationships organize attentional systems. A study of nearly 1,000 children indicated that those with secure attachment appeared to be protected from the effects of cumulative social contextual risk (and male gender) on attentional performance relative to their insecure counterparts (Belsky & Fearon, 2002; Fearon & Belsky, 2004). A further study found that infants with disorganized attachment also had difficulties with social attention coordination in interactions with their caregiver (Schölmerich, Lamb, Leyendecker & Fracasso, 1997). Cocaine-exposed children with disorganized attachment at 12 months showed the greatest dysfunctions of social attention coordination, not only with the caregiver but also with an experimenter, for example, initiating joint attention less often (Claussen, Mundy, Mallik & Willoughby, 2002). Evidence from late-adopted Romanian orphans with profoundly disorganized attachment suggests that severe attention problems are more common in this group than would be expected both in relation to other forms of disturbance and epidemiological considerations (e.g., Kreppner, O'Connor & Rutter, 2001).

We conclude that an enfeebled attentional control system is a likely consequence of attachment disorganization, perhaps linked with enfeebled affect representation; this enfeeblement undermines the development of mentalization as well as its appropriate functioning in later development. The pre-potent response is to attribute one's own mental state to the other. Attentional control is essential if children are to differentiate their own and others' thoughts, feelings, beliefs and desires. The disruption of attentional control is likely to account for many instances where we encounter temporary and selective disruptions of mentalization. Trauma likely further undermines attention regulation and is associated with chronic failures of inhibitory control (Allen, 2001).

The Stages of Acquiring Mentalization

The emergence of mentalizing follows a well-researched developmental line marked by four points.

(1) During the second half of the first year of life, the child begins to construct causal relations that connect actions to their agents and to the world. From about six months, infants recognize that animate objects are self-propelled and distinguish between biological and mechanical movement (Woodward, 1998). Joint attention and social referencing emerge at this time (Tomasello, 1999b). Infants also begin differentiating actions from their outcomes and think about actions as means to ends (Tomasello, 1999a). Infants around nine months begin to view actions in terms of the actor's underlying intentions (Baldwin, Baird, Saylor & Clark, 2001). This marks the beginning of their understanding of themselves as teleological agents who can choose the most efficient way to bring about a goal from a range of alternatives (Csibra

& Gergely, 1998). At this stage, however, agency is understood in terms of purely physical actions and constraints; mental states are not considered. Actors are expected by infants to behave rationally, given concrete goals and obvious physical constraints (Gergely & Csibra, 2003). We relate this nonmentalizing teleological understanding of actions to the mode of experience of agency that we often see in the physically self-destructive acts of individuals with borderline personality disorder who cannot accept anything other than a modification in the realm of the physical as a true index of the intentions of the other (Fonagy, Target & Gergely, 2000).

(2) During the second year, children develop a mentalistic understanding of agency: they and others are intentional agents whose actions are caused by prior states of mind such as desires (Wellman & Phillips, 2000), and their actions can bring about changes in minds as well as bodies, for example, by pointing (Corkum & Moore, 1995). Shared imaginative play is enjoyable and exciting for toddlers and may be the basis for the development of cooperative skills (Brown, Donelan-McCall & Dunn, 1996). Fifteen-month-old children can distinguish between the intended goal of an action and its accidental consequences (Meltzoff, 1995). The capacity for emotion regulation (e.g., frustration tolerance) comes to reflect the relationship with the primary caregiver (Calkins, Gill, Johnson & Smith, 1999). Most importantly, children begin to acquire an internal state language and the ability to reason non-egocentrically about feelings and desires in others (Repacholi & Gopnik, 1997). Ironically, mental state awareness becomes evident not only through the increase in joint goal-directed activity but also through teasing and provocation of younger siblings (Dunn, 1988). However, functional awareness of minds does not yet enable the child to represent mental states independent of physical reality and therefore the distinction between internal and external – appearance and reality – is not yet fully achieved (Flavell & Miller, 1998), making internal reality sometimes far more compelling and at other times inconsequential relative to an awareness of the physical world. We have referred to these states as psychic equivalence and pretend modes respectively (Fonagy et al., 2002), and they are exemplified in post-traumatic flashbacks and dissociative states as well as personality disturbance.

(3) Around three to four years of age, understanding agency in terms of mental causation begins to include the representation of epistemic mental states, that is, beliefs. The young child thus understands himself as a representational agent; he knows that people do not always feel what they appear to feel, and they show emotional reactions to events that are influenced by their current mood or even by earlier emotional experiences that were linked to similar events (Flavell & Miller, 1998). The pre-school child's representational mental states (Wellman, 1990) transform their social interactions; their understanding of emotions becomes associated with empathic behaviour (Zahn-Waxler, Radke-Yarrow, Wagner & Chapman, 1992) and more positive peer relations (Dunn & Cutting, 1999). At this stage, most children appreciate that human behaviour can be influenced by transient mental

states (such as thoughts and feelings) as well as by stable characteristics (such as personality or abilities), and this understanding creates the basis for a structure to underpin an emerging self-concept (Flavell, 1999). They also come to attribute mistaken beliefs to themselves and to others, enriching their repertoire of social interaction with tricks, jokes and deception (Sodian, Taylor, Harris & Perner, 1992). Extensive research shows that, by and large, children younger than three fail the false-belief task and, as age increases, they are increasingly likely to pass (Wellman, Cross & Watson, 2001); hence mentalizing abilities take a quantum leap forward around age four. The early acquisition of false belief is associated with more elaborate pretend play (Taylor & Carlson, 1997), greater connectedness in conversation (Slomkowski & Dunn, 1996), and more social competence (Lalonde & Chandler, 1995). At the same time, children shift from a preference for playing with adults to playing with peers (Dunn, 1994). This shift brings to a close the time when adult minds mediate mentalization and opens a lifelong phase of seeking to enhance the capacity to understand self and others in mental state terms through connectedness with individuals who share one's interests and humour.

(4) In the sixth year, children are able to organize memories of their intentional activities and experiences into a coherent causal-temporal framework, thereby establishing a temporally extended self (Povinelli & Eddy, 1995). This autobiographical extension of self ensures coherence across time, and this coherence is lost in severe personality disorder, in part because of the adverse impact of trauma on autobiographical memory (Fonagy & Target, 1997b). Full experience of agency in social interaction can emerge only when actions of the self and other can be understood as initiated and guided by assumptions concerning the emotions, desires and beliefs of both. Further skills that become part of the child's repertoire at this stage include grasping second-order theory of mind (the capacity to understand mistaken beliefs about beliefs), mixed emotions (e.g., understanding emotional conflict), the way expectations or biases influence interpretations of ambiguous events, and means of social deception (e.g., white lies). As these skills are acquired, the propensity to physical violence begins to decline (Tremblay, 2000) and relational aggression increases (Nagin & Tremblay, 2001).

Relationship Influences on the Acquisition of Mentalization

Our claim that attachment relationships are vital to the normal acquisition of mentalization flies in the face of nativist assumptions that children's social environments can trigger but cannot determine the development of theory of mind (Baron-Cohen, 1995). Some evidence suggests that the timetable of theory-of-mind development is fixed and universal (Avis & Harris, 1991), but the bulk of the evidence is inconsistent with the assumption of a universal timetable for the emergence of mentalization. More recent studies find ample evidence for substantial cultural differences, not just in the *rate* of emergence of theory-of-mind skills but also in the *order* of their emergence (Wellman et al., 2001). Similarly, although a study with a relatively small sample of twins suggested that theory-of-mind scores were powerfully influenced by genetic factors (Hughes & Cutting, 1999), a larger twin study (Hughes et al., 2005) showed that environmental factors explained the largest proportion of variance in performance and that a substantial proportion of the variance reflected non-shared environmental influences and was specific to theory of mind. The possible underlying proximal mechanisms considered by the authors included maternal speech and mind-mindedness, sibling interactions, and peer influences.

Nothing in these data is inconsistent with attachment relationships playing a major role in enhancing theory of mind. Importantly, we also know that infant attachment is rare among behaviours in showing little heritability in twin studies (e.g., Bokhorst et al., 2003) and the shared environmental influence accounts for a substantial proportion of the variance. These findings also hint that evolution left early development of emotionally invested ties and related social cognition maximally open to environmental influence and social heredity.

Consistent with this approach, many findings suggest that the nature of family interactions, the quality of parental control (e.g., Vinden, 2001), parental discourse about emotions (e.g., Meins et al., 2002), the depth of parental discussion involving affect (e.g., Dunn, Brown & Beardsall, 1991), and parents' beliefs about parenting (e.g., Ruffman, Perner & Parkin, 1999) are all strongly associated with the child's acquisition of a coherent conceptual apparatus for understanding behaviour in mentalistic terms. The role of family members in this developmental achievement is further highlighted by the finding that the presence of older siblings in the family improves the child's performance on a range of false-belief tasks (e.g., Ruffman, Perner, Naito, Parkin & Clements, 1998). In sum, the ability to give meaning to psychological experiences evolves as a result of our discovery of the mind behind others' actions, which develops optimally in a relatively safe and secure social context.

There is general agreement that, as well as increasing attachment security in the child, the "harmoniousness of the mother-child relationship contributes to the emergence of symbolic thought" (Bretherton, Bates, Benigni, Camaioni & Volterra, 1979, p. 224). Bowlby (1969) recognized the significance of the developmental step entailed in the emergence of "the child's capacity both to conceive of his mother as having her own goals and interests separate from his own and to take them into account" (Bowlby, 1969, p. 368). Peter Hobson (2002) described *the triangle of relatedness* as the source of alternative perspectives upon the world, which he considers to be lacking in autism and to be the foundation of symbolic thought.

Numerous studies demonstrate a relationship between secure attachment and mentalizing capacity. Attachment security with mother predicts concurrent metacognitive capacity in the child in the domains of memory, comprehension and communication (Moss, Parent & Gosselin, 1995). Our projective test of attachment security predicted belief-desire reasoning capacity in 42-month- to six-year-old children when age, verbal ability and social maturity were all controlled (Fonagy, Redfern & Charman, 1997). Furthermore, the belief–desire reasoning task at five and a half years can be predicted from attachment security with the mother in infancy (Fonagy, Steele, Steele & Holder, 1997). Moreover, infant–father attachment (at 18 months) also predicts children's performance, a pattern partially replicated by other studies (e.g., Symons & Clark, 2000).

Research also supports connections among early theory-of-mind development and mentalized affectivity in attachment relationships. Indeed, the capacity to reflect on intense emotion is one marker of secure attachment (Sroufe, 1996). Family-wide talk about negative emotions, often precipitated by the child's own emotions, predicts later success on tests of emotion understanding (Dunn & Brown, 2001). The number of references to thoughts and beliefs and the relationship specificity of children's real-life accounts of negative emotions correlate with early theory-of-mind acquisition, that is, false-belief performance (Hughes & Dunn, 2002). Similarly, parents whose disciplinary strategies focus on mental states (e.g., a victim's feelings or the non-intentional nature of transgressions) have children who succeed in theory-of-mind tasks earlier (Charman, Ruffman & Clements, 2002).

Relationship influences on the development of mentalization are probably limited and specific rather than broad and unqualified. Three key limitations to simplistic linking of mentalization and positive relationship quality should be kept in mind (Hughes & Leekham, 2004): First, the application of mentalization and the acquisition of theory-of-mind skills and mentalizing capacity can have adverse effects, such as opening the door to more malicious teasing (e.g., Dunn, 1988) or facilitating taking a lead in bullying others (Sutton, Smith & Swettenham, 1999) as well as increasing the individual's sensitivity to relational aggression (Cutting & Dunn, 2002). Possessing the capacity to mentalize neither guarantees that it will be used to serve pro-social ends nor assures protection from malign interpersonal influence.

Second, while positive emotion promotes the emergence of mentalization (Dunn, 1999), negative emotion can be an equally powerful facilitator. For example, children engage in deception that is indicative of mentalizing in emotionally charged conflict situations (Newton, Reddy & Bull, 2000).

Third, the impact of relationships on the development of mentalization is probably highly complex, involving numerous relational influences such as quality of language of mental states, quality of emotional interaction, themes of discourse, amount of shared pretend play, negotiations of conflict, humour in the family, and discourse with peers. These relationship influences, in turn, probably affect several components of the mentalizing function such as joint attention, understanding of affect states, capacity for emotion regulation, language competence, and competence with specific grammatical structures such as sentential complements (Hughes & Leekham, 2004).

UNDERSTANDING RELATIONSHIP INFLUENCES ON MENTALIZATION

Intersubjectivity beyond Infancy

The relationships among parental mentalizing, infant attachment security, and infant mentalizing are rooted in intersubjectivity – sharing of consciousness and sharing of minds. We have argued that the evidence for relational influences on mentalization is best explained by the assumption that the acquisition of theory of mind is part of an intersubjective process between the infant and caregiver (see Gopnik, 1993 for an elegant elaboration of such a model). In our view, the caregiver helps the child create mentalizing models through complex linguistic and quasi-linguistic processes that involve non-verbal as well as verbal aspects of social interaction within an attachment context (Brown, Hobson, Lee & Stevenson, 1997).

Infants by 12 months of age do not just participate in joint attention; they also actively attempt to establish it. For example, infants are not happy when an adult simply follows their pointing and looks to the object, looks to the infant with positive affect, or does nothing; they are satisfied only when the adult responds by looking back and forth from the object to the infant and comments positively, implying that this sharing of attention and interest was indeed their goal. Infants of 12 months happily point just to inform an adult of the location of a misplaced object they have no direct interest in (Liszkowski, Carpenter, Henning, Striano & Tomasello, 2004). Such declarative and informing motives are apparently purely social in their aims. Accordingly, modern developmental theory assumes a primary intersubjectivity, that knowledge about the world is shared knowledge. Correspondingly, the evolutionary underpinnings of human culture require that the infant turns to others for essential information about the world (Gergely & Csibra, 2005).

The small child assumes that his knowledge is knowledge held by all; what he knows is known by others and what others know is accessible to him. This deeply rooted expectation about shared knowledge has been called the *curse-of-knowledge* bias (Birch & Bloom, 2004). Thus young children report that other children will know facts that they themselves have just learned (Taylor, Esbensen & Bennett, 1994); unsurprisingly, three-year-olds are more likely than older children to assume this (Birch & Bloom, 2003). The curse-of-knowledge phenomenon accounts for the so-called egocentrism of young children. They cannot appreciate another person's perspective, not because they assume that everyone's perspective is the same as theirs, but rather because everyone knows the same things. Piaget's concept of egocentrism has exactly the opposite emotional valence to what is actually taking place: it is not the overvaluing of private knowledge but rather the undifferentiated experience of shared knowledge that hinders perspective taking (Birch & Bloom, 2003; Keysar, Lin & Barr, 2003). In short, we assume that everyone has the same knowledge that we do, because most of the beliefs that we have about the world were someone else's beliefs before we made them our own.

Children do not know fully that they are separate, that the internal world which they will eventually take ownership of – or at least claim privileged access to – is something private and individual. They do not know that they can choose whether to share their thoughts and feelings with their parents – or their therapist. This developmental configuration shapes unconscious fantasy and primes desire for oneness and merger. Perhaps toddlers are so prone to outbursts of rage and frustration in part because they expect other people to know what they are thinking and feeling and to see situations in the same way they do. Thus, crossing their intentions seems malign or wilfully obtuse rather than being the result of a different point of view; the denial of what they believe to be a shared reality is maddening. A developmental perspective on the narcissistic blow of Oedipus is the recognition forced upon the little boy by development that mother does not share his wish that they should marry.

Clinically, we are confronted daily with the recognition that our patients really do think in different ways. Stories we hear about stereotypical conflicts between women and men may rest on the difficulty that the one cannot conceive of the other not understanding situations as they do; the other really only pretends to disagree, not admitting to a shared reality. More routinely, the overwhelming expectation on the part of our patients of being totally understood must have a developmental root. The devastation of not having been accurately perceived – the rupture in the alliance – has therapeutic potential precisely because it forces analyst and patient beyond the illusion of shared consciousness and creates an opportunity for each to have a mind of their own, at least in the patient's experience.

Mentalization evolves out of the biological predisposition to a shared orientation to the representation of external reality. The child naturally turns to the caregiver to provide him with information about the nature of the world, internal and external. The mother approaches the crying baby with a question in her mind: "Do you want your nappy changed?" "Do you need a cuddle?" A sensitive mother is unlikely to address the situation without having the person in mind; she is unlikely to say to herself, "Are you wet around your bottom?" or "Have you been standing alone too long?" *The mentalizing caregiver can bridge the alternating focus on physical reality and internal state sufficiently for the child to identify contingencies between them.* From the caregiver's responsive behaviour, the child gradually concludes that he has desires, feelings and beliefs that determine his actions, and that others' reactions can be generalized to similar beings. Ultimately, the child arrives at the conclusion that the caregiver's reaction to him makes sense given internal states of desire or belief within himself.

In sum, unconsciously and pervasively, the caregiver ascribes a mental state to the child with her behaviour, treating the child as a mental agent. The child perceives and uses her responses in the elaboration of mental models of causation, and a core sense of selfhood organizes along these lines. We assume that this development is mostly a mundane process that is preconscious for both infant and parent, inaccessible to reflection or modification. Parents, however, execute this natural human function in different ways. Some are alert to the earliest indications of intentionality, while others may need stronger clues before they can perceive the child's mental state and modify their behaviour accordingly. Yet other parents consistently misread the infant's internal state; their expectations, based on past experience, dominate their mentalization of their infants and preclude accurate identification of intention. These biases preclude the possibility of contingent mirroring, and an emotional experience is mirrored which is incongruent with the child's constitutional experience. Yet other parents, as we have seen, fail to mark their mirroring and thus to alloy their emotional responses.

Subjectivity before Mentalization

What is the nature of subjectivity before the child recognizes that internal states are representations of reality? In describing the normal development of mentalizing in the child of two to five years (Fonagy & Target, 1996; Target & Fonagy, 1996), we suggest that children must make a transition from split modes of experience – psychic equivalence and pretend – to the integrated mode of mentalizing. In the *psychic equivalence mode*, the very young child equates the internal world with the external. What exists in the mind must exist out there and what exists out there must also exist in the mind. At this stage, there is no room for alternative perspectives; "How I see it is how it is." The toddler's or young pre-school child's insistence that "there is a tiger under the bed" is not allayed by parental reassurance. This psychic equivalence, as a mode of experiencing the internal world, can cause intense distress insofar as the experience of a fantasy as potentially real can be terrifying.

Psychic equivalence inevitably arises because, in the second and third year of life, children are as yet unable to distinguish mental experiences, for example, thinking about a sweet, from physical experiences, for example, having the sweet (e.g., Harris, Brown, Marriot, Whithall & Harner, 1991). Correspondingly, they do not yet understand that it is the brain and mind that are responsible for mental experiences like thinking, dreaming, wanting, pretending, knowing, imagining, and the like (e.g., Estes, Wellman & Wolley, 1989). Appearance *is* reality: children under four who do not yet know that a sponge that is shaped like a rock is really a sponge even though it *looks* like a rock (Flavell, Flavell & Green, 1987).

Functioning in the psychic equivalence mode is consistent with the fact that, developmentally, understanding desire precedes understanding beliefs (Wellman & Cross, 2001). In the pre-mentalizing teleological form of subjectivity, the toddler does not attribute to others knowledge or beliefs that differ from his own. In psychic equivalence mode there is no representational concept of desire; rather, a direct connection is assumed to exist between a person and a real object without positing an internal representation. These actional properties of people let them act in pursuit of goals, react to the environment, and interact with each other (Leslie, 1994). The mere physical presence of the object is equated with the wish. Both desire and perception are referential (about something) but not representational; goals and desires have direct volitional connections to the world (Astington, 2001).

Acquiring a sense of pretend in relation to mental states is therefore essential in liberating the child from psychic equivalence. In the *pretend mode*, while playing, the child knows that internal experience may not reflect external reality (e.g., Bartsch & Wellman, 1989; Dias & Harris, 1990). Yet the pretend mode has profound limitations of its own: then the internal state is thought to have no implications for the outside world. Hence ideally, at around four years old, the child integrates the psychic equivalence and pretend modes to arrive at the *mentalizing* or *reflective mode* in which mental states can be experienced as representations. Inner and outer reality can then be seen as linked, yet differing in important ways, no longer having to be either equated or dissociated from each other (Gopnik, 1993). Children discover that seeing-leads-to-knowing; if you have seen something in a box, you know something about what's in the box (Pratt & Bryant, 1990). They work out from gaze direction what a person is thinking about, thus making use of the eyes of another person to make a mentalistic interpretation (Baron-Cohen & Cross, 1992).

The child's experience of his mental states being reflected on, prototypically through secure play with a parent or older child, facilitates integration of the pretend and psychic equivalence modes. This interpersonal process is perhaps an elaboration of the complex mirroring proposed earlier. In playfulness, the caregiver (when he is "only pretending") gives the child's ideas and feelings a link with reality by indicating an alternative perspective outside the child's mind. The parent or older child also shows that reality may be distorted by acting upon it in playful ways, and through this playfulness a pretend but real mental experience may be introduced.

If the child's perception of mental states in himself and others thus depends on his observation of the mental world of his caregiver, then this sets a target for optimizing the facilitative power of early experience. Clearly, children require a number of adults with whom an attachment bond exists – who can be trusted and who have an interest in their mental state – to support the development of their subjectivity from a pre-mentalizing to a fully mentalizing mode. We must not place exclusive emphasis on parents (particularly mothers) in this regard. The evolutionary model holds that the child's brain is experience-expectant, dependent upon a range of benign adults willing to take the pedagogic stance towards their subjectivity. Thus, teachers, neighbours and older siblings as well as parental figures potentially play important roles in optimizing the child's capacity for mentalization – given their willingness to enter an attachment relationship with the child and an inclination to focus on the child's understanding of their own and others' states of mind. This pedagogy can happen through an almost unlimited set of methods, including shared pretend playing with the child (empirically shown to be associated with early mentalization) and many ordinary interactions such as conversations and peer interaction that will also involve shared thinking about an idea (Dunn & Brown, 2001). Importantly, this developmental process can be enhanced by professional interventions. In the Roots of Empathy Project in Canada, elementary-school children follow the development of an infant whom they see every day, an experience that reduces violence and bullying by creating a concern about mind in the infant. The child's social context also can be sensitized to mental states via family-based or school-based interventions (see Fearon and colleagues, Chapter 10 and Twemlow and Fonagy, Chapter 15). Such interventions improve children's behavioural control by strengthening their capacity to regulate affect, to control attentional processes, and to move away from pre-mentalistic, action-oriented modes of experience.

Disorganized Attachment and the Unmentalized Alien Self

Although mentalization may be evident in children whose attachment is disorganized, their mentalizing does not have the positive role in self-organization that it does in securely or even in insecurely attached (i.e., avoidant or resistant) children. The development of mentalizing self-organization requires exploring the mental state of a sensitive attachment figure who enables the child to find in his image of her mind a picture of himself motivated by feelings, beliefs and intentions. In contrast, not finding his own mental states represented in the mind of the other, the child with disorganized attachment intently scans the mental states of the other that threaten to undermine his agentive sense of self. These threatening mental states can create an alien presence within his self-representation that is so unbearable that his attachment behaviour becomes focused on re-externalizing these parts of the self onto attachment figures rather than on internalizing a capacity for containment of affects and other intentional states.

Even if they are interpersonally perceptive, infants with disorganized attachment fail to integrate their emotional awareness with their self-organization. A number of linked reasons may account for this failure: the child must use disproportionate resources to understand the parent's behaviour, at the expense of reflecting on self-states; the caregiver is likely to be less contingent in responding to the infant's self-state and shows systematic biases in her perception and reflection of his state; and the mental state of the caregiver may evoke intense anxiety through either frightening or fearful behaviour towards the child, including inexplicable fear of the child himself. These factors could combine to make children whose attachment system is disorganized become keen readers of the caregiver's mind under certain circumstances, yet poor readers of their own mental states.

DECOUPLING MENTALIZATION IN ATTACHMENT TRAUMA

Trauma-related Loss of the Capacity to Conceive of Mental States

Consistent with our hypothesis that childhood maltreatment undermines mentalization, adults with a history of childhood attachment trauma often appear to have an acquired failure to understand how others think or feel. Amalgamating the sequelae of a deeply insecure early environment, enfeebled affect representation and poor affect control systems, as well as a disorganized self-structure, trauma has profound effects on development: it inhibits the playfulness essential for the adequate unfolding of the interpersonal interpretive function (Dunn, Davies, O'Connor & Sturgess, 2000); it interferes directly with affect regulation and attentional control systems (Arntz, Appels & Sieswerda, 2000); and, most importantly, it can bring about an unconsciously motivated aversion to mentalizing. This motivated failure is a consequence of a defensive adaptive manoeuvre on the part of the child who protects himself from the frankly malevolent and dangerous states of mind of the abuser by decoupling the capacity to conceive of mental states, at least in attachment contexts (Fonagy, 1991). Moreover, we believe that adult social functioning is further impaired by childhood and adolescent adversity to the extent that adversity causes a breakdown of attachment-related mentalization (Fonagy et al., 2003a). There is considerable evidence that maltreated children have specific mentalization deficits and that individuals with borderline personality disorder are poor at mentalizing following severe maltreatment (Fonagy et al., 1996), in part because mentalizing deficits place some survivors of childhood adversity at greater risk for encountering adolescent adversity that compounds their developmental problems.

Traumatized patients' difficulty understanding themselves and others struck us forcibly over 15 years ago while treating borderline women and violent men (Fonagy, 1989), impressions reinforced by Anne-Marie Sandler's work at the Anna Freud Centre (Gerber, 2004; Perelberg, 1999). Research has shown that mentalizing capacity is undermined in a significant proportion of persons who have experienced trauma. For example, traumatized children cannot learn words for feelings (Beeghly & Cicchetti, 1994), and traumatized adults have more difficulty recognizing facial expressions (Fonagy et al., 2003a). Similar deficits in reflective function have been demonstrated in patients with post-traumatic stress disorder (Schechter et al., 2004).

What is the clinical picture like when trauma brings about a partial and temporary collapse of mentalization? We observe a lack of imaginativeness about the mental world of others and a naiveté or cluelessness about what others think or feel that can verge on confusion, concomitant with a lack of insight into the way that the traumatized person's own mind works. James, a young man physically abused throughout his childhood, describes thinking, "I keep doing these crazy things. Why am I doing these things? I was confused. I used to just sit down for hours sometimes and drive myself mad, thinking. And I just didn't get anywhere. It used to wind me up."

Yet many maltreated children become adequately functioning adults. While maltreatment places children at increased risk for developing psychopathology, only a small proportion will need mental health services (Widom, 1999). It is possible that early experience in an interpersonally hostile environment reduces individuals' opportunity fully to develop mentalizing skills, leaving them with inadequate capacities to identify and avoid risks for further interpersonal trauma. In dysfunctional attachment contexts, and especially when children are victims of abuse, they may learn to interpret parental initiation of communicative attention-directing behaviours as a cue that potentially harmful interactions are in the offing. Consequently, they may develop the defensive coping strategy of inhibiting the mentalistic interpretation of such cues; this may finally lead to the defensive disruption of their own metacognitive monitoring procedures in all subsequent intimate relationships (Fonagy, Target, Gergely, Allen & Bateman, 2003b).

Toth and colleagues have observed deficits in social cognition that point to impaired mentalizing capacity in maltreated preschoolers (Macfie et al., 1999); these children showed clear limitations in the representation of social cognition in a story-stem completion task where the story called for the relief of distress. A further study (Macfie, Cicchetti & Toth, 2001) showed that physically or sexually abused children manifested more dissociation, disruptions of identity, and incoherence of parental representations – all of which indicate impaired mentalizing capacities (Fonagy, 1997a). In maltreated children, social-cognitive capacities – particularly the complexity of the representation of the parent in conflict-laden settings – decreases with development, while the children's self-representation becomes increasingly simplified and exaggerated (Toth, Cicchetti, Macfie, Maughan & Vanmeenen, 2000). Most compelling are the effects of a randomized controlled intervention study in which preschooler parent psychotherapy was offered to maltreating families (Toth, Maughan, Manly, Spagnola & Cicchetti, 2002). This 12-month intervention aimed at elaborating and modifying the relationship between parent and child by linking current maternal conceptualization of relationships to the mother's childhood caregiving response. Compared to controls, the intervention group showed improvements in social-cognitive measures in a range of domains, including degree of maladaptiveness of maternal representation and the quality of self and mother–child relationship representations.

Equation of Inner and Outer

The collapse of mentalization in the face of trauma entails a loss of awareness of the relationship between internal and external reality and the re-emergence of earlier experiential modes (Fonagy & Target, 2000). In the psychic equivalence mode, the three-year-old's acute fear of a fantasy (the tiger under his bed) is highly compelling. Post-traumatic flashbacks are similarly compelling and resistant to reason; they feel dangerous until mentalized. Often trauma survivors simply refuse to think about their experience because thinking means reliving. They may show marked psychic equivalence even in other contexts. A severely physically and sexually abused man talked about writing letters from prison: "When you write to someone, it's like you're going in that letter, you put your hand in the letter, or your whole body's in the letter. And when they open the letter, the words, you are the words so you know, it's like you're outside, but you're still in, still in prison." Aspects of psychic equivalence overlap with descriptions of paranoid-schizoid forms of thinking as formulated by Wilfred Bion (1963) and symbolic equation as formulated by Hanna Segal (1957).

Separation from Reality

The pretend mode is a developmental complement to psychic equivalence. Not yet able to conceive of internal experience as mental, the child's fantasies are dramatically divided off from the external world. Small children cannot simultaneously pretend and engage with normal reality; asking them if their pretend gun is a gun or a stick spoils the game.

Following trauma and the constriction of mentalization, the intrusion of the pretend mode is evident in dissociative experiences. In dissociative thinking, nothing can be linked to anything; the principle of the pretend mode, in which fantasy is cut off from the real world, is extended so that nothing has implications (Fonagy & Target, 2000). The compulsive search for meaning (hyperactive mentalization), what James describes as "driving myself mad", is a common reaction against the sense of emptiness and disconnection that the pretend mode generates. Patients report blanking out, clamming up, or remembering their traumatic experiences only in dreams. The oscillation between psychic equivalence and pretend modes of experiencing the internal world is a hallmark of trauma.

"I Believe It when I See It"

A third pre-mentalistic aspect of psychic reality is the re-emergence of a teleological mode of thought, a mode of understanding the world that antedates language. Infants as young as nine months are able to attribute goals to people and to objects that seem to behave purposefully, but these goals are not yet truly mental inasmuch as they are tied to what is observable. The return of this teleological mode of thought is perhaps the most painful aspect of a subjectivity stripped of mentalization.

Following trauma, verbal reassurance means little. Interacting with others at a mental level has been replaced by attempts at altering thoughts and feelings through action. Trauma such as physical and sexual abuse is, by definition, teleological. Unsurprisingly, the victim feels that the mind of another can be altered only in this same mode, through a physical act, such as threat or seduction. Following trauma we all need physical assurances of security. A man who was severely physically maltreated described his feelings about being sent to live in a hostel at the age of 11 as follows: "I tried to make them understand that I was upset so I was throwing things quite a lot. I threw my bed out of the window. I broke all the windows in the room. It was the only way I could make them understand that I did not like it."

Hyperactivating Attachment

Attachment is normally the ideal training ground for the development of mentalization because it is safe and non-competitive. This biological configuration, which is so adaptive in the context of normal development, becomes immensely destructive in the presence of attachment trauma. Attachment trauma hyperactivates the attachment system because the person to whom the child looks for reassurance and protection is the one evoking fear. The devastating psychic impact of attachment trauma is the combined result of the inhibition of mentalization by attachment and the hyperactivation of the attachment system by trauma. This context demands extraordinary mentalizing capacities from the child; yet the hyperactivation of the attachment system inhibits whatever limited mentalizing capacity he retains.

The coincidence of trauma and attachment creates a biological vicious cycle. Trauma normally leads a child to try to get close to the attachment figure. This generates a characteristic dependency on the maltreating figure, with the real risk of an escalating sequence of further maltreatment, increased distress and an ever-greater inner need for the attachment figure. The inhibition of mentalization in a traumatizing, hyperactivated attachment relationship is conducive to a pre-mentalistic psychic reality, largely split into psychic equivalence and pretend modes. The memory of the trauma feels currently real so there is a constant danger of re-traumatization from inside. The traumatized child often begins to fear his own mind. Inhibiting mentalizing is an intrapsychic adaptation to traumatic attachment. The frankly malevolent mental state of the abuser terrifies the helpless child. The parent's abuse undermines the child's capacity to mentalize, because it is no longer safe for the child, for example, to think about wishing, if this implies recognizing his parent's wish to harm him.

To complicate matters, because the child with attachment trauma often phobically avoids the mind of the parent, he cannot use the model of the other to understand the self, and identity diffusion and dissociation often follows. Even more pernicious is the state when, desperate for some kind of self-awareness, psychic reality comes to be experienced through incorporating the other through pretend mode. A man we interviewed in his early twenties was brought up by his mother and a succession of stepfathers and particularly traumatized by the second. He described an episode when he was caught shoplifting and was brought home by the police:

> My stepfather tied me to the bed . . . and he got a screwdriver, and he was stabbing me in the hands with it, because they [the hands] were what stole . . . and I was just laughing at him, because I was . . . I don't know . . . And then he went downstairs, and he got a hammer and nails, and he nailed one of my hands to the board of the bed, like. Just stuck a nail straight through my hand, like. Like, so I was howling, I couldn't move, and the blood was . . . and I was screaming then. I had to cry then, I couldn't handle it. And after they had done it, my hands went numb, so I couldn't feel it. And I looked at my hands, and I started laughing at myself. And I felt I was going mad, like, cause I was going "Ha ha", you know, and I was thinking, "I had done that."

Of course this process, taking the perspective of the other intent on destroying him, is similar to Anna Freud's description of identification with the aggressor.

The Biology of Being Frazzled

The impact of trauma on mentalization is intermittent, for example, when the disappearance of mentalization results from the intensification of an attachment relationship in the course of an analysis. At other times, stress (e.g., touching on a sensitive issue) can trigger what feel like wild, unjustified reactions. Arnsten's dual arousal systems model, which she dubbed "the biology of being frazzled", delineates two complementary, independent arousal systems that play a part in the reciprocal relation between arousal and mentalizing: the pre-frontal and posterior cortical and subcortical systems (Arnsten, 1998; Arnsten, Mathew, Ubriani, Taylor & Li, 1999; Mayes, 2000). The system that activates frontal and pre-frontal regions inhibits the second arousal system that normally "kicks in" only at quite high levels of arousal, when pre-frontal activity goes off-line and posterior cortical and subcortical functions (i.e., more automatic or motor functions) take over.

The switch-point between the two arousal systems may be shifted by childhood trauma. Undoubtedly, as mentalization is mediated by the pre-frontal cortex, this switch accounts for some of the inhibition of mentalization in individuals with attachment trauma in response to increases in arousal that would not be high enough to inhibit mentalization in most of us. As a patient stated, "I just snap, you know what I mean. It's like a switch. But I don't like it, I hate it. But I just can't help myself for doing it."

This lowered threshold for switching off mentalizing implies that therapists must monitor the traumatized patient's readiness to hear comments about thoughts and feelings. As arousal increases, in part in response to interpretative work, traumatized patients cannot process talk about their minds. Transference interpretations at these times, however accurate they might be, are likely to be way beyond the capacity of the patient to hear. Work to reduce arousal must take priority so that the patient can again think of other perspectives (i.e., mentalize).

Projective Identification as a Matter of Life and Death

Internalizing the representation of another before the boundaries of the self are fully formed undermines the creation of a coherent sense of self. The infant is forced to internalize the other not as an internal object but as a core part of his self. If the caregiver fails to contain the infant's anxieties, metabolize them, and mirror the self-state, the infant, rather than gradually constructing a representation of his internal states, is forced to accommodate the object, an alien being, within his self-representation. Such incoherencies in self-structure not only characterize profoundly neglected children; the most sensitive caregiver is insensitive to the child's state of mind over 50% of the time, and we all have alien parts to our self-structure. The coherence of the self is somewhat illusory. This illusion is normally maintained by the continuous narrative commentary on behaviour that mentalization preconsciously provides, weaving our experiences together so that they make sense. In the absence of a robust mentalizing capacity in the wake of trauma, alien fragments in the self-structure are likely to be revealed in us all.

Of course, these introjections in traumatized individuals are coloured by the traumatic context in which they occur. A caregiver with terrifying intentions is internalized as part of the self. Momentary experiences of unbearable psychic pain emerge when the self feels attacked literally from within and overwhelmed by an experience of badness that is impossible to mitigate by reassurance. Experienced in the mode of psychic equivalence, the *feeling* of badness translates directly into *actual* badness from which, in a teleological mode of functioning, self-destructive action might appear to be the only escape – as acts of self-harm and suicide commonly attest.

The only way the person can deal with such introjects is by continually externalizing these alien parts of the self-structure into an other. Through projective identification the persecutory parts are experienced as being outside. Then the alien experiences are owned by another mind, so that another mind is in control of the parts of the self set upon its own destruction. Paradoxically, then, the need for projective identification is a matter of life and death for those with a traumatizing part of the self-structure, but the constellation creates a dependence on the object that has many features of addiction. Neuroscience helps explain how triggering the attachment system (by the need to find a container for traumatized, alien parts of the self) will once again inhibit mentalization. Unfortunately, this switch reduces the chance of either accepting alternative solutions or finding a non-teleological (non-action-oriented) solution.

The following verbatim extract from a male prostitute who was sexually abused by his stepfather and brothers illustrates the experience of externalizing the alien self:

> The more you experience, the more immune you become to anything. If you get lured into a gang of queers and then, you're abused, you don't fear queers no more. You just probably revenge against them. Because you can turn your mind into their activity and use it against them. I'm not getting into fights or anything like that, but I do happen to get into people's heads and hurt them, do you know what I mean?

In sum, maltreatment, or trauma more broadly, interacts with the domain- and situation-specific restrictions upon mentalization at two levels. First, maltreatment presents the young child with a powerful emotional disincentive for taking the perspective of others, because of the actual threat within the intentional stance of the abuser as well as the constraints upon self-development imposed by the parent's failure to understand and acknowledge the child's budding intentionality. Second, the child is deprived of the later resilience provided by the capacity to understand interpersonal situations (Fonagy, Steele, Steele, Higgitt & Target, 1994). Thus individuals who are traumatized by their family environment are vulnerable in terms of the long-term impact of the trauma, their reduced capacity to cope with it, and their difficulty in finding better relationships later. Severe developmental psychopathology and, ultimately, entrenched personality disorder, can be the outcome. Plainly, the earlier we can intervene to re-establish mentalizing in the context of secure attachment – be it in parental, marital or treatment relationships – the less likely that entrenched psychopathology will continually erode relationships, mentalizing capacity and subsequent development.

REFERENCES

Addis, D. R., McIntosh, A. R., Moscovitch, M., Crawley, A. P. & McAndrews, M. P. (2004). Characterizing spatial and temporal features of autobiographical memory retrieval networks: a partial least squares approach. *Neuroimage*, *23*, 1460–1471.

Adolphs, R. (2002). Neural systems for recognizing emotion. *Current Opinion in Neurobiology, 12*, 169–177.

Adolphs, R. (2003). Cognitive neuroscience of human social behaviour. *Nature Reviews, 4*, 165–178.

Adolphs, R., Damasio, H., Tranel, D., Cooper, G. & Damasio, A. R. (2000). A role for somatosensory cortices in the visual recognition of emotion as revealed by three-dimensional lesion mapping. *Journal of Neuroscience, 20*, 2683–2690.

Alexander, R. D. (1989). Evolution of the human psyche. In P. Mellars & C. Stringer (eds), *The Human Revolution: Behavioural and Biological Perspectives on the Origins of Modern Humans* (pp. 455–513). Princeton, NJ: Princeton University Press.

Alexander, R. D. (1990). *How Did Humans Evolve? Reflections on the Uniquely Unique Species* (Museum of Zoology Special Publication no. 1). Ann Arbor, MI: University of Michigan.

Allen, J. G. (2001). *Traumatic Relationships and Serious Mental Disorders*. Chichester, UK: John Wiley & Sons, Ltd.

Arnsten, A. F. T. (1998). The biology of being frazzled. *Science, 280*, 1711–1712.

Arnsten, A. F. T., Mathew, R., Ubriani, R., Taylor, J. R. & Li, B.-M. (1999). Alpha-1 noradrenergic receptor stimulation impairs prefrontal cortical cognitive function. *Biological Psychiatry, 45*, 26–31.

Arntz, A., Appels, C. & Sieswerda, S. (2000). Hypervigilance in borderline disorder: a test with the emotional Stroop paradigm. *Journal of Personality Disorders, 14*, 366–373.

Astington, J. W. (2001). The future of theory-of-mind research: Understanding motivational states, the role of language, and real world consequences. *Child Development, 72*, 685–687.

Avis, J. & Harris, P. (1991). Belief-desire reasoning among Baka children: evidence for a universal conception of mind. *Child Development, 62*, 460–467.

Bahrick, L. R. & Watson, J. S. (1985). Detection of intermodal proprioceptive-visual contingency as a potential basis of self-perception in infancy. *Developmental Psychology, 21*, 963–973.

Baldwin, D. A., Baird, J. A., Saylor, M. M. & Clark, M. A. (2001). Infants parse dynamic action. *Child Development, 72*, 708–717.

Baron-Cohen, S. (1995). *Mindblindness: An Essay on Autism and Theory of Mind*. Cambridge, MA; Bradford, England: MIT Press.

Baron-Cohen, S. (2003). *The Essential Difference: The Truth about the Male and Female Brain*. New York: Basic Books.

Baron-Cohen, S. & Cross, P. (1992). Reading the eyes: evidence for the role of perception in the development of a theory of mind. *Mind and Language, 6*, 173–186.

Bartels, A. & Zeki, S. (2000). The neural basis of romantic love. *Neuroreport, 11*, 3829–3834.

Bartels, A. & Zeki, S. (2004). The neural correlates of maternal and romantic love. *Neuroimage, 21*, 1155–1166.

Bartsch, K. & Wellman, H. M. (1989). Young children's attribution of action to beliefs and desires. *Child Development, 60*, 946–964.

Bartsch, K. & Wellman, H. M. (1995). *Children Talk about the Mind*. Oxford, UK: Oxford University Press.

Beeghly, M. & Cicchetti, D. (1994). Child maltreatment, attachment, and the self system: emergence of an internal state lexicon in toddlers at high social risk. *Development and Psychopathology, 6*, 5–30.

Belsky, J. (1999a). Interactional and contextual determinants of attachment security. In J. Cassidy & P. R. Shaver (eds), *Handbook of Attachment: Theory, Research and Clinical Applications* (pp. 249–264). New York: Guilford Press.

Belsky, J. (1999b). Modern evolutionary theory and patterns of attachment. In J. Cassidy & P. R. Shaver (eds), *Handbook of Attachment: Theory, Research and Clinical Applications* (pp. 141–161). New York: Guilford Press.

Belsky, J. & Fearon, R. M. (2002). Infant-mother attachment security, contextual risk, and early development: a moderational analysis. *Development and Psychopathology, 14*, 293–310.

Bion, W. R. (1962). A theory of thinking. *International Journal of Psychoanalysis, 43*, 306–310.

Bion, W. R. (1963). *Elements of Psycho-analysis*. London: Heinemann.

Birch, S. A. & Bloom, P. (2003). Children are cursed: an asymmetric bias in mental-state attribution. *Psychological Science, 14*, 283–286.

Birch, S. A. & Bloom, P. (2004). Understanding children's and adults' limitations in mental state reasoning. *Trends in Cognitive Sciences, 8*, 255–260.

Bogdan, R. J. (1997). *Interpreting Minds*. Cambridge, MA: MIT Press.

Bokhorst, C. L., Bakermans-Kranenburg, M. J., Fearon, R. M., van Ijzendoorn, M. H., Fonagy, P. & Schuengel, C. (2003). The importance of shared environment in mother-infant attachment security: a behavioral genetic study. *Child Development, 74*, 1769–1782.

Bowlby, J. (1969). *Attachment and Loss, Vol. 1: Attachment*. London: Hogarth Press and the Institute of Psycho-Analysis.

Braver, T. S., Barch, D. M., Gray, J. R., Molfese, D. L. & Snyder, A. (2001). Anterior cingulate cortex and response conflict: effects of frequency, inhibition and errors. *Cerebral Cortex, 11*, 825–836.

Brentano, F. (1973/1874). *Psychology from an Empirical Standpoint*. London: Routledge.

Bretherton, I., Bates, E., Benigni, L., Camaioni, L. & Volterra, V. (1979). Relationships between cognition, communication, and quality of attachment. In E. Bates, L. Benigni, I. Bretherton, L. Camaioni & V. Volterra (eds), *The Emergence of Symbols: Cognition and Communication in Infancy* (pp. 223–269). New York: Academic Press.

Brown, J. R., Donelan-McCall, N. & Dunn, J. (1996). Why talk about mental states? The significance of children's conversations with friends, siblings, and mothers. *Child Development, 67*, 836–849.

Brown, R., Hobson, R. P., Lee, A. & Stevenson, J. (1997). Are there "autistic-like" features in congenitally blind children? *Journal of Child Psychology and Psychiatry, 38*, 693–703.

Buccino, G., Lui, F., Canessa, N., Patteri, I., Lagravinese, G., Benuzzi, F., et al. (2004). Neural circuits involved in the recognition of actions performed by nonconspecifics: an FMRI study. *Journal of Cognitive Neuroscience, 16*, 114–126.

Cabeza, R. & Nyberg, L. (2000). Neural bases of learning and memory: functional neuroimaging evidence. *Current Opinion in Neurology, 13*, 415–421.

Calkins, S., Gill, K., Johnson, M. & Smith, C. (1999). Emotional reactivity and emotional regulation strategies as predictors of social behavior with peers during toddlerhood. *Social Development, 8*, 310–334.

Carpendale, J. & Chandler, M. J. (1996). On the distinction between false-belief understanding and subscribing to an interpretive theory of mind. *Child Development, 67*, 1686–1706.

Cavell, M. (1991). The subject of mind. *International Journal of Psycho-Analysis, 72*, 141–154.

Charman, T., Ruffman, T. & Clements, W. (2002). Is there a gender difference in false belief development? *Social Development, 11*, 1–10.

Cicchetti, D., Rogosch, F. A. & Toth, S. L. (2000). The efficacy of toddler-parent psychotherapy for fostering cognitive development in offspring of depressed mothers. *Journal of Abnormal Child Psychology, 28*, 135–148.

Claussen, A. H., Mundy, P. C., Mallik, S. A. & Willoughby, J. C. (2002). Joint attention and disorganized attachment status in infants at risk. *Development and Psychopathology, 14*, 279–291.

Conway, M. A. (1992). A structural model of autobiographical memory. In M. A. Conway, H. Spinnler & W. A. Wagenaar (eds), *Theoretical Perspectives on Autobiological Memory* (pp. 167–194). Dordrecht, The Netherlands: Kluwer Academic Publishers.

Conway, M. A. (1996). Autobiographical knowledge and autobiographical memories. In D. C. Rubin (ed.), *Remembering Our Past: Studies in Autobiographical Memory* (pp. 67–93). New York: Cambridge University Press.

Corkum, V. & Moore, C. (1995). Development of joint visual attention in infants. In C. Moore & P. Dunham (eds), *Joint Attention: Its Origins and Role in Development* (pp. 61–83). New York: Erlbaum.

Csibra, G. & Gergely, G. (1998). The teleological origins of mentalistic action explanations: a developmental hypothesis. *Developmental Science, 1*, 255–259.

Cutting, A. L. & Dunn, J. (2002). The cost of understanding other people: social cognition predicts young children's sensitivity to criticism. *Journal of Child Psychology and Psychiatry, 43*, 849–860.

Davidson, D. (1983). *Inquiries into Truth and Interpretation*. Oxford, UK: Oxford University Press.

Dennett, D. C. (1978). Beliefs about beliefs. *Behavior and Brain Sciences, 4*, 568–570.

Dennett, D. C. (1987). *The Intentional Stance*. Cambridge, MA: MIT Press.

Dias, M. G. & Harris, P. L. (1990). The influence of the imagination on reasoning by young children. *British Journal of Developmental Psychology, 8*, 305–318.

Dunn, J. (1988). *The Beginnings of Social Understanding*. Oxford, UK: Basil Blackwell Ltd and Cambridge, MA: Harvard University Press.

Dunn, J. (1994). Changing minds and changing relationships. In C. Lewis & P. Mitchell (eds), *Children's Early Understanding of Mind: Origins and Development* (pp. 297–310). Hove, UK: Lawrence Erlbaum Associates.

Dunn, J. (1999). Making sense of the social world: mindreading, emotion and relationships. In P. D. Zelazo, J. W. Astington & D. R. Olson (eds), *Developing Theories of Intention: Social Understanding and Self Control* (pp. 229–242). Mahwah, NJ: Lawrence Erlbaum Associates.

Dunn, J. & Brown, J. (2001). Emotion, pragmatics and developments in emotion understanding in the preschool years. In D. Bakhurst & S. Shanker (eds), *Jerome Bruner: Language, Culture, Self*. Thousand Oaks, CA: Sage Publications.

Dunn, J. & Cutting, A. (1999). Understanding others, and individual differences in friendship interactions in young children. *Social Development, 8*, 201–219.

Dunn, J., Brown, J. & Beardsall, L. (1991). Family talk abut feeling states and children's later understanding of others' emotions. *Developmental Psychology, 27*, 448–455.

Dunn, J., Davies, L. C., O'Connor, T. G. & Sturgess, W. (2000). Parents' and partners' life course and family experiences: links with parent-child relationships in different family settings. *Journal of Child Psychology and Psychiatry, 41*, 955–968.

Estes, D., Wellman, H. M. & Wolley, J. D. (1989). Children's understanding of mental phenomena. In H. Reese (ed.), *Advances in Child Development and Behaviour* (Vol. 22, pp. 41–87). New York: Academic Press.

Fearon, R. M. & Belsky, J. (2004). Attachment and attention: protection in relation to gender and cumulative social-contextual adversity. *Child Development, 75*, 1677–1693.

Ferrari, P. F., Gallese, V., Rizzolatti, G. & Fogassi, L. (2003). Mirror neurons responding to the observation of ingestive and communicative mouth actions in the monkey ventral premotor cortex. *European Journal of Neuroscience, 17*, 1703–1714.

Ferstl, E. C. & von Cramon, D. Y. (2002). What does the frontomedian cortex contribute to language processing: coherence or theory of mind? *Neuroimage, 17*, 1599–1612.

Flavell, J. H. (1999). Cognitive development: children's knowledge about the mind. *Annual Review of Psychology*, *50*, 21–45.

Flavell, J. & Miller, P. (1998). Social cognition. In D. Kuhn & R. Siegler (eds), *Cognition, Perception, and Language. Handbook of Child Psychology* (5th edn, Vol. 2, pp. 851–898). New York: John Wiley & Sons, Inc.

Flavell, J. H., Flavell, E. R. & Green, F. L. (1987). Young children's knowledge about the apparent-real and pretend-real distinction. *Developmental Psychology*, *23*, 816–822.

Fletcher, P. C., Happe, F., Frith, U., Baker, S. C., Dolan, R. J., Frackowiak, R. S., et al. (1995). Other minds in the brain: a functional imaging study of "theory of mind" in story comprehension. *Cognition*, *57*, 109–128.

Flinn, M., Geary, D. & Ward, C. (2005). Ecological dominance, social competition, and the coalitionary arms races: why humans evolved extraordinary intelligence. *Evolution and Human Behavior*, *26*, 10–46.

Fonagy, P. (1989). On tolerating mental states: theory of mind in borderline patients. *Bulletin of the Anna Freud Centre*, *12*, 91–115.

Fonagy, P. (1991). Thinking about thinking: some clinical and theoretical considerations in the treatment of a borderline patient. *International Journal of Psycho-Analysis*, *72*, 1–18.

Fonagy, P. (2001). *Early Intervention and the Development of Self-Regulation*. Paper presented at the Keynote address at the meeting of the Australian Association for Infant Mental Health, Perth, Australia, 30 August 2001.

Fonagy, P. (2003). The development of psychopathology from infancy to adulthood: the mysterious unfolding of disturbance in time. *Infant Mental Health Journal*, *24*, 212–239.

Fonagy, P. & Target, M. (1996). Playing with reality: I. Theory of mind and the normal development of psychic reality. *International Journal of Psycho-Analysis*, *77*, 217–233.

Fonagy, P. & Target, M. (1997a). Attachment and reflective function: their role in self-organization. *Development and Psychopathology*, *9*, 679–700.

Fonagy, P. & Target, M. (1997b). Perspectives on the recovered memories debate. In J. Sandler & P. Fonagy (eds), *Recovered Memories of Abuse: True or False?* (pp. 183–216). London: Karnac Books.

Fonagy, P. & Target, M. (2000). Playing with reality III: the persistence of dual psychic reality in borderline patients. *International Journal of Psychoanalysis*, *81*, 853–874.

Fonagy, P. & Target, M. (2002). Early intervention and the development of self-regulation. *Psychoanalytic Inquiry*, *22*, 307–335.

Fonagy, P., Edgcumbe, R., Moran, G. S., Kennedy, H. & Target, M. (1993). The roles of mental representations and mental processes in therapeutic action. *Psychoanalytic Study of the Child*, *48*, 9–48.

Fonagy, P., Gergely, G., Jurist, E. & Target, M. (2002). *Affect Regulation, Mentalization and the Development of the Self*. New York: Other Press.

Fonagy, P., Leigh, T., Steele, M., Steele, H., Kennedy, R., Mattoon, G., et al. (1996). The relation of attachment status, psychiatric classification, and response to psychotherapy. *Journal of Consulting and Clinical Psychology*, *64*, 22–31.

Fonagy, P., Redfern, S. & Charman, T. (1997). The relationship between belief-desire reasoning and a projective measure of attachment security (SAT). *British Journal of Developmental Psychology*, *15*, 51–61.

Fonagy, P., Steele, H., Moran, G., Steele, M. & Higgitt, A. (1991). The capacity for understanding mental states: The reflective self in parent and child and its significance for security of attachment. *Infant Mental Health Journal*, *13*, 200–217.

Fonagy, P., Steele, M., Moran, G. S., Steele, H. & Higgitt, A. (1992). The integration of psychoanalytic theory and work on attachment: the issue of intergenerational psychic processes. In D. Stern & M. Ammaniti (eds), *Attaccamento E Psiconalis* (pp. 19–30). Bari, Italy: Laterza.

Fonagy, P., Steele, M., Steele, H., Higgitt, A. & Target, M. (1994). Theory and practice of resilience. *Journal of Child Psychology and Psychiatry, 35*, 231–257.

Fonagy, P., Steele, H., Steele, M. & Holder, J. (1997). Attachment and theory of mind: overlapping constructs? *Association for Child Psychology and Psychiatry Occasional Papers, 14*, 31–40.

Fonagy, P., Stein, H., Allen, J., & Fultz, J. (2003a). *The Relationship of Mentalization and Childhood and Adolescent Adversity to Adult Functioning*. Paper presented at the Biennial Meeting of the Society for Research in Child Development, Tampa, FL.

Fonagy, P., Target, M. & Gergely, G. (2000). Attachment and borderline personality disorder: a theory and some evidence. *The Psychiatric Clinics of North America, 23*, 103–122.

Fonagy, P., Target, M., Gergely, G., Allen, J. G. & Bateman, A. (2003b). The developmental roots of borderline personality disorder in early attachment relationships: a theory and some evidence. *Psychoanalytic Inquiry, 23*, 412–459.

Fonagy, P., Target, M., Steele, H. & Steele, M. (1998). *Reflective-functioning Manual, Version 5.0, for Application to Adult Attachment Interviews*. London: University College London.

Frith, U. & Frith, C. D. (2003). Development and neurophysiology of mentalizing. *Philosophical Transactions of the Royal Society of London. Series B, Biological Sciences, 358*, 459–473.

Gallagher, H. L. & Frith, C. D. (2003). Functional imaging of "theory of mind". *Trends in Cognitive Sciences, 7*, 77–83.

Gallagher, H. L., Happe, F., Brunswick, N., Fletcher, P. C., Frith, U. & Frith, C. D. (2000). Reading the mind in cartoons and stories: an fMRI study of "theory of mind" in verbal and nonverbal tasks. *Neuropsychologia, 38*, 11–21.

Gallagher, H. L., Jack, A. I., Roepstorff, A. & Frith, C. D. (2002). Imaging the intentional stance in a competitive game. *Neuroimage, 16*(3 Pt 1), 814–821.

Gallese, V. (2003). The roots of empathy: the shared manifold hypothesis and the neural basis of intersubjectivity. *Psychopathology, 36*, 171–180.

Gallese, V., Fadiga, L., Fogassi, L. & Rizzolatti, G. (1996). Action recognition in the premotor cortex. *Brain, 119*(Pt 2), 593–609.

Gallese, V., Keysers, C. & Rizzolatti, G. (2004). A unifying view of the basis of social cognition. *Trends in Cognitive Sciences, 8*, 396–403.

Geary, D. C. (2005). *The Origin of Mind: Evolution of Brain, Cognition, and General Intelligence*. Washington, DC: American Psychological Association.

Gerber, A. J. (2004). *Psychodynamic Psychotherapy for Severe Personality Disorders: A Quantitative Study of Treatment Process and Outcome*. Unpublished PhD Thesis, University of London.

Gergely, G. (2001). The obscure object of desire: "Nearly, but clearly not, like me". Contingency preference in normal children versus children with autism. In J. Allen, P. Fonagy & G. Gergely (eds), *Contingency Perception and Attachment in Infancy, special issue of the Bulletin of The Menninger Clinic* (pp. 411–426). New York: Guilford Press.

Gergely, G. & Csibra, G. (2003). Teleological reasoning in infancy: the naive theory of rational action. *Trends in Cognitive Sciences, 7*, 287–292.

Gergely, G. & Csibra, G. (2005). The social construction of the cultural mind: imitative learning as a mechanism of human pedagogy. *Interaction Studies, 6*, 463–481.

Gergely, G. & Watson, J. (1996). The social biofeedback model of parental affect-mirroring. *International Journal of Psycho-Analysis, 77*, 1181–1212.

Gergely, G. & Watson, J. (1999). Early social-emotional development: contingency perception and the social biofeedback model. In P. Rochat (ed.), *Early Social Cognition:*

Understanding Others in the First Months of Life (pp. 101–137). Hillsdale, NJ: Erlbaum.

Goldman, A. I. & Sripada, C. S. (2005). Simulationist models of face-based emotion recognition. *Cognition, 94*, 193–213.

Gopnik, A. (1993). How we know our minds: the illusion of first-person knowledge of intentionality. *Behavioral and Brain Sciences, 16*, 1–14, 29–113.

Greene, J. & Haidt, J. (2002). How (and where) does moral judgment work? *Trends in Cognitive Sciences, 6*, 517–523.

Grienenberger, J., Kelly, K. & Slade, A. (2005). Maternal reflective functioning, mother-infant affective communication, and infant attachment: exploring the link between mental states and observed caregiving behaviour in the intergenerational transmission of attachment. *Attachment and Human Development, 7*, 299–311.

Gusnard, D. A., Akbudak, E., Shulman, G. L. & Raichle, M. E. (2001). Medial prefrontal cortex and self-referential mental activity: relation to a default mode of brain function. *Proceedings of the National Academy of Sciences of the United States of America, 98*, 4259–4264.

Hamann, S. (2003). Nosing in on the emotional brain. *Nature Neuroscience, 6*, 106–108.

Harman, C., Rothbart, M. K. & Posner, M. I. (1997). Distress and intention interactions in early infancy. *Motivation and Emotion, 21*, 27–43.

Harris, P. L., Brown, E., Marriot, C., Whithall, S. & Harner, S. (1991). Monsters, ghosts and witches: testing the limits of the fantasy/reality distinction in young children. *British Journal of Developmental Psychology, 9*, 105–123.

Hobson, P. (2002). *The Cradle of Thought: Explorations of the Origins of Thinking.* Oxford, UK: Macmillan.

Hofer, M. A. (2004). The emerging neurobiology of attachment and separation: How parents shape their infant's brain and behavior. In S. W. Coates & J. L. Rosenthal (eds), *September 11 – "When the Bough Broke", Attachment Theory, Psychobiology, and Social Policy: An Integrated Approach to Trauma.* New York: Analytic Press.

Holloway, R. L. (1996). Evolution of the human brain. In A. Lock & C. R. Peters (eds), *Handbook of Human Symbolic Evolution* (pp. 74–116). New York: Oxford University Press.

Hrdy, S. B. (2000). *Mother Nature.* New York: Ballentine Books.

Hughes, C. & Cutting, A. (1999). Nature, nurture and individual differences in early understanding of mind. *Psychological Science, 10*, 429–432.

Hughes, C. & Dunn, J. (2002). When I say a naughty word. Children's accounts of anger and sadness in self, mother and friend: longitudinal findings from ages four to seven. *British Journal of Developmental Psychology, 20*, 515–535.

Hughes, C. & Leekham, S. (2004). What are the links between theory of mind and social relations? Review, reflections and new directions for studies of typical and atypical development. *Social Behavior, 13*, 590–619.

Hughes, C., Jaffee, S. R., Happe, F., Taylor, A., Caspi, A. & Moffitt, T. E. (2005). Origins of individual differences in theory of mind: from nature to nurture? *Child Development, 76*, 356–370.

Insel, T. R. (1997). A neurobiological basis of social attachment. *American Journal of Psychiatry, 154*, 726–735.

Insel, T. R. (2003). Is social attachment an addictive disorder? *Physiology & Behavior, 79*(3), 351–357.

Jacobsen, T. & Hofmann, V. (1997). Children's attachment representations: longitudinal relations to school behavior and academic competency in middle childhood and adolescence. *Developmental Psychology, 33*, 703–710.

James, W. (1890). *Principles of Psychology.* New York: Henry Holt & Company.

Keysar, B., Lin, S. & Barr, D. J. (2003). Limits on theory of mind use in adults. *Cognition, 89*, 25–41.

Kochanska, G., Coy, K. C. & Murray, K. T. (2001). The development of self-regulation in the first four years of life. *Child Development, 72*, 1091–1111.

Kohler, E., Keysers, C., Umilta, M. A., Fogassi, L., Gallese, V. & Rizzolatti, G. (2002). Hearing sounds, understanding actions: action representation in mirror neurons. *Science, 297*, 846–848.

Koós, O. & Gergely, G. (2001). The "flickering switch" hypothesis: a contingency-based approach to the etiology of disorganized attachment in infancy. In J. Allen, P. Fonagy & G. Gergely (eds), *Contingency Perception and Attachment in Infancy, special issue of the Bulletin of The Menninger Clinic* (pp. 397–410). New York: Guilford Press.

Koren-Karie, N., Oppenheim, D., Dolev, S., Sher, S. & Etzion-Carasso, A. (2002). Mothers' insightfulness regarding their infants' internal experience: relations with maternal sensitivity and infant attachment. *Developmental Neuropsychology, 38*, 534–542.

Kreppner, J. M., O'Connor, T. G. & Rutter, M. (2001). Can inattention/overactivity be an institutional deprivation syndrome? *Journal of Abnormal Child Psychology, 29*, 513–528.

Lalonde, C. & Chandler, M. J. (1995). False belief understanding goes to school: on the social-emotional consequences of coming early or late to a first theory of mind. *Cognition and Emotion, 9*, 167–185.

Legerstee, M. & Varghese, J. (2001). The role of maternal affect mirroring on social expectancies in 2–3 month-old infants. *Child Development, 72*, 1301–1313.

Leslie, A. M. (1994). TOMM, ToBy, and agency: core architecture and domain specificity. In L. Hirschfeld & S. Gelman (eds), *Mapping the Mind: Domain Specificity in Cognition and Culture* (pp. 119–148). New York: Cambridge University Press.

Leslie, A. M. (2000). "Theory of Mind" as a mechanism of selective attention. In M. S. Gazzaniga (ed.), *The New Cognitive Neurosciences* (2nd edn, pp. 1235–1247). Cambridge, MA: The MIT Press.

Liszkowski, U., Carpenter, M., Henning, A., Striano, T. & Tomasello, M. (2004). Twelve-month-olds point to share attention and interest. *Developmental Neuroscience, 7*, 297–307.

Luquet, P. (1987). Penser-parler: Un apport psychanalytique a la theorie du langage. In R. Christie, M. M. Christie-Luterbacher & P. Luquet (eds), *La parole troublée* (pp. 161–300). Paris, France: Presses Universitaires de France.

Macfie, J., Cicchetti, D. & Toth, S. L. (2001). The development of dissociation in maltreated preschool-aged children. *Development and Psychopathology, 13*, 233–254.

Macfie, J., Toth, S. L., Rogosch, F. A., Robinson, J., Emde, R. N. & Cicchetti, D. (1999). Effect of maltreatment on preschoolers' narrative representations of responses to relieve distress and of role reversal. *Developmental Psychology, 35*, 460–465.

Maddock, R. J. (1999). The retrosplenial cortex and emotion: new insights from functional neuroimaging of the human brain. *Trends in Neurosciences, 22*, 310–316.

Main, M. (2000). The organized categories of infant, child and adult attachment: flexible vs. inflexible attention under attachment-related stress. *Journal of the American Psychoanalytic Association, 48*, 1055–1096.

Marty, P. (1990). *La psychosomatique de l'adulte*. Paris, France: Presses Universitaires de France.

Mayberg, H. S., Liotti, M., Brannan, S. K., McGinnis, S., Mahurin, R. K., Jerabek, P. A., et al. (1999). Reciprocal limbic-cortical function and negative mood: converging PET findings in depression and normal sadness. *American Journal of Psychiatry, 156*, 675–682.

Mayes, L. C. (2000). A developmental perspective on the regulation of arousal states. *Seminars in Perinatology, 24*, 267–279.

Meins, E. (1997). *Security of Attachment and the Social Development of Cognition*. London: Psychology Press.

Meins, E. & Fernyhough, C. (1999). Linguistic acquisitional style and mentalizing development: The role of maternal mind-mindedness. *Cognitive Development, 14*, 363–380.

Meins, E., Fernyhough, C., Fradley, E. & Tuckey, M. (2001). Rethinking maternal sensitivity: mothers' comments on infants' mental processes predict security of attachment at 12 months. *Journal of Child Psychology and Psychiatry, 42*, 637–648.

Meins, E., Fernyhough, C., Wainwright, R., Clark-Carter, D., Das Gupta, M., Fradley, E., et al. (2003). Pathways to understanding mind: construct validity and predictive validity of maternal mind-mindedness. *Child Development, 74*, 1194–1211.

Meins, E., Fernyhough, C., Wainwright, R., Das Gupta, M., Fradley, E. & Tuckey, M. (2002). Maternal mind-mindedness and attachment security as predictors of theory of mind understanding. *Child Development, 73*, 1715–1726.

Meltzoff, A. N. (1995). Understanding the intentions of others: re-enactment of intended acts by 18-month-old children. *Developmental Psychology, 31*, 838–850.

Miller, E. K. & Cohen, J. D. (2001). An integration of theory of prefrontal cortex function. *Annual Review of Neuroscience, 24*, 167–202.

Mitchell, R. W. (1993). Mental models of mirror self-recognition: two theories. *New Ideas in Psychology, 11*, 295–325.

Morton, J. & Frith, U. (1995). Causal modeling: a structural approach to developmental psychology. In D. Cicchetti & D. J. Cohen (eds), *Developmental Psychopathology. Vol. 1: Theory and Methods* (pp. 357–390). New York: John Wiley & Sons, Inc.

Moses, L. J., Baldwin, D. A., Rosicky, J. G. & Tidball, G. (2001). Evidence for referential understanding in the emotions domain at twelve and eighteen months. *Child Development, 72*, 718–735.

Moss, E., Parent, S. & Gosselin, C. (1995). *Attachment and Theory of Mind: Cognitive and Metacognitive Correlates of Attachment during the Preschool Period*. Paper presented at the biennial meeting of the Society for Research in Child Development, Indianapolis, IN, March-April.

Mundy, P. & Neal, R. (2001). Neural plasticity, joint attention, and a transactional social-orienting model of autism. In L. Masters Glidden (ed.), *International Review of Mental Retardation: Autism* (Vol. 23, pp. 139–168). San Diego, CA: Academic Press.

Nagin, D. S. & Tremblay, R. E. (2001). Parental and early childhood predictors of persistent physical aggression in boys from kindergarten to high school. *Archives of General Psychiatry, 58*, 389–394.

Neisser, U. (1988). Five kinds of self-knowledge. *Philosophical Psychology, 1*, 35–59.

Nelson, E. E., Leibenluft, E., McClure, E. B. & Pine, D. S. (2005). The social re-orientation of adolescence: a neuroscience perspective on the process and its relation to psychopathology. *Psychological Medicine, 35*, 163–174.

Newton, P., Reddy, V. & Bull, R. (2000). Children's everyday deception and performance on false-belief tasks. *British Journal of Developmental Psychology, 18*, 297–317.

Nimchinsky, E. A., Gilissen, E., Allman, J. M., Perl, D. P., Erwin, J. M. & Hof, P. R. (1999). A neuronal morphologic type unique to humans and great apes. *Proceedings of the National Academy of Sciences of the United States of America, 96*, 5268–5273.

Nitschke, J. B., Nelson, E. E., Rusch, B. D., Fox, A. S., Oakes, T. R. & Davidson, R. J. (2004). Orbitofrontal cortex tracks positive mood in mothers viewing pictures of their newborn infants. *Neuroimage, 21*, 583–592.

O'Connor, T. G. & Hirsch, N. (1999). Intra-individual differences and relationship-specificity of mentalizing in early adolescence. *Social Development, 8*, 256–274.

Oppenheim, D. & Koren-Karie, N. (2002). Mothers' insightfulness regarding their children's internal worlds: the capacity underlying secure child-mother relationships. *Infant Mental Health Journal, 23*, 593–605.

Panksepp, J. (1998). *Affective Neuroscience: The Foundations of Human and Animal Emotions*. Oxford, UK: Oxford University Press.

Perelberg, R. J. (ed.). (1999). *Psychoanalytic Understanding of Violence and Suicide*. London: Routledge.

Plotsky, P. M., Thrivikraman, K. V., Nemeroff, C. B., Caldji, C., Sharma, S. & Meaney, M. J. (2005). Long-term consequences of neonatal rearing on central corticotropin-releasing factor systems in adult male rat offspring. *Neuropsychopharmacology*, *38*, 2192–2204.

Posner, M. I. & Rothbart, M. K. (2000). Developing mechanisms of self-regulation. *Development and Psychopathology*, *12*, 427–441.

Povinelli, D. J. & Eddy, T. J. (1995). The unduplicated self. In P. Rochat (ed.), *The Self in Infancy: Theory and Research* (pp. 161–192). Amsterdam: Elsevier.

Pratt, C. & Bryant, P. E. (1990). Young children understand that looking leads to knowing (so long as they are looking into a single barrel). *Child Development*, *61*, 973–982.

Repacholi, B. M. & Gopnik, A. (1997). Early reasoning about desires: evidence from 14- and 18-month-olds. *Developmental Psychology*, *33*, 12–21.

Rizzolatti, G. & Craighero, L. (2004). The mirror-neuron system. *Annual Review of Neuroscience*, *27*, 169–192.

Ruffman, T., Perner, J., Naito, M., Parkin, L. & Clements, W. (1998). Older (but not younger) siblings facilitate false belief understanding. *Developmental Psychology*, *34*, 161–174.

Ruffman, T., Perner, J. & Parkin, L. (1999). How parenting style affects false belief understanding. *Social Development*, *8*, 395–411.

Rutter, M. & O'Connor, T. G. (2004). Are there biological programming effects for psychological development? Findings from a study of Romanian adoptees. *Developmental Psychology*, *40*, 81–94.

Saxe, R. & Kanwisher, N. (2003). People thinking about thinking people. The role of the temporo-parietal junction in "theory of mind". *Neuroimage*, *19*, 1835–1842.

Schechter, D. S., Coots, T., Zeanah, C. H., Davies, M., Coates, S., Trabka, K., et al. (2005). Maternal mental representations of the child in an inner-city clinical sample: violence-related posttraumatic stress and reflective functioning. *Attachment and Human Development*, *7*, 313–331.

Schechter, D. S., Zeanah, C. H., Myers, M. M., Brunelli, S. A., Liebowitz, M. R., Marshall, R. D., et al. (2004). Psychobiological dysregulation in violence-exposed mothers: salivary cortisol of mothers with very young children pre- and post-separation stress. *Bulletin of The Menninger Clinic*, *68*, 319–336.

Schölmerich, A., Lamb, M. E., Leyendecker, B. & Fracasso, M. P. (1997). Mother-infant teaching interactions and attachment security in Euro-American and Central-American immigrant families. *Infant Behavior and Development*, *20*, 165–174.

Schultz, R. T., Grelotti, D. J., Klin, A., Kleinman, J., Van der Gaag, C., Marois, R., et al. (2003). The role of the fusiform face area in social cognition: implications for the pathobiology of autism. *Philosophical Transactions of the Royal Society of London. Series B, Biological Sciences*, *358*, 415–427.

Segal, H. (1957). Notes on symbol formation. *International Journal of Psycho-Analysis*, *38*, 391–397.

Semendeferi, K. & Damasio, H. (2000). The brain and its main anatomical subdivisions in living hominoids using magnetic resonance imaging. *Journal of Human Evolution*, *38*, 317–332.

Siegel, D. J. (1999). *The Developing Mind: Toward a Neurobiology of Interpersonal Experience*. New York: Guilford Press.

Singer, T., Seymour, B., O'Doherty, J., Kaube, H., Dolan, R. J. & Frith, C. D. (2004). Empathy for pain involves the affective but not sensory components of pain. *Science*, *303*, 1157–1162.

Slade, A. (2005). Parental reflective functioning: an introduction. *Attachment and Human Development*, *7*, 269–281.

Slade, A., Grienenberger, J., Bernbach, E., Levy, D. & Locker, A. (2005). Maternal reflective functioning, attachment and the transmission gap: a preliminary study. *Attachment and Human Development*, *7*, 283–298.

Slomkowski, C. & Dunn, J. (1996). Young children's understanding of other people's beliefs and feelings and their connected communication with friends. *Developmental Psychology*, *32*, 442–447.

Sodian, B., Taylor, C., Harris, P. L. & Perner, J. (1992). Early deception and the child's theory of mind: false trails and genuine markers. *Child Development*, *62*, 468–483.

Sroufe, L. A. (1996). *Emotional Development: The Organization of Emotional Life in the Early Years*. New York: Cambridge University Press.

Stern, D., Sander, L., Nahum, J., Harrison, A., Lyons-Ruth, K., Morgan, A., et al. (1998). Non-interpretive mechanisms in psychoanalytic therapy: the "something more" than interpretation. *International Journal of Psycho-Analysis*, *79*, 903–921.

Sutton, J., Smith, P. K. & Swettenham, J. (1999). Social cognition and bullying: social inadequacy or skilled manipulation? *British Journal of Developmental Psychology*, *17*, 435–450.

Sylvester, C. Y., Wager, T. D., Lacey, S. C., Hernandez, L., Nichols, T. E., Smith, E. E., et al. (2003). Switching attention and resolving interference: fMRI measures of executive functions. *Neuropsychologia*, *41*, 357–370.

Symons, D. K. & Clark, S. E. (2000). A longitudinal study of mother-child relationships and theory of mind during the preschool period. *Social Development*, *9*, 3–23.

Target, M. & Fonagy, P. (1996). Playing with reality II: the development of psychic reality from a theoretical perspective. *International Journal of Psycho-Analysis*, *77*, 459–479.

Taylor, M. & Carlson, S. M. (1997). The relation between individual differences in fantasy and theory of mind. *Child Development*, *68*, 436–455.

Taylor, M., Esbensen, B. M. & Bennett, R. T. (1994). Children's understanding of knowledge acquisition: the tendency for children to report that they have always known what they have just learned. *Child Development*, *65*, 1581–1604.

Tomasello, M. (1999a). *The Cultural Origins of Human Cognition*. Cambridge, MA: Harvard University Press.

Tomasello, M. (1999b). Having intentions, understanding intentions, and understanding communicative intentions. In P. Zelazo, J. Astington & D. Olson (eds), *Developing Theories of Intention: Social Understanding and Self-Control* (pp. 63–75). Mahwah, NJ: Lawrence Erlbaum Associates.

Toth, S. L., Cicchetti, D., Macfie, J., Maughan, A. & Vanmeenen, K. (2000). Narrative representations of caregivers and self in maltreated pre-schoolers. *Attachment and Human Development*, *2*, 271–305.

Toth, S. L., Maughan, A., Manly, J. T., Spagnola, M. & Cicchetti, D. (2002). The relative efficacy of two interventions in altering maltreated preschool children's representational models: implications for attachment theory. *Development and Psychopathology*, *14*, 877–908.

Tremblay, R. E. (2000). The origins of violence. *ISUMA: Canadian Journal of Policy Research, Autumn Issue*, 19–24.

Tulving, E. (2002). Episodic memory: from mind to brain. *Annual Review of Psychology*, *53*, 1–25.

van Ijzendoorn, M. H. (1995). Adult attachment representations, parental responsiveness, and infant attachment: a meta-analysis on the predictive validity of the adult attachment interview. *Psychological Bulletin*, *117*, 387–403.

van Ijzendoorn, M. H. & van Vliet-Visser, S. (1988). The relationship between quality of attachment in infancy and IQ in kindergarten. *Journal of Genetic Psychology*, *149*, 23–28.

Vinden, P. G. (2001). Parenting attitudes and children's understanding of mind: a comparison of Korean American and Anglo-American families. *Cognitive Development*, *16*, 793–809.

Vogeley, K., Bussfeld, P., Newen, A., Herrmann, S., Happe, F., Falkai, P., et al. (2001). Mind reading: neural mechanisms of theory of mind and self-perspective. *Neuroimage*, *14*(1 Pt 1), 170–181.

Watson, J. S. (1995). Self-orientation in early infancy: the general role of contingency and the specific case of reaching to the mouth. In P. Rochat (ed.), *The Self in Infancy: Theory and Research* (pp. 375–393). Amsterdam, The Netherlands: Elsevier.

Wellman, H. M. (1990). *The Child's Theory of Mind*. Cambridge, MA: Bradford Books/MIT Press.

Wellman, H. M. & Cross, D. (2001). Theory of mind and conceptual challenge. *Child Development*, *72*, 702–707.

Wellman, H. M. & Phillips, A. T. (2000). Developing intentional understandings. In L. Moses, B. Male & D. Baldwin (eds), *Intentionality: A key to human understanding*. Cambridge, MA: MIT Press.

Wellman, H. M., Cross, D. & Watson, J. (2001). Meta-analysis of theory-of-mind development: the truth about false belief. *Child Development*, *72*, 655–684.

Wicker, B., Keysers, C., Plailly, J., Royet, J. P., Gallese, V. & Rizzolatti, G. (2003). Both of us disgusted in my insula: the common neural basis of seeing and feeling disgust. *Neuron*, *40*, 655–664.

Widom, C. S. (1999). Posttraumatic stress disorder in abused and neglected children grown up. *American Journal of Psychiatry*, *156*, 1223–1229.

Winnicott, D. W. (1965). *The Maturational Process and the Facilitating Environment*. London: Hogarth Press.

Winston, J. S., Strange, B. A., O'Doherty, J. & Dolan, R. J. (2002). Automatic and intentional brain responses during evaluation of trustworthiness of faces. *Nature Neuroscience*, *5*, 277–283.

Woodward, A. L. (1998). Infants selectively encode the goal object of an actor's reach. *Cognition*, *69*, 1–34.

Zahn-Waxler, C., Radke-Yarrow, M., Wagner, E. & Chapman, M. (1992). Development of concern for others. *Developmental Psychology*, *28*, 126–136.

Zhang, T. Y., Chretien, P., Meaney, M. J. & Gratton, A. (2005). Influence of naturally occurring variations in maternal care on prepulse inhibition of acoustic startle and the medial prefrontal cortical dopamine response to stress in adult rats. *Journal of Neuroscience*, *25*, 1493–1502.

Zilles, K., Dabringhaus, A., Geyer, S., Amunts, K., Qu, M., Schleicher, A., et al. (1996). Structural asymmetries in the human forebrain and the forebrain of non-human primates and rats. *Neuroscience and Biobehavioral Reviews*, *20*, 593–605.

4

MENTALIZING PROBLEMS IN CHILDHOOD DISORDERS

Carla Sharp

Aristotle (*Politics*, 1253a, 1278b) famously described humans as social *animals*. I emphasize "animals" because it so fittingly captures what we have since come to understand to be the evolutionary origins of social understanding. Our brains are hardwired to interact with other brains through our ability to mentalize. Over the last 15 years, evidence in support of a circumscribed neural circuitry underlying social cognition and human interaction has been accumulating (Adolphs, 2001, 2003; Brothers, 1990; Frith & Wolpert, 2004; see also Fonagy, Chapter 3). The application of this framework to further our understanding of child psychopathology began in the mid-1980s with Baron-Cohen's (Baron-Cohen, Leslie & Frith, 1985) work on the mentalizing deficits associated with autism and has since expanded to other disorders of childhood and adolescence.

While some clinicians may view these developments with trepidation, assuming that neurobiological evidence may render psychotherapy obsolete, others recognize the bidirectional relationship between brain development and environmental influences for most childhood disorders. Moreover, even in autism, which is traditionally assumed to be largely organic in its etiology, interventions with the aim of improving mentalizing are increasingly being developed (Muris et al., 1999). The explicit integration of mentalizing into child and adolescent clinical practice necessitates an overview of the mentalizing problems associated with psychological disorders in this age range. In providing such an overview, I will show how both nature and nurture contribute to mentalizing problems in childhood and adolescence.

Handbook of Mentalization-Based Treatment. Edited by J. G. Allen and P. Fonagy.
© 2006 John Wiley & Sons, Ltd.

Much controversy still exists regarding the exact boundaries for the mentalizing concept (see Allen, Chapter 1). I therefore begin by highlighting the particular features of mentalizing as reflected in developmental psychopathology research. A review of the mentalizing problems associated with childhood disorders follows next. I focus specifically on the two childhood disorders that are most clearly linked to impairments in mentalizing: autism and antisocial behavior disorders. My review of this literature is intended to illuminate how different aspects of mentalizing are reflected in the heterogeneity of these two childhood disorders. Finally, I consider the implications of this literature for the concept of mentalizing, its application in the treatment of child and adolescent disorders, and directions for future research.

A VIEW FROM DEVELOPMENTAL PSYCHOPATHOLOGY

The concept of mentalizing (Fonagy, 1991) had been used in psychoanalytic literature already during the 1970s, but only during the 1990s was the concept used interchangeably with the more common concept of "theory of mind" in the cognitive developmental literature. Theory of mind was coined by primatolo gists, Premack and Woodruff (1978), and adapted in developmental psychology to refer to the capacity to interpret the behavior of others within a mentalistic framework – that is, the child's ability to ascribe thoughts, feelings, ideas, and intentions to others and to employ this ability to anticipate and influence their behavior.

Most of the developmental research carried out during the 1980s and 1990s was done under the rubric of theory of mind. Specifically, the research made use of any of several variations of the false-belief task (Wimmer & Perner, 1983) either to map out the normative development of theory of mind in pre-schoolers or to demonstrate theory-of-mind deficits in autism. As Baron-Cohen (2000) proposed, false-belief tasks are first-order theory-of-mind tasks and involve inferring another person's mental state ("She thinks that . . .") as opposed to second-order theory-of-mind tasks, which involve the inference of embedded mental states (e.g., "He thinks that she thinks that . . .").

Over the last decade the construct of theory of mind and its false-belief paradigm have been criticized for being too narrow (Carpendale & Chandler, 1996). This has led some authors to opt for the term "mentalizing" instead, because it is slightly more general and not limited to specific tasks or age groups (O'Connor & Hirsch, 1999). One of the most fervent attempts to broaden the concept of theory of mind beyond the false-belief paradigm, beyond autism, and beyond the study of pre-schoolers, has come from Peter Fonagy and his coworkers (Fonagy, Gergely, Jurist & Target, 2002; Fonagy & Target, 2000; Sharp, Fonagy & Goodyer, 2006). In their definition, mentalizing can be used interchangeably with theory of mind or social intelligence, although it refers to more than just theory of mind.

Mentalizing refers to the process of taking the intentional stance (Dennett, 1978) – that is, treating people as intentional beings rather than objects without minds. Allen (2003) pointed out that mentalizing can be conscious or nonconscious. The former (explicit mentalizing) is closely related to language and thus strongly influenced by our verbal ability. The latter (implicit mentalizing) can happen instantaneously without us even being aware of it and may be seen as largely dissociable from general intellectual development (Scholl & Leslie, 2001). For instance, without consciously attending to facial expressions or body language, we are able to attribute mental states to others that help us explain and interpret behavior. Implicit mentalizing is therefore procedural and we do it all the time without thinking. As this chapter attests, research into mentalizing problems in children has focused on both implicit and explicit mentalizing.

To reiterate, mentalizing is more than just theory of mind. It is more than just the understanding that others hold beliefs and that those beliefs can motivate their behavior. Baron-Cohen (2003) therefore, chooses to divide mentalizing into two components: a cognitive component (theory of mind) and an empathizing component (the ability to know that others have feelings and that there are relations between beliefs, feelings, desires, and behavior). The successful mentalizer is therefore someone who not only passes cognitive mentalizing tasks (e.g., the false-belief task) but also manages to see the connections between thoughts and the effects of thoughts on feelings and desires.

Recently, mentalizing has broadened its parameters through the concept of interpretive theory of mind. In contrast to early research in mentalizing (which addressed the question of whether children *are able* to understand others' thoughts), recent studies have examined whether children *misperceive* others' thoughts, feelings, and intentions (O'Connor & Hirsch, 1999). In such studies, new methods of testing distortions, misperceptions, or biases in mentalizing are developed (Sharp et al., 2006). Researchers pursuing this line of research argue for a distinction between understanding that beliefs depend on having access to information (e.g., false-belief comprehension) and the more complex understanding that – even with access to the same information – people may interpret situations differently and thus end up with different beliefs, an insight achieved at around middle school-age (Carpendale & Chandler, 1996; Chandler & Carpendale, 1998; Chandler & Lalonde, 1996).

The concept of mentalizing also has broadened the concept of theory of mind in referring both to the process of reflecting on others' minds and the ability to reflect on one's own mind. We not only build models of others' minds, but also engage in continual self-monitoring ultimately to build models of our own mind.

Now that the features of mentalizing as they pertain to developmental psychopathology have been highlighted, we can proceed to examining the ways in which mentalizing can go awry during childhood and adolescence.

MINDBLINDNESS: THE CASE OF AUTISM

In his first formulation of autism as a syndrome, Kanner described a boy who on a crowded beach walked straight toward his goal irrespective of whether this involved walking over newspapers, hands, feet, or torsos, much to the discomfort of their owners (Baron-Cohen, 1997). It was as if the boy did not distinguish people from things. Since then, many clinicians and parents of autistic children have noticed the tendency of these children to – as one mother described it in a published account of life with her autistic daughter – gaze through people as if through glass. Claiborne Park (2001), the mother of Jessica Park, a celebrated artist, went on to describe Jesse's visual perception as so acute that she could assemble puzzles picture-side-down, while her ears were able to detect the faintest buzz, hum, or click of household appliances.

This seemingly localized deficit – viewing people without referring to their mental states in the absence of other cognitive deficits – led Baron-Cohen and his colleagues to coin the term *mindblindness* as an explanation for the social and communicative abnormalities associated with autistic-spectrum disorders (Baron-Cohen, 1997). A deficit in mentalizing is by no means the only cognitive feature of autistic-spectrum disorders; two other features include weak central coherence (Frith, 1989; Happé, 2000; Happé, 1997) and executive dysfunction (Russell, 1998). Nevertheless, impressive evidence suggests that the most profound and enduring mentalizing problems in childhood are associated with the autistic spectrum. Next I will review the evidence by situating mentalizing problems in autism within the context of normal developmental milestones.

The Stepping Stones of Mentalizing: Infancy and Toddlerhood

It is generally accepted that mentalizing in children is clearest for children three years and older (Wellman & Lagattuta, 2000). However, several researchers have proposed that, by age two, toddlers demonstrate an intentional understanding of persons (Bartsch & Wellman, 1995; Repacholi & Gopnik, 1997). In turn, this understanding is preceded by a range of precursors to intentional understanding that emerges during the first year of life. For instance, most parents remember the joy of witnessing for the first time the seemingly innate capacity of their infant to imitate facial expressions, signifying the first seeds of implicit mentalizing. Even at this young age, the mentalizing problems associated with autism are evident.

Autistic infants show a general lack of social interest, reduced levels of social engagement and social-communicative exchanges, limited eye contact, and less visual attention to social stimuli (Volkmar, Chawarska & Klin, 2005). At a time when most infants begin to more fully integrate object exploration with social interaction to become more intentional, those with autism seem to be less interested in people (Volkmar et al., 2005).

In two prospective studies, Baron-Cohen and colleagues found that toddlers who failed to show protodeclarative pointing, joint attention, and pretend play were likely to receive a diagnosis of autism at follow-up (Baron-Cohen, Allen & Gillberg, 1992; Baron-Cohen et al., 1996). These deficits remain present for children on the autistic spectrum, even beyond 40 months of age (Wimpory, Hobson, Williams & Nash, 2000). In addition, autistic children with a mental age below age three were shown to be less likely to attend to an apparently distressed adult (Sigman, Kasari, Kwon & Yirmiya, 1992) and to have difficulties imitating facial displays of emotion (Loveland & Tunali, 1994).

Around age two, play and imitation represent important developmental milestones (Meltzoff, 1995; Piaget, 1952; Vygotsky, 1980). Moreover, imitation demonstrates the early understanding of mental states, because imitating requires the mental or symbolic representation of a shared object (Leslie, 1987). Two-year-olds with autism are limited in these respects (Charman & Baron-Cohen, 1997; Charman, Swettenham, Baron-Cohen, Cox, Baird & Drew, 1997; Roeyers, Van Oost & Bothuyne, 1998) – a limitation that remains present for even older children with autism (Hobson & Lee, 1999; Loveland & Tunali, 1994; Smith & Bryson, 1994).

Although there is no doubt that autistic infants form attachment relationships with their parents (Dissanayake & Crossley, 1996, 1997; Gernsbacher et al., 2005; Rogers, Ozonoff & Maslin-Cole, 1993), the mentalizing deficits and delays just discussed inevitably result in diminished attachment behavior, and it is often this problem that motivates parents to seek professional help. Thus the neurobiological predisposition engenders autism, but the psychological effects for both child and parent render the problems clinically significant.

Theory-of-Mind Graduation Day: The Magic Age of Four

Many a journal article has been written to debate the issue of whether theory of mind develops in quantitative increments or qualitative leaps. It cannot be disputed that something magical seems to happen in the development of mentalizing abilities between ages three and four. Some authors have warned that this shift should not be seen as a theory-of-mind graduation day, and that mentalizing most definitely continues to develop throughout childhood. However, a recent meta-analysis of more than 500 false-belief conditions has shown that, overwhelmingly, children younger than three fail the false-belief task while, with increasing age, children become increasingly adept at passing (Wellman & Lagattuta, 2000). The development of mentalizing abilities therefore seems to be particularly salient around age four.

During this time children not only pass false-belief tasks but also are able to distinguish between mental experiences, for example, thinking about a cookie and physical experiences, for example, eating a cookie (Estes, 1998; Harris, Brown, Marriot, Whithall & Harner, 1991). Similarly, they know that it is the brain's and mind's function to do *mental* things like thinking, dreaming, wanting, pretending, knowing, and imagining (Estes, Wellman & Woolley, 1989; Wellman & Estes, 1986). They also know that a sponge that is shaped like a rock is really a sponge even though it *looks* like a rock (Flavell, Flavell & Green, 1983; Flavell, Green & Flavell, 1986, 1989) and that, if you have seen something in a box, you *know* something about what is in the box – the seeing-leads-to-knowing principle (Pratt & Bryant, 1990). They can work out from gaze direction what a person is thinking about, thus making use of the eyes of another person to make a mentalistic interpretation (Baron-Cohen & Cross, 1992). They also understand that emotions are not only caused by physical events but also by mental states such as desires or beliefs (Harris, Johnson, Hutton, Andrews & Cooke, 1989). For the first time, to the chagrin of their parents, they also start understanding and using deception (Sodian & Frith, 1992; Sodian, Taylor, Harris & Perner, 1992), a skill that relies on knowing both what others know and do not know.

Over the last 20 years much evidence testifying to impairment in the mentalizing skills just described has been reported for children on the autistic spectrum (Baron-Cohen, 2000). These children are less likely to make the mental–physical or appearance–reality distinctions, and they are less likely to understand the functions of the brain or mind (Baron-Cohen, 1989a). They perform less well on "seeing-leads-to-knowing" tests (Baron-Cohen & Goodhart, 1994), and they are worse at distinguishing mental from non-mental verbs (Baron-Cohen et al., 1994). They exhibit less spontaneous pretend play (Baron-Cohen, 1987), display difficulties in understanding complex mental states (Baron-Cohen, 1991), have trouble following gaze direction (Baron-Cohen, 1989b; Grice et al., 2005; Hobson, 1984; Leekam & Perner, 1991), and have reduced insight into deception (Baron-Cohen, 1992; Yirmiya et al., 1996). Finally, they are more likely to fail the acid test for a theory of mind, the false-belief task (Baron-Cohen et al., 1985; Perner, Frith, Leslie & Leekam, 1989; Swettenham, 1996).

Whereas the first-order theory-of-mind tasks correspond to what is expected of a normally developing four-year-old, second-order theory-of-mind tasks correspond to a six-year-old mental level (Baron-Cohen, 2000). Whereas normally developing six-year-olds are able to pass second-order theory-of-mind tasks, high-functioning autistic individuals tend to pass these only in adulthood (Bowler, 1992; Happé, 1993), and they may display difficulty in passing more complex mentalizing tasks even in adulthood (Baron-Cohen, 2000).

Knowing Me, Knowing You: The Problem of Self in Autism

Mentalizing not only refers to the ability to reflect on the contents of others' minds but also to having knowledge of one's own intentions, desires, and thoughts. Representing the contents of one's own mind is seen as tapping into the same meta-representational capacity required for representing the contents of another's mind (Frith & Frith, 1991). As such, the theory-of-mind account of autism does not make any special discrimination between the child with autism being able to monitor his own mental states or those of someone else (Phillips, Baron-Cohen & Rutter, 1998). Other researchers prefer to consider self-monitoring as distinct from mentalizing, rather than based on a common meta-representational capacity (e.g., Russell & Jarold, 1999). They prefer to view self-monitoring as an example of executive functioning.

Regardless, children with autism seem to have difficulties in monitoring their own intentions (Phillips et al., 1998); they are less likely to remember whether they themselves or someone else performed experimental tasks (Russell & Jarrold, 1999); and they are less likely than normal controls to correct their own erroneous responses, whether they received sensory feedback indicating their mistakes or not (Russell & Jarrold, 1998). These children therefore tend to conflate memories of their own actions with memories of the actions of others. As such, they are likely to develop a radically impoverished sense of themselves as owners of a unique history and mental life (Russell & Jarrold, 1999).

Final Considerations Regarding the Mindblindness Hypothesis of Autism

So far, this chapter has focused on the most severe and profound case of mentalizing problems: the case of mindblindness in autism. The fact that autism shows an 8:1 male-female ratio (Wing, 1981), coupled with findings suggesting superior mentalizing skills in females compared to males (Baron-Cohen, 2003; Bennett, Farrington & Huesmann, 2005), has led Baron-Cohen to advance the *extreme male brain* theory of autism (Baron-Cohen, 2002, 2003; Baron-Cohen & Hammer, 1997). Yet mentalizing deficits also have been demonstrated in persons with learning disabilities and other pervasive developmental disorders (Yirmiya, Erel, Shaked & Solomonica-Levi, 1998; Yirmiya & Shulman, 1996), suggesting that the mentalizing deficits in autism do not relate to a domain-specific impairment in social cognition *per se*, but rather should be attributed to a more domain-general cognitive deficit. Certainly, false-belief understanding correlates positively with measures of verbal IQ in both normally developing and autistic children (De Villiers, 2000; Happé, 1995; Tager-Flusberg, 2000; Tager Flusberg & Sullivan, 1994).

Although much work is still needed to tease out the overlap between mentalizing and related constructs such as executive functioning and verbal ability, the mindblindness hypothesis of autism benefits from recent findings in neuroscience that suggest dissociable neural circuitries underlying the capacity to mentalize (see Fonagy, Chapter 3). Might other groups of children apart from those with pervasive developmental disorders also suffer from mindblindness?

A THEORY OF "NASTY" MINDS: THE CASE OF CONDUCT DISORDER

Conduct disorder (CD) is a heterogeneous disorder, and subtypes have been identified (e.g., relationally versus physically aggressive and proactive versus reactive). For all subtypes of CD, problems are usually manifested in the context of social interaction. Thus, we naturally turn to the domain of social cognition as a framework for understanding the persistent and repetitive disregard these children and adolescents appear to have for the rights of others.

The issue of whether 6- to 12-year-old children with CD *can* read minds was put to rest a decade ago by Happé and Frith (1996), who investigated the cognitive component (false-belief understanding) of mentalizing in CD children. Although their teachers reported children to be impaired in their everyday use of social insight, they were as adept at passing false-belief tasks as expected for their age (see also Buitelaar et al., 1999).

Sutton, Reeves, and Keogh (2000) further explored the CD-mentalizing link by using theory-of-mind tasks appropriate for middle-school-age children. They demonstrated no relationship between mentalizing and disruptive behavior symptomology; on the contrary, they showed that bullies, who typically engage in indirect and proactive aggression (Griffin & Gross, 2004), are actually advanced in their mentalizing skills. Instead of viewing bullies as impaired or deficient in their social cognition, they suggested that these children become skilled mind readers in response to aversive environments characterized by harsh and inconsistent discipline.

The notion of advanced mentalizing may also be relevant for relationally aggressive girls. For instance, Crick and Grotpeter (1996) found that relationally aggressive girls tend to victimize their friends by eliciting intimacy and encouraging disclosure in order to acquire control, which in turn is used to manipulate the relationship by threatening to expose their friends' secrets to others. A certain level of mentalizing skill is required for such sophisticated social manipulation. It is therefore not surprising that indirect aggression relates positively to social intelligence in adolescence (Bjorkqvist & Osterman, 2000). Accordingly, we can conclude that, in contrast to the mindblindness associated with autism, antisocial children *can* read minds, but they do so inaccurately. They show an intact, but skewed theory of mind (Happé & Frith, 1996), in effect, a theory of "nasty" minds: they tend to assume by default negative intentions in others, or perhaps even to use knowledge of the contents of others' minds for the purposes of social manipulation or maltreatment.

I believe we have not paid sufficient attention in the mentalizing literature to the notion of *distorted mentalizing* (as opposed to nonmentalizing). Yet the idea of distorted thinking is well established in the cognitive information processing literature. For instance, the notion of a theory of nasty minds may not come as a surprise to those familiar with Dodge's (1993) social information processing model of aggression. In a series of studies spanning 20 years, Dodge and colleagues showed that, when confronted with a peer whose intentions are unclear, aggressive children selectively attend to hostile cues while ignoring mitigating cues in encoding information. When interpreting the meaning or intention behind peers' action, such children furthermore engage in *hostile-attribution bias*; they interpret cues as threatening rather than benign (Nasby, Hayden & DePaulo, 1979). These misinterpretations in mentalizing lead the child to pre-empt the effects of a perceived attack on the self by acting aggressively. The hostile-attribution bias is particularly characteristic of reactive ("hotheaded") compared with proactive aggressive children (Crick & Dodge, 1996). This distinction is important, because mentalizing abilities are affected differentially for children depending on the kind of antisocial behavior they display, thereby reflecting the heterogeneity of externalizing disorders and the multiple pathways by which children receive a diagnosis of disruptive behavior disorder.

The distorted mentalizing associated with antisocial behavior is not only evident when these children reflect on others' minds but also manifested when they reflect on their own mind. For instance, young adolescent girls who engage in a combination of relational and physical aggression have been found to attribute negative mental-state words to themselves, for example, "stupid," "mean," "bitchy," and "slutty" (Moretti, Holland & McKay, 2001). In contrast, when they are not divided according to type of aggression or gender, antisocial children often display inflated views of themselves (Hughes, Cavell & Grossman, 1997; Hughes, Cavell & Prasad Gaur, 2001; Rowe, Bullock, Polkey & Morris, 2001; Rudolph & Clark, 2001; Sharp, 2000; Sharp, Croudace & Goodyer, in press). Their mentalizing of self is therefore characterized by a self-protective bias that prevents them from processing negative feedback from others.

While the heterogeneity of antisocial behavior and child characteristics like gender certainly play a role in the types and variation of the mentalizing skills displayed by antisocial children, one should remain mindful of the fact that much of the research described above has focused on the cognitive component of mentalizing (theory of mind). Antisocial children indeed can read minds, albeit in a skewed fashion. In cases like indirect or relational aggression, they may even show superior mentalizing in the cognitive domain. Even so, a subgroup of antisocial children shows impairment with regards to the empathizing and implicit components of mentalizing, as discussed below.

"THUGS OR THINKERS?"[1]: THE CASE OF THE FLEDGLING PSYCHOPATH

Psychopathy is characterized by a combination of antisocial behavior, proneness to boredom, and impulsivity along with an interpersonal style of callousness, superficial charm, and a diminished capacity for remorse (Cleckley, 1941; Hare, 1991). Such individuals are more likely to engage in proactive aggression (Leistico & Salekin, 2003), defined as deliberate *instrumental* aggression directed at obtaining a specific goal, in contrast to *reactive* aggression, which refers to an angry, defensive response to frustration or perceived threat (Crick & Dodge, 1996). Although concerns about the diagnostic misuse of the concept have been documented (Edens, Skeem, Cruise & Cauffman, 2001; Seagrave & Grisso, 2002), the concept of psychopathy is gradually being applied to children, usefully distinguishing a subgroup of conduct-disordered children who may be at greater risk for more severe and pervasive antisocial behavior.

One of the major emerging theories of child psychopathy focuses on the notion of impoverished empathizing (e.g., Blair, 1995; Blair, Jones, Clark & Smith, 1997). Before considering this evidence it is worthwhile to note that mentalizing and empathizing are not synonymous; rather, like social intelligence and empathy, they reflect distinct but highly correlated constructs (Bjorkqvist & Osterman, 2000). Blair (1995) provides a helpful framework for understanding the overlap between empathy and mentalizing, defining empathy as an affective response more appropriate to someone else's situation than one's own. As an emotional response to someone else's state, empathy can be seen as a consequence of role taking. Role taking, in turn, requires the representation of another's internal state and thus involves mentalizing. As such, empathy is an emotional response to a representation of another's internal state (see also Allen, Chapter 1).

Research on adolescents with psychopathic tendencies has focused, in particular, on emotional reactions to a representation of the *distressed* internal state of another. Young adolescent boys have displayed decreased responsiveness to distress cues on both behavioral and physiological levels. For instance, Fisher and Blair (1998) showed that young adolescents with psychopathic tendencies do not show distinct emotional reactions to vignettes containing moral transgressions (during which a person expressed distress) versus conventional transgressions (during which a convention was broken but no one was distressed). Compared to normal controls, they furthermore report reduced responsiveness to sad and fearful but not angry facial expressions (Blair & Coles, 2001; Stevens, Charman

---

[1] Taken from Sutton (2001).

& Blair, 2001) and show less responsiveness to these stimuli as measured by electrodermal responses (Blair, 1999). When confronted with an emotional expression multimorph task, these children also exhibit difficulties in determining when a previously neutral face passes the threshold to turn into a discernable emotional expression; that is, an expression stimulus needs to be more intense before successful recognition (Blair, Colledge, Murray & Mitchell, 2001).

Blair's work attests to a selective impairment in the mentalizing of sad and fearful stimuli while no differences are found for other facial expressions like anger or happiness. To explain these findings Blair has developed the violence-inhibition model of psychopathic behavior (Blair, 1995; Fisher & Blair, 1998). The model is based on ethological findings suggesting that most social animals possess mechanisms for the control of aggression. We control our aggressive impulses by responding to submission (distress) cues from others in the same way a dog will cease fighting if its opponent bares its throat. Empathy should therefore provide immediate, proximal feedback that discourages both physical and relational aggression by making the perpetrator of the aggression aware of the pain suffered by the victim (Hastings, Zahn Waxler, Robinson, Usher & Bridges, 2000; Miller & Eisenberg, 1988). Because the amygdala is specifically involved in processing facial expressions of distress, it is likely to be the primary locus of dysfunction in psychopathic individuals (Blair & Frith, 2000; Blair, Morris, Frith, Perrett & Dolan, 1999).

Thus, young adolescents with psychopathic tendencies distinguish themselves from conduct-disordered youths and normal controls by performing poorly with regard to the emotional and implicit components of mentalizing. This circumscribed deficit in empathizing associated with antisocial behavior has been observed for children older than six years (Hastings et al., 2000). However, a developmental effect is evident here, given that aggressive or destructive toddlers have displayed *higher* arousal levels to distress in others, indicating higher levels of empathy compared to easy-to-manage toddlers (Gill & Calkins, 2003).

HARD-TO-MANAGE PRE-SCHOOLERS: "STOP SAYS THE RED LIGHT"

In addition to subtypes of antisocial behavior (e.g., reactive, proactive, and psychopathic) and child characteristics (e.g., gender) that relate to mentalizing problems in antisocial children, the developmental stage of the child plays a crucial role. Hughes and colleagues studied a group of hard-to-manage pre-schoolers and found that, at age four, these children were poorer at theory of mind, affective perspective taking, and executive-functioning tasks that entail planning and inhibitory control (Hughes, Dunn & White, 1998). Despite these group differences, mentalizing capacity (theory of mind and affective perspective taking) did not correlate with symptoms of disruptive behavior disorder (Hughes,

White, Sharpen & Dunn, 2000). Hughes and colleagues (2000) concluded that disruptive children's interpersonal problems owe more to failures in behavioral regulation (executive function) than to problems in social understanding *per se*.

Theory of mind is positively correlated with executive function in pre-schoolers (Hughes, 1998) and adults (Rowe et al., 2001) as well as in individuals with autism (Russell & Jarrold, 1999) and antisocial behavior (Blair, Colledge & Mitchell, 2001). Yet the relation between theory of mind and executive function has been the topic of vibrant debate. While some theorists argue that intact executive function is a prerequisite for the development of mentalizing (e.g., Russell, 1996, 1998), others believe that the development of mentalizing improves self-control (e.g., Carruthers, 1996; Perner & Lang, 2000; Perner, Lang & Kloo, 2002). The latter group argues that, with the formation of increasingly sophisticated mental concepts, children gain a better understanding of their own mentality. This gives children better control of their mental processes, resulting in improved behavioral and emotional regulation.

This latter position is in line with Fonagy and colleagues' view of infant development (Fonagy et al., 2002; Gergely, 2001; Gergely & Watson, 1996; see also Fonagy, Chapter 3). Infants learn to regulate their own behavior within the context of secure attachment and through the primary caregiver's capacity to mentalize her infant (Fonagy et al., 2002; Fonagy & Target, 1997). Several studies attest to the importance of such maternal *mind-mindedness* (Meins, 1997) for the development of children's mentalizing capacity and psychosocial development (Sharp et al., 2006). When a mother treats her infant as a mental agent – a psychological being with a mind – rather than as a mere creature with needs that must be satisfied, the infant is more likely to develop secure attachment (Fonagy et al., 1995, 1996). The child's secure attachment, in turn, promotes the child's own capacity to mentalize accurately (De Rosnay & Harris, 2002; Greig & Howe, 2001; Repacholi & Trapolini, 2004; Symons & Clark, 2000). Sophisticated mentalizing then helps children to control their mental processes and regulate both emotions and behavior, thereby reducing the risk for psychopathology.

CONCEPTUAL ISSUES AND CLINICAL APPLICATION

In this review of the mentalizing problems associated with childhood disorders, I have demonstrated that mentalizing is not all of one piece: mentalizing should not be treated as a unitary concept; thus a linear relationship between mentalizing and absence of psychopathology cannot be assumed.

Mentalizing is better viewed as an umbrella concept that refers to multiple constructs involved in treating others and ourselves as mental agents. Mentalizing is therefore operationalized in several different ways. In the case of autism, mentalizing has been operationalized by asking children to mentalize explicitly (e.g., the false-belief task) and implicitly (e.g., following eye-gaze direction), both of which show impairment. In studies of antisocial behavior disorders, children have shown impairment in implicit mentalizing (e.g., viewing distressing facial expressions without engaging in effortful appraisal processes), but not explicit mentalizing (e.g., the false-belief task).

Similarly, some studies have focused on the cognitive component of mentalizing (i.e., theory of mind) while others have focused on the emotional component of mentalizing (e.g., empathizing). While autistic children seem to be impaired on both, the difficulties in children with conduct problems and/or psychopathic tendencies seem to be specific to empathizing. Furthermore, some studies have based their design on skill-deficit models (e.g., by focusing on the presence or absence of mentalizing capacity in studies of autism), while other studies have used cognitive-distortion models as a framework (e.g., the hostile attributional bias studies for antisocial behavior disorders).

Mentalizing entails thinking about one's own thinking just as much as it entails thinking about others' thinking. Yet self and other processing is differentially linked, depending on the disorder under investigation. For instance, autistic children suffer from cognitive deficits in both self and other processing. In contrast, antisocial children show no such deficits, but rather display cognitive distortion in opposite directions; negative distortions in other-processing and positive distortions in self-processing.

We have also seen that child characteristics such as gender play a role in how mentalization problems manifest in children. There is evidence that girls are generally better mentalizers than boys, and it is tempting to use this difference to explain the over-representation of boys in both autism and antisocial disorders. However, in addition to reduced mentalizing capacity, the uneven distribution of different aspects of mentalizing and the inappropriate use of mentalizing also seem to be a liability for mental health. Recall the case of the bully who engages in proactive aggression or the group of relationally aggressive girls who show advanced mentalizing skills. We might view mentalizing as akin to IQ (intelligence quotient), a normally distributed latent variable that underlies many components. In such a model, average mentalizing would be considered as optimal in terms of psychosocial adjustment. Alternatively, we might view mentalizing as consisting of many divergent components that often relate orthogonally to each other. Any unifying statements about the relationship between mentalizing and psychopathology may thus be challenged by data relating to a differentially operationalized aspect of mentalizing.

Finally, for some disorders like autism, it is easier to conceptualize the mentalizing difficulties associated with the disorder as a result of a neurodevelopmental failure present at birth. For antisocial behavior disorders – or perhaps even personality disorders like psychopathy and borderline personality disorder – a stronger interaction between nature and nurture may be claimed. As described earlier, mentalizing problems may have their origin in the environmental circumstances of childhood that have hindered the adequate growth of these skills through processes of insecure attachment and inaccurate mind-mindedness on the part of the primary caregiver.

In sum, several distinct elements of mentalizing exist, and these show differential impairment for various groups and subtypes of child psychopathology. Future research should therefore acknowledge not only the heterogeneity of childhood disorders but also the heterogeneity of the construct of mentalizing. This refinement will stimulate novel approaches for applying this construct to other previously neglected disorders of childhood and adolescence. Another area for potential research is the application of mentalizing to the treatment of disorder in childhood and adolescence. Some mentalization-based treatment programs have been developed for borderline personality disorder (Bateman & Fonagy, 2004; see also Bateman & Fonagy, Chapter 9) and autism (Baron-Cohen & the Human Emotions Team, 2003). Aspects of mentalizing are also included in school-based preventative programs such as Promoting Alternative Thinking Strategies that have been shown to reduce antisocial behavior (Greenberg & Kusche, 1993; Greenberg, Kusche, Cook & Quamma, 1995; see also Twemlow & Fonagy, Chapter 15). The implications of these programs for children with psychopathic tendencies remain unexplored and should be prioritized, especially against the background of the stability of this disorder once fully developed, with its significant personal and societal costs.

Having begun this chapter with a reference to Aristotle's notion of social animals, I would like to end with Nick Humphrey's (1984) notion of humans as "homo psychologicus." Our animal ancestors have paved the way for us to be born psychologists. We are thus able to reflect on the mental states of self and other, which makes possible the most human and meaningful of behaviors: social interaction.

REFERENCES

Adolphs, R. (2001). The neurobiology of social cognition. *Current Opinion in Neurobiology, 11*, 231–239.

Adolphs, R. (2003). Investigating the cognitive neuroscience of social behavior. *Neuropsychologia, 41*, 119–126.

Allen, J. G. (2003). Mentalizing. *Bulletin of The Menninger Clinic, 67*, 91–112.

Baron-Cohen, S. (1987). Autism and symbolic play. *British Journal of Developmental Psychology, 5*, 139–148.

Baron-Cohen, S. (1989a). Are autistic children "behaviorists"? An examination of their mental-physical and appearance-reality distinctions. *Journal of Autism and Developmental Disorders, 19*, 579–600.

Baron-Cohen, S. (1989b). Perceptual role taking and protodeclarative pointing in autism. *British Journal of Developmental Psychology, 7*, 113–127.

Baron-Cohen, S. (1991). Do people with autism understand what causes emotion? *Child Development*, *62*, 385–395.

Baron-Cohen, S. (1992). Out of sight or out of mind? Another look at deception in autism. *Journal of Child Psychology and Psychiatry*, *33*, 1141–1155.

Baron-Cohen, S. (1997). *Mindblindness: An Essay on Autism and Theory of Mind*. Cambridge, MA: MIT Press.

Baron-Cohen, S. (2000). Theory of mind and autism: a fifteen year review. In S. Baron-Cohen, H. Tager-Flusberg & D. J. Cohen (eds), *Understanding Other Minds: Perspectives from Developmental Cognitive Neuroscience* (2nd edn, pp. 3–20). Oxford, England: Oxford University Press.

Baron-Cohen, S. (2002). The extreme male brain theory of autism. *Trends in Cognitive Sciences*, *6*, 248–254.

Baron-Cohen, S. (2003). *The Essential Difference: The Truth about the Male and Female Brain*. New York: Basic Books.

Baron-Cohen, S., Allen, J. & Gillberg, C. (1992). Can autism be detected at 18 months? The needle, the haystack, and the CHAT. *British Journal of Psychiatry*, *161*, 839–843.

Baron-Cohen, S., Cox, A., Baird, G., Swettenham, J., Nightingale, N., Morgan, K., et al. (1996). Psychological markers in the detection of autism in infancy in a large population. *British Journal of Psychiatry*, *168*, 158–163.

Baron-Cohen, S. & Cross, P. (1992). Reading the eyes: evidence for the role of perception in the development of a theory of mind. *Mind and Language*, *6*, 173–186.

Baron-Cohen, S. & Goodhart, F. (1994). The "seeing leads to knowing" deficit in autism: the Pratt and Bryant probe. *British Journal of Developmental Psychology*, *12*, 397–402.

Baron-Cohen, S. & Hammer, J. (1997). Is autism an extreme form of the "male brain"? *Advances in Infancy Research*, *11*, 193–217.

Baron-Cohen, S., Leslie, A. M. & Frith, U. (1985). Does the autistic child have a "theory of mind"? *Cognition*, *21*, 37–46.

Baron-Cohen, S., Ring, H., Moriarty, J., Schmitz, B., Costa, D. & Ell, P. (1994). Recognition of mental state terms. Clinical findings in children with autism and a functional neuroimaging study of normal adults. *British Journal of Psychiatry*, *165*, 640–649.

Baron-Cohen, S. & the Human Emotions Team. (2003). *Mindreading: The Interactive Guide to Emotions*. Jessica Kingsley Ltd.

Bartsch, K. & Wellman, H. M. (1995). *Children Talk about the Mind*. Oxford, England: Oxford University Press.

Bateman, A. W. & Fonagy, P. (2004). Mentalization-based treatment of BPD. *Journal of Personality Disorders*, *18*, 36–51.

Bennett, S., Farrington, D. P. & Huesmann, L. R. (2005). Explaining gender differences in crime and violence: the importance of social-cognitive skills. *Aggression and Violent Behavior*, *10*, 263–288.

Bjorkqvist, K. & Osterman, K. (2000). Social intelligence – empathy = aggression? *Aggression and Violent Behavior*, *5*, 191–200.

Blair, R. J. R. (1995). A cognitive developmental approach to morality: investigating the psychopath. *Cognition*, *57*, 1–29.

Blair, R. J. R. (1999). Responsiveness to distress cues in the child with psychopathic tendencies. *Personality and Individual Differences*, *27*, 135–145.

Blair, R. J. R. & Coles, M. (2001). Expression recognition and behavioural problems in early adolescence. *Cognitive Development*, *15*, 421–434.

Blair, R. J. R. & Frith, U. (2000). Neurocognitive explanations of the antisocial personality disorders. *Criminal Behaviour and Mental Health*, *10*, S66–S81.

Blair, R. J. R., Colledge, E. & Mitchell, D. G. V. (2001). Somatic markers and response reversal: is there orbitofrontal cortex dysfunction in boys with psychopathic tendencies? *Journal of Abnormal Child Psychology*, *29*, 499–511.

Blair, R. J. R., Colledge, E., Murray, L. & Mitchell, D. G. V. (2001). A selective impairment in the processing of sad and fearful expressions in children with psychopathic tendencies. *Journal of Abnormal Child Psychology, 29,* 491–498.

Blair, R. J. R., Jones, L., Clark, F. & Smith, M. (1997). The psychopathic individual: a lack of responsiveness to distress cues? *Psychophysiology, 34,* 192–198.

Blair, R. J. R., Morris, J. S., Frith, C. D., Perrett, D. I. & Dolan, R. J. (1999). Dissociable neural responses to facial expressions of sadness and anger. *Brain, 122*(Pt 5), 883–893.

Bowler, D. M. (1992). Theory of mind in Asperger syndrome. *Journal of Child Psychology and Psychiatry, and Allied Disciplines, 33,* 877–895.

Brothers, L. (1990). The social brain: a project for integrating primate behaviour and neuropsychology in a new domain. *Concepts in Neuroscience, 1,* 27–51.

Buitelaar, J. K., Van der Wees, M., Swabb Barneveld, H. & Van der Gaag, R. J. (1999). Theory of mind and emotion-recognition functioning in autistic spectrum disorders and in psychiatric control and normal children. *Developmental Psychopathology, 11,* 39–58.

Carpendale, J. & Chandler, M. J. (1996). On the distinction between false-belief understanding and subscribing to an interpretive theory of mind. *Child Development, 67,* 1686–1706.

Carruthers, P. (1996). Autism as mind-blindness: an elaboration and a partial defence. In P. Carruthers & P. K. Smith (eds), *Theories of Theory of Mind.* Cambridge, MA. Cambridge University Press.

Chandler, M. J. & Carpendale, J. (1998). Inching toward a mature theory of mind. In M. Ferrari & R. J. Sternberg (eds), *Self-Awareness: Its Nature and Development* (pp. 148–190). New York: Guilford Press.

Chandler, M. J. & Lalonde, C. (1996). Shifting to an interpretive theory of mind: 5- to 7-year-olds' changing conceptions of mental life. In A. Sameroff & M. Haith (eds), *Reason and Responsibility: The Passage through Childhood* (pp. 111–139). Chicago, IL: University of Chicago Press.

Charman, T. & Baron-Cohen, S. (1997). Brief report: prompted pretend play in autism. *Journal of Autism and Developmental Disorders, 27,* 325–332.

Charman, T., Swettenham, J., Baron-Cohen, S., Cox, A., Baird, G. & Drew, A. (1997). Infants with autism: an investigation of empathy, pretend play, joint attention, and imitation. *Developmental Psychology, 33,* 781–789.

Claiborne Park, C. (2001). *Exiting Nirvana: A Daughter's Life with Autism.* New York: Little Brown & Company.

Cleckley, H. (1941). *The Mask of Sanity.* St. Louis, MO: Mosby.

Crick, N. R. & Dodge, K. A. (1996). Social information-processing mechanisms on reactive and proactive aggression. *Child Development, 67,* 993–1002.

Crick, N. R. & Grotpeter, J. K. (1996). Relational aggression, gender, and social-psychological adjustment. *Child Development, 66,* 710–722.

De Rosnay, M. & Harris, P. L. (2002). Individual differences in children's understanding of emotion: the roles of attachment and language. *Attachment and Human Development, 4,* 39–45.

De Villiers, J. (2000). Language and theory of mind: what are the developmental relationships? In S. Baron-Cohen, H. Tager-Flusberg & D. J. Cohen (eds), *Understanding Other Minds: Perspectives from Developmental Cognitive Neuroscience* (pp. 83–123). Oxford, England: Oxford University Press.

Dennett, D. (1978). *The Intentional Stance.* Cambridge, MA: MIT Press.

Dissanayake, C. & Crossley, S. A. (1996). Proximity and sociable behaviours in autism: evidence for attachment. *Journal of Child Psychology and Psychiatry, and Allied Disciplines, 37,* 149–156.

Dissanayake, C. & Crossley, S. A. (1997). Autistic children's responses to separation and reunion with their mothers. *Journal of Autism and Developmental Disorders*, *27*, 295–312.

Dodge, K. A. (1993). Social-cognitive mechanisms in the development of conduct disorder and depression. *Annual Review of Psychology*, *44*, 559–584.

Edens, J. F., Skeem, J. L., Cruise, K. R. & Cauffman, E. (2001). Assessment of "juvenile psychopathy" and its association with violence: a critical review. *Behavioral Sciences and the Law*, *19*, 53–80.

Estes, D. (1998). Young children's awareness of their mental activity: the case of mental rotation. *Child Development*, *69*, 1345–1360.

Estes, D., Wellman, H. M. & Woolley, J. D. (1989). Children's understanding of mental phenomena. *Advances in Child Development and Behavior*, *22*, 41–87.

Fisher, L. & Blair, R. J. R. (1998). Cognitive impairment and its relationship to psychopathic tendencies in children with emotional and behavioral difficulties. *Journal of Abnormal Child Psychology*, *26*, 511–519.

Flavell, J. H., Flavell, E. R. & Green, F. L. (1983). Development of the appearance-reality distinction. *Cognitive Psychology*, *15*, 95–120.

Flavell, J. H., Green, F. L. & Flavell, E. R. (1986). Development of knowledge about the appearance-reality distinction. *Monographs of the Society for Research in Child Development*, *51*, i–v, 1–87.

Flavell, J. H., Green, F. L. & Flavell, E. R. (1989). Young children's ability to differentiate appearance-reality and level 2 perspectives in the tactile modality. *Child Development*, *60*, 201–213.

Fonagy, P. (1991). Thinking about thinking: some clinical and theoretical considerations in the treatment of a borderline patient. *International Journal of Psycho-Analysis*, *72*, 639–656.

Fonagy, P. & Target, M. (1997). Attachment and reflective function: their role in self-organization. *Development and Psychopathology*, *9*, 697–700.

Fonagy, P. & Target, M. (2000). Attachment and borderline personality disorder: a theory and some evidence. *The Psychiatric Clinics of North America*, *23*, 103–122.

Fonagy, P., Gergely, G., Jurist, E. L. & Target, M. (2002). *Affect Regulation, Mentalization, and the Development of Self*. New York: Other Press.

Fonagy, P., Leigh, T., Steele, M., Steele, H., Kennedy, R., Mattoon, G., et al. (1996). The relation of attachment status, psychiatric classification, and response to psychotherapy. *Journal of Consulting and Clinical Psychology*, *64*, 22–31.

Fonagy, P., Steele, M., Steele, H., Leigh, T., Kennedy, R., Mattoon, G., et al. (1995). Attachment, the reflective self, and borderline states: the predictive validity of the Adult Attachment Interview and pathological emotional development. In R. S. Goldberg (ed.), *Attachment Theory: Social, Developmental, and Clinical Perspectives* (pp. 233–278). New York: Analytic.

Frith, C. D. & Frith, U. (1991). Elective affinities between schizophrenia and childhood autism. In P. Bebbington (ed.), *Social Psychiatry: Theory, Methodology, and Practice* (pp. 20–34). New Brunswick, NJ: Transaction.

Frith, C. D. & Wolpert, D. M. (2004). *The Neuroscience of Social Interaction: Decoding, Imitating and Influencing the Actions of Others*. Oxford, England: Oxford University Press.

Frith, U. (1989). *Autism: Explaining the Enigma*. Oxford, England: Basil Blackwell.

Gergely, G. (2001). The obscure object of desire: "nearly, but clearly not, like me": contingency preference in normal children versus children with autism. *Bulletin of The Menninger Clinic*, *65*, 411–426.

Gergely, G. & Watson, J. S. (1996). The social biofeedback theory of parental affect-mirroring: the development of emotional self-awareness and self-control in infancy. *International Journal of Psycho-Analysis*, *77*(Pt 6), 1181–1212.

Gernsbacher, M. A., Dissanayake, C., Goldsmith, H. H., Mundy, P. C., Rogers, S. J. & Sigman, M. (2005). Autism and deficits in attachment behavior. *Science, 307,* 1201–1203; author reply 1201–1203.

Gill, K. L. & Calkins, S. D. (2003). Do aggressive/destructive toddlers lack concern for others? Behavioral and physiological indicators of empathic responding in 2-year-old children. *Developmental Psychopathology, 15,* 55–71.

Greenberg, M. T. & Kusche, C. A. (1993). *Promoting social and emotional development in deaf children: The PATHS project.* Seattle, WA: University of Washington Press.

Greenberg, M. T., Kusche, C. A., Cook, E. T. & Quamma, J. P. (1995). Promoting emotional competence in school-aged children: the effects of the PATHS curriculum. *Development and Psychopathology, 7,* 117–136.

Greig, A. & Howe, D. (2001). Social understanding, attachment security of preschool children and maternal mental health. *British Journal Developmental Psychology, 19,* 381–393.

Grice, S. J., Halit, H., Farroni, T., Baron-Cohen, S., Bolton, P. & Johnson, M. H. (2005). Neural correlates of eye-gaze detection in young children with autism. *Cortex, 41,* 342–353.

Griffin, R. S. & Gross, A. M. (2004). Childhood bullying: Current empirical findings and future directions for research. *Aggression and Violent Behavior, 9,* 379–400.

Happé, F. G. (1993). Communicative competence and theory of mind in autism: a test of relevance theory. *Cognition, 48,* 101–119.

Happé, F. G. (1995). The role of age and verbal ability in the theory of mind task performance of subjects with autism. *Child Development, 66,* 843–855.

Happé, F. G. E. (1997). Central coherence and theory of mind in autism: reading homographs in context. *British Journal of Developmental Psychology, 15,* 1–12.

Happé, F. (2000). Parts and wholes, meaning and minds: central coherence and its relation to theory of mind. In S. Baron-Cohen, H. Tager-Flusberg & D. J. Cohen (eds), *Understanding Other Minds: Perspectives from Developmental Cognitive Neurosciences* (pp. 203–222). Oxford, England: Oxford University Press.

Happé, F. G. E. & Frith, U. (1996). Theory of mind and social impairment in children with conduct disorder. *British Journal of Developmental Psychology, 14,* 385–398.

Hare, R. D. (1991). *The Hare Psychopathy Checklist – Revised Manual.* Toronto, Ontario: Multi-Health Systems.

Harris, P. L., Brown, E., Marriot, C., Whithall, S. & Harner, S. (1991). Monsters, ghosts and witches: testing the limits of the fantasy-reality distinction in young children. *British Journal of Developmental Psychology, 9,* 105–123.

Harris, P. L., Johnson, C., Hutton, D., Andrews, G. & Cooke, T. (1989). Young children's theory of mind and emotion. *Cognition and Emotion, 3,* 379–400.

Hastings, P. D., Zahn Waxler, C., Robinson, J., Usher, B. & Bridges, D. (2000). The development of concern for others in children with behavior problems. *Developmental Psychology, 36,* 531–546.

Hobson, R. P. (1984). Early childhood autism and the question of egocentrism. *Journal of Autism and Developmental Disorders, 14,* 85–104.

Hobson, R. P. & Lee, A. (1999). Imitation and identification in autism. *Journal of Child Psychology and Psychiatry, and Allied Disciplines, 40,* 649–659.

Hughes, C., Dunn, J. & White, A. (1998). Trick or treat? Uneven understanding of mind and emotion and executive dysfunction in "hard-to-manage" preschoolers. *Journal of Child Psychology and Psychiatry, and Allied Disciplines, 39,* 981–994.

Hughes, C., White, A., Sharpen, J. & Dunn, J. (2000). Antisocial, angry, and unsympathetic: "hard-to-manage" preschoolers' peer problems and possible cognitive influences. *Journal of Child Psychology and Psychiatry, and Allied Disciplines, 41,* 169–179.

Hughes, J. N., Cavell, T. A. & Grossman, P. B. (1997). A positive view of self: risk or protection for aggressive children? *Developmental Psychopathology, 9,* 75–94.

Hughes, J. N., Cavell, T. A. & Prasad Gaur, A. (2001). A positive view of peer acceptance in aggressive youth risk for future peer acceptance. *Journal of School Psychology*, *39*, 239–252.

Humphrey, N. (1984). *Consciousness Regained*. Oxford, England: Oxford University Press.

Leekam, S. R. & Perner, J. (1991). Does the autistic child have a metarepresentational deficit? *Cognition*, *40*, 203–218.

Leistico, A. R. & Salekin, R. T. (2003). The reliability and validity of the Risk, Sophistication-Maturity, and Treatment Amenability – Instrument (RST-i). *International Journal of Forensic Mental Health Services*, *2*, 101–117.

Leslie, A. M. (1987). Pretense and representation: the origins of "theory of mind". *Psychological Review*, *94*, 412–426.

Loveland, K. & Tunali, B. (1994). Narrative language in autism and the theory of affect in autism. *Development and Psychopathology*, *6*, 433–444.

Meins, E. (1997). *Security of Attachment and the Social Development of Cognition*. Hove, England: Psychology Press/Erlbaum, UK Taylor & Francis.

Meltzoff, A. N. (1995). Understanding the intentions of others: re-enactment of intended acts by 18-month-old children. *Developmental Psychology*, *31*, 838–850.

Miller, P. A. & Eisenberg, N. (1988). The relation of empathy to aggressive and externalizing/antisocial behavior. *Psychological Bulletin*, *103*, 324–344.

Moretti, M. M., Holland, R. & McKay, S. (2001). Self-other representations and relational and overt aggression in adolescent girls and boys. *Behavioral Sciences and the Law*, *19*, 109–126.

Muris, P., Steerneman, P., Meesters, C., Merckelbach, H., Horselenberg, R., van den Hogen, T., et al. (1999). The TOM test: a new instrument for assessing theory of mind in normal children and children with pervasive developmental disorders. *Journal of Autism and Developmental Disorders*, *29*, 67–80.

Nasby, W., Hayden, B. & DePaulo, B. M. (1979). Attributional bias among aggressive boys to interpret unambiguous social stimuli as displays of hostility. *Journal of Abnormal Psychology*, *89*, 459–468.

O'Connor, T. G. & Hirsch, N. (1999). Intra-individual differences and relationship-specificity of mentalizing in early adolescence. *Social Development*, *8*, 256–274.

Perner, J., Frith, U., Leslie, A. M. & Leekam, S. R. (1989). Exploration of the autistic child's theory of mind: knowledge, belief, and communication. *Child Development*, *60*, 689–700.

Perner, J. & Lang, B. (2000). Theory of mind and executive function: is there a developmental relationship. In S. Baron-Cohen, H. Tager-Flusberg & D. J. Cohen (eds), *Understanding Other Minds: Perspectives from Developmental Cognitive Neuroscience* (pp. 150–181). Oxford, England: Oxford University Press.

Perner, J., Lang, B. & Kloo, D. (2002). Theory of mind and self-control: more than a common problem of inhibition. *Child Development*, *73*, 752–767.

Phillips, W., Baron-Cohen, S. & Rutter, M. (1998). Understanding intention in normal development and in autism. *British Journal of Developmental Psychology*, *16*, 347–338.

Piaget, J. (1952). *The Origins of Intelligence in Children*. New York: International Universities Press.

Pratt, C. & Bryant, P. (1990). Young children understanding that looking leads to knowing (so long as they are looking into a single barrel). *Child Development*, *61*, 973–982.

Premack, D. & Woodruff, G. (1978). Does the chimpanzee have a "theory of mind"? *Behavioral and Brain Sciences*, *4*, 515–526.

Repacholi, B. M. & Gopnik, A. (1997). Early reasoning about desires: evidence from 14- and 18-month-olds. *Developmental Psychology*, *33*, 12–21.

Repacholi, B. & Trapolini, T. (2004). Attachment and preschool children's understanding of maternal versus non-maternal psychological states. *British Journal Developmental Psychology*, *22*, 395–415.

Roeyers, H., Van Oost, P. & Bothuyne, S. (1998). Immediate imitation and joint attention in young children with autism. *Developmental Psychopathology*, *10*, 441–450.

Rogers, S. J., Ozonoff, S. & Maslin-Cole, C. (1993). Developmental aspects of attachment behavior in young children with pervasive developmental disorders. *Journal of the American Academy of Child and Adolescent Psychiatry*, *32*, 1274–1282.

Rowe, A. D., Bullock, P. R., Polkey, C. E. & Morris, R. G. (2001). "Theory of mind" impairments and their relationship to executive functioning following frontal lobe excisions. *Brain*, *124*, 600–616.

Rudolph, K. D. & Clark, A. G. (2001). Conceptions of relationships in children with depressive and aggressive symptoms: social-cognitive distortion or reality? *Journal of Abnormal Child Psychology*, *29*, 41–56.

Russell, J. (1996). *Agency: Its Role in Mental Development*. Hove, Erlbaum, UK: Taylor & Francis Ltd.

Russell, J. (1998). How executive disorders can bring about an inadequate "theory of mind". In J. Russell (ed.), *Autism as an Executive Disorder* (pp. 256–299). Oxford, England: Oxford University Press.

Russell, J. & Jarrold, C. (1998). Error-correction in problems in children with autism: evidence for a monitoring impairment? *Journal of Autism and Developmental Disorders*, *29*, 177–188.

Russell, J. & Jarrold, C. (1999). Memory for actions in children with autism: self versus other. *Cognitive Neuropsychiatry*, *4*, 303–331.

Scholl, B. J. & Leslie, A. M. (2001). Minds, modules, and meta-analysis. *Child Development*, *72*, 696–701.

Seagrave, D. & Grisso, T. (2002). Adolescent development and the measurement of juvenile psychopathy. *Law and Human Behavior*, *26*, 219–239.

Sharp, C. (2000). *Biased Minds: Theory of Mind and Emotional-Behaviour Disorders of Middle Childhood*. Unpublished manuscript, University of Cambridge.

Sharp, C., Croudace, T. J. & Goodyer, I. M. (in press). A Latent Class Analysis of a child-focused mentalizing task in a community sample of 7–11 year olds. *Social Development*.

Sharp, C., Fonagy, P. & Goodyer, I. M. (2006). Imagining your child's mind: psychosocial adjustment and mothers' ability to predict their children's attributional response styles. *British Journal of Developmental Psychology: Special Issue on Conversation*, *24*, 197–214.

Sigman, M. D., Kasari, C., Kwon, J. H. & Yirmiya, N. (1992). Responses to the negative emotions of others by autistic, mentally retarded, and normal children. *Child Development*, *63*, 796–807.

Smith, I. M. & Bryson, S. E. (1994). Imitation and action in autism: a critical review. *Psychological Bulletin*, *116*, 259–273.

Sodian, B. & Frith, U. (1992). Deception and sabotage in autistic, retarded and normal children. *Journal of Child Psychology and Psychiatry, and Allied Disciplines*, *33*, 591–605.

Sodian, B., Taylor, C., Harris, P. L. & Perner, J. (1992). Early deception and the child's theory of mind: false trails and genuine markers. *Child Development*, *62*, 468–483.

Stevens, D., Charman, T. & Blair, R. J. R. (2001). Recognition of emotion in facial expressions and vocal tones in children with psychopathic tendencies. *Journal of Genetic Psychology*, *162*, 201–211.

Sutton, J. (2001). Bullies – things or thinkers? *The Psychologist*, *10*, 530–535.

Sutton, J., Reeves, M. & Keogh, T. (2000). Disruptive behaviour, avoidance of responsibility and theory of mind. *British Journal of Developmental Psychology*, *18*, 1–11.

Swettenham, J. (1996). Can children with autism be taught to understand false belief using computers? *Journal of Child Psychology and Psychiatry, and Allied Disciplines*, *37*, 157–165.

Symons, D. K. & Clark, S. E. (2000). A longitudinal study of mother-child relationships and theory of mind in the preschool period. *Social Development*, *9*, 2–23.

Tager-Flusberg, H. (2000). Language and understanding minds: connections in autism. In S. Baron-Cohen, H. Tager-Flusberg & D. J. Cohen (eds), *Understanding Other Minds: Perspectives from Developmental Cognitive Neuroscience* (pp. 124–149). Oxford, England: Oxford University Press.

Tager-Flusberg, H. & Sullivan, K. (1994). Predicting and explaining behavior: a comparison of autistic, mentally retarded and normal children. *Journal of Child Psychology and Psychiatry, and Allied Disciplines*, *35*, 1059–1075.

Volkmar, F., Chawarska, K. & Klin, A. (2005). Autism in infancy and early childhood. *Annual Review of Psychology*, *56*, 315–336.

Vygotsky, L. S. (1980). *Mind in Society*. Boston, MA: Harvard University Press.

Wellman, H. M. & Estes, D. (1986). Early understanding of mental entities: a reexamination of childhood realism. *Child Development*, *57*, 910–923.

Wellman, H. M. & Lagattuta, K. H. (2000). Developing understanding of mind. In S. Baron-Cohen, H. Tager-Flusberg & D. J. Cohen (eds), *Understanding Other Minds: Perspectives from Developmental Cognitive Neurosciences* (pp. 21–50). Oxford, England: Oxford University Press.

Wimmer, H. & Perner, J. (1983). Beliefs about beliefs: representation and constraining function of wrong beliefs in young children's understanding of deception. *Cognition*, *13*, 103–128.

Wimpory, D. C., Hobson, R. P., Williams, J. M. & Nash, S. (2000). Are infants with autism socially engaged? A study of recent retrospective parental reports. *Journal of Autism and Developmental Disorders*, *30*, 525–536.

Wing, L. (1981). Asperger's syndrome: a clinical account. *Psychological Medicine*, *11*, 115–130.

Yirmiya, N. & Shulman, C. (1996). Seriation, conservation, and theory of mind abilities in individuals with autism, individuals with mental retardation, and normally developing children. *Child Development*, *67*, 2045–2059.

Yirmiya, N., Solomonica-Levi, D., Shulman, C., & Pilowsky, T. (1996). Theory of mind abilities in individuals with autism, Downs Syndrome, and mental retardation of unknown etiology: the role of age and intelligence. *Journal of Child Psychology and Psychiatry*, *37*, 1003–1014.

Yirmiya, N., Erel, O., Shaked, M. & Solomonica-Levi, D. (1998). Meta-analyses comparing theory of mind abilities of individuals with autism, individuals with mental retardation, and normally developing individuals. *Psychological Bulletin*, *124*, 283–307.

5

A NEUROBIOLOGICAL PERSPECTIVE ON MENTALIZING AND INTERNAL OBJECT RELATIONS IN TRAUMATIZED PATIENTS WITH BORDERLINE PERSONALITY DISORDER

Glen O. Gabbard, Lisa A. Miller, and Melissa Martinez

Patients with borderline personality disorder (BPD) have long been recognized as creating extraordinary challenges for the clinicians who treat them (Bateman & Fonagy, 2004; Gabbard & Wilkinson, 1994; Gunderson, 2001). One of the major reasons for the treatment difficulty encountered is the repetition of patterns of relationships established in childhood and recreated in the therapeutic dyad. Moreover, problems with mentalizing make it difficult for patients to reflect on these patterns. Using splitting and projective identification as principal defense mechanisms (Kernberg, 1975), patients with BPD divide their internal world into a constellation of malevolent persecutors and idealized nurturers. These intrapsychic representations are then characteristically attributed to those with whom they form attachment relationships, such as treaters, lovers, friends, or coworkers. These recreations of internal object relationships are accompanied by extraordinary affective intensity. Those involved with someone with BPD often feel that the patient has gotten under their skin to the point where they feel coercively transformed by the patient. A therapist may feel, for example, "I'm not acting like myself" when treating a borderline patient (Gabbard & Wilkinson, 1994).

Handbook of Mentalization-Based Treatment. Edited by J. G. Allen and P. Fonagy.
© 2006 John Wiley & Sons, Ltd.

Many psycho-dynamic theories of etiology and pathogenesis have been advanced to explain the origins of these problematic relationships, including separation issues (Kernberg, 1975; Masterson & Rinsley, 1975; Mahler, Pine & Bergman, 1975), failure to develop a soothing internal object (Adler, 1985), and insecure modes of attachment that lead to a defect in the ability to mentalize (Bateman & Fonagy, 2004; see also Bateman & Fonagy, Chapter 9). These psycho-dynamic hypotheses have now been supplemented by a burgeoning literature based in neurobiology so that an integration of psycho-dynamic and neuroscience perspectives is within our grasp in the understanding of BPD. We would be naïve to think that neurobiology *explains* the intricacies of the unconscious internal world of borderline patients. However, data from neurobiology supplement findings from psycho-dynamic psychotherapy and help us understand possible mechanisms of therapeutic action in psychotherapeutic work. Neurobiology and psychoanalytic theory use different languages but mutually inform one another (Gabbard, 2005a). This examination of the interface of these two levels of explanation is an example of what Kendler (2001) has called *explanatory dualism*. While this type of dualism acknowledges that the mind is the activity of the brain rather than a separate substance, it also underscores the fact that there are two different ways of knowing or understanding that require two different levels of explanation.

BPD has a multifactorial etiology (Zanarini & Frankenburg, 1997). In this effort at bridging neurobiology and psycho-dynamic thinking, we are reviewing a literature on a subgroup of female patients with BPD who experience early abuse and neglect. Prospective research (Johnson, Cohen, Brown, Smailes & Bernstein, 1999) has clearly linked borderline symptoms in adults to childhood sexual abuse and neglect. However, significant numbers of borderline patients do not have such histories in the many retrospective studies that have been conducted. Here we will restrict our review to the role that early neglect and abuse play in the development of BPD and link it to both neurobiology and internal object relations.

HYPER-REACTIVITY OF THE HPA AXIS

One consequence of early interpersonal trauma with parents or caregivers is that borderline patients may have a persistent hyper-vigilance because they need to scan the environment for the possibility of others who may have malevolent intentions toward them. Neurobiological findings are confirming these sequelae of developmental trauma. Rinne and colleagues (2002) studied 39 female BPD patients who were given combined dexamethasone/corticotropin releasing hormone (CRH) tests using 11 healthy subjects as controls. Twenty-four of these women had a history of sustained childhood abuse, whereas 15 had no such history. The results showed that the chronically abused BPD patients had significantly enhanced adrenocorticotropic hormone (ACTH) and cortisol responses to the dexamethasone/CRH challenge compared with non-abused subjects. In addition, there were no significant differences between non-abused BPD subjects and normal controls. They concluded that a history of sustained childhood abuse is associated with hyper-responsiveness of ACTH release, suggesting that this hyper-reactive physiological state is relevant to this subgroup of traumatized borderline patients but not necessarily to those who lack such histories. Sustained childhood abuse appears to increase the CRH receptors' sensitivity.

Knowledge of the hyper-responsiveness of the HPA axis fits well with our understanding of the pattern of internal object relationships in BPD. Because we understand that internal object relationships are created through building blocks of self-representations, object representations, and affects linking the two, we can infer that an anxious and hyper-vigilant affect state would be linked to a perception of others as persecuting and the self as victimized (Gabbard, 2005b). Hence there is an expectation of malevolence in the environment, and the borderline patient may misread the intentions of others as persecuting in a way that creates repetitive conflict with others. States of arousal undermine the capacity to accurately mentalize the internal states of others (see Fonagy, Chapter 3). Hyper-vigilant misperceptions appear to be related to amygdala hyperactivity, and a review of recent research in that area is illuminating.

THE ROLE OF THE AMYGDALA

One function of the amygdala is to increase vigilance and to facilitate an individual's evaluation of the potential for novel or ambiguous situations (Donegan et al., 2003). A functional magnetic resonance imaging (fMRI) study (Herpertz et al., 2001) comparing six female BPD patients with six female control subjects found that the amygdala on both sides of the borderline patients' brains showed enhanced activation compared to that in the control group. The investigators concluded that the perceptual cortex in a borderline patient may be modulated through the amygdala in such a way that attention to emotionally relevant environmental stimuli is increased.

Two different studies (Donegan et al., 2003; Wagner & Linehan, 1999) examined how borderline patients react to standard presentations of faces compared to control subjects. In one study (Herpertz et al., 2001) borderline patients showed significantly greater left amygdalar activation to facial expressions of emotion compared with normal control subjects. Of even greater importance, though, was the tendency for borderline subjects, in contrast to controls, to attribute negative attributes to neutral faces. Persons with expressionless faces were regarded as threatening, untrustworthy, and possibly plotting to do something nefarious. A hyperactive amygdala may be involved in the predisposition to be hyper-vigilant and overreactive to relatively benign emotional expressions. This misreading of neutral facial expressions is clearly related to the transference misreadings that occur in psychotherapy of borderline patients and in the recreation of "bad object" experiences in their lives. It is also connected to the common observation of therapists that the usual professional boundaries and therapeutic neutrality are experienced by BPD patients as cruel and withholding (Gabbard & Wilkinson, 1994).

As Donegan and colleagues (2003) point out, the perception of threat may actually elicit reactions in others that confirm what is being projected. When the therapist, for example, feels falsely accused, he or she may react with irritation, which may subsequently elicit higher levels of amygdalar activity. This form of projective identification is a common experience that therapists report in the treatment of borderline patients.

> A 24-year-old female borderline patient began a session by complaining about the therapist's upcoming vacation. She said to the therapist, "You generally give me over a month's advance notice when you are going to be gone, and this time you told me only two weeks ahead. You know how difficult your vacations are for me. Why did you wait so long to let me know?" The therapist, feeling on the defensive, replied by saying, "I don't think I always give you at least a month's notice." The patient became more insistent: "Oh, yes, you do. I keep track of these things." The therapist then responded, "Well, I'm not sure that's true, but it's possible I wanted to avoid the reaction I usually get from you when I say I have to take a vacation." The patient felt hurt and said to the therapist, "See? You *did* delay in letting me know because you want to avoid how I feel. I'm sorry if my feelings of neediness were too much for you."

In this vignette, the therapist appears to put off announcing vacation as a way of avoiding the emotional outburst she expects from the patient. Inadvertently, however, she confirms the patient's sense that she is malevolent by not taking into account the patient's need for greater notice and also confirms the patient's view of herself as in some way noxious.

Studies using magnetic resonance imaging (MRI) techniques with borderline patients and controls have demonstrated reduced hippocampal and amygdalar volumes in BPD versus those of control groups (Driessen et al., 2000; Schmahl, Vermetten, Elzinga & Bremner, 2003; Tebartz van Elst et al., 2003). While the role of stress and trauma in reducing hippocampal volume has been observed in many studies, the exact relationship between early trauma and the decreased volumes in the amygdala is unclear. Genetic factors may be at work as well. Hariri and colleagues (2002) found that normal individuals with one or two copies of the short allele of the serotonin transporter (5-HTT) promoter gene demonstrate greater amygdalar neuronal activity in response to fearful stimuli compared to individuals homozygous for the long allele. Further research on 5-HTT status in borderline patients would be helpful to explore this hypothesis.

THE PRE-FRONTAL CORTEX: "TOP-DOWN" REGULATION

The foregoing focus on such subcortical structures as the amygdala only partly addresses the clinical phenomena associated with BPD. The regulatory functions of cortical structures must be taken into account as well. Our emphasis on the amygdala and HPA axis examines borderline object relations from a perspective described in the literature as bottom-up (reflexive) regulation (Berston, Sarter & Cacioppo, 2003). Consideration of top-down regulation by the pre-frontal cortex is equally important in understanding the interpersonal difficulties and affective dysregulation seen in patients with BPD (Herpertz et al., 2001).

Both the medial and orbital pre-frontal cortex have direct, reciprocal connections with areas of the brain that are crucial to emotion, and both have an inhibiting effect on the amygdala (Hariri, Mattay, Tessitore, Fera & Weinberger, 2003; LeDoux, 2002; Rausch, Shin & Wright, 2003). The dorsolateral pre-frontal cortex also appears to exert a modulatory influence upon the amygdala indirectly via its direct connections with the medial and orbital pre-frontal cortices (Hariri et al., 2003; LeDoux, 2002).

Investigators postulate that dual brain pathology involving increased activity in the amygdala and decreased activity in the pre-frontal regions may be central to understanding borderline phenomena. In two studies (Lyoo, Han & Cho, 1998; Tebartz van Elst et al., 2003), reductions in medial and orbital frontal lobe volumes have been noted in the brains of borderline patients. Of particular interest in the fMRI study by Tebartz van Elst and colleagues was that the left orbitofrontal volumes correlated significantly with amygdala volumes. Hence the weakening of pre-frontal inhibitory controls may actually contribute to the hyper-reactivity of the amygdala. This combination may be related to the common clinical situation where a borderline patient cannot seem to control or shut off intense emotional responses.

THE PRE-FRONTAL CORTEX AND MENTALIZATION

The pre-frontal cortex is crucial for mentalization, that is, the ability to assign separate mental states to self and others in order to explain and predict behavior (Gallagher et al., 2000). A securely attached caregiver passes on secure attachment and the capacity to mentalize to the infant. The caregiver ascribes mental states to the child, treats the child as someone with agency, and helps the child to create internal working models. The end result is that a child can read the expression on another's face and know what that person is feeling without extensive conscious effort to figure out the meaning of the facial expression. Research has linked BPD patients with insecure attachment (Alexander et al., 1998; Allen, 2001; Patrick, Hobson, Castle, Howard & Maughan, 1994; Stalker & Davies, 1995). The failure to resolve trauma appears to distinguish the BPD group from others. Early childhood trauma leads to defensive withdrawal from the mental world on the part of the victim. Hence some patients with BPD who have had severe trauma cope with the abuse by avoiding reflection on the content of the caregiver's mind. This defensive shutdown may be needed to avoid thinking about the caregiver as a malevolent individual or the self as deserving of abuse. It may also prohibit resolution of abusive experiences (Fonagy, 2001).

As Fonagy has reviewed in detail (see Chapter 3), imaging studies suggest that mentalization involves a network of different functionally related brain regions working in concert (Baron-Cohen et al., 1999; Calarge, Andreasen & O'Leary, 2003; Frith & Frith, 1999; Gallagher et al., 2000). Such brain structures appear to include orbital (Grezes, Frith & Passingham, 2004; Ramnani & Miall, 2004) and medial pre-frontal regions (Abu-Akel, 2003; Gallagher et al., 2000; Grezes et al., 2004; Ramnani & Miall, 2004; Frith & Frith, 1999, 2003; Gallagher & Frith, 2003), mirror neurons originating in the ventral pre-motor cortex (Abu-Akel, 2003; Grezes et al., 2004; Ramnani & Miall, 2004), temporal lobe structures, including the temporal poles (Frith & Frith, 2003; Gallagher & Frith, 2003) and amygdala (Abu-Akel, 2003; Baron-Cohen et al., 1999; Fine, Lumsden & Blair, 2001), temporo-parietal regions, including the superior temporal sulcus (Abu-Akel, 2003; Grezes et al., 2004; Ramnani & Miall, 2004; Frith & Frith, 2003; Gallagher et al., 2000; Gallagher & Frith, 2003) and fusiform gyrus (Gallagher et al., 2000), and the cerebellum (Abu-Akel, 2003; Calarge et al., 2003). Of these structures, functional neuroimaging studies most consistently demonstrate activation of the medial pre-frontal cortex during mentalization tasks (Abu-Akel, 2003; Frith & Frith, 2003; Gallagher et al., 2000). As noted above, neuroimaging studies of borderline patients demonstrate abnormalities in many of these brain regions, including the medial pre-frontal cortex, the orbital pre-frontal cortex, and amygdala. Theories involving simulation and internalized self/object representations suggest ways in which these structures may work together in the process of mentalization.

SIMULATION THEORY AND MENTALIZATION

Current evidence supports the notion that mentalization relies, in part, upon internal simulations of the perceived emotions and mental states of others (Abu-Akel, 2003; Adolphs, 2002; Grezes et al., 2004; Ramnani & Miall, 2004). This hypothesis is strengthened by studies that demonstrate that imitating facial expressions of others induces the emotional content of those expressions in the imitator (Adolphs, Damasio, Tranei, Cooper & Damasio, 2000).

Mirror neurons in the ventral pre-motor cortex appear to automatically trigger unconscious internal simulations of the observed behaviors of others so that the observer may reconstruct their mental states and emotions (Abu-Akel, 2003; Adolphs, 2001; Grezes et al., 2004). Mirror neurons are activated by *either* performance of goal-directed behaviors, like grasping or frowning, or observation of them in others (Adolphs, 2001; Buccino, Binkofski & Riggio, 2004; Gallese, 2003; Grezes et al., 2004; Hari et al., 1998; Tai, Scherfler, Brooks, Sawamoto & Castiello, 2004). Gallese (2003) hypothesizes that there is a broad array of mirror-matching mechanisms present in the human brain that enable intersubjective communication and attribution of intentionality.

For example, representations of the frowning facial expression of another person may register in the superior temporal sulcus and fusiform gyrus of the observer (Abu-Akel, 2003; Adolphs, 2002). Non-conscious, temporo-parietal representations of the frowning facial expression may activate mirror neurons in the pre-motor cortex (Abu-Akel, 2003; Adolphs, 2002), which appear automatically to trigger unconscious simulations of frowning in the observer (Grezes et al., 2004; Ramnani & Miall, 2004; Tai et al., 2004). Simulations of frowning are believed to trigger the associated feeling and mental states such as anger (Abu-Akel, 2003).

Research suggests that conscious discernment of feeling states of self and others relies on the encoding of such *feeling state representations* in the insula and SSII regions of the right somatosensory cortex (Adolphs, 2001; Damasio, 2003; Damasio et al., 2000; Critchley, Mathias & Dolan, 2001; Singer et al., 2004). The SSll and insular regions appear to be important in generating non-conscious neural representations of feeling states associated with different emotions (Adolphs et al., 2000; Damasio et al., 2000). Investigators propose that the medial pre-frontal cortex reads the neural representations of self and other feeling states conveyed by SSll and insular regions (Damasio et al., 2000; Singer et al., 2004). This observation is relevant to the role of the medial pre-frontal cortex (e.g., anterior cingulate cortex and paracingulate gyrus) in conscious attention to emotional states of the self and others (Devinsky, Morrell & Vogt, 1995; Stuss & Knight, 2002).

INTERNALIZED SELF/OBJECT REPRESENTATIONS AND MENTALIZATION

The amygdala, with reciprocal connections to both the sensory cortices and the pre-frontal cortices, may also participate in the generation of internalized mental state representations of both the self and others (Abu-Akel, 2003; Schore, 1997, 2003). Non-conscious representations of self and others in parieto-temporal regions, such as the superior temporal sulcus and fusiform gyrus, are matched up with self and other representations based on prior experience, which are linked with the orbital pre-frontal cortex by affects generated by the amygdala based on prior learning (Schore, 1997, 2003). An important function of the orbital pre-frontal cortex, relevant to mentalizing capacity, is to decode the reward and punishment value of emotions and behaviors of self and others (Kringelbach & Rolls, 2004; Rolls, 2004; Soloff et al., 2003). It is also involved in both the learning of these values and the reversal of that learning. The orbitofrontal cortex is particularly responsive to facial emotional expressions, and it is important in attachment processes (Schore, 1997).

These functions of the orbital pre-frontal cortex are critical to the ability to predict the intentions and motives of others, and the impact of one's behaviors upon the mental states of others (Abu-Akel, 2003; Schore, 1997; Kringelbach & Rolls, 2004). Schore (1997) contends that these self and other representations conveyed to the orbital pre-frontal cortex, along with their associatively linked affects (conveyed from the amygdalae to the orbital pre-frontal cortex), are integrated in the orbital pre-frontal cortex as internalized object relations – that is, a self-representation, an object representation, and a linking affect state.

ABNORMALITIES OF THE PRE-FRONTAL CORTEX IN PATIENTS WITH BPD

Understanding how the pre-frontal cortex regulates affect states via direct inhibitory modulation, and via mechanisms involving mentalization, may shed light on the dysfunctional affect regulation seen in patients with BPD. Functional neuroimaging studies of BPD patients demonstrate abnormalities in regions of the medial and orbital pre-frontal cortex (Schmahl et al., 2003; Soloff et al., 2003). Dysfunction of these pre-frontal regions may be associated with reduced pre-frontal serotonergic function (Soloff et al., 2003), but the etiology is unknown. As noted previously, a recent structural imaging study showed significantly reduced volumes of the medial and orbital pre-frontal cortex in patients with BPD (Tebartz van Elst et al., 2003). These pre-frontal abnormalities may correlate with impaired recognition of emotional states of self and others, feelings of psychic emptiness, an urge to self-mutilate, emotional affect dysregulation, and the impulsivity so commonly seen in patients with BPD (Soloff et al., 2003; Tebartz van Elst et al., 2003). Medial pre-frontal cortical dysfunction induced by transcranial magnetic stimulation has been associated with lengthening of reaction times to pictures of angry expressions in normal subjects (Adolphs, 2002), supporting the concept that the medial pre-frontal cortex is important to shutting off negative affect states (Schmahl et al., 2003).

Simulation theory may partially explain impaired mentalization in borderline patients. Generating internal simulations of perceived emotions and mental states of others in traumatized BPD patients relies upon neural networks in which abusive self and object representations are encoded. Additionally, the proposed dual brain pathology of pre-frontal cortex and limbic circuits (Tebartz van Elst et al., 2003) may further contribute to conditioning of negative affect states to self and other representations, also leading to negative interpretive biases such as those in reaction to neutral faces (Donegan et al., 2003).

The centrality of separation anxiety and abandonment themes in patients with BPD also has been studied using positron emission tomography (PET) imaging by Schmahl and colleagues (2003). These investigators studied 20 women with a history of childhood sexual abuse and 20 controls while they listened to scripts describing neutral and personal abandonment events. These investigators noted that, similar to rhesus monkeys exposed to maternal separation, the BPD women exposed to memories of abandonment showed evidence of increased activation of the right dorsolateral pre-frontal cortex. Hence the investigators postulate that stress associated with maternal separation activates the same pre-frontal brain regions as memories of childhood abandonment in these patients. They also propose that the reduced right medial pre-frontal activation may reflect the inability, in BPD patients, to shut down negative emotions.

Our discussion of the role of pre-frontal cortex and amygdalar abnormalities in BPD patients highlights important considerations involving regions of aberrant activation in functional neuroimaging studies. For example, when we see increased or decreased activation of the amygdala in functional neuroimaging studies, there are multiple possibilities to consider other than that the amygdala is intrinsically abnormal. For example, distorted self-object neural representations may activate a normally functioning amygdala. Alternatively, aberrant amygdalar activation may be related to dysfunction in another brain region, such as a hypo-functioning pre-frontal cortex, or the problem may lie in diffuse systems that interact with widespread brain regions including the pre-frontal cortex and amygdala, such as the serotonergic system.

Most of our attention up to this point has been directed to the pre-frontal cortex and the amygdala. However, learning from experience involves structures which encode memory, notably, the hippocampus. We now turn to these considerations and their influence on the repetition of problematic object relations.

IMPAIRMENTS IN MEMORY RELATED TO HIPPOCAMPAL ABNORMALITIES

The relationships of BPD patients are characterized by a repetitive quality suggesting that these patients have difficulty learning from experiences. Could there be a disturbance in memory that contributes to this difficulty? As the studies summarized up to this point have illustrated, hippocampal abnormalities are commonly noted in BPD. The hippocampus is involved in the formation and retrieval of implicit and explicit memories. Whereas implicit memories are activated unconsciously, explicit memories are activated consciously (Solms & Turnbull, 2002). The neural networks created in the process of forming and retrieving memories are dependent upon which cells are stimulated. In other words, cells that fire together, wire together (Hebb, 1949).

The four stages involved in forming and accessing memories include encoding, consolidation, storage, and retrieval. When new information is acquired, it is initially encoded. With time, this information is consolidated and stored. The process of consolidation involves entrenching memories into deeper and deeper levels of storage. When necessary, this information is retrieved for further use (Solms & Turnbull, 2002).

Among the multiple hormones and neurotransmitters involved in the formation of memories, glucocorticoids appear to play a pre-eminent role. Numerous studies suggest that increased levels of glucocorticoids can impair or enhance the formation of memories depending on the content of the memory, the duration of exposure to elevated glucocorticoid levels, and the temporal relationship between exposure to elevated glucocorticoid levels and the item to be learned (McGaugh & Roozendaal, 2002). Whereas acute increases in glucocorticoid exposure can enhance memory consolidation, they can also impair memory encoding and retrieval. This effect on memory occurs through direct impairment of a process called *long-term potentiation* (LTP; Grossman, Buschsbaum & Yehuda, 2002).

In LTP, receptors are activated and a cascade of events is initiated that eventually results in the strengthening of synaptic connections between neurons. These synaptic connections are essential for the encoding, consolidation, storage, and retrieval of memories. Changes in systemic glucocorticoid levels can interfere acutely with the process of LTP (Grossman et al., 2002) and thus interfere with the process of forming memories. Hence, borderline patients who have experienced early childhood trauma and have a hyper-reactive HPA axis, leading to elevated systemic glucocorticoid levels, may have difficulty forming and retrieving declarative memories.

Elevated glucocorticoid levels can affect the physical structures involved in memory formation and retrieval as well. Sustained exposure to elevated glucocorticoid levels leads to neuronal degeneration in the CA3 hippocampal region in vervet monkeys and rats (McEwen & Magarinos, 2001; McKittrick et al., 2002; Sapolsky, Uno, Rebert & Finch, 1990). Increased endogenous glucocorticoid production resulting from stressful conditions causes dendritic pruning in animals (McKittrick et al., 2002; Watanabe, Gould & McEwen, 1992). Therefore, the possibility exists that patients with a history of early life trauma, which could result in alterations of endogenous glucocorticoid levels due to stress, might subsequently suffer from memory impairments and structural damage to the hippocampus (Bremner et al., 1997; Gabbard, 2005a; Stein, Koverola, Hanna, Torchia & McClarty, 1997).

As noted above, patients with a history of BPD and early life trauma have smaller hippocampal and amygdalar volumes than those without a history of BPD (Driessen et al., 2000; Schmahl et al., 2003; Tebartz van Elst et al., 2003).

These decreased volumes could be due to multiple etiologies such as neuronal cell death, neuronal atrophy, inhibited neurogenesis, or dendritic pruning (Grossman et al., 2002), possibly related to elevated glucocorticoid levels. Stress connected with childhood trauma and neglect may induce elevations of cortisol and decreased levels of brain-derived neurotrophic factor (BDNF). Exposure to elevated glucocorticoid levels may contribute to excitotoxicity and subsequent neuronal cell death, while lower levels of BDNF may result in decreased neurogenesis (Schmahl et al., 2003).

However, this correlation between BPD and smaller hippocampal and amygdalar volumes does not definitively prove a traumatic etiology. While it is possible that these smaller volumes could result from damage occurring over time, which subsequently results in the development of BPD, it is also possible that people with smaller hippocampal and/or amygdalar volumes may be more predisposed to having this disorder. Frodl and colleagues (2004) found that smaller hippocampal volumes are associated with the long variant of the serotonin transporter polymorphism in major depression, suggesting the possibility that patients with BPD may also have a genetic predisposition to smaller hippocampal volumes.

In any case, patients with BPD appear to have specific memory impairments. Smaller hippocampal and temporal lobe size have been associated with poorer memory performance regardless of diagnosis (Grossman et al., 2002). Stevens and colleagues (2004) compared 22 female subjects with BPD to 25 matched controls on tests of working memory and perception. The BPD subjects suffered from impairments in working memory and perceptual speed when compared with the controls. Impaired non-verbal executive functioning and non-verbal memory have been noted in patients with BPD when compared to controls as well (Dinn et al., 2004).

Neural networks that survive the pruning that occurs during development serve as templates, or models, around which all later memories are organized. These networks are called *trunk circuits*, and they are activated on a regular basis even if the events that originally created them are not consciously recalled (Solms & Turnbull, 2002). In fact, access to memories created during childhood may not be possible as the brain functions differently during different stages of development. In addition, traumatic memories may not be encoded in a form that leaves them accessible to subsequent conscious recall due to the hippocampal dysfunction occurring during the traumatic event, such as impairment of the LTP process (Solms & Turnbull, 2002).

Perception of reality is based on what one has learned about the world and thus what one remembers. Reality is constructed based on expectations of what it should be, which are based on our memories. One example of this is the blind spot, the location in the retina where the optic nerve enters and exits the eye. Because there are no receptors in this specific area, there is a hole in one's vision. This hole, however, does not interfere with one's perception of the world as this region is filled in with what one expects to see (Solms & Turnbull, 2002).

Patients with BPD, like everyone else, thus perceive others in accordance with the internalized models contained in their trunk circuits. The memory that informs expectations may be both explicit (i.e., conscious) and implicit (i.e., unconscious). The "how to" of relatedness is encoded early in life in implicit procedural memory as a set of unconscious internal object relationships of self, others, and affect states connecting them (Westen & Gabbard, 2002). These internalized models of relationships are played out repeatedly in a manner that often seems obligatory. In a psychotherapeutic setting, borderline patients often enact these patterns without being able to articulate them in a way that makes them understandable in light of previous experience.

These patterns also are repeated outside of the therapy, and one of the greatest challenges in the therapy is trying to help the borderline patient reflect on the meaning of the patterns and learn from them (i.e., mentalize). Patients often actively resist connections of this sort. A therapist said to a female borderline patient who had a long series of unhappy relationships that the man she was now dating was similar to the previous man she dated, who ended up neglecting her and cheating on her. The patient responded with great intensity and told the therapist in no uncertain terms, "I don't want to talk about him. He's in the past. I don't ever want to think about him again." This type of temporal splitting (Gabbard, 2005b), in which the patient actively keeps apart past object relationships and present object relationships, may contribute to the tendency for borderline patients not to learn from previous experience. What we are also suggesting is that anatomical changes in the hippocampus may be linked to difficulties remembering specifics of past relationships which are requisite to process the potential for repeating past relationship patterns.

As stated earlier, the borderline patient may need to choose a partner who seems like a good receptacle for the terrifying parts of the self. Alternatively, these patients may need to transform the romantic partner into a bad object through projective identification as a way of externalizing an abusive internal object so that someone else must be in control of frightening impulses (Gabbard, 2005b). The obligatory nature of the repetition of these patterns can be understood through a mechanism of getting another person to "own" aspects of the borderline patient.

> A 29-year-old borderline patient came to conjoint therapy with her husband because of chronic arguments and fights that stopped just short of physical altercations. In the course of the therapy, the husband of the patient made a poignant statement illustrating the extent to which he felt transformed by the patient's behavior: "I keep telling her over and over again, I am *not* your abusive father. I don't want to hurt you, hit you, or be mean to you. But it's like no matter what I do, she sees me as somehow mistreating her. I'm at a loss as to what to do. I feel like giving up."

This vignette illustrates that while borderline patients may unconsciously select partners who are suitable templates for transformation into abusive objects, they also may transform others into a figure that fits their expectations of reality based on past experience. As noted previously, amygdalar hyperactivity in association with reduced cortical regulation may cause them to misconstrue facial expressions or behavior in a way that overreads malevolence in benign actions. Through projective identification, they may nudge the partner into confirming the expectations derived from the past.

REWARD CIRCUITS

Therapists often wonder why such maladaptive relationships are so compelling to the borderline patient. Another mechanism may involve reward circuitry. In his studies of addiction, Insel (2003) has suggested that social attachment or pair bonding may have circuitry in common with addictive disorders. Dopamine release in the nucleus accumbens is associated with both reward and addictive behaviors. Studies of pair bonding in mammals suggest that a dopamine agonist can induce partner preferences. Research has even shown that a partner preference could be facilitated with a D2 agonist infused directly into the nucleus accumbens. A D2 antagonist infused in the same location blocks development of a partner preference in the presence of mating (Insel, 2003). We might hypothesize that the familiar relationships experienced by borderline patients are in some way soothing because they tap into circuitry that releases dopamine and functions like the gratification of an addiction.

Projections from the amygdala to the nucleus accumbens may also be involved in mediating amygdalar effects on memory consolidation. If memories and attachment are associated with reward, then the task of weakening old circuits becomes daunting. BPD patients may be neurochemically rewarded for activating old circuits and old internalized objects.

fMRI studies have shown that both romantic and maternal love activate regions of reward circuitry, as well as regions specific to each kind of attachment (Bartels & Zeki, 2004). While this reward circuitry is activated the brain regions associated with negative emotions and the evaluation of others' emotions and intentions are deactivated. This pattern of activation and deactivation encourages attachment without the critical assessment of others, and may contribute to the repeated strong attachments borderline patients develop with abusive others. In other words, the capacity to mentalize is deactivated when the patient falls in love (see also Fonagy, Chapter 3).

CONCLUDING COMMENTS

We have outlined a number of neurobiological correlates with the object relationship patterns of patients diagnosed with BPD. A hyper-reactive HPA axis may be associated with heightened perception of threat in the environment. Excessive amygdalar activity appears to contribute to the misinterpretation of neutral faces as potentially malevolent. This bottom-up regulation appears to be supplemented by impaired top-down regulation from the pre-frontal cortex due to decreased volume and hypo-activity of that region. Abnormalities of the pre-frontal cortex may also influence impaired mentalization in patients with borderline psychopathology. Hippocampal abnormalities may be relevant to the problems these patients have in learning from previous relationships and applying that knowledge to current relationships. Finally, reward circuitry associated with the nucleus accumbens and dopamine may make the patterns tenaciously resistant to treatment. The elucidation of neurobiological underpinnings helps us understand the tenacity with which these patterns are maintained and the need for extended psychotherapeutic and pharmacological intervention to alter these patterns. Indeed, one of the implications of this understanding is that extended psychotherapeutic intervention is necessary to see substantial changes in these relational patterns.

Another implication is that selective serotonin reuptake inhibitors (SSRIs) may be useful as an adjunct to psychotherapy. Because serotonin has an inhibitory effect on behavior, the impulsivity characteristic of borderline patients may in part relate to this altered serotonergic activity (Siever & Davis, 1991). Moreover, Rinne and colleagues (2003) found that one of the SSRIs, fluvoxamine, reduced the hyper-reactivity of the HPA axis in borderline patients. Hence SSRIs may facilitate psychotherapy by reducing "affective noise" such as hyper-vigilant anxiety, intense anger, or dysphoria that interferes with mentalizing (Gabbard, 2005a).

Several other implications for psychotherapy derive from this understanding. Much of dynamic psychotherapy links past patterns with current patterns. If hippocampal dysfunction and/or damage are present, then formation and retrieval of memories become more challenging. Moreover, representations of object relationships are not "things" stored in memory, but connections among nodes of a network that have been activated together for many years (Gabbard & Westen, 2003). These potentials for reactivation exist in a heightened state of potential, and a great deal of time is necessary to weaken links between nodes in this network that have fired together for a long time. What we call structural change in psychotherapy involves a relative deactivation of problematic links in activated networks and an increased activation of new, more adaptive connections. By strengthening the new and more adaptive circuits and weakening activation of old circuits, the newer circuits ultimately override the old circuits. Working in parallel with this change in circuitry is an increased capacity for conscious self-reflection and mentalization that allows the patient to override unconscious patterns once they are recognized (Gabbard & Westen, 2003). The challenge of overriding old patterns when they have an addiction-like appeal to the patient is a formidable one, and further research on these mechanisms is badly needed.

REFERENCES

Abu-Akel, A. (2003). A neurobiological mapping of theory of mind. *Brain Research. Brain Research Reviews*, *43*, 29–40.

Adler, G. (1985). *Borderline Psychopathology and Its Treatment*. New York: Jason Aronson.

Adolphs, R. (2001). The neurobiology of social cognition. *Current Opinions in Neurobiology*, *11*, 231–239.

Adolphs, R. (2002). Neural systems for recognizing emotion. *Current Opinions in Neurobiology*, *12*, 169–177.

Adolphs, R., Damasio, H., Tranei, D., Cooper, G. & Damasio, A. R. (2000). A role for somatosensory cortices in the role of visual recognition of emotions as revealed by 3-dimensional lesion mapping. *Journal of Neuroscience*, *20*, 2683–2690.

Alexander, P. C., Anderson, C. L., Brand, B., Schaeffer, C. M., Grelling, B. Z. & Kretz, L. (1998). Adult attachment and long-term effects in survivors of incest. *Journal of Child Abuse and Neglect*, *22*, 45–61.

Allen, J. G. (2001). *Traumatic Relationships and Serious Mental Disorders*. Chichester, UK: John Wiley & Sons, Ltd.

Baron-Cohen, S., Ring, H. A., Wheelwright, S., Bullmore, E. T., Brammer, M. J. & Simmons, A., et al. (1999). Social intelligence in the normal and autistic brain: an fMRI study. *European Journal of Neuroscience*, *11*, 1891–1898.

Bartels, A. & Zeki, S. (2004). The neural correlates of maternal and romantic love. *Neuroimage*, *21*, 1155–1166.

Bateman, A. & Fonagy, P. (2004). *Psychotherapy for Borderline Personality Disorder: Mentalization-Based Treatment*. Oxford/New York: Oxford University Press.

Berston, G. G., Sarter, M. & Cacioppo, J. T. (2003). Ascending visceral regulation of cortical affective information processing. *European Journal of Neurology*, *18*, 2103–2109.

Bremner, J. D., Randall, P., Vermetten, E., Staib, L., Bronen, R. A. & Mazure, C., et al. (1997). Magnetic resonance imaging based measurement of hippocampal volume in posttraumatic stress disorder related to childhood physical and sexual abuse – a preliminary report. *Biological Psychiatry*, *41*, 23–32.

Buccino, G., Binkofski, F. & Riggio, L. (2004). The mirror neuron system and action recognition. *Brain and Language*, *89*, 370–376.

Calarge, C., Andreasen, N. C. & O'Leary, D. S. (2003). Visualizing how one brain understands another: a PET study of theory of mind. *American Journal of Psychiatry*, *160*, 1954–1964.

Critchley, H. D., Mathias, C. J. & Dolan, R. J. (2001). Neuroanatomical basis for first- and second-order representations of bodily states. *Nature Neuroscience*, *4*, 207–212.

Damasio, A. (2003). *Looking for Spinoza: Joy, Sorrow, and the Feeling Brain* (1st edn.). New York: Harcourt.

Damasio, A. R., Grabowski, T. J., Bechara, A., Damasio, H., Ponto, L. L. B., Parvizi, J., et al. (2000). Subcortical and cortical brain activity during the feeling of self-generated emotions. *Nature Neuroscience*, *3*, 1049–1056.

Devinsky, O., Morrell, M. J. & Vogt, B. A. (1995). Contributions of anterior cingulate cortex to behavior. *Brain*, *118*, 279–306.

Dinn, W. M., Harris, C. L., Aycicegi, A., Greene, P. B., Kirkley, S. M. & Reilly, C. (2004). Neurocognitive functioning in borderline personality disorder. *Progress in Neuropsychopharmacological Biological Psychiatry*, *28*, 329–341.

Donegan, N. H., Sanislow, C. A., Blumberg, H. P., Fulbright, R. K., Lacadie, C. & Skudlarski, P., et al. (2003). Amygdala hyperreactivity in borderline personality disorder: implications for emotional dysregulation. *Biological Psychiatry*, *54*, 1284–1293.

Driessen, M., Herrmann, J., Stahl, K., Zwaan, M., Meier, S. & Hill, A., et al. (2000). Magnetic resonance imaging volumes of the hippocampus and the amygdala in women with borderline personality disorder and early traumatization. *Archives of General Psychiatry*, *57*, 1115–1122.

Fine, C., Lumsden, J. & Blair, R. J. R. (2001). Dissociation between "theory of mind" and executive functions in a patient with early left amygdala damage. *Brain*, *124*, 287–298.

Fonagy, P. (2001). *Attachment Theory and Psychoanalysis*. New York: Other Press.

Frith, C. D. & Frith, U. (1999). Interacting minds – a biological basis. *Science*, *286*, 1692–1695.

Frith, U. & Frith, C. D. (2003). Development and neurophysiology of mentalizing. *Philosophical Transactions of the Royal Society of London*, *358*, 459–473.

Frodl, T., Meisenzahl, E. M., Zill, P., Baghai, T., Rujescu, D., Leinsinger, G. et al. (2004). Reduced hippocampal volumes associated with the long variant of the serotonin transporter polymorphism in major depression. *Archives of General Psychiatry*, *61*, 177–183.

Gabbard, G. O. (2005a). *Psychodynamic Psychiatry in Clinical Practice* (4th edn.). Washington, DC: American Psychiatric Press.

Gabbard, G. O. (2005b). Mind, brain, and personality disorders. *American Journal of Psychiatry*, *162*, 648–655.

Gabbard, G. O. & Westen, D. (2003). Rethinking therapeutic action. *International Journal of Psychoanalysis*, *84*, 823–841.

Gabbard, G. O. & Wilkinson, S. (1994). *Management of Countertransference with Borderline Patients*. Washington, DC: American Psychiatric Press.

Gallagher, H. L. & Frith, C. D. (2003). Functional imaging of "theory of mind." *Trends in Cognitive Sciences*, *7*, 77–83.

Gallagher, H. L., Happe, F., Brunswick, N., Fletcher, P. C., Frith, U. & Frith, C. D. (2000). Reading the mind in cartoons and stories: an fMRI study of "theory of mind" in verbal and nonverbal tasks. *Neuropsychologia*, *38*, 11–21.

Gallese, V. (2003). The roots of empathy: the shared manifold hypothesis and the neural basis of intersubjectivity. *Psychopathology*, *36*, 171–180.

Grezes, J., Frith, C. D. & Passingham, R. E. (2004). Inferring false beliefs from the actions of oneself and others: an fMRI study. *Neuroimage*, *21*, 744–750.

Grossman, R., Buschsbaum, M. S. & Yehuda, R. (2002). Neuroimaging studies in post-traumatic stress disorder. *Psychiatric Clinics in North America*, *25*, 317–340.

Gunderson, J. G. (2001). *Borderline Personality Disorder: A Clinical Guide*. Washington, DC: American Psychiatric Press.

Hari, R., Forss, N., Avikainen, S., Kirveskari, E., Salenius, S. & Rizzolatti, G. (1998). Activation of human primary motor cortex during action observation: a neuromagnetic study. *Proceedings of the National Academy of Sciences*, *95*, 15061–15065.

Hariri, A. R., Mattay, V. S., Tessitore, A., Fera, F. & Weinberger, D. R. (2003). Neocortical modulation of the amygdala response to fearful stimuli. *Biological Psychiatry*, *53*, 494–501.

Hariri, A. R., Mattay, V. S., Tessitore, A., Kolachana, B., Fera, F., Goldman, D. et al. (2002). Serotonin transporter genetic variation and the response of the human amygdala. *Science*, *297*, 400–403.

Hebb, D. O. (1949). *Organization and Behavior*. New York: John Wiley & Sons, Inc.

Herpertz, S. C., Dietrich, T. M., Wenning, B., Krings, T., Erberich, S. G., Willmes, K. et al. (2001). Evidence of abnormal amygdala functioning in borderline personality disorder: a functional MRI study. *Biological Psychiatry*, *50*, 292–298.

Insel, T. R. (2003). Is social attachment an addictive disorder? *Physiology and Behavior*, *79*, 351–357.

Johnson, J. G., Cohen, P., Brown, J., Smailes, E. M. & Bernstein, D. P. (1999). Childhood maltreatment increases risk for personality disorders during early adulthood. *Archives of General Psychiatry*, *56*, 600–606.

Kendler, K. S. (2001). A psychiatric dialogue on the mind and body problem. *American Journal of Psychiatry*, *158*, 989–1000.

Kernberg, O. F. (1975). *Borderline Conditions and Pathological Narcissism*. New York: Jason Aronson.

Kringelbach, M. L. & Rolls, E. T. (2004). The functional neuroanatomy of the human orbitofrontal cortex: evidence from neuroimaging and neuropsychology. *Progress in Neurobiology*, *72*, 341–372.

LeDoux, J. (2002). *Synaptic Self: How Our Brains Become Who We Are*. New York: Penguin Putnam, Inc.

Lyoo, I. K., Han, M. H. & Cho, D. Y. (1998). A brain MRI study in subjects with borderline personality disorder. *Journal of Affective Disorders*, *50*, 235–243.

Mahler, M. S., Pine, F. & Bergman, A. (1975). *The Psychological Birth of the Human Infant: Symbiosis and Individuation*. New York: Basic Books.

Masterson, J. F. & Rinsley, D. B. (1975). The borderline syndrome: the role of the mother in the genesis and psychic structure of the borderline personality. *International Journal of Psychoanalysis*, *56*, 163–177.

McEwen, B. S. & Magarinos, A. M. (2001). Stress and hippocampal plasticity: implications for the pathophysiology of affective disorders. *Human Psychopharmacology*, *16*, S7–S19.

McGaugh, J. L. & Roozendaal, B. (2002). Role of adrenal hormones in forming lasting memories in the brain. *Current Opinions in Neurobiology*, *12*, 2005–2010.

McKittrick, C. R., Magarinos, A. M., Blanchard, D. C., Blanchard, R. J., McEwen, B. S. & Sakai, R. R. (2002). Chronic social stress reduces dendritic arbors in CA3 of hippocampus and decreases binding to serotonin transporter sites. *Synapse*, *36*, 85–94.

Patrick, M., Hobson, R. P., Castle, D., Howard, R. & Maughan, B. (1994). Personality disorder and the mental representation of early experience. *Developmental Psychopathology*, *6*, 375–388.

Ramnani, N. & Miall, R. C. (2004). A system in the human brain for predicting the actions of others. *Natural Neuroscience*, *7*, 85–90.

Rausch, S. L., Shin, L. M. & Wright, C. I. (2003). Neuroimaging studies of amygdala function in anxiety disorders. *Annals of the New York Academy of Sciences*, *985*, 389–410.

Rinne, T., de Kloet, E. R., Wouters, L., Goekoop, J. G., DeRijk, R. H. & van den Brink, W. (2002). Hyperresponsiveness of hypothalamic-pituitary-adrenal axis to combined dexamethasone/corticotropin-releasing hormone challenge in female borderline personality disorder subjects with a history of sustained childhood abuse. *Biological Psychiatry*, *52*, 1102–1112.

Rinne, T., de Kloet, E. R., Wouters, L., Goekoop, J. G., de Rijk, R. H. & van den Brink, W. (2003). Fluvoxamine reduces responsiveness of HPA axis in adult female BPD patients with a history of sustained childhood abuse. *Neuropsychopharmacology*, *28*, 126: 132.

Rolls, E. T. (2004). The functions of the orbitofrontal cortex. *Brain and Cognition*, *55*, 11–29.

Sapolsky, R. N., Uno, H., Rebert, C. S. & Finch, C. E. (1990). Hippocampal damage associated with prolonged glucocorticoid exposure in primates. *Journal of Neuroscience*, *10*, 2897–2902.

Schmahl, C. G., Elzinga, B. M., Vermetten, E., Sanislow, C., McGlashan, T. H. & Bremner, J. D. (2003). Neural correlates of memories of abandonment in women with and without borderline personality disorder. *Biological Psychiatry*, *54*, 142–151.

Schmahl, C. G., Vermetten, E., Elzinga, B. M. & Bremner, J. D. (2003). Magnetic resonance imaging of hippocampal and amygdalar volume in women with childhood abuse and borderline personality disorder. *Psychiatry Research*, *122*, 193–198.

Schore, A. (1997). A century after Freud's project: is a rapprochement between psycho-analysis and neurobiology at hand? *Journal of the American Psychoanalytic Association*, *45*, 808–840.

Schore, A. N. (2003). *Affect Regulation in the Repair of the Self*. New York: W. W. Norton.

Siever, L. J. & Davis, K. L. (1991). A psychobiological perspective on the personality disorders. *American Journal of Psychiatry*, *148*, 1647–1658.

Singer, T., Seymour, B., O'Doherty, J., Kaube, H., Dolan, R. J. & Frith, C. D. (2004). Empathy for pain involves the affective but not sensory components of pain. *Science*, *303*, 1157–1162.

Solms, M. & Turnbull, O. (2002). *The Brain and the Inner World: An Introduction to the Neuroscience of Subjective Experience*. New York: Other Press.

Soloff, P. H., Meltzer, C. C., Becker, C., Greer, P. J., Kelly, T. M. & Constantine, D. (2003). Impulsivity and prefrontal hypometabolism in borderline personality disorder. *Psychiatry Research*, *123*, 153–163.

Stalker, C. A. & Davies, F. (1995). Attachment organization and adaptation in sexually abused women. *Canadian Journal of Psychiatry*, *40*, 234–240.

Stein, M. B., Koverola, C., Hanna, C., Torchia, M. G. & McClarty, B. (1997). Hippocampal volume in women victimized by childhood sexual abuse. *Psychological Medicine*, *27*, 951–959.

Stevens, A., Burkhardt, M., Hautzinger, M., Schwarz, J. & Unckel, C. (2004). Borderline personality disorder: impaired visual perception and working memory (Abstract only). *Psychiatry Research*, *125*, 257–267.

Stuss, D. & Knight, R. (2002). *Principles of Frontal Lobe Function*. New York: Oxford University Press.

Tai, Y. F., Scherfler, C., Brooks, D. J., Sawamoto, N. & Castiello, U. (2004). The human premotor cortex is "mirror" only for biological actions. *Current Biology*, *14*, 117–120.

Tebartz van Elst, L., Hesslinger, B., Thiel, T., Geiger, E., Haegele, K., Lemieux, L., et al. (2003). Frontolimbic brain abnormalities in patients with borderline personality disorder: a volumetric magnetic resonance imaging study. *Biological Psychiatry*, *54*, 163–171.

Wagner, A. W. & Linehan, M. M. (1999). Facial expression recognition ability among women with borderline personality disorder: implications for emotion regulation? *Journal of Personality Disorders*, *13*, 329–344.

Watanabe, Y., Gould, E. & McEwen, B. S. (1992). Stress induces atrophy of apical dendrites of hippocampal CA3 pyramidal neurons. *Brain Research*, *588*, 341–345.

Westen, D. & Gabbard, G. O. (2002). Developments in cognitive neuroscience, II. Implications for the concept of transference. *Journal of the American Psychiatric Association*, *50*, 99–113.

Zanarini, M. C. & Frankenburg, F. R. (1997). Pathways to the development of borderline personality disorder. *Journal of Personality Disorders*, *11*, 93–104.

PART III

INCORPORATING MENTALIZING IN ESTABLISHED TREATMENTS

6

INTEGRATING MENTALIZATION-BASED TREATMENT AND TRADITIONAL PSYCHOTHERAPY TO CULTIVATE COMMON GROUND AND PROMOTE AGENCY

Richard L. Munich

Mentalization-based treatment is a contemporary form of psycho-dynamic psychotherapy that aims to enhance the capacity for mentalizing, a more imaginative and interpretive way of thinking about the mental life of self and others, and ultimately to promote the individual's agency for illness, treatment, and self (Allen, 2003; Bateman & Fonagy, 1999, 2001; Bleiberg, 2001; Fonagy & Target, 1997; Munich, 2003). At its center is the concept of mentalized affectivity, that is, the identification and modulation of – and ultimately the freedom to choose the type of expression for – various feeling states (Fonagy, Gergely, Jurist & Target, 2002; Lane & Garfield, 2005). In some psychoanalytic circles an often heard criticism of mentalization is that it is nothing new, representing a condensation of more traditional notions such as psychological mindedness and empathy and more contemporary ones such as mindfulness and inter-subjectivity (see Allen, Chapter 1 and Holmes, Chapter 2). Another suggestion is that there is very little difference between enhancing the capacity for mentalizing and cognitively based practices (see Björgvinsson & Hart, Chapter 7).

In this chapter I will discuss how a traditionally trained psychotherapist thinks about mentalizing and mentalization-based therapy. This discussion is strongly

Handbook of Mentalization-Based Treatment. Edited by J. G. Allen and P. Fonagy.
© 2006 John Wiley & Sons, Ltd.

influenced by working with difficult-to-treat patients who are typically recalcitrant or resistant to treatment, or who have had multiple treatment failures and struggle with treatment compliance (Munich & Allen, 2003). In a clinical vignette, I will recount a problematic application of my version of mentalization-based treatment and the special difficulty of working with impaired capacity for mentalized affectivity. Then, in the context of recent discussions about forging common ground in the practice of psychotherapy (Gabbard & Weston, 1995, 2003), I will outline how a traditional psychotherapist conceives of the context and certain technical aspects of this new model that aims to increase mentalizing and personal agency.

DECONSTRUCTING MENTALIZATION

In attempting to implement more mentalization-based treatments with some of our patients, I have found it useful to imagine a web or a hierarchy of mental operations, in particular, those mental arrangements or steps that might be considered pathways to mentalizing. Such a pathway or hierarchy begins with acting and reacting, a pattern most often useful in dangerous situations conducive to fight or flight; but this pattern is essentially dysfunctional in most interpersonal situations because it is characterized by rigid and stereotypical thinking. This is thinking that is pre-empted by strong and usually un-regulated emotional responsiveness, more like what is seen and experienced in an intense argument as compared to an organized debate.

The next step in the hierarchy is a more temperate and flexible cognitive reaction characterized by focused attention and the identification of an affect, at first its somatic equivalents. This step involves noticing or awareness of the reaction. As would easily be recognized by most therapists who work with patients who are difficult to treat, this may be the most difficult step to promote. It is the step that is most profoundly affected by developmental disturbances, brain impairment, and severe mental illness. This is also a step faintly reminiscent of Piaget's (1954) shift from concrete to formal operations in early adolescence.

The capacity to reflect and think flexibly requires attentional control and affect regulation (see Fonagy, Chapter 3). Noticing one's reactions is a precursor to psychological mindedness, the ability to move below the surface, literal content of communications and to think about one's thinking and feeling. Psychological mindedness is closely related to empathy and a realistic attunement to another. Empathy involves thinking while feeling with and about another person, and it is mentalized affectivity that provides the mental space for empathic attunement. Mentalizing, the final step, includes empathy and mentalized affectivity, but adds the dimension of symbolic, imaginative, and interpretive thinking about the mental life of the self and other and their interrelationship. This hierarchy is represented in Figure 6.1.

MENTALIZING PROPER

symbolic, imaginative and interpretive thinking about self and other;
representational/autobiographical agency

EMPATHY AND REALISTIC ATTUNEMENT

psychological mindedness; mentalized affectivity; thinking while feeling

REFLECTIVE AND FLEXIBLE THINKING

affect regulation; attentional control; thinking about thinking and feeling

AWARENESS OF REACTING

identifying the emotion; attentional focus; pushing the "pause button"

ACTING AND REACTING

rigid and stereotypical thinking; high emotional arousal

Figure 6.1 Stages in mentalizing

Another caveat about mentalizing is inspired by the work of the late Jacques Derrida, who theorized that to know more about a construct, one must deconstruct it by determining what is excluded from it. In the case of mentalizing, I refer here to fundamental notions from psycho-dynamic psychiatry such as intra-psychic conflict, defense, and resistance, and the symbolizing function of mental life – stocks in trade of the psycho-dynamic approach to patients and their psychopathology. Although mentalization-based treatment is based in attachment theory that valorizes two-person psychology, in practice it may do so at the expense of important aspects of the patient's internal world and certain mental processes. Mentalization-based treatment is reinforced by a focus on the here-and-now relationship with the therapist as opposed to more traditional notions of transference.

Whereas the practice of mentalization-based treatment emphasizes the description of current mental states over insight into intra-psychic conflict and past, internalized object relations, then a concern about its preoccupation with the surface, its potential relation to a cognitive approach, and its limited intention to promote structural change may be worth considering. In the following example, I present material that highlights many of the aforementioned concerns, especially harkening back to an old-fashioned controversy in psycho-dynamic psychiatry, the difference between conflict and deficit in the etiology of dysfunction (London, 1973). The material is presented here as an example of the difficulty promoting mentalized affectivity in an increasing number of non-psychotic patients who present to us with a dramatically compromised or inhibited reflective capacity. Have these patients never learned to mentalize as a result of *deficits* in the creation of a secure base in attachment, or are there various *conflicts* that interfere with requisite mental processes?

The case material is also, *pari passu*, an example of how a patient's persistent difficulty mentalizing can lead to a failure in the therapist's mentalizing, opening up important questions about the role of transference and counter-transference and their relationship to projection, projective identification, and the concepts of enactment and inter-subjectivity.

CASE REPORT

Background

Steven is a mid-thirties, single, Caucasian male who was self-referred to an inpatient unit for his second admission to evaluate and treat paranoid thinking and self-sabotaging behavior. Discharged from the unit six months previously, he had done quite well for several months managing his depression and substance abuse while working as a marketing researcher for a software manufacturing company. Two months prior to readmission he was "dumped" by the latest in a long series of girlfriends and felt overwhelmed by a course he was taking at school. He relapsed with crack cocaine, marijuana, and significant amounts of alcohol. Additionally, he had persistent thoughts of hurting himself and took a leave from the latest in a long series of jobs; he entered the hospital feeling like a "complete loser" and quite frightened that his chronic drug usage was causing the disintegration of his thinking.

History

Steven is the only son of a high-achieving lawyer mother and financially successful businessman father, both of whom came from modest backgrounds. Except for a year-long conflict with his third-grade teacher that led to an extensive workup and a failed trial of Ritalin, along with a more or less absent father, Steven consistently described his childhood in positive terms. He acknowledged being a loner and recounted being mostly stoned on marijuana from mid-adolescence onward, nevertheless, completing high school and college in excellent standing. During late adolescence he began working with a psychiatrist who provided medication and support, often referring him to various psychotherapists over the next 20 years. Steven describes this support as helpful, but following graduation from college he spent the next several years using cocaine and wending his way through two masters' degrees and various failed employments. One early job lasted for nearly five years, but each new foray ended in discouragement, depression, and relapse. His personal life sounded bleak and rather desperate. He received extensive treatment at three major centers for substance abuse before his current hospitalization, ruefully acknowledging that he always did better in a treatment center.

Even though he had been more or less forced into the hospital and generated considerable frustration in the treatment team, Steven considered his first inpatient stay of approximately two months a success. An important dynamic process that emerged on the unit and in his twice-weekly psychotherapy sessions with me was a remarkable ability to elicit help and advice, the uselessness of which he was quickly able to demonstrate. It seemed to take very little, furthermore, to precipitate feelings of self-denigration and blame, hopelessness, and despair; and nothing really happened until the team more or less agreed with him that things were going nowhere, implicitly indicating that Steven had to assume some greater responsibility for his illness and treatment. This suggestion was coincidentally echoed in the psychotherapy where it took several sessions for me to realize and reflect back that, much like his report of previous psychotherapies, insight and interpretation were not followed by any noticeable continuity or change. Nevertheless, something about these confrontations seemed to mobilize a more reflective stance and self-directed activity, and Steven somehow pulled himself together for discharge.

Hospital and Psychotherapy Course: Second Admission

Steven presents as an intelligent and attractive man. One is immediately aware of an intense and beseeching eye contact that is compromised, however, by a permanently raised left eyebrow and right lip that convey an edge ranging from supercilious and mocking to arch and engaging. The mental-status examination indicates that he is essentially with it; and, except for some muted affect, his stated hopelessness and despair are not matched with vegetative signs and symptoms.

The diagnoses on admission and readmission were the same: major depressive disorder, recurrent; alcohol, cannabis, and cocaine dependence; dysthymia; and personality disorder NOS with dependent and narcissistic features. In this second hospital stay, he was continued on his medications, Risperdal and Wellbutrin.

Although cravings for substances along with hopelessness and despair were still prominent, the tenor and tone of Steven's second hospital stay were quite different from the first. He seemed less defensive, more genuine, and more willing to participate in his treatment; accordingly, the treatment team was generally more optimistic. Because the relapse and his request for re-hospitalization were precipitated by the disruption of a relationship, and because of his long history of failed relationships, I thought that this difficulty ideally would be an early focus in the psychotherapy. This plan was reinforced when Steven began complaining – eight days after admission and midway through our second session – about the intrusive and thoughtless behaviors of his roommate; but in this second session I mainly focused on Steven's continual use of de-clarifying expressions like "just want to go to bed," "to be honest with you, doc," and "you know . . ."

Remembering from our sessions during the first admission that I would often explore the implications of such verbal usages made it somewhat easier for Steven to appreciate that these linguistic habits tended to cover over or minimize issues as well as to reflect considerable internal uncertainties for him. With a lot of help, he acknowledged that these uncertainties also kept anyone from knowing what was going on, protected his space, and – despite his expressed wish to have close relationships – heightened the edge that kept people distant. More consistent with the principles of a directive and cognitively based treatment, I explained to Steven that his treatment would be severely compromised until he could acknowledge that his conscious wish for close relationships was in conflict with his investment in maintaining his apparent edge and interpersonal distance. Steven responded as if he did not know what I was talking about.

I felt hopeful, however, as we were able to continue in the next two sessions with Steven's ambivalence about relationships. This hope was reinforced as he first defended against and then with some persistence on my part was able to experience and even describe some sadness about the news that his therapist from home was moving out of town. Steven was then able to identify irritability, ensuing cravings for cocaine, and even some paranoid-like thinking as *maybe*, *perhaps*, connected *somehow* to that sadness. He was more certain, though, that using drugs cleared his mind of virtually all feelings, and we worked hard to identify exactly what made the more mundane feelings associated with sadness and loss so difficult to deal with. I remained concerned, however, about how often Steven seemed to be confusing feelings with behavior and how quickly any feeling was translated into a call for action or resolution. More technically, as in the earlier descriptions of his rhetoric, his projection of unwanted affect created pressure for the therapist to respond. Further examples of this process included such nudging statements as: "OK. I do feel sad, but what am I supposed to do about it?" Or, "So, wouldn't anyone feel sad about something like that?" Or, "How has my feeling sad right now solved anything?" By such means, he finessed my encouragement to have him simply sit with or describe this affective experience, continually obviating my best efforts.

In the next (fifth) session, Steven complained that he was getting very little from treatment and felt like leaving the hospital. After being asked if this complaint also applied to our psychotherapy, he responded that it probably did and that he could not remember the last session; upon prompting, he stated he could not feel sad and did not remember the last time he cried. Feeling sad and not a little frustrated myself, I worked hard to help him consider the possibility that his feelings of resignation were actually "easier" for him to live with than sadness. In this context, I continued, hopelessness and despair were old friends, very useful in mobilizing help and support. The patient appreciated rationally that he had much to be sad about, and he quickly wondered if early and extensive experience with substances had compromised his capacity to feel or tolerate sadness. It was during these interchanges that I felt most immediately Steven's energy to create a more or less compelling plea for help that arranged for all of his therapists to provide suggestions and advice in place of sitting with and working through his various dilemmas and difficult mental states.

Nevertheless, in the next two sessions Steven reported feeling somewhat better and essentially stuck with his difficulty identifying the internal signs of sadness. There were as well more intellectualized interchanges about whether or not mental states as contrasted with life circumstances had any role in his difficulty. Gradually, and partly as a result of untoward events in his peer group, he was able to report how easily he could feel hurt, and then quickly angry, and then just as quickly helpless and despairing. Fortunately, both in the treatment team and in the therapy, no one at this point was jumping in to fix things; instead, we were primarily encouraging the patient to sit with his feelings and see what came up. In spite of these modest advances, the note from my seventh psychotherapy session concluded with continued pessimism about Steven's capacity to reflect about his mental life.

The Fateful Eighth Session

My pessimism was obviously still at work during the very difficult eighth session during which, for virtually the first time in my long career as a psychotherapist with difficult patients, I felt a strong impulse to ask Steven to leave the session – and I communicated this feeling to him. Unlike Winnicott's putting his patient out of the office for therapeutic reasons, what felt like a temporary loss of a therapeutic stance on my part came about as Steven described himself as seething at – and having "nailed" – another patient during a group session for bringing up something critical about him. As I attempted to help figure out what about the feeling had led to his verbal assault on the other patient, I used the term "boiling mad." The patient countered, "No, I wasn't boiling mad, I was *seething*." I tried to correct myself, but the patient kept insisting that I had it wrong. Finally, I told the patient that I was finding the situation impossible: here I was trying very hard to help him sort out what he was feeling and what about feelings led to action, and even in the face of my acknowledging my not using his exact words he was arguing about what seemed to me a meaningless choice of words. Continuing in this vein, I said this kind of nit-picking had happened many times before, but this time it really made me want to end the session on the spot.

Steven was stunned. "Really," he said, "I've never seen you like this!" I told him I rarely *was* like this and felt pretty upset; that what he seemed unable to do in spite of my best efforts was think about his angry feeling: he would only let himself feel it very briefly and act or figure out ways to stop the feeling. I went on to say that, in this case, disagreement about the choice of words ended the possibility of understanding how his mind might be working, following which the angry feeling was assumed by me who then wanted to distance myself from him. There was a long silence as I began to regain my composure, but not, I might add, diminishing my strong feeling about what had happened. Finally, I was able to suggest that it was unlikely that Steven wanted to create this much distance from someone who could be helpful, but that many such problems he experienced with maintaining relationships might be an unintended side effect of his nit-picking, overly concrete, passive, and defensive style. I reiterated that this style was a way to avoid contemplating feeling states.

Immediately following the session, feeling quite undone, guilty, and un-therapeutic, I sought consultation from the patient's psychiatrist team leader, during which time I learned for the first time that his primary clinician, an experienced social worker, had in fact sent him twice from her office. Furthermore, he continued, the leader of his dialectical behavior therapy group, a group dedicated to imparting principles of mindfulness and emotional regulation, had often had the same experience. This information, however, was only mildly reassuring.

The Aftermath

Because of a long weekend, I did not see Steven again for five days. Remarkably, he began the next session by saying he had been thinking about our last session for several days. I told him that I had as well, and he responded with surprise. He thought the session was pretty amazing, and over the weekend had begun to see how regularly and effectively he arranged to change the subject, and to get the other person off track and away from anything he himself might be feeling. He seemed especially intrigued with the idea that, despite his professed loneliness, driving people away was often an unintended side effect of his efforts that I characterized as his "going concrete" on me. He went on to say, "To be honest with you, Dr Munich, I really don't know how to think about my feelings." Furthermore, he thought that as a result of the sessions he was actually feeling worse. I acknowledged that allowing himself to feel more could actually feel worse but in the long run could be better – pallid reassurance, alas, for person with severe addictive tendencies.

In subsequent sessions Steven seemed to have less of an edge and seemed slightly more reflective. He noted that he had some success sitting with his cravings without doing anything, and he reported that he cried for the first time in years. He spontaneously returned to his third-grade experience and could not remember anyone asking him about or even empathizing with his experience at that time;

they simply sent him off to doctors. For the first time in nearly two dozen psychotherapy sessions over two separate hospital stays, he was able to share ambivalent feelings about his parents with me. In spite or maybe even because of our fateful moment, he acknowledged feeling heard and even cared about by me.

As for me, I worked hard to understand what was going on that led to such a strong response to Steven's arguing with me about words. For a while, I thought it had something to do with how hard I was working in the sessions compared to Steven and my discouragement, perhaps as a projective identification from him, about how little progress toward a more reflective stance he could take. Nevertheless, our work continued until his discharge and included his very tentative and moving revelation that some of his difficulty opening up further related to feeling that we would not be able to continue working together.

The initial self-analytic interpretation of my reaction diminished a few weeks later when discussing the session with a colleague. Something she said reminded me of my own struggles growing up with an aphasic, impatient, and temper-ridden father who I often helped find the right word. I was immediately then in touch with the terror I felt when he would become frustrated with me for finding the wrong word as well as the anger I felt but never had the chance to express because of that terror. When wondering if it would have been better to have maintained a more interpretive or at least more holding stance with Steven rather than revealing the experience of my frustration, it felt as if I had no choice at the time. I was momentarily in a more reactive mode, without flexible thinking or necessary affect regulation, leading to what some might characterize as an enactment, an example of a regression in the hierarchy leading to mentalizing.

From a more traditional transference-focused point of view, I was provoked to act in a way that at the very least brought Steven's absent father into play, while the anger in my counter-transference served to express deeply forbidden impulses toward my own father, that is, getting him out of play. From an object relations point of view, my response indicated to the patient that he had made a significant impact upon me, that I cared about him in a very real sense, and that I was going to stick by him.

As it turned out, my outburst likely had more of a deleterious effect on me. I did not, in fact, end the session; and my overall response may have even had many elements of mentalized affectivity. That is, I was able to experience and utilize the experience of an intense burst of anger to suggest to Steven what it may have meant and implied about him, his own provocativeness and inadvertent distancing manoeuvres. One way to think about the events of the fateful eighth session is that it is exactly what we are trying to help our patients do. Speaking hopefully, it may have promoted some aspects of our work; however, it is obviously difficult to recommend such a spontaneous and very personal response to a colleague or student. One thing that can be recommended, however, is what

Schlesinger (1995) indicates when he says that it is less what happens right now that matters than what happens next in a therapeutic exchange. Like many of our interventions, its effect must await a longer-term perspective in the patient's future psychotherapeutic, interpersonal, and adaptive functioning.

DISCUSSION

Much like what is implied by the concept of mentalized affectivity, Lane and Garfield (2005) hypothesize that the greater awareness one has of their affective state, the greater the chance for modulating that state and regulating the reactions that precede and follow it. Without being explicit about it, most psychotherapists, especially those working with the more difficult-to-treat patients, work toward assisting them to identify mental states and enhance awareness of them. Awareness of one's mental state is a prerequisite to the restoration of flexible thinking, stimulation of non-guilty reflectivity, promotion of an active consideration of the inner worlds of self and other (mentalizing), and the enhancement of personal authority and agency.

To these ambitious ends we first recommend maintaining a clear therapeutic framework and interpersonal boundary that includes the implications and awareness of transference and counter-transference reactions. In addition to this very standard and traditional position, we also advocate active and interactive listening that prioritizes theoretical flexibility over technical neutrality. In other words we utilize whatever theoretical perspective can help us achieve the goal of engaging the patient and catalyzing a therapeutic process. At this point in the development of our field we borrow from many sources: a focus on process over the content and surface over the depth has echoes of ego psychology; contemporary object relations theory and self-psychology bring us the two-person point of view and the notion of empathy; exploring the patient's relationships is central for the interpersonalists and relational therapists; dialectical behavior therapy and attachment theory have given us mindfulness and mentalization, crucial for affect regulation; and finally, a more cognitive-behavioral approach provides an educational and psycho-educational point of view that offers alternatives to rigid or personalized thinking.

In this same vein, one might think of the theoretical disputes of the 1980s and 1990s about the nature of borderline psychopathology as representing conflicting points of view about the clinical presentations of very different kinds of patients. For example, a therapist utilizing an Adler-Buie "holding" approach for a patient with borderline personality disorder featuring inappropriate and intense anger along with impulsiveness and aggressive self-destructiveness would be overwhelmed in rapid fashion. The approach advocated by Kernberg, transference-focused psychotherapy, would make an effort to deal with these same volatile issues early in the contract-setting phase of treatment (Yeomans, Selzer & Clarkin,

1992), but such efforts might intimidate a more fragile patient. Or a patient with unstable interpersonal relations, micropsychoses, and schizoid phenomena might benefit more from a therapist with an object relations point of view than one who is focusing on interpretations of defensive operations (Horwitz et al., 1996; Munich, 1993).

Similar flexibility is seen in traditional psychotherapeutic approaches to patients with psychotic disorders wherein, depending on where the patient is at any given moment, one might practice the flexible psychotherapy proposed by Fenton (2001), the personal psychotherapy of Hogarty (Hogarty et al., 1995), or more traditional therapies as practiced by Fromm-Reichman, Sullivan, and Searles (Munich, 1987). In short, patients might benefit from techniques derived from different theoretical points of view, whether employed by different therapists or by the same therapist at different times during the process. Good therapists do what works (Pine, 1984, 1985).

After active and interactive listening, the next recommendation to promote mentalizing involves describing the here-and-now mental state, focusing more on how the patient's mind is working than on its content and more on its surface than on its depth. These processes are detected, of course, in the music and flow of the narrative, nuance of expression, and patterns of interaction with the therapist. Techniques that support this focus on mental content include paying close attention to stereotypical rhetorical usages; providing contingent responsiveness; helping the patient identify reliable signals of affect – and especially confusions of thought, affect, and action; radically validating trauma; forcing a moment of reflection; playing back to moments that triggered strong responses, especially those that occur in the session; and judiciously using irony and confrontation (Lear, 2003). Insofar as mental processes are usually working to restore equilibrium or to maintain the status quo, it may be less important what the therapist observes or interprets at a given moment than what he or she does next to follow up and increase the possibilities for change (Schlesinger, 1995, 2003; Stern et al., 1998).

As mentioned, these interventions are reinforced by offering cognitively based alternatives to rigid or personalized thinking. These alternatives must be appropriately graded and not offered prematurely so that the patient thinks of them as overwhelming or quick fixes that come from the outside rather than from the inside, thus promoting ownership and agency both for illness and recovery. Important reinforcements that do come from outside an interactive individual psychotherapy include educational and psycho-educational exercises, group and family therapy, and the habilitative and rehabilitative provision of skills for recognizing and coping with dysfunctional mental processes.

One non-psychotherapeutic technique that I have found useful in conducting psychotherapy are occasional "lecturettes." For example, it is often useful to

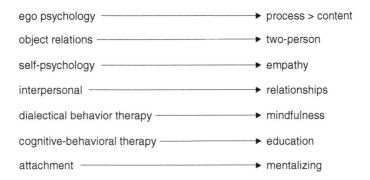

Figure 6.2 Origins of contemporary psychotherapeutic practice

explain to patients the difference between the private and personal aspects of a feeling and its public and political aspects. In the reactive state, these aspects are often conflated, and the expression of the affect is out of the patient's control. Indicating that our work aims to have them notice a feeling, let it reverberate, and examine its vicissitudes, makes it much easier to decide whether it could be publicly effective. Often, as is well known, feeling more does not always mean feeling better, and this also needs elucidation.

Elements of the common ground integrating mentalization-based treatment with traditional psychotherapy are shown graphically in Figure 6.2.

The ever widening scope of psychotherapeutic goals includes everything from making the unconscious conscious, delineating the internal self and object world, resolving intra-psychic conflict, providing a corrective emotional experience, mitigating disabling symptoms, modifying dysfunctional character patterns, enhancing self-esteem and enlarging the capacity to love and work. Mentalization-based therapy contributes to the achievement of all these goals, promoting mentalizing capacity by focusing on here-and-now mental states.

CONCLUSION

Utilizing an example of a complex therapeutic moment, I have attempted to demonstrate the elements of the concept of mentalizing as well as some therapeutic techniques that serve to enhance the capacity to mentalize. Implicit in the discussion of these techniques is the notion that mentalization-based treatment is a natural outgrowth of existing trends in psychotherapeutic technique, contributing to and consolidating a growing common ground of practice. It may be that focusing on efforts to help patients describe their mental contents rather than the interpretation of intra-psychic conflict is especially useful in enabling patients with restricted and inflexible thinking to become more reflective.

REFERENCES

Allen, J. (2003). Mentalizing. *Bulletin of The Menninger Clinic, 67,* 91–112.

Bateman, A. & Fonagy, P. (1999). The effectiveness of partial hospitalization in the treatment of borderline personality disorder – a randomized controlled trial. *American Journal of Psychiatry, 156,* 1563–1569.

Bateman, A. & Fonagy, P. (2001). Treatment of borderline personality disorder with psychoanalytically oriented partial hospitalization: an 18 month follow-up. *American Journal of Psychiatry, 158,* 36–42.

Bleiberg, E. (2001). *Treating Personality Disorders in Children and Adolescents: A Relational Approach.* New York: Guilford Press.

Fenton, W. (2001). Individual psychotherapies in schizophrenia. In G. O. Gabbard (ed.), *Treatments of Psychiatric Disorders* (3rd edn, Chapter 34, Vol. 1, pp. 1045–1064), Washington, DC: American Psychiatric Press.

Fonagy, P. & Target, M. (1997). Attachment and reflective function: their role in self-organization. *Development and Psychopathology, 9,* 679–700.

Fonagy, P., Gergely, G., Jurist, E. L. & Target, M. (2002). *Affect Regulation, Mentalization, and the Development of the Self.* New York: Other Press.

Gabbard, G. (2003). Countertransference: the emerging common ground. *International Journal of Psycho-Analysis, 76,* 475–485.

Gabbard, G. & Weston, D. (1995). Rethinking therapeutic action. *International Journal of Psycho-Analysis, 84,* 823–841.

Hogarty, G. E., Kornblith, S. J. & Greenwald, D. et al. (1995). Personal therapy: a disorder-relevant psychotherapy for schizophrenia. *Schizophrenia Bulletin, 21,* 379–393.

Horwitz, L., Gabbard, G. O., Allen, J. G., Frieswyk, S. H., Colson, D. B., Newsom, G. E., et al. (1996). *Borderline Personality Disorder: Tailoring the Therapy to the Patient.* Washington, DC: American Psychiatric Press.

Lane, R. & Garfield, D. A. S. (2005). Becoming aware of feelings: integration of cognitive-developmental, neuroscientific, and psychoanalytic perspectives. *Neuro-Psychoanalysis, 7,* 1–66.

Lear, J. (2003). *Therapeutic Action: An Earnest Plea for Irony.* New York: Other Press.

London, N. J. (1973). An essay of psychoanalytic theory: two theories of schizophrenia: I. Review and critical assessment of the two theories. *International Journal of Psycho-Analysis, 54,* 169–193.

Munich, R. (1987). Conceptual trends and issues in the psychotherapy of the schizophrenia. *American Journal of Psychotherapy, 61,* 23–37.

Munich, R. (1993). Conceptual issues in the psychoanalytic psychotherapy of patients with borderline personality disorder. In W. Sledge & A. Tasman (eds), *Clinical Challenges in Psychiatry* (Chapter 3, pp. 61–88), Washington, DC: American Psychiatric Press.

Munich, R. (2003). Efforts to preserve the mind in contemporary hospital treatment. *Bulletin of The Menninger Clinic, 67,* 167–187.

Munich, R. & Allen, J. G. (2003). Psychiatric and sociotherapeutic perspectives on the difficult-to-treat patient. *Psychiatry, 66,* 346–357.

Piaget, J. (1954). *The Construction of Reality in the Child.* New York: Basic Books.

Pine, F. (1984). The interpretive moment. *Bulletin of The Menninger Clinic, 48,* 54–71.

Pine, F. (1985). *Developmental Theory and Clinical Process.* New Haven: Yale University Press.

Schlesinger, H. (1995). The process of interpretation and the moment of change. *Journal of the American Psychoanalytic Association, 43,* 662–685.

Schlesinger, H. (2003). *Texture of Treatment: On the Matter of Psychoanalytic Technique.* Hillsdale: Analytic Press.

Stern, D., Sander, L., Nahum, J., Harrison, A., Lyons-Ruth, K., Morgan, A., et al. (1998). Non-interpretive mechanisms in psychoanalytic therapy: the "something more" than interpretation. *International Journal of Psycho-Analysis*, *79*, 903–921.

Yeomans, F. E., Selzer, M. A. & Clarkin, J. F. (1992). *Treating the Borderline Patient: A Contract-Based Approach*. New York: Basic Books.

7

COGNITIVE BEHAVIORAL THERAPY PROMOTES MENTALIZING

Thröstur Björgvinsson and John Hart

Bateman and Fonagy defined mentalizing as

> making sense of the actions of oneself and others on the basis of intentional mental
> states, such as desires, feelings, and beliefs. It involves the recognition that what
> is the mind is in the mind and reflects the knowledge of one's own and other's
> mental states as mental states. (2004, p. 36)

They proposed that a lack of capacity to mentalize underlies borderline
personality disorder and perhaps most psychopathology, and they developed
mentalization-based therapy to enhance mentalizing capacity. Nonetheless,
Bateman and Fonagy explicitly note that there may be many roads to facilitate
mentalizing capacity and that facilitating mentalizing may be a common
thread throughout effective psychotherapeutic interventions (see also Munich,
Chapter 6).

Consistent with Bateman and Fonagy's (2004) view, we build an explicit bridge
between cognitive behavioral therapy (CBT) and mentalizing, and we contend
that interventions employed in CBT are effective in promoting mentalizing. We
begin by noting how some concepts from cognitive therapy dovetail with mentalizing and then illustrate how cognitive therapy interventions enhance mentalizing
capacity.

Handbook of Mentalization-Based Treatment. Edited by J. G. Allen and P. Fonagy.
© 2006 John Wiley & Sons, Ltd.

COGNITIVE THEORY

Although many cognitive and behavior models for therapeutic changes have been developed, Dobson (2001) identified three fundamental propositions that all CBTs share: cognitive activity affects behavior; cognitive activity may be monitored and altered; and desired behavioral change may be effected through cognitive change. Many pertinent theories have been developed, including cognitive therapy (Beck, 1964, 1976), rational emotive behavior therapy (Ellis, 1962), and mindfulness-based cognitive therapy (Segal, Williams & Teasdale, 2004). In this chapter, when we refer to CBT, we are considering evidence-based therapies that share the three fundamental propositions Dobson (2001) identified.

We agree with Allen's (Chapter 1) emphasizing the verb, mentalizing, to reflect cognitive or mental activity. In a similar vein Hayes, Strosahl and Wilson (1999) wrote,

> When we speak of "minds" we are referring here to individuals' repertoire of public and private verbal activities (using our technical definition of verbal): evaluating, categorizing, planning, reasoning, comparing, referring, and so on. Although we will use the noun form, the mind is not a thing. The brain is a thing, replete with white and gray matter, midbrain structures, and so on, but the mind is a repertoire, not a place. "Minding" would be a more accurate, if cumbersome, description. (p. 49)

Thus mentalizing is construed as an activity, involving a set of skills, in which people engage in effective and adaptive functioning when relating to others as well as to themselves.

Mentalizing can be implicit or explicit as skills can be declarative or procedural. From a social-cognition standpoint, Fiske and Taylor (1991) described people as *cognitive misers*, that is, as being unable to process the infinite number of perceptions, interactions, and events that occur throughout the day. Owing to the cognitive limitations in fully processing every situation, we take shortcuts. Although these shortcuts are intended to be an effective use of cognitive resources, accuracy is often sacrificed. From this viewpoint, effective mentalizing is often done implicitly. Effective implicit mentalizing involves the automatic selection of behavioral responses and assumptions based on such mental processes as intuition, prototypes and exemplars, or heuristic biases; these can be quick, efficient, and even protective when we must respond immediately to threatening or dangerous stimuli. However, such responses can be – and often are – completely wrong, at which time more explicit processes are needed. Explicit mentalizing can override impulsive and risky urges that might get us into trouble, and mentalizing can prevent us from jumping to conclusions before we embark on an ill-advised behavioral course. Cognitive therapy is concerned with hitting the metaphorical pause button (Allen, 2005); patients are asked to stop and think. "What went through your mind before that happened?" is a common question cognitive therapists ask to make automatic thought processes more explicit. Cognitive therapy thus promotes mentalizing in making patients more aware of the nature and function of their negative thinking.

As the foregoing implies, we are not only cognitive misers but also *motivated tacticians* (Fiske, 2004; Fiske & Taylor, 1991). Depending on our motivation, we can switch from implicit, resource-saving cognitive miserliness to more thoughtful and thorough strategies for forming impressions and undertaking actions. To be effective, we think only as hard as we must according to our evaluation of the situational context. For example, we tend to be more motivated to size up thoroughly our new internist than the person who comes to install our cable television. Yet a person who had a previous traumatic experience with an assailant posing as service person coming to their home would be motivated to make a more thorough assessment. Effective mentalizers are able to adapt, being sensitive and flexible in utilizing cognitive resources to navigate their interpersonal environment.

This selective marshaling of cognitive resources implies that explicit thought is necessary to employ effective strategies. Yet Ferguson and Bargh (2004) review recent research that indicates that automatic attitudes also can be sensitive to context and flexible to novel situations. They suggest that automatic attitudes are functional in that they provide us with evaluative information about an object within the current situation that is sensitive to the meaning of the object and its relevance to our goals. Moreover, they assert that we seem to have the ability to automatically appraise and evaluate novel objects by integrating, outside of our awareness, evaluative information from multiple sources to deliver an evaluation about the whole object. Nonetheless, automatic attitudes about other persons, which involve implicit mentalizing skills, do not do all the work; the importance of developing explicit attitudes also has been demonstrated.

How do people become effective implicit mentalizers? Much of our behavior has been shaped by contingency-based learning, such as the successive approximations of trial-and-error and practice that are employed in acquiring the target skill of riding a bicycle. Other kinds of responding are more rule-driven, which allows us to respond to stimuli in precise and effective ways when the slower contingency-based learning would be maladaptive or even dangerous. We do not use contingency-based learning to avoid certain types of danger, because it would be too slow and ineffective. We typically employ rule-governed behavior when behavioral consequences are subtle, future-oriented, cumulative, or probabilistic. Rules are often remote from contingency learning inasmuch as they are hypothetical and probabilistic (Hayes et al., 1999). Rule-governed behaviors allow us to be effective cognitive misers, saving effortful thinking for the various important matters that may arise throughout the day. According to Skinner (1974), rule-following behavior is the veneer of society, whereas contingency-shaped behavior "comes from the depths of the personality or mind" (p. 140). Artists, composers, and poets may follow rules by imitating the work of others, but they exercise their creative expression by acting in idiosyncratic ways and are reinforced by their natural excitement or joy. As Picasso reportedly once quipped, "Good taste is the enemy of creativity."

Yet Hayes and associates (1999) pointed out that rule-governed behavior is not without disadvantages. A number of studies demonstrate that excessive use of rule-governed behavior can lead to insensitivity to the environment. Rule-governed behavior is less sensitive to changes in the environment than behavior guided by immediate experience. Rule-governed behavior often leads to rigidity and diminishes flexible thinking and behavioral responses. Flexibility requires mindfulness, a concept that overlaps with mentalizing (see Allen, Chapter 1). Langer (1989) developed her concept of mindlessness through a series of studies of the pitfalls that automatic responding and inflexible thinking entail. In a now famous study, Langer and her associates instructed a research subject to make copies on a photocopier. An experimental confederate was instructed to interrupt with one of three requests: "Excuse me, may I use the Xerox machine?" "Excuse me, may I use the Xerox machine because I have to make copies?" Or, "Excuse me, may I use the copy machine because I am in a rush?" Subjects let the confederate interrupt when any reason was given, despite the nonsensical nature of the request to make copies since that is the only plausible reason to use a copy machine. Why one would be mindless in such a situation has been the source of much investigation and conjecture. Mindlessness and being miserly often have unfortunate consequences. Mindlessness can take us out of the moment and cause us to miss important experiences that are out of the routine. A more mindful approach is more open, aware, and flexible, such that it can lead us in a new and creative direction.

Langer's concept of mindfulness is similar to our understanding of explicit mentalizing. According to Langer and Moldoveanu (2000), mindfulness consists of several interrelating elements: openness to novelty; alertness to distinction; sensitivity to different contexts; implicit, if not explicit, awareness of multiple perspectives; and orientation to the present. To the extent that the object of attention is personal or interpersonal, all these facets of mindfulness are consistent with mentalizing. In Langer's construct, mindfulness is a psychological state that uses basic skills and information to guide our behavior in the present rather than automatically, like a computer program. As philosophers Prinz & Clark (2004) wrote, "A mind whose ideas are mixed like bricks rather than chemicals would be an inhuman mind, and it would be a mind unfit for this world" (p. 61).

One key facet of mentalizing and mindfulness is self-awareness, which encompasses our capacity to become the object of our own attention and depends on actively identifying, processing, and storing information about the self (Morin, 2005). According to Trapnell and Campbell (1999), thinking about the self can take two forms: self-rumination and self-reflection. Self-rumination has been linked to negative mood, whereas self-reflection is associated with more positive moods. The difference can be depicted in the statements "Oh no, *why* did I do that?" as opposed to "Huh, I wonder why I did *that*?" Self-reflection implies motivation stimulated by interest and curiosity in thinking about oneself in contrast to the guilt, anger, and disappointment that is characteristic of self-rumination. Grant (2001) extended this motivational theme to another closely related concept, psychological mindedness (PM), "a form of metacognition: a predisposition to engage acts of affective and intellectual inquiry into how and why oneself and/or others behave, think, and feel in the way that they do" (p. 12). We contend that mentalizing represents the skills necessary to foster and utilize PM as Grant construed it. Furthermore, Grant argued that "The proposed model of PM is of relevance to clinical practice because the self-monitoring and self-evaluation of one's cognitions, emotions, and behaviors is central to the successful practice of CBT" (p. 14). Hence CBT requires and enhances mentalizing capacity and PM.

Allen (2003) proposed that "We are not behaviorists; we learn intuitively to postulate hidden mental causes to make sense of behavior, and behavior makes no sense otherwise" (p. 98). We disagree. We are cognitive-behaviorists. What is the benefit of knowing the mental states of others if not to anticipate the behavior of others? We assume the benefit of the feeling of being loved by one's significant other is the security of the predictability that he or she continue to behave lovingly toward us in the future. Despite the acknowledged improbability of a spouse acting lovingly toward their mate without having loving mental states, nonetheless what would be the difference? Mentalizing about our significant others may be the glue that holds loving experiences together.

COGNITIVE THERAPY

The distinction between effective and ineffective mentalizing is fuzzy; does the behavior or the consequence define the concept? Allen (Chapter 1) points out that mentalizing is a value-laden concept, entangled with ethics and virtue. This further complicates the picture: how badly or ineffectively does one have to think about another person in order to be an ineffective mentalizer or to not mentalize at all? How distorted or maladaptive can the person's thoughts be before he or she becomes an ineffective mentalizer? A successful con man or swindler may be skilled in considering the thoughts, feelings, and desires of others with the intention to deceive. Is the swindler mentalizing? Not entirely, according to Allen's view. Recognizing that mentalizing is a skill with many gradations, we follow his lead that mentalizing entails adaptive and flexible mental activity compatible with moral and ethical considerations, and we will use the word in this sense.

We have argued that mentalizing indicates that the person has acquired sets of skills. He or she is able to apply flexible thinking across various situations, is socially adept, is able to be empathic, and is capable of dealing effectively with interpersonal challenges. How does one foster mentalizing in persons who are deficient in applying these skills? How do we address maladaptive or distorted thinking about other persons, negative automatic thoughts that arise in interpersonal situations, or the tendency to jump to conclusions? Challenging maladaptive thinking patterns is the centerpiece of cognitive therapy (Clark & Beck, 1999). Beck and Weishaar (1989) define this centerpiece as a "collaborative process of empirical investigation, reality testing, and problem solving between therapist and patient. The patient's maladaptive interpretations and conclusions are treated as testable hypotheses" (p. 285). Cognitive therapy is an ongoing, fluid process in which collaboratively planned interventions are intended to become part of the patient's way of experiencing the world and himself or herself. Challenging the maladaptive negative thoughts extends beyond examining the *content* of a belief or the truth and falsity of any particular thought to how the *process* of thinking functions within a person's life and the world that he or she lives in.

Cognitive therapy focuses on supporting the patient to challenge maladaptive thinking through collaborative empiricism and on helping patients evaluate the evidence for their interpretations or meaning-making conclusions. We challenge patients' assumptions or negative thoughts by asking them to consider questions such as: "What is the evidence that he or she did not like you?" "How do you know that the person was angry with you?" "If the person were angry with you, then how would you cope with the situation?" This process is not intended to arrive at any particular correct answer inasmuch as there are many possibilities; rather, the process provides practice in flexible and creative thinking about alternative thoughts and strategies in response to a disturbing situation. In the process, patients develop a keener sense of how their mind works and how the ways their mind works influence their thoughts, feelings, and behavior.

Conceptualizing a patient within cognitive theory takes into consideration aspects of the patient's past that have contributed to the formation of the most central or deep-seated maladaptive core self-beliefs or schemas (Beck, 1976; Beck et al., 1979). Beck postulated that, when these maladaptive core beliefs or schemas are activated by negative life events, these beliefs fuel symptoms of depression. These symptoms are maintained by automatic negative thoughts and maladaptive behaviors (e.g., procrastination and avoidance). According to Beck (1964, 1976), these core beliefs or schemas tend to fall into two broad categories: helplessness and un-lovability (see J. S. Beck, 1995 for detailed discussion). Specifically, Beck postulated that these maladaptive schemas or beliefs can be organized around four views: self, others, the world, and the future. Persons, Davidson and Tompkins (2000) argued that the most prominent maladaptive beliefs or schemas pertain to self and others – the territory of mentalizing. Depressed patients, for example, are likely to have distorted and negative core beliefs or schemas, such as "I am inadequate," "I am inept," or "I am a failure." These patients often experience automatic negative thoughts about various situations triggered by serious life events, such as "I cannot handle this!" or "Why bother? This isn't going to work." These automatic negative thoughts that stem from distorted schemas in turn fuel depressive mood, hopelessness, and procrastination.

Cognitive therapy emphasizes the *automatic* aspect of maladaptive thoughts that often arise without the awareness of the patient, without any effort or intention. Several techniques, which are beyond the scope of this paper, have been developed to address automatic negative thoughts (see J. S. Beck, 1995; Persons et al., 2000). It is important to note, as Gluhoski (1994) admonished, that cognitive therapy is not merely a collection of techniques. Rather, the patient and therapist develop a collaboration intended to promote an inquisitive, exploratory attitude toward thinking – in effect, a mentalizing attitude. Two main therapeutic tools are frequently used to challenge automatic thoughts (a process called *cognitive restructuring*): the Socratic method and the thought record. The Socratic method entails guided questioning to help patients become more aware of their maladaptive interpretations of events. The thought record, which mirrors Beck's cognitive theory, entails documenting the situation that triggered the automatic negative thoughts in conjunction with emotions and behaviors. Most importantly, the thought record promotes alternative ways of thinking about events, reinforcing the experience of multiple mental perspectives. Several different versions of the thought records exist, and it is unclear what particular method is most effective (Beck, 1995; Persons et al., 2000). Clearly, however, employing thought records in some form is effective in alleviating depressive symptoms (DeRubeis & Crits-Christoph, 1998).

To illustrate how cognitive therapy potentially facilitates mentalizing, we present a case illustration of a patient who became very defensive when he met with his inpatient treatment team at The Menninger Clinic. The treatment team had told this middle-aged lawyer that he used humor and intellectualization to avoid emotional experience. The patient had said that he genuinely wanted help, to be understood, and to collaborate with the treatment team members to reach these goals. In cognitive therapy terms, we established that he had an intense, pervasive fear and avoidance of humiliation and embarrassment; therefore, he had a strong urge to be right. This is illustrated in the example below, where the patient became angry when there was a diversion from his expectation; a trivial issue became major power struggle. The core belief or schema that was activated in the following illustration was his basic sense of inadequacy and vulnerability. This core belief was reflected in his conditional assumptions, "If I am wrong, then I will get criticized" and "If people disagree with me then they are out to get me." Conditional assumptions are typically expressed in contingent "if–then" statements. Maladaptive if–then statements are associated with imperatives or rigid rules of thought and behavior not only for the patient but also for those in the patient's interpersonal world. For example, this patient had the imperative that no one *should ever* get the best of him and that he *must never* be wrong.

The following illustrates a therapeutic interaction between the patient and his cognitive therapist following a meeting with the treatment team.

PATIENT:	"When I meet with my team I get very defensive, and yesterday I got very angry. In our individual meeting, my doctor said that I needed to stay in the hospital one week longer, but later in the clinical rounds she said that I only needed to stay a couple of days."
COGNITIVE THERAPIST:	"And that made you angry?"
PATIENT:	"Yes, so I called her on it."
COGNITIVE THERAPIST:	"What reason would she have to say that?"
PATIENT:	"She was just trying to save face in the team."
COGNITIVE THERAPIST:	"So it came down to her own thoughts and feelings about herself being more important than your treatment. Is that how you understood it?"
PATIENT:	"Well she was wrong. What she said was one week and I wanted to make sure the rest of the treatment team knew it."
COGNITIVE THERAPIST:	"So what I understand you to be saying is that you wanted to make sure that the treatment team knew that you were right?"
PATIENT:	"Yeah, this is like we discussed before. If I am wrong I feel embarrassed or humiliated."
COGNITIVE THERAPIST:	"And what does it mean to be embarrassed?"
PATIENT:	"I don't know. I may have forgotten. If it's a work deal, then I can get angry and go on the attack. If I'm with friends, then I just make a big joke out of it."
COGNITIVE THERAPIST:	"Do you think it was the doctor's intention to embarrass or humiliate you?"
PATIENT:	"I guess it felt like it, but my experience of her is that she is not the kind of person to do that."
COGNITIVE THERAPIST:	"So, your initial thoughts and feelings about what was going on actually turned out to be contrary to how you experience your doctor?"
PATIENT:	"Yeah."
COGNITIVE THERAPIST:	"So I wonder why you reacted so strongly on your first interpretation of this situation, rather than basing it on your previous experience with your doctor?"

PATIENT:	"I guess that's what I'm here for. It wouldn't be too hard to figure out that this has something to do with my dad, who always thought I was wrong and didn't hold back from telling me."
COGNITIVE THERAPIST:	"Did this seem similar to experience you might have had with your father?"
PATIENT:	"My doctor is obviously not my father."
COGNITIVE THERAPIST:	"Do you think your approach to this was effective?"
PATIENT:	"Oh no, it was completely ineffective – I got nowhere."

This illustration demonstrates the patient's misreading the mind of his doctor, a failure of mentalizing. He attributed motivations and intentions to his doctor that were contrary to his previous experience of her. The patient's core belief is that he is inept or inadequate. When this basic belief is activated, he feels embarrassed and inadequate. This patient feels vulnerable when he is wrong or makes mistakes. Therefore, he operates under the conditional assumption that, if he is wrong, he will be criticized. Feeling criticized, he becomes overwhelmed with embarrassment and humiliation. The therapy did not focus primarily on the content of his thoughts that led to the threat of embarrassment or humiliation (e.g., viewing his doctor as if she were his father); rather, the interventions emphasized the patient's relationship to these feelings, that is, what these emotions mean to him, how he interprets them, what behaviors they trigger, and what other interpretations he might consider. In addition, the therapist focused on the function of his thoughts and feelings and how they thwarted him in reaching his stated goals ("I got nowhere"). His goals shifted from being understood and maintaining a collaborative, helping relationship with his doctor and treatment team to avoiding embarrassment and humiliation. The therapist then challenged the patient to explore if he was willing to commit to his stated goal of being understood and working together and at the same time allowing himself to experience the feelings of embarrassment and humiliation.

Another theme was at work with this patient: he was willing to sacrifice accuracy for coherence. Despite the fact that he was arguing over whether he was right or not, he was willing to overlook the accuracy of his actual experience of his doctor for the sake of maintaining the coherence of his basic belief system. That is, he maintained that people would take advantage of him, particularly when he perceived that he was being questioned, challenged, or otherwise not taken seriously. Research by Swann and his associates (Swann, Rentfrow & Guin, 2002) has demonstrated that we are motivated by self-verification. That is, to satisfy needs for prediction and control, we seek to evaluate ourselves in ways that will verify our existing self-concept. We will distort information not to make ourselves feel more positive but rather to gain a better sense of consistency and coherence as to what we already believe about ourselves. This is all well and good if the self-views are positive but, according to Swann, people will gain a better sense of security and predictability even if they confirm negative beliefs about themselves if they hold a generally negative self-concept. The patient we described seemed to be motivated to confirm his self-concept that he was a vulnerable person, not be taken seriously, easily humiliated, and basically ineffective in getting his needs met. His petty and argumentative attitude was directed toward verifying negative core beliefs about himself.

Although people are motivated to seek self-verification, this motivation can be overridden when they feel it is in their best interest. A fundamental task of cognitive therapy is to help people become more effective motivated tacticians. To experience himself in a new light, the patient must be willing to feel the tension and negative feelings that dissonance with his self-concept creates. We encouraged the patient to reappraise his feelings as part and parcel of a desired process of change rather than automatically deflecting disconfirming evidence of negative self-beliefs. Cognitive therapy helped this patient to develop the adaptive notion that people can have flexible thinking or be able to take others' perspectives. Hence we were encouraging him to have others' minds in mind, that is, to mentalize.

Segal, Williams and Teasdale (2002, 2004) have developed a cognitive therapy for depression enhanced by mindfulness training, an approach that overlaps considerably with mentalizing (Allen, 2006). In this therapy, patients are trained to purposefully pay attention to the present moment in specific, non-judgmental ways. Mindfulness training involves learning de-centering skills in which patients come to realize that thoughts are just thoughts and not fully representative of one's reality. One of the tenets of mindfulness-based cognitive therapy holds that negative thoughts underlying a dysphoric mood involve critical processing modes that are automatic in nature. These critical processing modes have become automatic through well-practiced, habituated, cognitive routines; but they are nonetheless extremely dependent on highly controlled central processing attentional resources. Mindfulness training endeavors to shift to a cognitive-processing mode that is fully in the present and attentive to moment-to-moment experience regardless of the emotional valence. According to Segal and his colleagues, this mindfulness mode encourages the free and open experience of thoughts, feelings, and bodily functions; hence it reduces the experiential avoidance that constitutes various forms of psychopathology.

Keeping in mind Bateman and Fonagy's (2004) definition of mentalizing as "making sense of the actions of oneself and others on the basis of intentional mental states, such as desires, feelings, and beliefs" (p. 36), we propose that experiential avoidance is commensurate with ineffective mentalizing – particularly with what Fonagy and colleagues (2002) call mentalized affectivity, namely, feeling and thinking about feeling simultaneously. Pivotal in experiential avoidance is the intolerance of emotion. In Leahy's (2003) cognitive behavioral model, our responses to feeling states are organized around emotional schemas. By definition, schemas organize abstract forms of behavior, desires, attitudes, and attributions in contrast to the more prolonged process of recalling a multitude of specifics that guide even the most basic social interaction (Moscowitz, 2004). Leahy (2003) advanced a model in which emotional experience reflects universal concepts and processes while allowing for individual differences in particular beliefs and response strategies. The nature of these beliefs and strategies will determine how problematic emotional experiences will become.

Habitually, the socially phobic person ineffectively mentalizes the emotional schemas of others. For example, persons with social phobia often hold the belief that being anxious means being weak or incompetent; consequently, they may misread the minds of others by assuming that others hold this same set of beliefs. Under the scrutiny of others, an emotional schema can be activated that guides an ineffective response associated with various safety behaviors. A socially phobic person may wish to be approached by others in a social situation but may expend a great deal of energy in looking calm, cool, and collected – an effort that comes off looking aloof and angry. Such a person will look unapproachable, reinforcing negative beliefs about self and others. The initial detection of anxious feelings will signal vulnerability to negative evaluation.

Consider the case of a college instructor who had socially anxious reactions during his classes. He believed that, if his students knew he was anxious, then they would conclude that he was ineffective as teacher, because teachers that are anxious do not know what they are talking about. Despite this man's best effort to hide his emotional state, he was unable to do so. One of his particularly troubling and uncontrollable physiological symptoms was profuse sweating – prominently on his forehead – that was hard to hide even if, as a safety behavior, he wore short-sleeve shirts in the middle of the winter. To promote effective mentalizing, he was encouraged to reflect on alternative perspectives from his vantage point as well as that of his students. Because of his intolerance of uncertainty, no amount of challenging maladaptive assumptions would produce the certainty to which he aspired. In fact he became quite good at recognizing and challenging his maladaptive assumptions by becoming a better mind reader. Nonetheless he retained residual anxiety whenever he entered a classroom. Practicing mindfulness skills helped him observe and accept his experience of anxiety. To address directly his emotional avoidance, exposure techniques were employed. These techniques activated his emotional schemas, facilitating both acceptance and change. Thus, in a variety of ways, the treatment improved his mentalizing capacity.

Thus we are working with what Leahy (2003) called *individuals' theory of emotions*, that is, the theories built on the basis of emotional experience. Individuals build theories about a variety of mental activities, including intrusive thoughts, recurring traumatic imagery, the nature of worry, or the meaning of panic symptoms. For example, the cognitive activity of worry serves to reduce the physiological response of anxious arousal, including such physiological responses as heart and respiration rates as well as galvanic skin temperature (Borkovec, Alcaine & Behar, 2004). Worry is linguistic in nature and is typically experienced as self-talk. The relative left-hemisphere activation involved in anxious self-talk might help to dampen right-hemisphere processing of more intensely emotional experience associated with imagery and visceral responses. Worry is reinforced by patient's excessive focus on catastrophic fears that rarely come true, thus reinforcing the perceived protective nature of worry. In addition, worry is a mental activity that interferes with active problem solving; chronic worriers would rather fret than engage in effective activities. CBT encourages people to engage in real and effective problem solving despite increased anxiety. Hence, excessive worriers are not being effective in keeping their mind in mind. And excessive worries about avoided situations prevent them from experiencing disconfirming evidence that is invaluable in modifying their rigidly held schemas.

Emotions provide us with information concerning the state of affairs of others, our environment, and ourselves. Emotional awareness – mentalized affectivity – promotes change, and avoidance of emotion blocks change. Inadequate or maladaptive emotional processing inhibits our ability to communicate effectively about what is on our minds. Constricted emotions and impaired emotion regulation makes emotional experience a poor source of information and not useful in navigating patients' internal and external worlds. Emotional avoidance often takes the form of maladaptive covert and overt strategies to avoid unwanted and intolerable emotional experience as seen in the form of unnecessarily risky behaviors, obsessive-compulsive rituals, substance abuse, and so forth (Holland, 2003).

Mentalization-based treatments build on creating *agency* within the patient and a framework for understanding their mind as they keep other persons' minds in mind (see Allen, Chapter 1 and Munich, Chapter 6). One of the main strengths of cognitive behavior therapy is the easily understood framework it provides for therapy. In our experience, patients are very receptive to this framework; it makes intuitive sense and provides a platform to tackle maladaptive thinking patterns. The collaborative work that takes place is aimed at helping the patient be his or her own cognitive behavioral therapist (Heimberg & Becker, 2002).

CONCLUSION

Plainly, the ability to understand the minds of others as well to have some clarity about what is happening in one's own mind promotes adaptive functioning. In this chapter, we have conceptualized mentalizing as a psychological process that uses sets of cognitive skills that promote personal wellbeing and adaptive interpersonal functioning. In addition, we have illustrated how one might construe the therapeutic action of CBT as promoting mentalizing; in effect, cognitive therapy provides highly structured ways of practicing mentalizing.

"Mentalizing" has become a part of the vernacular of The Menninger Clinic. Even without full appreciation of the concept's roots in psychoanalysis, attachment theory, and developmental psychopathology (Fonagy et al., 2002), patients and staff members seem to use "mentalizing" in a meaningful pragmatic way to describe a more flexible and reflective style of thinking. Hence, as we construe it, CBT interfaces well with the institution's emphasis on mentalizing as well as providing systematic and well-researched strategies that effectively promote mentalizing.

REFERENCES

Allen, J. G. (2003). Mentalizing. *Bulletin of The Menninger Clinic, 67*, 91–112.

Allen, J. G. (2005). *Coping with Trauma: Hope through Understanding* (2nd edn). Washington, DC: American Psychiatric Publishing.

Allen, J. G. (2006). *Coping with Depression: From Catch-22 to Hope.* Washington, DC: American Psychiatric Publishing.

Bateman, A. W. & Fonagy, P. (2004). Mentalization-based treatment of BPD. *Journal of Personality Disorders, 18*, 36–51.

Beck, A. T. (1964). Thinking and depression: II. Theory and therapy. *Archives of General Psychiatry, 10*, 561–571.

Beck, A. T. (1976). *Cognitive Therapy and the Emotional Disorders.* New York: International Universities Press.

Beck, A. T. & Weishaar, M. E. (1989). Cognitive therapy. In R. J. Corsini & D. Wedding (eds), *Current psychotherapies* (4th edn, pp. 285–320). Itasca, IL: Peacock.

Beck, A. T., Rush, J., Shaw, B. & Emery, G. (1979). *Cognitive Therapy of Depression.* New York: Guilford.

Beck, J. S. (1995). *Cognitive Therapy: Basics and Beyond.* New York: Guilford.

Borkovec, T. D., Alcaine, O. M. & Behar, E. (2004). Avoidance theory of worry and generalized anxiety disorder. In R. G. Heimberg, C. L. Turk & D. S. Mennin (eds), *Generalized Anxiety Disorder: Advances in Research and Practice* (pp. 77–109). New York: Guilford.

Clark, D. A. & Beck, A. T. (1999). *Scientific Foundations of Cognitive Theory and Therapy of Depression.* New York: John Wiley & Sons, Inc.

DeRubeis, R. J. & Crits-Christoph, P. (1998). Empirically supported individual and group psychological treatments for adult mental disorders. *Journal of Consulting and Clinical Psychology, 66*, 37–52.

Dobson, K. S. (2001). *Handbook of Cognitive-Behavioral Therapies* (2nd edn) New York: Guilford.

Ellis, A. (1962). *Reason and Emotion in Psychotherapy.* New York: Stuart.

Ferguson, M. J. & Bargh, J. A. (2004). Sensitivity and flexibility: exploring the knowledge function of automatic attitudes. In L. F. Barrett & P. Salovey (eds), *The Wisdom of Feeling: Psychological Processes in Emotional Intelligence* (pp. 383–405). New York: Guilford.

Fiske, S. T. (2004). *Social Beings: A Core Motives Approach to Social Psychology.* New York: John Wiley & Sons, Inc.

Fiske, S. T. & Taylor, S. E. (1991). *Social Cognition*. New York: McGraw-Hill.

Fonagy, P., Gergely, G., Jurist, E. & Target, M. (2002). *Affect Regulation, Mentalization, and the Development of the Self*. New York: Other Press.

Gluhoski, V. L. (1994). Misconceptions of cognitive therapy. *Psychotherapy*, *31*, 594–600.

Grant, A. M. (2001). Rethinking psychological mindedness: metacognition, self-reflection and insight. *Behavior Change*, *18*, 8–17.

Hayes, S. C., Strosahl, K. D. & Wilson, K. G. (1999). *Acceptance and Commitment Therapy: An Experiential Approach to Behavior Change*. New York: Guilford.

Heimberg, R. G. & Becker, R. E. (2002). *Cognitive-Behavioral Group Therapy for Social Phobia: Basic Mechanisms and Clinical Strategies*. New York: Guilford.

Holland, S. J. (2003). Avoidance of emotion as an obstacle to progress. In R. L. Leahy (ed.), *Roadblocks in Cognitive-Behavioral Therapy: Transforming Challenges into Opportunities for Change* (pp. 116–134). New York: Guilford.

Langer, E. J. (1989). Mindfulness. Reading, MA: Addison-Wesley.

Langer, E. J. & Moldoveanu, M. (2000). The construct of mindfulness. *Journal of Social Issues*, *56*, 1–11.

Leahy, R. L. (2003). Emotional schemas and resistance. In R. L. Leahy (ed.), *Roadblocks in Cognitive-Behavioral Therapy: Transforming Challenges into Opportunities for Change* (pp. 91–115). New York: Guilford.

Morin, A. (2005). Possible links between self-awareness and inner speech: theoretical background, underlying mechanisms, and empirical evidence. *Journal of Consciousness Studies*, *12*, 115–134.

Moscowitz, G. B. (2004). *Social Cognition: Understanding Self and Others*. New York: Guilford.

Persons, J. B., Davidson, J. & Tompkins, M. A. (2000). *Essential Components of Cognitive-Behavior Therapy for Depression*. Washington, DC: American Psychological Association.

Prinz, J. & Clark, A. (2004). Putting concepts to work: some thoughts for the twenty-first century. *Mind and Language*, *19*, 57–69.

Segal, Z. V., Williams, J. M. G. & Teasdale, J. D. (2002). *Mindfulness-Based Cognitive Therapy for Depression: A New Approach to Preventing Relapse*. New York: Guilford.

Segal, Z. V., Williams, J. M. G. & Teasdale, J. D. (2004). Mindfulness-based cognitive therapy: theoretical rationale and empirical status. In S. C. Hayes, V. M. Follette & M. M. Linehan (eds), *Mindfulness and Acceptance: Expanding the Cognitive-Behavioral Tradition* (pp. 45–65). New York: Guilford.

Skinner, B. F. (1974). *About Behaviorism*. New York: Vintage.

Swann, W. B., Rentfrow, P. J. & Guin, J. S. (2002). Self-verification: the search for coherence. In M. Leary & J. Tagney (eds), *Handbook of Self and Identity* (pp. 367–383). New York: Guilford.

Trapnell, P. D. & Campbell, J. D. (1999). Private self-consciousness and the five-factor model of personality: distinguishing rumination from reflection. *Journal of Personality and Social Psychology*, *76*, 284–304.

8

ENHANCING MENTALIZING CAPACITY THROUGH DIALECTICAL BEHAVIOR THERAPY SKILLS TRAINING AND POSITIVE PSYCHOLOGY

Lisa Lewis

Mentalizing (Fonagy, 1991; Fonagy, Gergely, Jurist & Target, 2002) is emerging as a concept that unites a broad range of psychotherapeutic interventions and thus functions as a bridging concept, much like therapeutic alliance does (Bateman & Fonagy, 2004). Mentalizing refers to awareness of mental states and processes in oneself and other persons, in short, holding mind in mind. Promoting mentalizing is posited to be a core facet of effective psychotherapeutic interventions for a wide range of psychological disorders.

Although dialectical behavior therapy (DBT; Linehan, 1993a) and mentalization-based therapy (MBT; Bateman & Fonagy, 2004) are alternative evidence-based approaches to treating borderline personality disorder (BPD), this chapter explains how we construe the psycho-educational intervention of DBT skills training as promoting mentalizing in the service of emotion regulation. In addition, the chapter presents our evolving efforts to augment DBT skills training with advances in positive psychology (Seligman, 2003). By incorporating positive psychology into psycho-education, we are highlighting the significance of mentalizing positive emotions as well as negative emotions in the process of emotion regulation.

Handbook of Mentalization-Based Treatment. Edited by J. G. Allen and P. Fonagy.
© 2006 John Wiley & Sons, Ltd.

MENTALIZING AND EMOTION REGULATION

Fonagy and colleagues (2002) conceptualize emotion regulation in terms of *mentalized affectivity*. Emotion regulation entails revaluing and not simply modulating emotions; as we explain it to patients, we identify and make sense of the emotions we are feeling, modulate them, and then express our emotions. Implicit in this definition is the desirability of bringing cognitive processes to bear on the experience of raw, bodily emotion. We employ the metaphor of "hitting the pause button" to allow reflective thought to intervene between the event that precipitates an emotional reaction and the behavior prompted by that emotion (Allen, 2005).

Mentalized affectivity entails an optimum balance of emotion and cognition, for example, feeling and thinking about feeling at the same time. When emotion is too intense, mentalizing collapses and gives way to emotionally driven, stereotypic behavior. When emotion is too suppressed, mentalizing is uninformed and sterile. We integrate this perspective with DBT skills training by linking mentalizing to Linehan's (1993b) concept of *wise mind*, that is, the optimal integration of reason and emotion.

In addition to integrating cognition and emotion, the clinical applications described here are intended to help patients find an optimum balance of negative emotion and positive emotion. As we explain it to patients, these two classes of emotion have different forms of adaptive value (Fredrickson, 2003; Seligman, 2002). Generally, negative emotions prompt behavior related to survival of the individual; when events threaten our lives and cause us to be anxious, we flee; when events hurt and anger us, we attack. Positive emotions such as joy, interest, compassion, and pleasure also promote survival of the species; they are intimately involved in promoting attachment relationships that are instrumental in successful communal and procreative behaviors.

Finally, the clinical applications described in this chapter are intended to alter patients' fundamental stance in relation to emotional experience (Allen, 2005). Rather than viewing negative emotions as something to be rid of as quickly as possible and positive emotions as something to be pursued at nearly any cost, we encourage patients to reflect on the meanings of emotions in the context of current and past experiences of the world and of close relationships, in particular. In other words, patients are encouraged to consider that meaning can be found and created through the process of reflecting on emotion while in the midst of emotional experience.

To recapitulate, with the concept of mentalized affectivity in mind, we employ psycho-educational interventions to augment a wide range of treatment modalities that facilitate emotion regulation. Understandably, many dysphoric patients equate emotion regulation with squelching negative emotions. We encourage them to think differently about emotion. We explain the balance of cognition and emotion in optimal functioning; the value of reducing vulnerability to the experience of disproportionately intense negative motions while increasing the capacity for the experience and tolerance of a range of positive emotions; and, most importantly, developing the capacity to find meaning in emotion so as to bear the entire range of emotions elicited by living life fully as gracefully – and gratefully – as one can.

INCORPORATING POSITIVE PSYCHOLOGY INTO DBT SKILLS TRAINING

The field of positive psychology has generated a burgeoning body of research findings that can be incorporated into the way DBT skills are taught, with the goal of cultivating the patients' capacity for mentalized affectivity. DBT skills training employs a psycho-educational model that is conducive to inclusion of explicit education about research findings.

Incorporating research findings from positive psychology enhances patients' motivation to cultivate the capacity for mentalizing emotionally in two respects. First, sharing the research findings intrigues patients about the meaning of emotion, promoting a fundamental shift in how they think about their own emotional experience. They begin viewing emotion no longer as something that simply happens to them or descends upon them – or exists as mere epiphenomena of neurons firing. They learn to view emotions as harbingers of meaning. In this context, we also make use of the ego psychological perspective: ideally, emotions carry a signal function that engages the ego in the processes of reality testing and reflection (Rapaport, 1953). Second, incorporating these research findings into DBT skills training provides the participants with tangible evidence of the potential benefits of practicing skills. And, as with any skill, the key to successful DBT skills mastery is practice and more practice. Educating patients about research findings can increase their motivation to make effective everyday use of DBT skills to balance emotion and reason and to balance positive and negative emotional experience, thereby cultivating mentalizing capacity.

This chapter summarizes the convergence of DBT skills training and positive psychology with mentalizing, then illustrates our efforts to promote mentalized affectivity with three domains of DBT skills: modulating negative emotion, increasing positive emotion, and enhancing interpersonal effectiveness.

DBT Skills Training

Linehan (1993a) developed DBT to treat BPD, a disorder in which emotion-regulation problems are paramount. DBT has been demonstrated to be an effective treatment for BPD, even when comorbid with other conditions such as eating disorders or substance abuse (Linehan et al., 1999, 2002; Telch, Agras & Linehan, 2001). Linehan views the emotion-regulation problem in BPD as involving disproportionately intense emotional responses to situations along with extreme difficulty calming and returning to baseline. She proposes that this core problem of emotion dysregulation develops from a combination of neurobiological vulnerability and exposure to an invalidating environment. Linehan's emphasis on emotional invalidation dovetails with the mentalizing perspective (Fonagy et al., 2002; see also Fonagy, Chapter 3): invalidation entails a failure to hold the child's mind in mind in the context of emotional arousal, typically in relation to heightened attachment needs.

Consistent with the patient's core problem of emotion dysregulation, Linehan describes three dialectics in BPD (Linehan & Manning, 1999). In these dialectics, conflict or paradox is produced by the tension of two opposing propositions, the thesis and the antithesis. The dialectical method is an effort to resolve these conflicts through rational discussion that recognizes the truth in opposites.

The first dialectic in the patient is the tension between the polarities of apparent competence versus active passivity. The position of apparent competence is attained at the cost of suppression of all or nearly all emotion and, as such, it cannot be sustained and eventually gives way to its polar opposite: active passivity. In this latter state, persons with BPD are awash in emotion to the point that they feel virtually incapable of doing anything on their own behalf. Suggesting what they might do to help themselves meets with the lament, "I can't!" This is not an act or a pose; it is rooted in neurobiologically demonstrable deficits (see Gabbard and colleagues, Chapter 5). The person is experiencing such a strong upsurge of painful emotion that no constructive personal action seems possible in the moment. Mentalizing capacity has collapsed; the individual can neither understand the emotional state or its basis nor regulate the emotion through active coping.

The second dialectic is defined at its two poles by unrelenting crisis and inhibited experiencing, including inhibited grieving. Individuals with BPD often find it difficult to experience emotion in the context that elicits it; the experience of grief in the context of loss is particularly intolerable as it is experienced as a deep well from which one will never emerge intact. The suppressed grief and anxiety over anticipated losses emerge in the form of reacting to normal life problems and relationship disruptions as though they were crises.

The third dialectic is defined at one pole by emotional vulnerability and at the other by self-invalidation. Individuals with BPD show an exquisite emotional vulnerability to feeling hurt, shamed, and angered by the ordinary behaviors and communications of others. Yet, at the same time, they tolerate a steady stream of quite vicious self-invalidating statements. The self-invalidation parallels early failure in mentalizing on the part of caregivers; individuals with BPD are unable to hold an accurate appraisal of their own mind in mind.

Given the vulnerability to emotion dysregulation entailed in these internal dialectics, the patient with BPD is in need of a treatment that explicitly teaches skills to better regulate emotions, that is, to experience, tolerate, and express them. Hence Linehan (1993b) developed skills-training groups to augment individual psychotherapy; these groups are a psycho-educational component of DBT that lends itself to incorporation into our inpatient setting with several-week lengths of stay.

Positive Psychology

The roots of the positive psychology movement extend back several decades (Ryff, 2003), but the field has gained coherence and momentum under Seligman's initiative. As Seligman (1998) summarized, "Psychology is not just the study of weakness and damage, it is also the study of strength and virtue. Treatment is not just fixing what is broken, it is nurturing what is best within ourselves" (p. 2). In sum, clinical psychology has made great advances in the diagnosis and treatment of psychopathology; yet the elimination of excess negative mood does not necessarily yield happiness or flourishing but rather may result merely in emptiness and languishing (Seligman, 2004).

Persons with many forms of psychopathology experience excess negative mood and a paucity of positive mood. For example, depression is characterized by negative affects including anxiety, sadness, guilt, irritability, and hopelessness coupled with a decrement in the ability to experience pleasure in previously enjoyable activities (Allen, 2006). Post-traumatic stress disorder is characterized by an excess of anxiety symptoms coupled with attenuation of positive emotions evident in decreased ability to feel love along with diminished hope and a sense of a foreshortened future (American Psychiatric Association, 1994; Litz & Gray, 2002). Thus, positive psychology complements traditional clinical psychology by promoting methods to help us clinicians and our patients rise above zero and to begin flourishing.

Modulating Negative Emotion

DBT Distress-Tolerance skills are used when patients are faced with a distressing life event that they can do nothing to change for the better in the present moment. Distress-Tolerance skills are not about changing things; they are about bearing unavoidable pain in life as gracefully as possible, and without resorting to doing something that will make a bad situation worse (Linehan, 1993b). One Distress-Tolerance skill is the "half-smile" (i.e., Duchenne smile). This smile involves a gentle upturning of the corners of the mouth, but the smile must also reach the eyes; there is also a slight elevation of the cheeks and a gentle crinkling of the skin at the corners of the eyes – the place where laugh lines develop if one smiles often enough.

In teaching the half-smile to DBT skills-training group participants, we present Fredrickson's (1998, 2003) research demonstrating that positive experiences, such as smiling, quell or undo the cardiovascular stress induced by negative emotions. For example, Fredrickson and Levenson (1998) induced participants to feel negative emotion by watching a sad or frightening film clip. Participants who spontaneously smiled or were later induced to smile by watching an amusing film clip showed a much more rapid slowing of pulse rate and a more rapid return to non-stress levels of blood pressure and pulse amplitude. We also describe Ekman and Davidson's (1993) EEG research to explain that not all smiles are the same. Fifteen participants in their study demonstrated good ability to differentially contract the zygomatic major and orbicularis oculi muscles. Only when both sets of muscles contracted together in a half-smile did the pattern of brain activation match the pattern observed during spontaneous smiling. As we explain it to patients, by deliberately arranging our face in the half-smile, we strongly activate the left frontal and anterior temporal regions that are associated with an experience of pleasure.

We also explain to patients how intensifying levels of distressing affect erodes the capacity to be in wise mind, that is, the capacity for mentalized affectivity – feeling and thinking about feeling simultaneously. For example, fear narrows thinking to a particular set of behavioral repertoires that promote varying degrees of flight and avoidance, depending on the intensity of the fear (Fredrickson & Branigan, 2005; Fredrickson & Joiner, 2002). As we explain it, the degree and quality of mentalizing involved, relative to the degree of actual threat, renders the action more or less adaptive. When the threat is extreme and concrete, the narrowing of thinking associated with fight, flight, and freeze behaviors has clear survival value. More ordinary interpersonal problems, however, are best resolved through mentalizing. If we are afraid of strangers and refuse to leave our home, there is little mentalizing activity intervening between the fear and the avoidance; the narrowing of thinking has been too extreme relative to the risk. If instead we determine that it is best to gradually get to know people before deciding on complete trust or complete mistrust, our mentalizing tempers our fear and promotes avoidance only when the person truly poses danger.

Participants have no problem generating multiple examples from their lives that attest to the reality of these research findings on the effects of negative emotion on mentalizing capacity. They can give instance after instance when, in the face of an event that caused them great distress, they lost the ability to reflect on their emotion and instead engaged in emotionally driven, maladaptive behaviors. The emotionally driven behaviors made the bad situation worse (e.g., flying into a rage when their boss gave them a less than perfect performance appraisal).

Using the half-smile can thus help improve distress tolerance by activating brain patterns that produce pleasure, thereby titrating down the level of distressing emotion and enabling participants to mentalize more effectively. Then participants are in the frame of mind where they can begin to use other Distress-Tolerance skills, such as finding the meaning in emotional pain, a DBT Distress-Tolerance skill compatible with mentalized affectivity. Patients can use their mentalizing capacity to practice skills that, in Linehan's (1993b) terms, enable them to bear gracefully and get through the unavoidable distress encountered in building a life worth living. Emotional pain that is faced and borne eventually recedes, whereas pain that is avoided typically becomes protracted (Robins, Schmidt & Linehan, 2004).

Increasing Positive Emotion

As already noted, the DBT Emotion-Regulation skills module is designed to help patients understand the meanings and functions of emotions, to reduce their vulnerability to excess negative emotion and emotional suffering, and to increase their experience of positive emotions. The DBT skill, Build Positive Experiences, promotes positive emotion through homework assignments that engage patients in activities from the Adult Pleasant Events Schedule (Linehan, 1993b).

Whereas intense negative emotion impairs mentalizing capacity, positive emotion promotes the kind of flexibility in thinking that we associate with the mentalizing attitude (see Allen, Chapter 1, and Haslam-Hopwood and colleagues, Chapter 13). In this context, we educate patients about some additional positive psychology research findings. For example, Fredrickson and colleagues' (2005) research indicates that positive emotions broaden our perceptual and cognitive capacities, whereas negative emotions narrow our perceptual and cognitive capacities. More specifically, one study revealed that participants who were induced to experience positive emotion were able to generate a much longer and broader range of activities that they would like to do at that time than participants who were induced to have a negative mood. In a related vein, Isen and colleagues (1987, 1991) randomly divided practicing physicians into a group who received a small bag of candy and those who did not; the candy successfully induced a positive mood. Then all the physicians spoke out loud as they went through the chart of a patient with complex liver disease. Those physicians who were induced to have a more positive mood took a broader view of the case, showing more integrative and accurate diagnostic reasoning than the physicians who were not.

To underscore the cognitive benefits of positive emotion, we describe to patients the gist of admittedly complex research findings on the laterality of emotion; this research provides some glimpses as to why negative emotions narrow thought–action repertoires while positive emotions broaden them. As persons move from the avoidance emotions (e.g., fear, disgust, or shame) into the approach emotions (e.g., joy or amusement), the right hemisphere activation associated with the avoidance emotions is retained but increasing recruitment of left-hemisphere activation also becomes evident (Asthana & Mandal, 2001; Hamann, Ely, Hoffman & Kilts, 2002; Workman & Peters, 2000). We speculate that these neurophysiological shifts reflect different levels of flexibility in cognition and action. Negative emotions narrow thought-action repertoires, progressively collapsing mentalizing relative to the intensity of danger and emotion present so as to promote rapid initiation of survival behaviors evident in fight, flight, and freeze responses. On the other hand, the recruitment of left-hemisphere activation with positive emotions might facilitate broadening of thought–action repertoires. Thus positive emotion not only facilitates resilience in the form of rapid recovery from distress-related physiological arousal but also promotes flexible and nuanced prosocial behaviors that enhance survival through stable social group formation and increased procreation opportunities (Tugade & Fredrickson, 2004; Tugade, Fredrickson & Barrett, 2004). To reiterate, negative and positive emotions serve different functions (Levenson, 1999): negative emotion signals a zero sum game where someone is going to win and someone is going to lose; whereas positive emotions signal positive sum games where both people can win (Aron, Norman, Aron, McKenna & Heyman, 2000; Fredrickson, 1998; Levenson, 1994; Tooby & Cosmides, 1990).

We also employ principles from positive psychology to engage participants in a very broad form of mentalizing, namely, reflecting about their life. We describe Seligman's (2002) research indicating that there are three pathways to an authentically happy life: the *pleasant* life is one of sensory pleasures and positive emotions; the *engaged* life is one of using our signature strengths and talents in a way that produces the experience of absorption and flow (Csikszentmihalyi, 1997); and the *meaningful* life is one in which we invest in something larger than ourselves (e.g., family, community, an environmental cause, a church, or God). We encourage patients to consider the extent to which the pleasant events they engage in, in doing their 'build positive experiences' homework, relate to these three different facets of an authentically happy life.

To recapitulate, with a focus on developmental psychopathology, we put much effort into the painful side of mentalized affectivity, aspiring to help patients become more attuned to negative emotions, ascribe meaning to them, express them, and regulate them. We are convinced that mentalizing is the cornerstone of effective interpersonal problem solving. Yet we not only wish to help patients address problematic patterns of behavior that contribute to insecure attachment but also wish to help them develop a positive exploratory attitude toward mentalizing: we encourage open-mindedness and curiosity about themselves and others, consideration of multiple perspectives on mental states, and a playful attitude toward this exploration. Positive psychology can be brought to bear on these aspirations as it has demonstrated that experiencing positive emotions broadens our perceptual and cognitive styles, making them more inclusive, synthetic and flexible (Fredrickson & Branigan, 2005).

Enhancing Interpersonal Effectiveness

The DBT Interpersonal Effectiveness skill module is designed to help patients learn how to initiate and maintain healthy relationships, maintain self-respect in relationships, and communicate objectives and emotions to others in respectful and clear ways. Plainly, mentalizing capacity is critical to these goals and, conversely, the exercise of the skills engages patients in mentalizing. To illustrate, Linehan (1993b) employs the acronym, GIVE, for a set of skills that are especially important in initiating and maintaining healthy relationships: G stands for being Gentle and temperate in our approach to the other person (i.e., no attacks, threats, or judgmental moralizing); I stands for acting Interested by listening, not interrupting, and making eye contact; V stands for Validating by explicitly acknowledging an understanding and appreciation of where the other is coming from, even if one does not share the same perspective; and E stands for using an Easy manner that incorporates a little humor and light-heartedness. All these facets of interacting are consistent with mentalizing in the context of a secure attachment relationship.

The DBT skills-training group fosters GIVE skills by means of teaching, modeling, and role playing. We also incorporate some research findings from positive psychology here. Expressing positive emotions and experience in relationships, as prescribed by GIVE, correlates significantly with job success, academic success, and – most pertinently – the quality and longevity of attachment relationships, that is, friendships and marriages (Seligman, 1990; Seligman & Schulman, 1986). A ratio of 5:1 positives to negatives is needed in marriages, and a ratio of 3:1 in the workplace (Losada & Heaphy, 2004). A caveat: researchers recommend not exceeding a ratio of 13:1, which can come across as Pollyannaish sappiness (Fredrickson, 2004).

Again, GIVE skills require mentalizing in relation to the other and the self. Monitoring how effectively one is being gentle, interested, validating, and easygoing requires both implicit and explicit reading of a host of reciprocal cues in the unfolding relationship. For example, as we explain it to patients, I may think I am acting interested but, if I am mentalizing well, I might pick up cues that indicate my partner in the relationship is likely feeling smothered; then I may need to check this hypothesis out explicitly or check it out implicitly by toning down my expressions of interest and noting whether my partner's comfort level seems to increase.

DBT, MBT, AND BPD

As noted in the introduction, DBT (Linehan, 1993a) and MBT (Bateman & Fonagy, 2004) are two evidence-based approaches to treating emotion-regulation problems in patients with BPD. While we clinicians at The Menninger Clinic are incorporating an explicit focus on mentalizing into many arenas of treatment, we continue to rely on DBT skills training to provide patients with much-needed tools for regulating their profound dysphoria. The concept of mentalized affectivity provides a conceptual framework for this psycho-educational intervention that renders it coherent with our general treatment approach. This conceptual coherence is crucial for both patients and staff members; without it, multimodal treatment in an inpatient setting such as ours can become fragmented.

As this chapter has explicated, mentalized affectivity does not entail exercising intellect to quell experience and expression of painful emotions. Consistent with treatment as a whole, we employ DBT skills training to cultivate reflective capacity in the midst of emotional experience and the development of an appreciation for the signal and existential meanings of emotional experience in the context of present and past relationships. Understandably, but unfortunately, positive emotion has been given short shrift in clinical work, and cultivating mentalized affectivity with respect to positive experience is especially crucial for patients with BPD, many of whom struggle with severe depression in relation to a history of trauma in attachment relationships (Allen, 2001, 2005). Positive psychology is a promising development that we are striving to exploit more fully in this context. Yet cultivating greater capacity for mentalized affectivity is especially challenging in working with such patients, because attachment trauma is most pernicious in undermining mentalizing capacity and, thereby, the development of the capacity for emotion regulation (Fonagy & Target, 1997). Thus it is no accident that we find a useful convergence of DBT with our interest in mentalizing, and our patients need all the help we can give them – from any quarter.

REFERENCES

Allen, J. G. (2001). *Traumatic Relationships and Serious Mental Disorders*. Chichester, UK: John Wiley & Sons, Ltd.

Allen, J. G. (2005). *Coping with Trauma: Hope through Understanding* (2nd edn). Washington, DC: American Psychiatric Publishing.

Allen, J. G. (2006). *Coping with Depression: From Catch-22 to Hope*. Washington, DC: American Psychiatric Publishing.

American Psychiatric Association (1994). *Diagnostic and Statistical Manual of Mental Disorders* (4th edn). Washington, DC: American Psychiatric Association.

Aron, A., Norman, C. C., Aron, E. N., McKenna, C. & Heyman, R. E. (2000). Couple's shared participation in novel and arousing activities and experienced relationship quality. *Journal of Personality and Social Psychology*, 78, 273–284.

Asthana, H. S. & Mandal, M. K. (2001). Visual-field bias in the judgement of facial expression of emotion. *Journal of General Psychology*, 128, 21–29.

Bateman, A. W. & Fonagy, P. (2004). Mentalization-based treatment of BPD. *Journal of Personality Disorders*, 18, 36–51.

Csikszentmihalyi, M. (1997). *Finding Flow*. New York: Basic Books.

Ekman, P. & Davidson, R. J. (1993). Voluntary smiling changes regional brain activity. *Psychological Science*, 4, 342–345.

Fonagy, P. (1991). Thinking about thinking: Some clinical and theoretical considerations in the treatment of a borderline patient. *International Journal of Psycho-Analysis, 72,* 639–656.

Fonagy, P. & Target, M. (1997). Attachment and reflective function: their role in self-organization. *Development and Psychopathology, 9,* 679–700.

Fonagy, P., Gergely, G., Jurist, E. L. & Target, M. (2002). *Affect Regulation, Mentalization, and the Development of the Self.* New York: Other Press.

Fredrickson, B. L. (1998). What good are positive emotions? *Review of General Psychology, 2,* 300–319.

Fredrickson, B. L. (2003). The value of positive emotions. *American Scientist, 91,* 330–335.

Fredrickson, B. L. (2004). Authentic Happiness Coaching Program, Master Class 5. (Teleconference).

Fredrickson, B. L. & Branigan, C. (2005). Positive emotions broaden the scope of attention and thought-action repertoires. *Cognition and Emotion, 19,* 313–333.

Fredrickson, B. L. & Joiner, T. (2002). Positive emotions trigger an upward spiral toward emotional well-being. *Psychological Science, 13,* 172–175.

Fredrickson, B. L. & Levenson, R. W. (1998). Positive emotions speed recovery from the cardiovascular sequelae of negative emotions. *Cognition and Emotion, 12,* 191–220.

Hamann, S. B., Ely, T. D., Hoffman, J. M. & Kilts, C. D. (2002). Ecstasy and agony: activation of the human amygdala in positive and negative emotions. *Psychological Science, 13,* 135–141.

Isen, A. M. (1987). Positive affect, cognitive processes and social behavior. *Advances in Experimental Social Psychology, 20,* 203–253.

Isen, A. M., Rosenzweig, A. S. & Young, M. J. (1991). The influence of positive affect on clinical problem solving. *Medical Decision Making, 11,* 221–227.

Levenson, R. W. (1994). Human emotions: a functional view. In P. Ekman & R. Davidson (eds), *The Nature of Emotion: Fundamental Questions* (pp. 123–126). New York: Oxford University Press.

Levenson, R. W. (1999). The intrapersonal functions of emotion. *Cognition and Emotion, 13,* 481–504.

Linehan, M. M. (1993a). *Cognitive-Behavioral Treatment of Borderline Personality Disorder.* New York: Guilford Press.

Linehan, M. M. (1993b). *Skills Training Manual for Treating Borderline Personality Disorder.* New York: Guilford Press.

Linehan, M. M. & Manning, S. (1999). *Dialectical Behavior Therapy Intensive Training Seminar.* Seattle, WA.

Linehan, M. M., Dimeff, L. A., Reynolds, S. K., Comtois, K. A., Shaw Welch, S., Heagerty, P., et al. (2002). Dialectical behavior therapy versus comprehensive validation plus 12-step for the treatment of opioid dependent women meeting criteria for borderline personality disorder. *Drug and Alcohol Dependence, 67,* 13–26.

Linehan, M. M., Schmidt, H., Dimeff, L. A., Craft, C., Kanter, J. & Comtois, K. A. (1999). Dialectical behavior therapy for patients with borderline personality disorder and drug-dependence. *American Journal on Addictions, 8,* 279–292.

Litz, B. T. & Gray, M. J. (2002). Emotional numbing in post-traumatic stress disorder: current and future research directions. *Australian and New Zealand Journal of Psychiatry, 36,* 198–204.

Losada, M. & Heaphy, E. (2004). The role of positivity and connectivity in the performance of business teams: a nonlinear dynamics model. *American Behavioral Scientist, 47,* 740–765.

Rapaport, D. (1953). On the psychoanalytic theory of affects. *The Collected Papers of David Rapaport (1967).* New York: Basic Books.

Robins, C. J., Schmidt, H. & Linehan, M. M. (2004). Dialectical behavior therapy. Synthesizing radical acceptance with skillful means. In S. C. Hayes, V. M. Follette &

M. M. Linehan (eds), *Mindfulness and Acceptance: Expanding the Cognitive Behavioral Tradition* (pp. 30–44). New York: Guilford Press.

Ryff, C. D. (2003). Corners of myopia in the positive psychology parade. *Psychological Inquiry, 14*, 153–159.

Seligman, M. E. P. (1990). *Learned Optimism.* New York: Simon & Schuster.

Seligman, M. E. P. (1998). President's column: building human strength: psychology's forgotten mission. *APA Monitor, 29*, 2.

Seligman, M. E. P. (2002). *Authentic Happiness.* New York: Simon & Schuster.

Seligman, M. E. P. (2003). Foreword: the past and future of positive psychology. In C. L. Keyes & J. Haidt (eds), *Positive Psychology and the Life Well-Lived.* Washington, DC: American Psychological Association.

Seligman, M. E. P. (2004). Authentic Happiness Coaching Program, Master Class 1. (Teleconference).

Seligman, M. E. P. & Schulman, P. (1986). Explanatory style as a predictor of productivity and quitting among life insurance agents. *Journal of Personality and Social Psychology, 50*, 822–838.

Telch, C. F., Agras, W. S. & Linehan, M. M. (2001). Dialectical behavior therapy for binge eating disorder. *Journal of Consulting and Clinical Psychology, 69*, 1061–1065.

Tooby, J. & Cosmides, L. (1990). The past explains the present: emotional adaptations and the structure of ancestral environments. *Ethology and Sociobiology, 11*, 375–424.

Tugade, M. & Fredrickson, B. L. (2004). Resilient individuals use positive emotions to bounce back from negative emotional experiences. *Journal of Personality and Social Psychology, 86*, 320–333.

Tugade, M., Fredrickson, B. L. & Barrett, L. F. (2004). Psychological resilience and positive emotional granularity: examining the benefits of positive emotions on coping and health. *Journal of Personality, 72*, 1161–1181.

Workman, L. & Peters, S. (2000). Lateralization of perceptual processing of pro- and anti-social emotions displayed in chimeric faces. *Laterality, 5*, 237–249.

PART IV

MENTALIZATION-BASED THERAPY

9

MENTALIZING AND BORDERLINE PERSONALITY DISORDER

Anthony Bateman and Peter Fonagy

In this chapter we will discuss briefly the concept of mentalization as applied to borderline personality disorder (BPD), consider the changing views of BPD as a severe and enduring personality disorder, and argue that a focus on mentalization as a core component of treatment provides the best chance of successful outcome not only because it addresses the central problem of the patient but also because it reduces the likelihood of causing harm in a group of patients who may be particularly sensitive to inapt psychotherapeutic interventions.

MENTALIZATION

Mentalizing entails making sense of the actions of oneself and others on the basis of intentional mental states, such as desires, feelings and beliefs. It involves the recognition that what is in the mind is in the mind, and reflects knowledge of one's own and others' mental states as mental states. In effect, mentalizing refers to making sense of each other and ourselves, implicitly and explicitly, in terms of subjective states and mental processes. It is a capacity that is acquired gradually over the first few years of life in the context of safe and secure child–caregiver relationships. Consequently, there is ample opportunity for the process to be disrupted. Our premise is that unstable or reduced mentalizing capacity is a core feature of BPD and, as such, to be successful, any treatment must have mentalization as its focus or at the very least stimulate development of mentalizing as an epiphenomenon.

Handbook of Mentalization-Based Treatment. Edited by J. G. Allen and P. Fonagy.
© 2006 John Wiley & Sons, Ltd.

We have discussed our developmental model of BPD in detail elsewhere (Bateman & Fonagy, 2004; Fonagy, 2002; Fonagy, Target, Gergely & Bateman, 2003). Essentially it is focused around the development of the social-affiliative system, which we consider to be driving many higher-order social-cognitive functions that underpin interpersonal interaction, specifically in an attachment context. We considered four of these to be of primary importance: affect representation and, related to this, affect regulation; attentional control, also with strong links to the regulation of affect; the dual arousal system involved in maintaining an appropriate balance between mental functions undertaken by the anterior and posterior portions of the brain; and, finally, mentalization, a system for interpersonal understanding within the attachment context. To psycho-analytic readers, the focus on attachment and a range of neurocognitive mechanisms may sound insufficiently dynamic to be considered in the context of a psycho-analytic theory of borderline pathology. However, we would maintain that our model is dynamic insofar as we consider the above capacities to evolve in the context of the primary caregiving relationships experienced by the child and to be vulnerable to extremes of environmental deficiency as exemplified by severe neglect, psychological or physical abuse, childhood molestation, or other forms of maltreatment.

We suggest that the aforementioned four mechanisms, including mentalizing, are in place normally to control or obscure the potential for a much more primitive form of subjectivity. This form of subjectivity is dominated by modes of representation of internal states and the relationship of internal and external, which are observable in the mental functioning of young children. These processes, in combination with the profound disorganization of self-structure, explain many facets of borderline personality functioning. We do not attribute a central role to trauma, although we expect that in individuals made vulnerable by early inadequate mirroring and disorganized attachment to highly stressful psycho-social experiences in an attachment context, trauma will play a key role in both shaping the pathology and directly causing it by undermining the capacity for mentalization. We see this capacity as having the power to hold back modes of primitive mental functioning in those who are subjected to the same kinds of experience but who suffered little or no adverse effects. It makes conceptual sense, therefore, that mentalizing should be a focus for therapeutic intervention if we are to help borderline patients bring primitive modes of mental functioning under better regulation and control. But before we discuss treatment it is necessary to understand the longitudinal course of BPD, because it is against this background that treatment is applied and potentially can provide great benefit or induce considerable harm.

THE COURSE OF BPD

We expect BPD to have an enduring quality. Early follow-up studies, despite noting some improvements, highlighted the inexorable nature of the "disease", talking of "burnt out" borderlines and hinting less at recovery than at a disease process, which ran a long-term course (e.g., Stone, 1990). Therapeutic nihilism was justified by the intensity and incomprehensibility of emotional pain, the often dramatic self-mutilation, and the degree of ambivalence in interpersonal relationships that was considered as beyond understandable. Not surprisingly, in the face of apparently wilful disruption of any attempt at helping, mental health professionals assumed the condition to be resistant to therapeutic help.

Two carefully designed, fully powered prospective studies have highlighted the inappropriateness of the attitudes that confined individuals with severe PD to the margins of even generous healthcare systems (Shea et al., 2004). The majority of BPD patients experience a substantial reduction in their symptoms far sooner than previously assumed. After six years, 75% of patients diagnosed with BPD severe enough to require hospitalization achieve remission by standardized diagnostic criteria (Zanarini, Frankenburg, Hennen & Silk, 2003). Patients with BPD *can* undergo remission – a concept that heretofore had been solely used in the context of Axis I pathology. About 50% remission rate has occurred by four years, but the remission is steady (10–15% per year). Recurrences are rare, perhaps no more than 10% over six years. This contrasts with the natural course of many Axis I disorders, such as affective disorder, where improvement may be somewhat more rapid but recurrences are common. In the Collaborative Depression Study, 30% of the patients had not recovered at one year, 19% at two years and 12% at five years (Keller et al., 1992).

While improvements of BPD are substantial, it should be noted that symptoms such as impulsivity and associated self-mutilation and suicidality show dramatic change – not affective symptoms or social and interpersonal functioning. The dramatic symptoms (self-mutilation, suicidality, quasi-psychotic thoughts, often seen as requiring urgent hospitalization) recede, but abandonment concerns, sense of emptiness, relationship problems and vulnerability to depression are likely to remain present in at least half the patients. When dramatic improvements occur, they sometimes occur quickly, quite often associated with relief from severely stressful situations (Gunderson et al., 2003). It seems that certain co-morbidities undermine the likelihood of improvement (Zanarini, Frankenburg, Hennen, Reich & Silk, 2004); the persistence of substance use disorders decreases the likelihood of remission, suggesting that the latter must be treated.

CHANGING EXPECTATIONS ABOUT THE EFFECTIVENESS OF TREATMENT

Dialectical behaviour therapy (DBT) was the first treatment to challenge the atmosphere of therapeutic nihilism. This imaginative, complex but well-manualized treatment approach captured the attention of the field. It broke new ground in recommending validation rather than confrontation of the patient's experience, offering skills training to fill the void that generates self-harming and suicidal behaviour, and integrating spirituality (aspects of Zen Buddhism) into a highly potent multi-faceted behavioural treatment protocol. Three randomized-controlled trials (RCTs; Linehan et al., in press; Linehan, Armstrong, Suarez, Allmon & Heard, 1991; Verheul et al., 2003) reported dramatic reductions in suicide attempts. The number of suicide attempts in those treated with DBT decreased to just over seven compared to over 33 in the treatment-as-usual control group. When compared with an active control group, the benefit of DBT is still evident although less clearly marked. In Linehan's most recent larger-scale RCT, both DBT and treatment by non-behavioural therapists (nominated as experts in treating BPD) reduced the number of non-suicidal para-suicidal acts over 18 months. Nevertheless, DBT achieved numbers needed to treat (NNT) of around four for suicidal behaviours, use of services and avoiding dropouts (National Education Alliance conference report). But, while DBT has powerful effects on the management of behavioural problems associated with impulsivity, its effects on mood state and interpersonal functioning are more limited (Scheel, 2000).

Our own evidence base remains small as far as treatment outcome is concerned; yet replication studies are underway, and an increasing number of practitioners are using mentalization techniques in treatment, such that more information will become available soon. Our original RCT of treatment of BPD in a partial-hospital 18-month programme offering individual and group psycho-analytic psychotherapy (Bateman & Fonagy, 1999, 2001) showed significant and enduring changes in mood states and interpersonal functioning. The benefits, relative to treatment as usual, were large (NNTs around two) and were observed to increase during the follow-up period of 18 months, rather than staying level as with DBT. This continuing improvement may be a hallmark of psycho-dynamic treatment. The effective components of this complex treatment programme remain unclear, although the common feature of all the different treatment elements was mentalization. In the study, patients received a range of treatments along with group and individual therapy, which included psychodrama and other expressive therapies along with some psycho-education early in treatment. To determine if the focus on mentalizing is a key component effecting change and to see if a more modest treatment programme may be effective in a less severe group of borderline patients, we are currently undertaking an RCT of individual and group psychotherapy alone offered in an outpatient programme. Results are not yet available.

The only head-to-head comparison of psycho-dynamic and dialectical behaviour therapy was recently reported by the Cornell Medical College Group (Clarkin et al., 2004a; Clarkin, Levy, Lenzenweger & Kernberg, 2004b). In what is probably until now the most carefully controlled study of psychotherapy for BPD, the Cornell group found significant improvements in impulsivity-related symptoms as well as mood and interpersonal functioning measures. The trial contrasted transference-focused psychotherapy, DBT, and supportive psychotherapy. There was significant and equal benefit from all the interventions, although early dropout rates were higher for DBT than for the other treatments.

Additional non-randomized controlled trials have shown various implementations of psycho-dynamic, supportive and cognitive-behavioural therapies to be somewhat effective (see Bateman & Tyrer, 2004). Possibly important negative findings to emerge from the literature concern the greater efficacy of briefer periods of hospitalization (Chiesa, Fonagy, Holmes & Drahorad, 2004), the general ineffectiveness of brief hospital admissions motivated by suicide threats (Paris, 2004), and the value of combining inpatient admissions with structured psychotherapeutic interventions (Bohus et al., 2004). Evidence that medication will reduce the risk of suicide or attempted suicide is scarce (Lieb, Zanarini, Schmahl, Linehan & Bohus, 2004). Evidence shows, however, that low-dose atypical antipsychotics and SSRIs are helpful in addressing emotional dysregulation, anxiety and impulsive behavioural dyscontrol, and that these medications might assist in making patients accessible to psycho-social interventions (Tyrer & Bateman, 2004). The trials, however, usually involve only moderately ill patients, and many do not stay on medication for sustained periods.

THE REALITY OF IATROGENIC HARM

A real puzzle emerges from this brief overview of recent findings on the natural course and treatment outcome of BPD. If, as it seems from the studies cited, a range of well-organized and coordinated treatments are effective for BPD, and in any case in the vast majority of cases BPD naturally resolves within six years, how can it be that clinicians across the globe have traditionally agreed about the treatment-resistant character of the disorder? Earlier surveys indicated that 97% of patients with BPD who presented for treatment in the United States received outpatient care from an average of six therapists. An analysis of outcomes measured two to three years later suggest this treatment as usual is at best only marginally effective (see Lieb et al., 2004). How can we square such findings with what we know of potential treatment effects and the new data on the natural course of the disorder?

It seems to us that there is no way to avoid the conclusion that some psycho-social treatments practised currently, and perhaps even more commonly in the past, have impeded the borderline patient's capacity to recover following the natural course of the disorder and advantageous changes in social circumstances. In Michael Stone's (1990) classic follow-up of patients treated nearly 40 years ago, 66% recovery rate was only achieved in 20 years (four times longer than reported in more recent studies). Has the nature of the disorder changed? Have treatments become that much more effective? Both seem unlikely explanations. The known efficacy of pharmacological agents, new and old, cannot account for this difference (Tyrer & Bateman, 2004); the evidence-based psycho-social treatments are not widely available. It is, sadly, far more likely that the apparent improvement in the course of the disorder is accounted for by harmful treatments being less frequently offered. This change might stem more from the changing pattern of healthcare, particularly in the United States (Lambert, Bergin & Garfield, 2004), than from clinicians' recognizing the possibility of iatrogenic deterioration and thereby avoiding damaging side effects.

IATROGENESIS, PSYCHOTHERAPY AND BPD

As part of the regular scrutiny of side effects, pharmacological studies routinely explore the potential harm that a well-intentioned treatment may cause. In the case of psycho-social treatments we all too readily assume – as Hans Eysenck (1952) did a half-century ago – that at worst such treatments are inert but, in any case, they are unlikely to do harm. This may indeed be the case for most disorders where psychotherapy is used as part of a care plan.

Yet there may be particular disorders where psychological therapy represents a significant risk to the patient. Whatever the mechanisms of therapeutic change might be – emotional, cognitive, creation of a coherent narrative, modification of distorted cognitions, emotional experience of a secure base, or the rekindling of hope – traditional psychotherapeutic approaches depend for their effectiveness on the capacity of the individual to consider their experience of their own mental state alongside its re-presentation by the psychotherapist. The appreciation of the difference between one's own experience of one's mind and that presented by another person is a key element. It is the integration of one's current experience of mind with the alternative view presented by the psychotherapist that must be at the foundation of a change process. The capacity to understand behaviour in terms of the associated mental states in self and other (the capacity to mentalize; Fonagy, Gergely, Jurist & Target, 2002; Bateman & Fonagy, 2004) is essential for the achievement of this integration (see also Fonagy, Chapter 3).

While most people without major psychological problems are in a relatively strong position to make productive use of an alternative perspective presented by the psychological therapist, those individuals who have a very poor appreciation of their own and others' perception of mind are unlikely to be able to derive benefit from traditional (particularly insight-oriented) psychological therapies. We have argued that individuals with BPD have an impoverished model of their own and others' mental function, and we have accumulated some evidence to support this view (Bateman & Fonagy, 2004). They have schematic, rigid and sometimes extreme views, which make them vulnerable to powerful emotional storms and apparently impulsive actions, and which create profound problems of behavioural regulation, including affect regulation. The weaker an individual's sense of their own subjectivity, the more difficult it is for them to compare the validity of their own perceptions of the way their mind works with what a "mind expert" presents. When presented with a coherent and perhaps even accurate view of mental function in the context of psychotherapy, they are not able to compare the picture offered to them with a self-generated model, and they may all too often accept uncritically or reject wholesale alternative perspectives.

These divergent responses can be generated by any psychological therapy. Both cognitively based and dynamically oriented therapies offer causal explanations for underlying mental states. These therapies can give ready-made answers and provide illusory stability by inducing a process of quasi-mentalizing in which patients take on the explanations without question and make them their own. Conversely, both types of perspective can be summarily and angrily dismissed as overly simplistic and patronizing, which in turn fuels a sense of abandonment, feelings of isolation and desperation. Even focusing on how the patient feels can have its dangers. A person who has little capacity to discern the subjective state associated with anger cannot benefit from being told both that they are feeling angry and the underlying cause of that anger. This assertion addresses nothing that is known or can be integrated. It can only be accepted as true or rejected outright, but in neither case is it helpful. The dissonance between the patient's inner experience and the perspective given by the therapist, in the context of feelings of attachment to the therapist, leads to bewilderment, which, in turn, leads to instability as the patient attempts to integrate the different views and experiences. Unsurprisingly, this results in more rather than less mental and behavioural disturbance.

EFFECTIVE TREATMENT

So what is the psychiatrist or other mental health professional supposed to do? The problem is compounded by the fact that attachment and mentalization are loosely coupled systems existing in a state of partial exclusivity (see Fonagy, Chapter 3). While mentalization has its roots in the sense of being understood by an attachment figure, mentalizing is also more challenging to maintain in the context of an attachment relationship – including the relationship with the therapist – for those individuals whose problem is fundamentally one of attachment disturbance (Gunderson, 1996). Recent intriguing neurobiological findings have highlighted how the activation of the attachment system tends temporarily to inhibit or decouple the normal adult's capacity to mentalize (Bartels & Zeki, 2004). Elsewhere we have proposed, on the basis of research findings as well as clinical observation, that individuals with BPD have hyperactive attachment systems as a result of their history and/or biological predisposition (Fonagy & Bateman, 2006). This impairment may account for their compromised mentalizing capacity.

Mentalizing as the Key to Successful Treatment

It follows from the evidence outlined above that the recovery of mentalizing capacity in the context of attachment relationships must be a primary objective of all psycho-social treatments for BPD. But we suggest that patients with BPD are particularly vulnerable to side effects of psychotherapeutic treatments that activate the attachment system. Yet, without activation of the attachment system, borderline patients will never develop a capacity to function psychologically in the context of interpersonal relationships, an incapacity that is at the core of their problems. Hence the psychiatrist or other mental health professional must tread a precarious path between stimulating a patient's attachment and involvement with treatment while helping him maintain mentalization. Treatment will only be effective to the extent that it is able to enhance the patient's mentalizing capacities without generating too many negative iatrogenic effects as it stimulates the attachment system. This balance may be achieved by encouraging exploration and identification of emotions within multiple contexts, particularly interpersonal ones, and by helping the patient establish meaningful internal representations, while avoiding premature conscious and unconscious explanations. We now turn to this strategy to illustrate a few aspects of technique that we believe allow patients to develop their own understanding. If iatrogenic effects are to be minimized, the principle to follow is to move through levels of intervention from identifying positive mentalizing, through clarification, affect elaboration and judicious confrontation to mentalizing the transference itself – without jumping too far ahead. The therapist follows as well as guides, asks as well as answers; there should be no fast forward but rather frame-by-frame progression with rewind and explore.

MENTALIZING TECHNIQUES FOR BPD

The overall aim of mentalization-based therapy (MBT) is to develop a therapeutic process in which the mind of the patient becomes the focus of treatment (Bateman, 2004). The objective is for the patient to find out more about how he thinks and feels about himself and others, how that dictates his responses, and how "errors" in understanding himself and others lead to actions in an attempt to retain stability and to make sense of incomprehensible feelings. As we have previously mentioned, it is not for the therapist to "tell" the patient about how he feels, what he thinks, how he should behave, or what the underlying reasons are – conscious or unconscious – for his difficulties. We believe that any therapy approach that moves towards "knowing" how a patient "is", how he should behave and think, and "why he is like he is" is likely to be harmful. Therapists must ensure that they retain an approach that focuses on the mind of their patients as they are experiencing themselves and others at any given moment. This is easier said than done, and many therapists are pushed off course by transference and counter-transference processes, which result in interventions that are at best non-mentalizing but more often anti-mentalizing. We have therefore developed what we hope are memorable techniques for therapists to follow, especially when they feel that they "don't know what to do". These are general principles, and the skill of the therapist is to apply them consistently but flexibly – particularly when in the line of fire.

Identifying and Exploring Positive Mentalizing

The appropriate use of praise adds to a reassuring atmosphere created within therapy. The therapist should not become a "cheer leader" supporting the patient from the touchline but rather should stand alongside the patient, provoking curiosity about motivations and demonstrating how understanding and explaining to oneself and others improves emotional satisfaction and control of mood states. Positive attitudes are commonly used in therapy to instil hope and to demonstrate that change is possible, but the principle to follow is to use praise only to highlight positive mentalizing and to explore its beneficial effects.

The therapist alights on how the patient has understood a complex interpersonal situation, for example, and examines how this may have helped him not only to understand how he felt but also to recognize the other person's feelings.

> The patient explained, "My mother phoned me and asked me to come to help her pack before she went on holiday. I told her I wasn't going to do that and she retorted that I had always been a selfish girl given all that she had done for me – which of course upset me. This time though I didn't put the phone down but told her that I couldn't help her pack because I had to go to work. She made me feel guilty about that but I said that it was too late for me to ask for time off. In the end, I was able to say that I would also miss her because of all she did for me."

> The therapist said, "You sound like you really managed to explain something to her this time. How did that make you feel?" Later he explored how the patient thought her mother felt about the whole conversation. The patient and her mother had managed to say goodbye to each other in a constructive way, which seemed to leave them both feeling satisfied at the end of the phone call.

Judicious praise of mentalizing strengths is balanced by identification of non-mentalizing fillers. Trite explanations, dismissive statements, assumptions, rationalizations, and so forth should all be identified and tackled as they arise (see Munich, Chapter 6). Most non-mentalizing fillers lack any obvious practical success in furthering a relationship and in developing understanding of situations or oneself. This needs to be highlighted.

Clarification and Affect Elaboration

Clarification is self-explanatory and requires little elucidation here. It is the tidying up of behaviour that has resulted from a failure of mentalization. In order to tidy up, important facts have to be established and their relationship to underlying feelings identified. Actions should always be traced to feelings whenever possible by rewinding the events and establishing the moment-by-moment process leading to an action. Within this process the therapist should be alert to any failures to "read minds" in himself or his patient and, when this is apparent in a story, to question it and to seek an alternative understanding of the mentalizing failure. Open-ended questions, restating facts, focusing on moment-to-moment events are common clarification techniques.

A 22-year-old patient reported that he had left his university course. He had failed to attend lectures and seminars for a few weeks, preferring to stay at home and smoke cannabis. The first time he re-attended his tutor asked him where he had been. Taking offence, the patient told the tutor, "Stick your course up your ass!" – and then walked out. He had not returned after that.

The therapist asked the patient to go back to the point at which he had stopped attending the university lectures and traced the events leading up to his absence. Having spent considerable time looking at preceding events and tracing the pathway to the patient's eventual return to university, the therapist alighted on the obvious failure of mentalization when the student shouted at his tutor and walked out. In the transcription of the tape, the therapist makes many comments such as: "Take me through what happened." "Not so quickly. Can you go slowly there and tell me what was in your mind at the time?" "Just to be clear: you felt that your tutor was criticizing you and sneering about your lack of attendance?" "Looking back, do you think that he could have meant what he said any other way?" "Have there been other times when you have felt he didn't like you?" These are all attempts to clarify the pathway leading up to the failure of mentalization while linking it to what was going on in his mind at the time.

It transpired that his understanding of his tutor's mind was that he was being censorious when in fact, an alternative understanding was that his tutor was expressing concern for him and showing that he had missed him. In an attempt to link the patient's experience of the motivation of the tutor to the action, the therapist asked what the tutor would have had to say and perhaps have thought about him for him to have felt differently and not to have acted so precipitously.

The exploration in our view is not enough to effect change and, having developed this level of clarity, the therapist needs to move with the patient towards mentalizing the transference. In this case the area of affective importance was the student's hurt and humiliation, which, when explored, revealed a powerful narcissistic experience; he required admiration to remain stable.

Affect elaboration requires the therapist to explore empathically the feeling states of the patient and not to be deflected from the task by manifest feelings. Many patients will express feelings during the session or talk about how they felt under specific circumstances, and MBT focuses particularly on the affective state of the patient so this is encouraged. It is important to elicit feelings during non-mentalizing interactions; affects disrupt mentalizing. As the patient becomes increasingly bewildered about feelings, his mental agitation increases, quickly overwhelming his capacity to be reflective. Physical agitation, actions, panic and defensive manoeuvres result. Identifying feelings and placing them in context helps to reduce the perplexity of the patient and reduces the likelihood that feelings must be managed through self-harm or other actions.

Many patients exhibit emotions that are unlikely to induce sympathy in others. The expression of such feelings should become a focus of therapy if it seems likely that the overtly expressed emotion covers a feeling that is more likely to provoke a caring or concerned response from someone else. A common example of this process is the use of anger and hostility to cover more problematic feelings such as longing for closeness and intimacy. Here the therapist should make careful use of counter-transference feelings, which may be the first indication of the patient's underlying state.

Challenge or "Stop and Stand"

Stop and stand or challenge defines the action of the therapist at the point at which mentalization fails and he interrupts the session to insist that the patient focuses on the moment of rupture so as to reinstate mentalizing in the patient and sometimes within himself. The therapist calls a halt and seeks to stimulate reflection about an aspect of the dialogue, which has become muddling, perplexing, or appears to indicate that the patient is making massive assumptions and basing decisions on them. Stop and stand should always be accompanied by exploration of the underlying feeling state and not a cognitive analysis of the logic of the dialogue. This is the point at which the therapist can go no further without sorting out some aspect of the patient's behaviour and, in particular, an aspect of the patient's mental process that justifies their experience and excuses their stance.

The complaining patient

A patient complained throughout the session that no one understood his problems. He had made a number of written complaints about the ill treatment that he had received from mental health professionals whom he felt had never really believed his reports of neglect as a child and so had not taken his problems seriously. Because he could function to some extent and was gainfully employed, they had told him that he was all right and didn't need further help. As he talked about this he continually pointed out to the therapist that she did not understand, and treatment with her was going to be useless.

THERAPIST: So I suppose that if I don't understand it will make it difficult for you to come to see me, especially if it means to you that I am not going to take your problems seriously.

PATIENT (challenging tone):   You can't understand because you have never experienced what I have. You weren't ill treated as a child, were you? I think I will have to go to one of those user groups where everyone has had the same experience. At least, they might know how I feel.

THERAPIST: How do you know?

PATIENT: How do I know what?

THERAPIST: That I never experienced emotional neglect as a child?

PATIENT: Well you didn't.

THERAPIST: It seems, then, that you feel justified in your formal complaints to the hospital that all these mental health professionals should not have made all sorts of assumptions about you being OK and not needing help. But when it comes to you making assumptions about me and basing your attitude to me on those assumptions it is somehow OK ... I am someone who can be dismissed as just another person who will not be able to understand because you assume that I have not experienced neglect.

PATIENT: That's different.

THERAPIST: In what way is it different?

PATIENT: It is.

THERAPIST: Is it? How come it is a matter for formal complaint to the hospital board that other people make assumptions about your difficulties and then act on them but it is all right for you to do so about me?

The reader may feel that the therapist was becoming a little too challenging in this session, but the therapist felt strongly that this was a core element of the patient's difficulties: as soon as he found underlying feelings problematic, he became dismissive of others without reflection, lost the ability to mentalize momentarily and, accordingly, left relationships with his feelings un-addressed and a grudge that no one understood him. The session continued to focus on this area. The stop and stand had reinstated some reflection by the patient whose mostly pre-conscious assumption about the therapist was now conscious and on the table for discussion as something that might stimulate feelings that would lead him inexorably towards leaving therapy and repeating his previous interactions with therapists – and possibly writing a further letter of complaint. The therapist moved on to identify the patient's fears of never being understood and his current feeling that the therapist would never be able to understand his wish to be understood as a person who had his own needs and desires, who required support and emotional care, and who was not someone who could manage and get on with his life without help (see below).

Mentalizing the Transference

Mentalizing the transference refers to the therapist's attempt to highlight the underlying motive that underpins the patient's current mental state. It is the most complex aspect of the extent to which it is easy for the therapist to break the fundamental rule of not telling the patient what is "really going on". As soon as the therapist seeks to identify unconsciously determined motives, it is all too easy for him to begin making assumptions about the cause of the current patient/therapist interaction, for example, as a repetition of an earlier object relationship. In fact, mentalizing the transference is an attempt to demonstrate alternative perspectives, contrasting the patient's perception of what is happening with another likely explanation. This is more easily done in a group when other patients may have alternative perspectives about the patient's experience (either of the therapist or someone else in the group), rather than in individual therapy when the contrast is only between that of the patient and the therapist.

The principle: in order to harness the transference successfully, and to stimulate mentalizing rather than defensiveness, the therapist must link selected aspects of the treatment situation to both the current mental state and the underlying affect of the patient while retaining the mentalizing stance of "not knowing".

The complaining patient, continued

We eventually established that the patient felt that people throughout his life had failed to understand how misunderstood he felt as a person. He was seen by others as someone who could acquit himself well and who needed little support. This hurt had turned to bitterness over time and, currently, he was sensitive to any suggestion that he had some capabilities. Recognition of some of his abilities, such as his academic prowess, was not a compliment but rather evidence that his difficulties were not being taken seriously.

THERAPIST: Perhaps you had already decided in your mind before you arrived that I was going to be another person who would not realize that you had problems that needed to be taken seriously.

PATIENT: It did occur to me that you would be the same sort as the other lot because you work for the same hospital – so why should you be any different?

THERAPIST: I can see that, if it's your experience over a long time, it's easy to assume that it's going to happen again. But it seems that everyone has become a misunderstander of you and what is wrong.

PATIENT: I cannot think of anyone who has understood.

THERAPIST: You seem so certain that no one can, it's almost that you have to have it so. I wonder how it would have to be for you to feel that someone did understand?

PATIENT: They'd have to be like me, I suppose.

THERAPIST: Not have their own thoughts and feelings or even different ideas?

PATIENT: The only person who has come near to it was someone in an abuse group who seemed to think just what I thought and had all the same sort of experience. I got close to her but it all went wrong.

THERAPIST: Perhaps you end up having to have it that no one will understand so that you can keep your distance, and now you want to make sure that I can't do anything so that it goes wrong before you feel anything.

PATIENT: What are we going to do in all the sessions that we have? I've talked about everything already. I don't want to sit here saying nothing. If that happens, I'll end up feeling I'm supposed to be all right and everyone thinks that I'm just getting on with things and don't need anything. But I do.

In this transcript, the therapist is attempting to stimulate the patient to think further about the motives underlying his current experience of being misunderstood. He does not focus on all the previous experiences of being misunderstood, which might only serve to invalidate the patient's current experience; rather, he emphasizes possible underlying unconscious motives for seeing him in a schematic way. To some extent it worked. The rest of the session focused on the patient's uncertainty about the level of trust he was able to develop in others and how that uncertainty forced him to keep a distance from others including the therapist.

CONCLUSIONS

Although we have merely presented a range of mentalizing techniques for illustrative purposes, the principal aims are always the same: to reinstate mentalizing at the point at which it is lost, to stabilize mentalizing in the context of an attachment relationship, to minimize the likelihood of adverse effects, and to allow patients to discover themselves and others through a mind considering a mind. Careful focus on the patient's current state of mind will achieve these aims. As one patient said,

> Before I did all this it never even occurred to me that what I did or thought had any effect on anyone else. Sometimes I still think that life was better, because sometimes I don't like what other people think. But it does make life more interesting.

REFERENCES

Bartels, A. & Zeki, S. (2004). The neural correlates of maternal and romantic love. *Neuroimage*, *21*, 1155–1166.

Bateman, A. (2004). Mentalization based treatment of borderline personality disorder. *Journal of Personality Disorders*, *18*, 35–50.

Bateman, A. & Fonagy, P. (1999). The effectiveness of partial hospitalization in the treatment of borderline personality disorder – a randomised controlled trial. *American Journal of Psychiatry*, *156*, 1563–1569.

Bateman, A. W. & Fonagy, P. (2001). Treatment of borderline personality disorder with psychoanalytically oriented partial hospitalization: an 18-month follow-up. *American Journal of Psychiatry*, *158*, 36–42.

Bateman, A. W. & Fonagy, P. (2004). *Psychotherapy for Borderline Personality Disorder: Mentalization-Based Treatment*. Oxford, England: Oxford University Press.

Bateman, A. W. & Tyrer, P. (2004). Psychological treatment for personality disorders. *Advances in Psychiatric Treatment*, *10*, 378–388.

Bohus, M., Haaf, B., Simms, T., Limberger M. F., Schmahl, C., Unckel, C., et al. (2004). Effectiveness of inpatient dialectical behavioral therapy for borderline personality disorder: a controlled trial. *Behaviour Research and Therapy*, *42*, 487–499.

Chiesa, M., Fonagy, P., Holmes, J. & Drahorad, C. (2004). Residential versus community treatment of personality disorders: a comparative study of three treatment programs. *American Journal of Psychiatry*, *161*, 1463–1470.

Clarkin, J. F., Levy, K. N., Lenzenweger, M. F. & Kernberg, O. F. (2004a) The Personality Disorders Institute/Borderline Personality Disorder Research Foundation randomized control trial for borderline personality disorder: progress report. *Annual Meeting of the Society for Psychotherapy Research*, Rome, Italy.

Clarkin, J. F., Levy, K. N., Lenzenweger, M. F. & Kernberg, O. F. (2004b). The Personality Disorders Institute/Borderline Personality Disorder Research Foundation randomized control trial for borderline personality disorder: rationale, methods, and patient characteristics. *Journal of Personality Disorders*, *18*, 52–72.

Eysenck, H. J. (1952). The effects of psychotherapy: an evaluation. *Journal of Consulting Psychology*, *16*, 319–324.

Fonagy, P. (2002). Understanding of mental states, mother-infant interaction, and the development of the self. In J. Maldonado Duran (ed.) *Infant and toddler mental health: Models of clinical intervention with infants and their families* (pp. 57–74). Washington, DC: American Psychiatric Publishing.

Fonagy, P. & Bateman, A. (2006). Mechanisms of change in mentalization based therapy with BPD. *Journal of Clinical Psychology*. *62*, 411–430.

Fonagy, P., Gergely, G., Jurist, E. L. & Target, M. (2002). *Affect Regulation, Mentalization and the Development of the Self*. New York: Other Press.

Fonagy, P., Target, M., Gergely, G., Allen, J. G. & Bateman, A. (2003). The developmental roots of borderline personality disorder in early attachment relationships: a theory and some evidence. *Psychoanalytic Inquiry*, *23*, 412–458.

Gunderson, J. G. (1996). The borderline patient's intolerance of aloneness: Insecure attachments and therapist availability. *American Journal of Psychiatry*, *153*, 752–758.

Gunderson, J. G., Bender, D., Sanislow, C., Yen S., Bame Rettew J., Dolan-Sewell R., et al. (2003). Plausibility and possible determinants of sudden "remissions" in borderline patients. *Psychiatry*, *66*, 111–119.

Keller, M. B., Lavori, P. W., Mueller, T. I., Endicott, J., Coryell, W., Hirschfeld, R. M., et al. (1992). Time to recovery, chronicity, and levels of psychopathology in major depression: a 5-year prospective follow-up of 431 subjects. *Archives of General Psychiatry*, *49*, 809–816.

Lambert, M., Bergin, A. E. & Garfield, S. (2004). Introduction and historical overview. In M. Lambert (ed.), *Bergin and Garfield's Handbook of Psychotherapy and Behavior Change* (pp. 3–15). New York: John Wiley & Sons, Inc.

Lieb, K., Zanarini, M. C., Schmahl, C., Linehan, M. M. & Bohus, M. (2004). Borderline personality disorder. *Lancet*, *364*, 453–461.

Linehan, M. M., Armstrong, H. E., Suarez, A., Allmon, D. & Heard, H. L. (1991). Cognitive-behavioural treatment of chronically parasuicidal borderline patients. *Archives of General Psychiatry*, *48*, 1060–1064.

Linehan, M. M., Comptois, K. A., Murray, A. M., Brown, M. Z., Gallop, R. J., Heard, H. L., Korslund, K. E., Tutek, D. A., Reynolds, S. K., Lindenboim, M. S. (in press). Two-year randomized trial and follow-up of dialectical behavioural therapy versus therapy by experts for suicidal behaviors and borderline personality disorder. *Archives of General Psychiatry*.

Paris, J. (2004). Is hospitalization useful for suicidal patients with borderline personality disorder? *Journal of Personality Disorders*, *18*, 240–247.

Scheel, K. (2000). The empirical basis of dialectical behavior therapy: summary, critique, and implications. *Clinical Psychology Science and Practice*, *7*, 68–86.

Shea, M. T., Stout, R. L., Yen, S., Pagano, M. E., Skodol, A. E., Morey, L. C. et al. (2004). Associations in the course of personality disorders and Axis I disorders over time. *Journal of Abnormal Psychology*, *113*, 499–508.

Stone, M. H. (1990). *The Fate of Borderline Patients: Successful Outcome and Psychiatric Practice*. New York: Guilford Press.

Tyrer, P. & Bateman, A. (2004). Drug treatments for personality disorders. *Advances in Psychiatric Treatment*, *10*, 389–398.

Verheul, R., Van Den Bosch, L. M., Koeter, M. W., De Ridder, M. A., Stijnen, T. & Van Den Brink, W. (2003). Dialectical behaviour therapy for women with borderline personality disorder: 12-month, randomised clinical trial in The Netherlands. *British Journal of Psychiatry*, *182*, 135–140.

Zanarini, M. C., Frankenburg, F. R., Hennen, J. , Reich, D. B. & Silk, K. R. (2004). Axis I comorbidity in patients with borderline personality disorder: 6-year follow-up and prediction of time to remission. *American Journal of Psychiatry*, *161*, 2108–2114.

Zanarini, M. C., Frankenburg, F. R., Hennen, J. & Silk, K. R. (2003). The longitudinal course of borderline psychopathology: 6-year prospective follow-up of the phenomenology of borderline personality disorder. *American Journal of Psychiatry*, *160*, 274–283.

10

SHORT-TERM MENTALIZATION AND RELATIONAL THERAPY (SMART): AN INTEGRATIVE FAMILY THERAPY FOR CHILDREN AND ADOLESCENTS

Pasco Fearon, Mary Target, John Sargent, Laurel L. Williams, Jacqueline McGregor, Efrain Bleiberg, and Peter Fonagy

Short-term mentalizing and relational therapy (SMART) is a relatively new therapeutic endeavor designed to take the theory and clinical base of mentalization and use it to create a framework for doing clinical work with children and adolescents and their families. While many of the techniques, methods of assessment, and interventions that are used in SMART share much in common with other therapeutic approaches, there are certain features that are quite distinct and flow more or less directly from the conceptual framework of mentalization (Bateman & Fonagy, 2004a; Fonagy, Gergely, Jurist & Target, 2002; Fonagy & Target, 1998). Furthermore, we believe that this framework goes beyond the generation of specific therapeutic maneuvers in offering a coherent set of principles and ideas that weave together many of the key elements and insights of other therapeutic approaches. In our view, this capacity for mentalization theory to tie together conceptually a range of different relationship processes – which are arguably critical to therapeutic change – makes this approach attractive.

In this chapter, we will provide an outline of SMART, focusing particularly on the conceptualization of clinical material from a mentalizing perspective and the key therapeutic orientations and interventions that, together, crystallize the essence of the approach. The chapter begins by addressing a number of "why"

Handbook of Mentalization-Based Treatment.   Edited by J. G. Allen and P. Fonagy.
© 2006 John Wiley & Sons, Ltd.

questions about the format of SMART and describes some of the similarities and differences between SMART and other therapies for children and adolescents. Next we give an overview of the clinical model and its procedures. We conclude with a discussion of some of the strengths and limitations of the approach as it currently stands.

FORMAT OF SMART

Why Short-Term?

Unlike the extensive evidence base concerning the value of short-term treatments for adult psychological problems (Roth & Fonagy, 2005), the extent to which a short-term focus might be more beneficial for children and adolescents is less clear-cut. Thus, when developing SMART, there was less of a clear steer from the evidence base regarding the optimal length for an effective therapy. Certainly, cognitive behavioral therapy (CBT) for anxiety and depression, which is generally short-term, has been most comprehensively evaluated and appears to be effective to a considerable degree (Fonagy, Target, Cottrell, Phillips & Kurtz, 2002; Kazdin, 2003). Thus, there is certainly reason to believe that effective psychological intervention can be undertaken within a relatively short-term circumscribed frame. Nevertheless, an explicit aim of SMART was to produce a relatively generic child and adolescent mental health intervention that had the capacity to be helpful for a wide range of presenting problems in a wide range of clinical contexts. The often waxing and waning pattern of childhood psychological problems could be taken to indicate that longer-term work would be needed in many if not most cases. Furthermore, the reality of much of everyday clinical practice is that referred cases are typically complex and involve a conjunction of multiple psychosocial problems and vulnerabilities. These were the kinds of therapeutic scenarios that SMART was intended to address. However, rather than interpreting these facts to indicate the need for longer treatment, we designed SMART to shift the focus away from solving a (possibly lengthy) list of problems and toward addressing the processes that currently limit family members' capacity to support each other and to find their own solutions to the problems that they face.

The philosophy of SMART is based on the view that, to promote longer-term resilience in a family – particularly in the context of multiple psychological and social problems – directly relieving symptoms may be a less critical therapeutic goal than promoting means of coping, particularly in relation to the quality and supportiveness of family attachment relationships. As such, in addition to the obvious pragmatic benefits of short-term treatment for clinicians and families alike, SMART actively uses a short-term focus to articulate to the family the clinician's belief that they can acquire or rediscover skills that will help family members support each other more effectively and tackle problems in the short and long term. By the end of treatment, then, the aim is not only to offer solutions in relation to the problems identified but also for the family to feel that they are in a position to solve problems themselves and to be better equipped in the future to tackle new ones. Although there is scope for longer-term versions of SMART, the manual in its current incarnation assumes a period of treatment ranging from 6 to 12 sessions.

Why Relational?

Put simply, mentalization refers to the capacity to interpret the behavior of others and oneself in terms of underlying mental states, like feelings, thoughts, beliefs, and desires (Harris, 1992; Wimmer & Perner, 1983). Although these skills are obviously useful for a variety of reasons, they are of paramount importance as the foundation of our capacity for relatedness. Mentalization forms the basis of one's explicit or implicit sense of being connected psychologically with others, of knowing them, of being loved and cared for by them, and of being understood. Mentalization drives the way that people behave toward other people, which, in turn, shapes developing representations of oneself in relationship with others. Arguably, these psychological factors, closely associated with secure attachment, are critical elements in a broad definition of resilience (Egeland, Carlson & Sroufe, 1993; Fonagy, Steele, Steele, Higgitt & Target, 1994; see also Stein, Chapter 16). Thus, mentalization is all about relationships: the reasons people have feelings and thoughts about each other and the two-way links between these feelings and thoughts and their behavior toward each other. Mentalization is relationship-specific: an individual's capacity to mentalize is inadequately assessed outside of the context of specific relationships. It is this interdependence of relationships and mentalizing that forms the backbone of SMART. Practically speaking, SMART focuses on relationship problems and mentalizing solutions. The therapist uses the relationship problems identified by the family as a constant compass for steering the family toward considering how thoughts, feelings, and behavior are connected within the family and how an understanding of them might suggest new and more positive ways of relating.

A further aspect of SMART emphasizes its relational nature: unlike some therapies, but certainly like others, SMART explicitly uses the therapeutic relationship to further develop mentalizing within the family. Although relationship processes (such as the therapeutic alliance) in psychotherapy have been less extensively studied in children and adolescents compared to adults, there is now a significant literature on this topic. A recent meta-analysis (Shirk & Karver, 2003) concluded on the basis of 23 child outcome studies that perceptions of the therapeutic alliance in child and adolescent psychotherapy are consistently, albeit modestly, associated with treatment outcome. This association was rather stronger for children with externalizing behavior problems compared to internalizing ones (Shirk & Karver, 2003). Of course, methodological limitations (particularly the method and scope of measurement) in all these studies mean that they are likely to under-estimate the significance of the therapeutic relationship in treatment outcome. Indeed, many authors have argued that the therapeutic alliance is especially important in child psychotherapy and that it may indeed be the primary vehi-cle for therapeutic change (Freud, 1946; Goldfried, 1998). Nevertheless, not all child and adolescent therapies place the therapeutic relationship at the center of therapeutic process or offer a theoretical and explanatory framework that provides a common home for thinking about these as well as other clinical processes.

By placing relational processes and the interplay between mental states and behavior that mediate them at the heart of the model, SMART provides a natural way to talk about the therapeutic relationship in the same breath as other signif-icant relational processes that the family are concerned about. As we describe in more detail later, this new relationship often provides a unique opportunity for the family to be spontaneously open and curious about mental states in a way that sometimes happens less naturally in connection with more familiar ones. The acquisition of mentalization is based on one person having another's mind in mind. This experience can be initiated, modeled, reinforced, practiced, and generalized from the therapeutic context to the family's everyday interactions.

What Are the Similarities and Differences Between SMART and Other Therapies?

As Kazdin (2003) has pointed out, there are at least 550 apparently different psy-chological therapies used by practitioners working with children and adolescents; hence any commentary on the similarities and differences between SMART and other therapies must be extremely selective. Nevertheless, it is particularly help-ful to think about the connections between SMART and three other general schools because they represent areas of thinking that inspired much of our work on SMART. In particular, SMART was strongly influenced by psycho-dynamic psychotherapy, CBT, and systemic therapy (each of these being areas that at least one of the authors routinely works with).

There are several features of SMART that bear many similarities with – and indeed were directly inspired by – psycho-dynamic theory and practice. Most importantly, like much of psycho-dynamic practice, SMART focuses strongly on drawing attention to, and encouraging thinking about, family members' inner experiences, conflictual feelings, and repetitive patterns of behavior. Further-more, SMART also encourages families to think about the developmental origins of patterns of behavior and thinking, and how early experiences may imbue later ones with important meanings not necessarily recognized by other people. SMART departs from psycho-dynamic practice most clearly in not making use of symbolic interpretation or considering the role of unconscious conflict. Rather,

SMART works with relatively here-and-now psychological content and focuses on the way that behavior can be understood in folk-psychological terms (Harris, 1992) such as beliefs, desires, feelings, and thoughts.

The similarities between SMART and CBT are relatively self-evident. The focus on thought processes as mediators between experience and behavior is the same in both approaches. Furthermore, there are quite a number of therapeutic interventions in SMART that were adapted more or less directly from CBT interventions for children (e.g., Stallard, 2002). However, there are several differences between SMART and CBT. Firstly, SMART does not make reference to cognitive distortions, thinking errors, attentional biases, or schemas (e.g., see Wells, 1997). Secondly, SMART is intrinsically a family therapy in the sense that it is designed for more than one individual. Of course, there are family instantiations of cognitive therapy (e.g., Howard & Kendall, 1996), and in this case the differences between the approaches become smaller. Furthermore, SMART explicitly focuses on interactive processes between two or more members of the family and how mental states make sense of these interactions, for example, "Perhaps X was angry because he didn't like being thought about by Y as childish." "Perhaps X thought Z was intending to be hurtful, so he felt upset and shouted, which made Z think ..." Related to this, while SMART does consider the way that an individual understands his or her own mental states, there is a very strong emphasis on how family members think about each others' thoughts and feelings. Again, modifications to CBT for families, which are less well known, involve similar interactive connections but rather focus on thinking errors and cognitive distortions (Howard & Kendall, 1996). SMART conceptualizes interactive and relational problems between family members exclusively in terms of difficulties with mentalizing, which bring about misapprehensions about the thoughts, feelings, and beliefs of others (or oneself). One straightforward but significant consequence of this difference of emphasis: SMART uses a language about family relationships that is natural and familiar while also being compelling and resonant. To reiterate, a further difference is that SMART makes much greater use of the therapeutic relationship.

It is particularly useful to consider the similarities and differences between SMART and systemic family therapy. There are many thematic similarities and shared values between these two therapeutic approaches, so only a small proportion of these can be discussed here. At the theoretical level, both systemic therapy (excluding social deconstructionist schools) and SMART see the identified child's problem as a manifestation of a poorly functioning family system, albeit in the case of SMART chiefly in the area of failures of mentalization. One major technical component of SMART, which borrows much from systemic family therapy, is the way in which it encourages family members to be curious about what other members of the family might be thinking and feeling. This line of discussion often has a marked resemblance to circular questioning (e.g., "What's it like for Danny, do you think, to hear your mum say that? How might he feel about that?"). In some ways, SMART and systemic family therapy also share a common view about the value of working from people's strengths and the importance of avoiding a pathologizing discourse in therapy (see Pote, Stratton, Cottrell, Shapiro & Boston, 2003). However, it would also be fair to say that SMART does make clear reference to problems within the family and difficulties with mentalizing in a way that some practitioners of systemic family therapy might try to avoid. Like some formulations of systemic family therapy, SMART also seeks to explore family beliefs and to reframe beliefs that appear constraining to the family in a more positive way (Pote et al., 2003). However, SMART does this with an exclusive focus on the nature of mental state processes and how they operate within the family. In that sense, the content of a systemic reframe could be quite different from one used in SMART, although the intention is often similar. Perhaps the most important difference is that, unlike systemic family therapy, SMART uses a model that is articulated fully to the family. Consequently, SMART has a more directive and psycho-educational component, and it encourages families to join the therapist in using the model to understand and improve family relationships. The intention behind SMART is thus that families will learn about the nature of mentalizing, see how it operates in their family, and use what they have learned to tackle current and future relational difficulties.

OVERVIEW OF SMART

Basic Clinical Model

A key starting point in SMART is the conceptual model, that is, the underlying theory or framework that motivates the therapeutic efforts that the clinician and family will embark upon. This model is critical not just for clinicians to understand for their own thinking and planning but also for families to understand so they can think about, practice, internalize, talk about, and make use of the ideas contained in SMART themselves. Consequently, it is essential that the therapist has a firm understanding of this model and can communicate it in a clear, uncomplicated, and compelling way.

There are several key concepts in the SMART mentalizing model. The first concerns the nature of mentalizing itself. Fundamentally, the therapy is based on the assumption that problems in family relationships derive at least in part from the family's difficulties with mentalizing, that is, difficulties in the capacity that all human beings over a certain age have in spontaneously and often intuitively making sense of the actions of themselves and others by reference to mental states such as beliefs, desires, thoughts, and feelings. What this means in practical terms is that the therapist and the family are engaged in a process of trying to understand each other more clearly through observing and discussing the connections between thinking, feeling, and behavior. Of course, this process is challenging because mental states are, by their very nature, opaque; they cannot be "read" directly. Instead, mentalizing requires automatic or conscious attention to, or explicit discussion of, behavior in relation to context, prior history, and the process by which individuals come to have thoughts and feelings about the world. Mentalizing is thus a complex and uncertain facility for a variety of reasons: a person can act according to a belief that is wrong; beliefs arise through complicated interactions among sensory perceptions, memory, and motivation and thus may change for many reasons – perhaps because the environment has changed or because some hidden mental process has occurred; and because beliefs are just representations of reality, people can have very different beliefs and feel very different emotions about apparently similar things. In light of the uncertainties inherent in thinking about mental states in others, a healthy appreciation of the limits of one's knowledge is absolutely central to good mentalizing. Thus, the heart of effective mentalizing is not so much a skill as it is a way of approaching relationships that reflects an expectation that one's own thinking has limits and may be enlightened, enriched, and changed by learning about the mental states of other people. This curious stance is the ultimate foundation of the SMART approach, which the therapist tries to demonstrate and encourage in families experiencing relational difficulties.

A second key component of the model is the idea that stress of various kinds, and the consequent emotional arousal, interferes with mentalizing (Bateman & Fonagy, 2004b; see also Fonagy, Chapter 3). This is a critical element for several reasons. Firstly, it provides a way of communicating to families that their difficulties with mentalizing are understandable within the context of the stressors that they face. Secondly, it provides an extremely important guideline to the therapist about the extent to which she can expect effective mentalizing to take place during sessions (or at home). If someone within the family (or the whole family) is highly emotionally aroused, it can be extremely difficult for them to mentalize, particularly if that mentalizing is of the effortful, conscious variety (as opposed to more immediate or automatic mentalizing). Titrating the focus of the work with this caveat in mind is an extremely important point of practice for the therapist – and it is also useful for the family to think about.

The third key component of the model concerns the interplay between mentalizing, stress, and behavior and how these can lead to interactions among family members that are unsupportive and unsatisfactory. This process usually can be understood as a kind of vicious cycle, as illustrated in Figure 10.1.

The general principle outlined in Figure 10.1 is that non-mentalizing makes the behavior of others or oneself hard to comprehend, which undermines one's capacity to formulate an effective (i.e., supportive and helpful) response. Stressful, emotion-laden interactions leave the person in question without a psychological means of influencing the other; instead they revert to attempting to control the other's behavior (or their own) as a kind of second-line strategy. Controlling behavior leads to interactions that are perceived by the other as hostile,

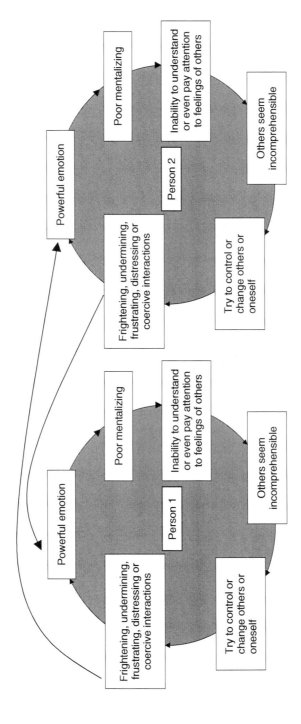

Figure 10.1 Cycles of non-mentalizing interactions

unsupportive, or coercive (to name a few possibilities); this, in turn, triggers strong feelings in the other person. These evoked feelings then prevent the other from mentalizing effectively, and a similar negative cycle is set in motion and sustained. Often, these non-mentalizing interactions are highly repetitive and predictable for all concerned; they become part of the fabric of their relationship and their expectations for each other. In time, these interactions may become so familiar and over-learned that non-mentalizing occurs without a triggering emotion to initiate it.

With these principles in mind, the clinician is charged with the task of making the model seem relevant so that the family can see, more or less rapidly, why SMART might be a useful and sensible treatment. The therapist must do this both explicitly and implicitly. Explicitly, the therapist strives to explain the ideas contained in mentalizing theory as clearly and plainly as possible, using important examples initially provided by the family as well as examples subsequently arising during sessions. Implicitly, the therapist strives to demonstrate mentalizing to the family by showing an interest and curiosity about mental states (and sometimes quite deliberately paying less attention to non-mentalizing dialogue), a respect for and consideration of individuals' mental states (e.g., "I noticed, Sally, that you have been quite quiet, and I was wondering what you were thinking about"), and excitement about discovering mental state processes could be very helpful for finding new solutions to problems with which the family is grappling.

Assessment and Case Conceptualization

Just like any other therapy, assessment in SMART is an ongoing and evolving process. Indeed, to a significant extent, understanding mentalizing and associated relational problems is presumed to be a major part of the mechanism of change in SMART. Nevertheless, the early sessions typically are dedicated primarily to developing a formulation or working hypothesis about how mentalizing does and does not work effectively within the family and how this might relate to salient relational processes (strengths and weaknesses). Thus, in practice, the structure of assessment in SMART is essentially generic, addressing the following issues:

- the nature and emergence of the referred problem(s) including detailed account of recent example(s);
- contextual characteristics and fluctuations of the problem(s);
- the referred child's or the family's attempts to deal with it;
- each family member's understanding of the problem(s);
- the effects of the symptoms on family and others; and
- outside help sought and previous treatment(s).

In the course of eliciting the family's story in this way, the therapist pays particular attention to indicators of mentalizing (described in more detail below) and probes for mentalizing from members of the family with questions such as

- What do you think your child might have been thinking when he/she became scared/upset/angry/argumentative (as appropriate)?
- What were you thinking during the situation? How did you feel?
- Why do you think your child's reaction was different or similar to yours?
- What do you think your husband/wife/sibling might have been thinking? How did he/she feel? Can you comment on differences or similarities?
- What do you think your child might have thought you felt about it? How might this have made him/her feel?
- Would you have wanted this scenario to work out differently? In what ways?

In this way, the therapist is alert to spontaneous mentalizing (or its absence) that takes place during the assessment process, and the therapist pushes members of the family to mentalize as well, so that the therapist can be reasonably sure that any lack of mentalizing was not simply a result of the way family members implicitly interpreted what the therapist was looking for. It follows from our model of mentalization that the questions aimed at identifying the relational problems and difficulties within the family can be illuminated with the same kind of questioning that may be most useful in identifying mentalizing problems. The therapist aims to assess mentalizing within family dyads rather than individuals. Doing this systematically is a rather laborious process; thus, in the process of creating a picture of the nature of mentalization within a family system, our manual recommends observing spontaneous discourse alongside asking specific questions that require mentalizing.

Across the course of the assessment, the therapist is aiming eventually to arrive at some general understanding of the strengths and weaknesses in mentalizing in the family, the nature of the main relational problems, and how these might be connected. Once the therapist is reasonably confident in this set of working hypotheses, he or she shares them with the family in order to get feedback and to elicit their agreement that work based along those lines would be a useful direction for them to pursue.

Types and Indications of Mentalizing and Non-Mentalizing

When SMART therapists start piecing together a working hypothesis about mentalizing within the family, they begin by considering areas of strength. In particular, therapists are on the lookout for the use of mentalizing language that is tentative, respectful, and reflects appropriate care not to overreach the limits of one's knowledge about the mental states of others. Another positive indicator of mentalizing is when family members show curiosity about other people's perspectives and adopt an expectant attitude that their understanding will be elaborated or expanded by what is on other people's minds. More indirectly, there are several indications of mentalizing: family members are flexible in their thinking and do not get stuck in one point of view; family members are playful and use gentle humor; problem solving is undertaken in a give-and-take fashion that bears in mind others' viewpoints; two-way communication largely consists of each individual describing their experience (e.g., "This is what I think or feel when such and such happens"); family members demonstrate responsibility and "ownership" over their behavior rather than conveying a sense that their behavior "happens" to them; and family members behave in a way that implicitly takes account of how other people might be thinking or feeling.

For each person in the family, the therapist tries to consider the extent to which signs of positive mentalizing (or approximations thereof) have been observed. This information is extremely important because it may indicate areas of strength upon which they can build during the therapy. It is also very important because it provides an opportunity for the therapist to give each family member positive feedback, which is ideally related to mentalizing (but any positive feedback is better than none).

Next, the therapist must also consider indicators of non-mentalizing that were apparent during the assessment process. There are several ways in which mentalization may fail, which in turn generate, maintain, reinforce, or exacerbate relational difficulties. We distinguish four general types of failure in mentalizing: concrete understanding, context-specific loss of mentalizing, pseudo-mentalizing, and misuse of mentalizing.

Concrete understanding refers to a general failure to appreciate the feelings of oneself or others as well as the relationships among thoughts, feelings, and actions. The typical features of concrete understanding are:

Difficulty recognizing or paying attention to emotions.

- Difficulty observing one's own thoughts and feelings, identifying changes in them, or recognizing their representational nature (they are not absolute reflections of reality).
- Understanding behavior in "concrete" terms, for example, in terms of external circumstances or other behaviors rather than in terms of internal states (e.g., "We had a fight because it was hot") rather than recognizing the thoughts, feelings, and behaviors that mediated any possible contextual influences like temperature.
- Excessive preoccupation with detail (who did what, when, exactly what time it was), with external agents (the school, the neighborhood), or with rules or prescriptions (e.g., this is how Johnny should behave because I say so, or because that's how children should behave).

- Not recognizing the impact of one's thoughts, feelings, and actions on others.
- Not being able to be flexible and to play with different ways of thinking about situations.
- Acting without thinking or avoidance of thinking.

A parent–child relationship may be described as concrete if the parent reacts to behavior without being aware of the feelings or wishes that are motivating the child's behavior. Thus the parent might be angry, over-reactive, blaming, and prescriptive. The child's mental states are obscured, not noticed, or treated as unimportant; or they are frankly mysterious to the parent. This form of failure may also happen when there is an identified problem (e.g., attention deficit hyperactivity disorder (ADHD) or a physical condition) and either the condition is ignored or every behavior is explained on the basis of it.

This concretization also can arise from passive resignation or withdrawal of awareness from the child's mental states over a period of time on the part of the parent. Thus, as in the previous examples, the parent's approach has become unthinking, concrete, and behavioral. The parent may be depressed or overwhelmed and too tired to focus on the child unless situations escalate to a point when the parent falls back on a stock response without trying to understand the psychological state of the child.

Context-specific loss of mentalizing is a situationally specific loss, typically associated with immediate stress. Given sufficient pressure, most people can lose their capacity to think about thoughts and feelings in others. Sometimes, dramatic temporary failures of mentalization can arise during emotionally intense interchanges or in relation to particular thoughts and feelings. Under such circumstances, grossly inaccurate and malevolent feelings can be attributed to the other person (e.g., in an argument, thinking that someone is deliberately trying to upset you, ruin your plans, or mess up your life). In some individuals or relationships, or in some family systems, relatively ordinary stresses appear to be able to trigger this kind of catastrophic non-mentalizing reaction. In the heat of an argument, the parent might become convinced, for example, that the child is deliberately provoking him or her.

In some cases, specific non-mentalizing reactions are more enduring and there is a context-specific ignoring of the child's state of mind. The parent is thus able to be responsive and attuned to the child at some times but not others. Hence, for reasons probably unknown to the child, the parent is highly variable in attention and interest. A parent may be preoccupied at certain times with work crises, or find it difficult to think about one child's feelings when another is "acting up," or have a "blind spot" around a particular feeling or conflict.

Pseudo-mentalizing refers to a type of difficulty where there is apparent thoughtfulness that lacks some essential features of genuine mentalizing. For example, there may be a tendency to express absolute certainty about the thoughts and feelings of the other without recognition of the inherent uncertainty about knowing someone else's mind or appreciation for what it is like to have someone else define what is on one's own mind. Pseudo-mentalizing is often highly selective or self-serving. Thoughts and feelings in others or the self are recognized only as long as these are consistent with the individual's self-interest or preferences. The most important marker of pseudo-mentalizing, however, lies in the limited implications the individual draws from an apparently mentalistic understanding. Genuine mentalizing will always direct action. Pseudo-mentalizing either appears independent of the individual's actions (i.e., has no effect) or follows actions and serves as justification rather than a part of planning.

Pseudo-mentalizing takes four forms.

(1) Preserving a developmentally early view: in these instances the parent or child continues to think of the other person from an earlier perspective. For example, a parent may not be able to consider his or her adolescent's burgeoning sexuality or need for autonomy.

(2) Intrusive mentalizing: in this case the separateness or opaqueness of minds is not respected within a family; someone thinks they know what another person thinks or feels. More perniciously, sometimes elements of the parent's image of the child's mind might be correct, but the subtle differences between what the parent expresses and what the child is likely to feel reveal that they are not in touch with the thoughts and feelings of the child. In any case, they are unaware of the impact that being told what he or she thinks and feels can have on the child.

(3) Overactive, inaccurate mentalizing: in this scenario parents often invest a lot of energy in thinking or talking about how people in the family think or feel, but this has little or no relationship to the other person's reality. There can be an idealization of "insight" for its own sake or reliance on psychobabble.

(4) Completely inaccurate attributions: at the more extreme end of pseudo-mentalizing, consistently bizarre attributions may be made about another's thinking (e.g., "You are trying to drive me crazy," "Your grandma is in league with your father against us"), or objective realities will be denied (e.g., "You provoked me," "You fell down the stairs – I never hit you") or the child's feelings (e.g., "You enjoyed it when I touched you like that," "You don't care about whether your dad is here or not," "You don't care about me," "You would be glad if I was dead").

These examples, of course, are very similar to the kinds of breakdowns in mentalizing that may occur at peak stress during an argument but, in this case, the hostile pseudo-mentalizing is chronic and generalized. In these cases children may be so traumatized by parents' misperceptions, and the threat that parents' mental state represents to their welfare, that they will seek to inhibit their own capacity to mentalize altogether.

Misuse of mentalizing refers to instances where the mental states attributed by a person to others (or less commonly to themselves) appear accurate, but the use to which this knowledge is put is malevolent, undermining, and hurtful. Such misuses of mentalizing may involve parents' using their understanding of a child's distress as ammunition in a parental conflict, or using their understanding deliberately to shame or belittle a child in front of others.

Once therapists have a good understanding of areas of strength and weakness for each family member, their next task is to select amongst these in terms of their relevance and amenability to intervention. Most importantly, therapists need to develop a hypothesis about how the mentalizing difficulties they have identified are implicated in the main relational problems presented by the family. Ideally, this can be understood in quite interactive terms along the lines shown in Figure 10.1. Thus therapists should be able to arrive at a fairly clear picture of strengths in mentalizing, difficulties with mentalizing, connections between mentalizing problems and problematic interactions, and how these mentalizing problems maintain and contribute to relational difficulties. Armed with these hypotheses (which will evolve and change), therapists are ready to plan and conduct SMART. The therapeutic basis of SMART is focused on improving mentalizing where there are difficulties and working with the family on the main relational difficulties using mentalizing techniques to highlight their role in the "status quo" and to open up new possibilities for change.

Core Therapeutic Approach

During the assessment and intervention stages of SMART therapy, specific core SMART maneuvers are the primary skills needed to flesh out the therapist's understanding of the mentalizing capabilities within the family and to assist the family in improving those capabilities. As we noted earlier, the heart of good mentalizing is not so much the capacity to always accurately read one's own or another's inner states, but rather a way of approaching relationships that reflects an expectation that one's own thinking and feeling may be enlightened, enriched, and changed by learning about the mental states of other people. In this respect, mentalizing is more like an attitude than a skill, an attitude that is inquiring and respectful of other people's mental states, aware of the limits of one's knowledge of others, and reflects a view that understanding the feelings of others is important for maintaining healthy and mutually rewarding relationships. This stance is the ultimate foundation of the approach that the therapist tries to demonstrate and thereby encourage. The therapist thus aims to be highly respectful of the genuine feelings of others (when other family members may well disavow them in themselves or others), inquisitive about what those feelings might be as well as what thoughts, meanings, and related experiences are attached to them. The therapist always strives to act under the assumption that every individual's actions within the family are entirely understandable if the feeling that motivates them is fully recognized. The therapist works hard to communicate this mentalizing stance to the family as a whole. By doing so, and through the core mentalizing techniques, the therapist aims to help the family make sense of what feelings are experienced by each family member, what thoughts are connected with these feelings, how these feelings are communicated within the family, and ways in which miscommunication or misunderstanding (or lack of understanding) of these feelings leads to interactions that maintain family problems.

The SMART therapist must strike a careful balance between allowing the family to interact in the ways they normally would and being directive and intervening at critical moments. On the one hand, it is important to let the family inter-act fairly naturally, because the therapist needs to understand fully the way the family typically interacts, and the therapist and family need to share a set of common experiences of relevant family processes that accurately characterize the key problems that all can refer to and discuss meaningfully. On the other hand, non-mentalizing interactions never produce significant changes in family interactions; so simply allowing these interactions to occur is not therapeutic in any meaningful sense. When the therapist has a clear idea of the nature of the mentalizing difficulties and has a good example of a connected relational prob-lem or interaction to work with, the therapist intervenes to shift attention away from non-mentalizing material and introduces a mentalizing intervention. As the therapist models mentalizing while facilitating its emergence within the family, it is important that he or she studiously avoids undermining mentalizing by adopt-ing the "know-it-all" expert role and, even worse, modeling non-mentalizing by declaring with certainty what anyone is feeling or thinking. Maintaining an inquisitive stance might be one of the hardest aspects of SMART practice, particularly for experienced therapists whose model offers them clear probable descriptions about the states of mind of clients – including unconscious motives; yet, in line with the manual, the therapist must resist the temptation to explore feelings and areas of thinking that are far beyond the conscious experience of the client.

Throughout SMART, the therapist is aiming to work toward a shared under-standing of mentalizing within the family; when introducing an intervention, the therapist tries to provide a mentalizing "context" or explanation (which will be connected with the shared formulation). For example, after observing a non-mentalizing interaction, the therapist might say to the family:

> It seems that when Sally does w, David, you find it very hard to understand what exactly she is feeling and why, and without this understanding her behavior does not seem to make sense. This then makes you feel really x, and so you do y. Likewise, Sally, when David then does this, it seems like you find it hard to understand exactly what he is feeling that makes him behave like this. And then that makes you feel z and it goes round in circles. Everyone seems to be finding it hard to understand where everyone else is coming from.

This kind of rationale illustrates how mentalizing difficulties are implicated in a relational or interactive difficulty and provides a rationale for introducing one of the mentalizing interventions. Although there are a large (and growing) number of possible ways of intervening to promote mentalizing, we have identified seven that we consider central to SMART. Their centrality reflects the fact that the therapist will use these interventions very frequently as they form the fabric into which other more discrete interventions (like mentalizing games) are woven. The seven core SMART interventions are:

(1) *Identifying, highlighting, and praising examples of skillful mentalizing.* Families more or less frequently demonstrate mentalizing in sessions. When they do, particularly if the example is relevant to the way the therapist understands mentalizing to be problematic in the family, the therapist communicates to the family how interested she is in this, how impressive and significant she thinks it is, and why. The therapist may, for example, intervene and pause a conversation, then draw the family's attention to the mentalizing that was observed. The therapist may say, "Sorry, I just want to come back to something here because I think it might be really important. Joanna, I noticed a moment ago you said to Johnny x and it seemed like he really noticed and liked how interested you were in his point of view ..."

(2) *Sharing and provoking curiosity.* As noted above, the most important feature of a mentalizing stance is respect for and curiosity about the minds of others and an attitude that learning about how others are thinking and feeling will be enlightening. The therapist thus models this attitude as frequently as possible, by asking about how others are feeling or what they might be thinking – and by not making assumptions about either of these. Thus, the therapist may say, "This is interesting. I wonder, Sally, what it feels like for you when your dad does x?" "Let me see if I got this right: are you saying that when your dad does x that makes you feel y, and you think to yourself z?" If the therapist wants to share a hypothesis about what someone might be feeling, he or she qualifies this by saying, "I'm not sure I've got this right, so please tell me, but I was wondering whether Sally might feel x. Is that right, Sally?"

(3) *Pausing and searching.* During a non-mentalizing interaction, the therapist stops the interaction and deliberately slows it down, noting that he or she is very interested in exactly what each person is feeling as this interaction unfolds. The therapist then lets the interaction slowly move forward, checking with each person exactly what the action of the other person makes them feel and what it makes them think. In other words, the therapist stops a non-mentalizing interaction and tries to help the family piece together the sequence of mental states, emotions, and behaviors that occurred during that interaction, along the lines of the interactive model in Figure 10.1. Having done so, the therapist sometimes follows up by asking the relevant parties to try to empathize with one person's feelings, perhaps by asking them to recall a time when they felt similarly or by asking them to role-play the

other person. All attempts by family members to add typical non-mentalizing narratives considered next are actively limited by the therapist.

(4) *Identifying preferred non-mentalizing narratives.* When non-mentalizing occurs, a person often has a characteristic style of non-mentalistic thinking and speaking that they use to try to explain another person's (or their own) behavior. If this process appears to be blocking a shift to a more mentalizing perspective, the therapist highlights that, for example, the family seems to get in quite similar repetitive conversations that don't seem to get anywhere. This observation may form the basis for a move to a mentalizing intervention and provides a shared reference, so that later on the therapist is able to say, "It feels a bit like we're getting into one of those round-in-circles conversations again" (or whatever label is most fitting). When done with gentle humor this approach can be a very effective way of drawing attention to, and hopefully changing, non-mentalizing interactions.

(5) *Identifying and labeling hidden feeling states.* During family discussions of a problem-relevant situation, the therapist actively elicits a feeling state or, if one is mentioned but not dwelt on, the therapist highlights the importance of this feeling. The therapist actively encourages family members to label their feelings and, when they have done so, to reflect on what that must be like for them. In addition, the therapist strives to search for subtleties in emotional experience that are not routinely expressed. For example, the therapist might say, "You say you were feeling angry; were there any other feelings you had at that time?" Often, simple probes like this will elicit a richer, and less hostile or hurtful, picture of someone's thinking. Ultimately, the therapist aims to learn from the person in question what would need to happen to allow them to not feel this way and, more specifically, how this person would need other members of the family to think about them such that they would help them feel differently.

(6) *Using hypotheticals and counterfactuals.* The therapist aims to activate the family's capacity to think about states of mind. This is tantamount to increasing the level of abstraction at which the family functions, particularly at times of stress. A relatively easy way of achieving this goal is using hypotheticals, or "What if?" questions, often building on the client's implicit assumptions. An extension of this technique is asking clients to conceive of states of mind diametrically opposed to the assertion they have made. For example, the therapist might say, "You said that you expect David would leave if you said x. What if he did not leave? What do you think might have been going on in his mind if he decided not to leave?"

(7) *Therapist's making use of self.* Therapists ask families to focus and express feelings that have triggered non-mentalizing responses. Therapists encourage family member to be direct, honest, and vulnerable with each other. Therapists use their own experience of current interactions to communicate openly, clearly, and honestly about their own mental states and the way these are affected by the behavior and interactions of others. This requires tremendous trust and courage of all participants. The therapist's willingness

to enter intense, personal conversations bringing his or her own honesty, conviction, commitment, and vulnerability greatly affects the outcome by modeling the integrity that the therapist attempts to promote in all family members.

These seven core techniques are used repeatedly throughout SMART when trying to raise the general level of mentalizing in the family and when attempting to grapple with a specific relational or interactive problem highlighted by the case formulation. In addition to these techniques, the therapist also makes use of between-session tasks and mentalizing games.

Between-Session Tasks and Mentalizing Games

While the therapist engages with non-mentalizing interactions that occur during sessions (or that are reported by the family between sessions) using the seven core approaches described earlier, there are also circumstances where a change of tack is required: using structured activities and games. First, depending on the style of the family, direct engagement with a relational problem can be quite threatening, so illustrating mentalizing principles and processes using less direct means can be a very helpful starting point. Second, commonly, a highly repetitive, over-learned non-mentalizing interaction proves hard to shift, either because family members become too emotionally aroused too quickly, or because perspectives and reactions have become too rigid. Rather than continuing to pursue the same fruitless avenue, the SMART therapist actively changes gear and introduces a game or structured task, which represents a novel experience for the family where routine ways of responding and thinking are less automatically elicited. Finally, structured games and tasks represent an effective way of encouraging further thinking about mentalization between sessions; these activities bring families together and engage them in talking and relating in new ways. These mentalizing games and tasks are similar to the kinds of activities employed in other therapies, but the focus is exclusively on what they illustrate about how thoughts, feelings, and behavior are connected within the family.

Space does not permit presenting all these activities; instead we will describe two to give a flavor of how they work. The first game, which can be used in session or out, is called the "feeling hot-potato" game. The game begins with the child picking a card upon which is written a basic emotion (scared, angry/mad, happy, and sad). For each card, the child has to model what she does when she feels this emotion (in the style of "charades"), either by pulling a face or acting it out (e.g., stomping around or curling the lower lip). The child is told that all the adults have to remember what he or she has acted out, and they are given one chance each to practice with help and feedback from the child. Then, once all the emotions have been done, the game really starts. The child is given a ball and told to throw it to someone in the room while calling out an emotion. The person catching the ball has to reproduce the action that the child demonstrated for this emotion, before he/she can pass the ball on to the next person. When passing on the ball he/she calls out another emotion, which the next person has to reproduce, and so on. At each throw of the ball, the child judges whether the action demonstrated by the adult was good enough before the ball can be passed on. The game can be repeated in relation to the emotional reactions of other members of the family. This simple activity is designed to do several things. First, as noted above, it is a change of pace or atmosphere (toward being more fun) that children and parents often appreciate. It also represents an opportunity for parents and children to actively concentrate on, show an interest in, and have fun with how everyone behaves when they feel different emotions within the family.

A second game that focuses on perspective taking is called the "trading places" game. Parents play at being their children and imagining how they might think and feel in various situations (and the therapist uses movie examples like "Freaky Friday" or "Big" to explain the premise to the children). The child then identifies a situation for the parents to be in (e.g., going to a school function, doing chores, or facing bedtime) and the parents think themselves into the role of their children, particularly emphasizing their thoughts and emotions. The child then listens to the parents struggle with the task and gives feedback (e.g., "warmer" or "colder"). The child is encouraged to help the parents out by telling them what to think, say, and feel, which the parents must copy. This game is often fun and provides valuable opportunities for parents to recognize and think about what they do not know about how their children think and feel. It also gives children a chance to be in a position of authority regarding their thoughts and feelings, and it illustrates to them how their parents can be open to learning new things about them.

Throughout treatment, the SMART therapist uses structured tasks and games strategically, in relation to the emerging conceptualization of the case. Between-session activities are used routinely so that the family continues to think about mentalization outside the sessions, so that the rate of progress of the work is maximized.

CONCLUDING REMARKS

SMART is a new treatment that, we believe, shows promise as a relatively generic mental health treatment for children and adolescents. Several aspects of SMART make it attractive to mental health professionals who work with children and adolescents. SMART explicitly works from a model based in attachment theory, and hence provides a framework for addressing the role of attachment relationships in children's emotional and behavioral problems. The wealth of evidence that most if not all psychological problems involve disturbed family relationships and insecure attachment relationships strongly suggests that a therapy that places these kinds of processes at the center of the endeavor should have considerable potential. SMART is a generic therapy, and training in SMART assists in the acquisition of generic therapeutic skills (see Williams and colleagues, Chapter 11). Moreover, it is possible that the acquisition of mentalization is an active component of a number of therapies; thus focusing on this aspect of family functioning in a sense provides a distillation of a number of clinical intervention models.

Of course, as we noted earlier, a number of other therapies also target relational process. We described some of the similarities and differences between SMART and other therapies, but perhaps the clearest relates to the capacity of mentalizing theory to tie together interventions and ideas from a wide range of therapeutic approaches into a coherent set that can be explicitly shared with families and taught as lifelong skills. Part of the philosophy of SMART is about helping families acquire conceptual tools for thinking about how members of the family relate to each other, how these relationships influence each other, and the vital role that mental states play in making sense of these relationship processes. In that sense, SMART implicitly communicates to the family a sense of optimism that the family can cope on its own with some brief support and that they will learn skills and ways of thinking that may be useful to them in many situations and periods of their lives beyond the problem that brought them to treatment at this point in time. Furthermore, SMART provides a natural way to talk about and make use of the therapeutic relationship, and it provides a clear account of why therapeutic alliance factors are so important in treatment outcome (Shirk & Karver, 2003).

While we believe that SMART has a lot of potential, formal evaluation of its efficacy has yet to be completed, and there is a great deal of work to be done in terms of delineating the range of appropriate targets (e.g., types of problem and age of child). Currently, a manualized version of SMART has been used with children as young as seven and up to late adolescence. Generally speaking, we have noted that, with younger children, relatively limited mental state understanding significantly restricts the way in which the therapist can operate (i.e., having to place greater emphasis on promoting parental mentalizing); currently, we do not treat children less than seven years of age. SMART also has been used with a variety of different clinical presentations, including oppositional behavior, aggression, anxiety, and depression. Nevertheless, it is currently unclear which presentations would not be appropriate cases for SMART. We certainly have found that more complex, high-risk cases necessarily require the SMART therapist to work closely with other colleagues and either to step out of model when necessary (e.g., when assessing risk) or to bring in other colleagues to take up aspects of the case that do not specifically fall within the remit of SMART.

A further matter of debate concerns who should be invited to attend treatment sessions. Our strong inclination, given the relational focus of SMART, has always been to make strenuous efforts to invite all relevant family members, even when parents have separated. However, we acknowledge that this aspiration can be very challenging, particularly in non-specialist centers serving highly disadvantaged populations. The extent to which the model might need to be adapted in cases where some family members are unwilling or unable to attend treatment (and the possible value of inviting others to treatment at later stages) are currently issues under discussion. A further area for development in SMART is the creation of systematic methods for assessing treatment integrity. While the therapy is manualized, we do not currently have objective measures of therapist adherence (although work on this is underway).

Evaluations and further treatment development efforts are currently underway in the United States (Houston, Texas) and the United Kingdom (London). We hope this new mentalization-based treatment will be an effective addition to the arsenal of therapies available to clinicians working with distressed young people and their families.

REFERENCES

Bateman, A. W. & Fonagy, P. (2004a). Mentalization-based treatment of BPD. *Journal of Personality Disorders, 18*, 36–51.

Bateman, A. W. & Fonagy, P. (2004b). *Psychotherapy for Borderline Personality Disorder: Mentalization Based Treatment.* Oxford, England: Oxford University Press.

Egeland, B., Carlson, E. & Sroufe, L. A. (1993). Resilience as a process. *Development and Psychopathology, 5*, 517–527.

Fonagy, P. & Target, M. (1998). Mentalization and the changing aims of child psychoanalysis. *Psychoanalytic Dialogues, 8*, 87–114.

Fonagy, P., Gergely, G., Jurist, E. L. & Target, M. (2002). *Affect Regulation, Mentalization, and the Development of the Self.* New York: Other Press.

Fonagy, P., Steele, M., Steele, H., Higgitt, A. & Target, M. (1994). The Emmanuel Miller Memorial Lecture 1992: the theory and practice of resilience. *Journal of Child Psychology and Psychiatry, and Allied Disciplines, 35*, 231–257.

Fonagy, P., Target, M., Cottrell, D., Phillips, J. & Kurtz, Z. (2002). *What Works for Whom? A Critical Review of Treatments for Children and Adolescents.* New York: Guilford Press.

Freud, A. (1946). *The Psychoanalytic Treatment of Children.* London: Imago Publishing.

Goldfried, M. R. (1998). A comment on psychotherapy integration in the treatment of children. *Journal of Clinical Child Psychology, 27*, 49–53.

Harris, P. L. (1992). From simulation to folk psychology: the case for development. *Mind and Language, 7*, 120–144.

Howard, B. L. & Kendall, P. C. (1996). Cognitive-behavioral family therapy for anxiety-disordered children: a multiple-baseline evaluation. *Cognitive Therapy and Research, 20*, 423–443.

Kazdin, A. E. (2003). Psychotherapy for children and adolescents. *Annual Review of Psychology, 54*, 253–276.

Pote, H., Stratton, P., Cottrell, D., Shapiro, D. & Boston, P. (2003). Systemic family therapy can be manualized: Research process and findings. *Journal of Family Psychotherapy, 25*, 236–262.

Roth, A. & Fonagy, P. (eds). (2005). *What Works for Whom? A Critical Review of Psychotherapy Research* (2nd edn). New York: Guilford Press.

Shirk, S. R. & Karver, M. (2003). Prediction of treatment outcome from relationship variables in child and adolescent therapy: a meta-analytic review. *Journal of Consulting and Clinical Psychology, 71*, 452–464.

Stallard, P. (2002). *Think Good – Feel Good: A Cognitive Behaviour Therapy Workbook for Children and Young People.* Chichester, United Kingdom: John Wiley & Sons, Ltd.

Wells, A. (1997). *Cognitive Therapy of Anxiety Disorders: A Practical Manual and Conceptual Guide.* Chichester, United Kingdom: John Wiley & Sons, Ltd.

Wimmer, H. & Perner, J. (1983). Beliefs about beliefs: representation and constraining function of wrong beliefs in young children's understanding of deception. *Cognition, 13*, 103–128.

11

TRAINING PSYCHIATRY RESIDENTS IN MENTALIZATION-BASED THERAPY

*Laurel L. Williams, Peter Fonagy, Mary Target, Pasco Fearon,
John Sargent, Efrain Bleiberg, and Jacqueline McGregor*

All mental health disciplines struggle with the challenge of cultivating clinical skills in prospective psychotherapists. In the last several years, the effectiveness of training psychiatry residents in psychotherapy has come under increasing scrutiny, as evidenced by the Accreditation Council for Graduate Medical Education (ACGME) mandate for core competencies in specific therapy modalities. The ACGME has undergone a philosophical shift from a focus on fulfilling programme requirements to evaluating actual success as evidenced by competence in therapy (Andrews & Burruss, 2004), a seemingly Herculean task.

This chapter describes our evolving training programme for psychiatric residents in mentalization-based therapy (MBT). This programme is intended to foster therapeutic skills that we consider crucial to a wide range of specific therapy modalities. We begin by highlighting some general challenges in psychotherapy training and noting the potential advantages of a mentalization-based approach. Then we describe our pilot project in training psychiatry residents and our long-range plan to evaluate its effectiveness.

CHALLENGES IN PSYCHOTHERAPY TRAINING

Training psychiatry residents is founded on the venerable master–apprentice model, exemplified by the tenet, "See one, do one, teach one." Rarely in psychotherapy training, however, do trainees witness a full treatment by a master;

Handbook of Mentalization-Based Treatment. Edited by J. G. Allen and P. Fonagy.
© 2006 John Wiley & Sons, Ltd.

nor are trainees' treatments fully observed. Typically, supervision is based on trainees' process notes and their recollection of session content. This entirely verbal approach risks the transmission of declarative knowledge without the corresponding procedural skills (Binder, 1999).

In the context of comparative research regarding the effectiveness of different brands of therapy – cognitive behavioral therapy, interpersonal psychotherapy, and dialectical behavior therapy – clinicians have developed manuals to ensure consistency in the delivery of the treatment. To the extent that research protocols for treatments of depression and anxiety have a higher response rate in comparison to placebo, the manuals have been successful. Unlike psycho-dynamic therapy, these manualized therapies lend themselves to adherence scales and treatment-review scales that can be monitored to assess overall adherence and, by implication, competence in the delivery of the treatment (Milne, 1999).

In principle, treatment manuals could be a boon to psychotherapy training by virtue of providing a high level of structure and specific guidelines. Yet the initial excitement regarding manualized therapies has been tempered by research showing a generally weak relationship between adherence to prescribed techniques and treatment outcomes (Binder, 1999). Moreover, although therapists in research protocols consistently gain competence, and patients generally have significant reductions in symptoms, once these therapies are scrutinized in the non-research settings, patient gains drop precipitously. Furthermore, treatment manuals may facilitate teaching specific techniques but not their skilful use, only repeating the problem of transmitting declarative but not procedural knowledge. Ultimately, the flexible application of knowledge will be the hallmark of a competent and effective therapist (Binder, 1999; Roth & Fonagy, 2005); manuals cannot teach creativity. All these concerns about manualized therapies are amplified by the labour-intensive nature of the training, which imposes further strain on the already strapped budgets of academic training facilities.

Alternatively, psychotherapy training might capitalize on the well-established contribution of the therapeutic relationship to treatment outcome (Beitman, 2004), which implies that training should focus on the teaching of basic relationship skills (Summers & Barber, 2003). These relationship skills are manifested in the development of a therapeutic alliance, which is central to treatment outcome (Beitman, 2004). Bordin (1979), for example, operationalized the concept of therapeutic alliance in terms of three components: shared goals, recognition of the tasks each person is to perform, and an attachment bond. There is some debate, however, about our ability to teach relationship skills that contribute to the therapeutic alliance (Summers & Barber, 2003).

We propose that therapists' mentalizing skills are central to establishing and maintaining an effective treatment relationship and a therapeutic alliance as Bordin (1979) construed it. Thus, we are developing a training programme to foster therapists' mentalizing capacities in the treatment process. We aim not only to promote therapists' attentiveness to mental states in their patients but also to increase their awareness of their own mental states in the conduct of psychotherapy.

TRAINING IN MENTALIZATION-BASED THERAPY

Our psychotherapy training programme is designed to enable psychiatric residents to conduct Short-Term Mentalization and Relational Therapy (SMART), an approach to family therapy developed in a consortium comprised of the Anna Freud Centre, University College London, and the Menninger Department of Psychiatry and Behavioral Sciences at the Baylor College of Medicine (see Fearon and colleagues, Chapter 10). This programme teaches mentalizing theory and skills to moderately experienced trainees (generally third and fourth postgraduate-year residents) who have some background in psycho-dynamic, cognitive behavioral, and structural family therapy. In part, we modelled our training after Binder's (1999) approach, which includes structured exercises that replicate clinical practice.

Trainees meet for a two-day training module during which they are immersed in the theory of mentalization and the therapy protocol. The initial training includes discussion of the concept of mentalizing, viewing illustrative video-tapes of SMART, and role-playing clinical interactions. The video clips provide examples of accurate mentalizing, various mentalizing deficits, and specific techniques that promote mentalizing. Role-playing is essential to learn how MBT differs from other therapeutic approaches, and it provides an opportunity to practice interventions with experienced trainers. After completing the initial training module, trainees take on clinical cases and videotape their weekly sessions. Supervision to date has revolved around reviewing videotapes with a focus on mentalizing strengths and difficulties in family members and in the therapist. Trainees and supervisors also plan interventions that would maximize the family's mentalizing abilities.

Although the treatment has not undergone any fundamental changes since its inception in 2002, we have continually revised the SMART manual and the training in response to problems psychiatry residents show in developing skill in conducting the treatment. As our predecessors in psychotherapy training have observed, translating declarative knowledge into procedural knowledge is a daunting challenge. Just as we have struggled to clarify what makes the *concept* of mentalizing unique (see Allen, Chapter 1), we struggle to delineate what makes mentalization-based *therapy* unique. Commonly, on the first day of training most of the trainees nod their heads and comment, "Oh, but I already do that [in brand-x therapy] now." The discussion of mentalization-based interventions also brings forth debate about whether the concept of mentalizing is any different from myriad others, including alliance, attachment, empathy, reflective functioning, projection, transference, counter-transference, cognitive therapy, gestalt theory, and so on. Yet when the time comes for role-playing using the mentalization-based approach, the trainees who equated mentalizing with everything else become frozen and comment, "This really is different from [brand-x therapy]!" Learning the treatment is more difficult than it initially appears. Interestingly, experienced and novice therapists share this opinion. After going through two training modules over the past two years, trainees continue to struggle to keep mentalizing in the forefront during their work with families. They are cognitively aware of their lack of mentalizing in the sessions, even before they come to supervision to review their videotapes.

Our early attempts to train residents in mentalization-based therapy only underscored the principle that trainees can understand the concept but be unable to apply it skilfully in practice. Unsurprisingly, what suppresses mentalizing in families suppresses it in therapists: emotional distress. When no one in the room feels sufficiently secure to mentalize, the therapy takes on a mechanistic quality that hinders the establishment and maintenance of the alliance. In our early efforts, the lack of an alliance was obvious to therapists, family members, and supervisors. Families did not appear to make any appreciable changes, even when they remained committed for the entire 8- to 12-session protocol. We recognized a need to revamp the training.

Our failure to help trainees translate knowledge into practice suggested that we trainers were not mentalizing adequately. In consultation with the trainees, we realized that certain elements in the training needed more emphasis if our efforts to teach mentalizing therapy were to be successful. As a result of these considerations, we focused our third training module – the manual, training, and supervision – on relationship skills. Although we are always keen to discuss the conceptual nuances of mentalization, we recognize that our main goal must be to cultivate therapists' ability to freely mentalize in a room of emotionally distressed family members. Procedural knowledge is paramount. Thus in the third training module we spent a greater portion of the training in role-playing, consistent with Binder's (1999) recommendations:

> The concert stage is probably not the best place to first practice basic piano technique, however, and the therapy session may not be the best place to first practice basic therapy technique. Procedural knowledge appears to be most efficiently acquired in learning situations that provide active involvement of the learner, who is exposed to a prearranged sequence of progressively more complex clinical problems, knowledge, and methods. (p. 715)

Role-playing is a vital instrument in mentalization-based therapy, because it provides an opportunity for trainees to practise mentalizing, just as structured activities are essential to provide patients with mentalizing practice in psycho-educational groups (see Haslam-Hopwood et al., Chapter 13). Hindered by performance anxiety, most trainees cringe at the thought of role-playing. Some sit in silence; others spend an inordinate amount of time "clarifying" the task in order to avoid it. This avoidance provides the trainer with an opportunity to teach *in vivo* how emotional distress suppresses mentalizing. Watching the experienced trainers ("see one") approach the task from a mentalizing perspective and then taking over the therapist role ("do one") in the trainer's presence initiates the trainee to the mentalizing stance. On the basis of this recent experience, we have decided to move from individual supervision to group supervision and to incorporate role-playing into the supervisory process. We will maximize procedural learning by utilizing videotapes to identify problems trainees are having in mentalizing with their families; these problems will provide a basis for role-playing with their colleagues in the presence of their supervisor.

Now entering our third year of training in mentalization-based therapy, we have borrowed shamelessly from previous training modules created by experienced clinician–educators; thus much of what we do in teaching mentalizing is not new. We believe that four elements are essential to teaching mentalizing skills and their artful application in family therapy. First, the training works best with real-life examples of mentalizing strengths and deficits as well as specific mentalizing techniques applied during times of high emotional distress in family members. Second, the training must shift frequently between watching an expert in mentalizing therapy and practising the mentalizing assessment and interventions. Shifting from observing to practising must occur not only during the initial training but also throughout the subsequent supervisory process. Third, the value of videotapes cannot be overestimated; mentalizing and its failures must be observed in action. Finally, the therapist's mentalizing capacity must remain in the forefront. Supervision must attend to therapists' attunement to mental states in themselves and the family members as well as their capacity to use that attunement skilfully to further the clinical process. In selecting candidates for conducting mentalization-based therapy, supervisors must distinguish between transient failures of mentalizing (e.g., with certain types of clients or in particular emotional states or attachment contexts) and pervasive limitations in mentalizing capacity.

BEING SMART ABOUT SMART

The entire theoretical framework upon which SMART is based speaks volumes about how the SMART protocol should be learned. In a sense, training in SMART is fourth-order mentalizing insofar as it entails the trainer's thoughts about the trainee's thoughts about the parent's thoughts about the child's thoughts (or the child's about the parents'). In this sense, this chapter may be considered fifth-order mentalizing on the part of the authors. Of course, this is no different from the training of people who work with therapy groups or other family therapy models: while not explicitly focused on mentalization, they address the multi-layered attributions, perceptions and relational dynamics among people who have come for help. The theory, however, also is quite clear that this kind of intellectual exercise is far more likely to yield pseudo-mentalization than genuine understanding. With that caution in mind, we tentatively point to five principles that we have found important to delivering effective training.

The first – and most radical – principle is shifting expectations about what interventions should aim to achieve. Many clinicians come to the training with the notion that there is a magic formula that unlocks understanding or shifts behaviour. Trying to impose a regime that merely asks questions (instead of providing answers) is counterintuitive and might even feel unprofessional. The trainer has to be prepared to recognize that the trainees' expectations of SMART may create disappointment and anxiety about having enough to offer to the family.

The second principle concerns the dialectic about providing structure. A frame of reference is essential for all therapists in order to handle the confusing and pressurizing interactions within the family. Evidence shows that manualized, structured interventions are more effective than unstructured ones, probably because – regardless of the specific recommendations – the presence of a structure to some degree protects the therapist from unconsciously colluding with the organized resistance to change within the family system and each individual within it (Fonagy, 1999). However, imposing a structure is inherently mindless, and the premature imposition of structure may directly undermine mentalizing, as it implies that the therapist already knows what is in the patient's mind, without the need for communication. A good example of the misapplication of structure is recovered-memory therapies, where the therapist presumes to know not only the patient's reaction to an experience but also the nature of that experience – before the patient could have conscious awareness (Fonagy & Target, 1997). In fact, any singular developmental model of psychopathology carries the inherent risk of reductionism, as focus on any specific developmental stage or type of influence is unlikely to offer a full explanation of the subsequent pathology.

In implementing SMART training, clinicians are purposely not discouraged from using other models that they bring to SMART treatment, for example, medical, social work, or psycho-dynamic ways of thinking. However, they are trained to superimpose the explicitly inquisitive stance and to actively override their theoretical presumptions, and to engage the family in enquiring about mental states. So, for example, if the therapist has an intuition, instead of stating this as a fact or interpretation, they will ask the family to consider the idea and to see whether it fits with their own impressions. The same inquisitive stance applies to the method of training: rather than mindlessly imposing this approach, the trainer asks the trainee to question why they might adopt a particular non-inquisitive approach (e.g., a medical or behavioural approach) and to think about what impact this is likely to have on the family. Thus, in the training also we deal with the dialectic between structure and open enquiry.

The third principle of training is prioritizing practice over theory. As mentalization is such a core aspect of everyday social cognition and ideally every kind of clinical work, it is understandably easy for trainees to feel that they have acquired the skill once they have acquired the concept. This of course, parallels the way families can react by short-cutting thinking by making an overarching behavioural comment such as "We do that all the time". As with families, the SMART therapist tries to elicit the behavioural evidence for these generalizations that close down questioning. In SMART training, the trainer requests trainees to demonstrate how their approach is already a mentalizing one. This can be done only in carefully constructed role-plays using the fishbowl model, where other participants observe the target therapist interacting with a role-played family. An alternative strategy, of course, is to watch videotapes and ask about what the assumptions of the therapist might be. Any practical exercise has a reflective aspect. This is necessary in order that trainees do not get drawn into various lines of discussion that families will tend to provoke, such as advice and blaming.

The fourth principle is that passivity on the part of the therapist mostly cannot change existing levels of mentalization. Training promotes the idea of an active therapist, who constantly tests out assumptions by questioning, reacting, seeking further information, suggesting exercises, and so on. This creates a continual interplay between members of the family and the therapist around the subject of each person's different feelings and perspectives. Inherent in a passive stance is a non-questioning of assumptions; we assume that many current assumptions being made by the family are either pseudo-mentalizing or non-mentalizing, and these need to be challenged actively. This extends to the training as well. The trainer must actively engage with the current practice of the trainee and illustrate the actively questioning stance, the stance that the trainee needs to adopt with a family. There is an interplay between modelling a mentalizing stance within the training and what needs to happen frequently within the family sessions. The family members will observe the therapist modelling mentalizing with different individuals; they will understand that this is something they are not doing enough and can do more, and that new things are learned through it.

A final principle is that mentalizing is mostly non-conscious, and just as the families are not aware when they fail to mentalize, so therapists cannot be expected to monitor themselves. Thus, the routine use of video and of ongoing supervision using these videos is essential. But unlike in psycho-dynamic psychotherapy, for example, where the supervision is focused on content, SMART supervision focuses on the manner in which the therapist interacts with the family.

For example, is the therapist turning too much to the most mentalizing family members (often the children) for assistance, rather than working to enhance the mentalization of those who are having more trouble? Are such opportunities being lost, and are non-mentalizing fillers being too readily accepted? The use of video is essential, but it is not very important which bit of video is chosen, as these aspects of interaction are likely to be fairly consistent.

FUTURE DIRECTIONS

As all the above attests, training in mentalization-based therapy is a work in progress. We enrolled 25 participants in our third training module, and their feedback was highly positive. Their responses to evaluation forms indicated that participants generally felt that the mentalization approach to therapy was well explained; the role-playing was helpful; they left the training with a good understanding of SMART; and they felt confident that they could begin conducting SMART with supervision.

The challenges of investigating the effectiveness of SMART and the effectiveness our training programme are thoroughly intertwined. The first step will be to obtain standardized assessments of mental health problems from children and parents at admission, termination and follow-up. Next steps will entail comparisons of mentalization-based therapy with a waiting-list control and then with other standard therapies. Concomitantly, we will need to develop measures of mentalizing capacity suitable for children and adults. These measures will enable us to determine the extent to which SMART uniquely enhances mentalizing capacity and the extent to which gains in mentalizing translate into improvements in standardized measures of mental health.

REFERENCES

Andrews, L. & Burruss, J. (2004). *Core Competencies for Psychiatric Education Defining, Teaching, and Assessing Resident Competence* (pp. 3–10). Washington, DC: American Psychiatric Publishing.

Beitman, B. (2004). Psychotherapy research: "Horse Race" versus process. *Journal of Psychiatric Practice, 10*, 386–388.

Binder, J. (1999). Issues in teaching and learning time-limited psychodynamic psychotherapy. *Clinical Psychology Review, 19*, 705–719.

Bordin, E. S. (1979). The generalizability of the psychoanalytic concept of the working alliance. *Psychotherapy: Theory, Research and Practice, 16*, 252–260.

Fonagy, P. (1999). Achieving evidence-based psychotherapy practice: a psychodynamic perspective on the general acceptance of treatment manuals. *Clinical Psychology: Science and Practice, 6*, 442–444.

Fonagy, P. & Target, M. (1997). Perspectives on the recovered memories debate. In J. Sandler & P. Fonagy (eds), *Recovered Memories of Abuse: True or False?* (pp. 183–216). London: Karnac Books.

Milne, D. (1999). Effectiveness of cognitive therapy training. *Journal of Behavior Therapy and Experimental Psychiatry*, *30*, 81–92.

Roth, A. & Fonagy, P. (2005). *What Works for Whom? A Critical Review of Psychotherapy Research* (2nd edn). New York: Guilford.

Summers, R. & Barber, J. (2003). Therapeutic alliance as a measurable psychotherapy skill. *Academic Psychiatry*, *27*, 160–165.

12

TREATING PROFESSIONALS IN CRISIS: A MENTALIZATION-BASED SPECIALIZED INPATIENT PROGRAM[1]

Efrain Bleiberg

Treating high achieving, well-educated individuals whom Munich (1989) described as "very important persons" (VIPs) presents clinicians with unique challenges. This group includes attorneys; physicians and mental health professionals; business executives and entrepreneurs; professional athletes; artists; and priests, rabbis, and ministers among others. The treatment of these patients challenges clinicians' skill, sensitivity, and integrity; their ability to sustain professional boundaries and to maintain effective communication and cohesiveness within treatment teams and clinical institutions; and their capacity to respond ethically and therapeutically in the face of their own emotional reactions (Group for the Advancement of Psychiatry, 1973; Munich, 1989; Saari & Johnson, 1975; Stroudmire & Rhoads, 1983).

The Professionals in Crisis program at The Menninger Clinic is designed to minimize the dysfunctional impact of the patient's position, power, prestige, wealth, or knowledge on the treatment process – an impact whose legacy of poor outcomes has warranted the cautionary descriptor of "the VIP Syndrome" (Munich, 1989; Group for the Advancement of Psychiatry, 1973; Weintraub, 1964). This chapter discusses a treatment model organized around the systematic promotion of mentalizing in the patients, their treaters, and the culture of

---

[1] This chapter is based on the article 'Treating Professionals in Crisis: A Framework Focused on Promoting Mentalizing', published in The Bulletin Menninger Clinic (2003, 67(3), pp. 212–226). Reproduced by permission of Guilford Press.

Handbook of Mentalization-Based Treatment. Edited by J. G. Allen and P. Fonagy.
© 2006 John Wiley & Sons, Ltd.

the treatment program. The chapter defines the goals and objectives of this mentalization-based inpatient treatment program and reviews its specific components and interventions.

HOW PROFESSIONALS IN CRISIS COME TO TREATMENT

The modal patient in the Professionals in Crisis program is a high-achieving individual who has completed college and postgraduate education in a professional field. Some patients lack formal professional education and have risen to executive positions in the business world or have become self-made entrepreneurs, professional athletes, entertainers, or artists. Others are religious leaders, physicians, or non-physician mental health professionals whose work involves caring for others' spiritual, physical, or psychological needs.

Katsavdakis, Gabbard and Athey (2004) reviewed records of 334 health professionals who were evaluated and/or treated at The Menninger Clinic between 1985 and 2000. This subgroup represented about 10% of admissions to the Professionals in Crisis program. Of these patients, 67% were male, the average age was 45, and 71% were working up to the time of admission. Forty-six percent were referred by their psychotherapist, 11% by a licensing board, and 22% by a physicians' health program. The rest were self-referred or referred by a friend, a colleague, a primary care physician or a family member.

The modal Professionals in Crisis patient is in his or her early thirties to mid-to-late fifties and presents a characteristic constellation of mutually reinforcing problems. Most commonly, this constellation includes various combinations of the following psychiatric disorders: depression; bipolar disorder; eating disorder; anxiety disorder, including social phobia and posttraumatic stress disorder (PTSD); substance abuse or dependency; other addictive disorders, such as pathological gambling and sexual addiction; and personality disorders including narcissistic, borderline, histrionic, paranoid, and compulsive personality disorder or, more commonly, personality disorder with a mixture of the above mentioned features. In Katsavdakis and colleagues' sample, the most common primary diagnosis was major depression (47% of patients). Furthermore, in approximately 40% of all Professionals in Crisis patients, addictive disorders figure prominently in the decision to seek help.

Many patients feel burned-out at work or have violated the professional boundaries and codes of ethics of their professions. Their marriages are often in crisis, and they cannot obtain comfort or support from friends or colleagues. Feeling jaded and hopeless, unable to find love or meaning in life, they consider suicide or discover increasingly more destructive and self-destructive means to numb their pain and despair. Yet they delay seeking treatment or discontinue treatment abruptly and prematurely. When they do engage in treatment, they minimize their difficulties; rationalize even their most maladaptive and outrageous behavior; and seek to control, manipulate, intimidate, denigrate, or seduce their treaters, who typically struggle with feelings of helplessness, anger, contempt, or intimidation along with unacknowledged competitiveness, envy, or identification. Such counter-transference can lead to corruption of treatment and failure to maintain therapeutic boundaries, as patients demand special treatment and a special relationship. Concomitantly, the patients end up as stuck in their treatment as they are stuck in their life.

The patients' characterological – and characteristically rigid – patterns of coping with stress and conflict and of relating to others are a key factor in determining the need for a specialized treatment program. They require a setting with clinicians who are experienced in managing the special appeal and complexity of high-achieving individuals. Steyn (1980) and Munich (1989) make the point that many of the patterns of behavior that impede effective use of treatment in VIPs are deteriorations or exaggerations of behaviors that have contributed to the VIPs gaining and sustaining their position. Thus, writes Munich, "These patients' aggressiveness, drive, and imagination become assultiveness, restlessness, and grandiosity; soberness and attention to detail become self-denigration, helplessness, and worthlessness; and vigilance becomes a concern about conspirators" (p. 581). Munich concludes that VIPs often fear that treatment will alter those aspects of their personality that they believe account for their success. Personality traits indeed are a core aspect of personal identity, the thread that weaves a person's way of "knowing" and creating a narrative of his or her experiences and the compass that guides the person's efforts to respond to adaptive demands. But, as just noted, the personality traits of the Professionals in Crisis patients are also typically traits that have been instrumental in their professional success and adaptation to the culture and the ethos promoted by their professional field.

As an example of how personality traits and a professional culture become intertwined, Gabbard (1985, 2005) describes compulsiveness, perfectionism, and an exaggerated sense of responsibility associated with guilt feelings and self-doubt as typical characteristics of the physician's personality. Gabbard argues that individuals with such compulsive and perfectionistic traits are attracted to medical and research careers and other professional pursuits, because these traits facilitate meeting the demands of professional education and careers and are, in turn, reinforced by the culture and ideals of many professional fields. For example, during medical education, students confront the ideal of physicians being expected to think of everything, to know everything, and to do everything – perfectly. Physicians are inescapably burdened with life-or-death responsibilities and face relentless demands on their time, leaving little room for family or leisure. Compulsive and perfectionistic traits, like other constellations of personality traits discussed below, both reinforce and are reinforced by the stressors and adaptive demands of professional life. Then traits become intimately woven into the person's sense of identity and their sources of satisfaction, self-esteem, and relationships.

Suspiciousness and hypersensitivity to social cues and, not infrequently, frank paranoid traits are another common characteristic of the personality of Professionals in Crisis patients. As in the case of compulsiveness and perfectionism, a heightened sensitivity and increased capacity to read social cues are significant assets to those who become leaders in society, business, and the professions. Secret or overt feelings of shame and narcissistic vulnerability, and a dysfunctional narcissistic solution to such vulnerability, loom large behind compulsive and paranoid personality constellations.

Gabbard (2005) and Flett and Hewitt (2002) identify a set of beliefs and dispositions underlying compulsiveness and perfectionism that bear the hallmarks of narcissistic vulnerability (Bleiberg, 2001): an intolerance of helplessness or dependency and the associated tendency to deny and disown these feelings, paradoxically coexisting with an intense need for external validation; the conviction that others will value them only if they are perfect, and yet, the belief that the better they perform, the more will be expected of them; a need to control others rooted in a fear of losing control; an abiding terror that closeness, intimacy, and emotional expression will render them helpless, dependent, and vulnerable to ridicule, rejection, and humiliation; and the expectation that a state of flawlessness and utter perfection not only will bring approval and self-esteem but also will forever protect them from their secret conviction of being defective and unworthy of love.

A similar set of concerns serve as underpinnings of the suspiciousness and hyper-vigilance of paranoid individuals, whose attention is directed to internal or interpersonal signals of danger. These situations involve the anticipation of rejection, humiliation, passivity, or loss of control as well as the expectation of becoming overwhelmed with one's own needs or exposed as weak, dependent, helpless, or defective. Shame, the prototypical affect of narcissistic vulnerability, figures prominently as a signal of danger for paranoid individuals. Shame also fuels the rage, grandiosity, arrogance, and devaluation of others that are rooted in efforts to cover a hidden sense of defectiveness and vulnerability.

Dr A., for example, was described as a "disruptive physician" by the hospital where he practiced. The hospital's medical director reported that Dr A. was "our best doctor and our worst doctor." He was highly regarded for his clinical skills and his encyclopedic knowledge of his specialty, and he was much admired for his capacity to comfort patients in the midst of a medical emergency. Yet he was also prone to explosions of rage during which he insulted and humiliated patients who dared to inquire about his country of origin (he was a child of immigrant parents) or who wondered about the medical school he attended, a question that conveyed to him the expectation to uncover his "inferior" foreign medical training. In reality, he had attended a well-regarded mid-western medical school and felt constantly chagrined and embarrassed that he had not gone to an Ivy League institution. His grandiosity, arrogant bluster, and pedantic self-assurance were then in obvious display. Far less evident were the secret shame and the terror he felt of being exposed as inadequate or falling short of his own impossible standards. When he found out that his wife was having an affair with a relative who tormented, abused, and humiliated him as a child, he was unable to bear the rage and humiliation; then he attempted suicide.

Other professionals, on the other hand, reach a crisis point by more openly displaying their helplessness and vulnerability, while keeping secret the sense of power and control they derive from their apparent helplessness. Ms B., a successful corporate attorney, responded to her experience of feeling ignored or loathed for her "neediness" by engaging in self-mutilation and purging. In treatment she came to appreciate the multiple functions and gains afforded by cutting or burning herself, gains that she must relinquish if she were to choose to interrupt such patterns. She felt real rather than empty. She compelled others' engagement without risking rejection or the humiliation of being ignored. She could safely get back at those she felt had wronged her, without having to own her aggression. She felt a sensual, thrilling rush of excitement when she cut herself. She confirmed her moral superiority as a victim of injustice. But, most powerfully, she felt "in control of hope" as she "produced" the conditions that triggered the healing process in her lacerated skin.

These patterns of crisis, dysfunction, and despair include three common elements:

(1) Patients rely on a key coping strategy to deal with specific internal and/or interpersonal signals of danger: *the inhibition of mentalization* (Allen, 2001; Bleiberg, 2001; Fonagy, Gergely, Jurist & Target, 2002; Bateman & Fonagy, 2003).

(2) There are two consequences of this selective and context-specific inhibition of mentalizing. First, there is a temporary loss of the sense of agency and "ownership" over one's behavior as exemplified by Ms B. and Dr A. and in those who "find themselves" abusing drugs or engaged in other addictive patterns; such patients experience their behavior as "happening" to them. Paradoxically, they also experience a total certainty and sense of power, control, and invincibility, well articulated by Ms B. or experienced by Dr A. during his rageful rants. Second, the inhibition of mentalizing is associated with a transient loss of empathy, self-reflectiveness, and the ability to engage in two-way social communication. Other persons are no longer human beings whose behavior can have multiple meanings and whose mental states can be potentially understood, "played" with, and potentially changed by sharing one's own perspective. Instead, others' behavior admits only one interpretation, such as the malevolent and humiliating intent Dr A. assumed from a question about his origins. Mental states, such as hope, are experienced and treated as concrete "things" like Ms B.'s healing wounds. Psychological exchanges are replaced with non-mentalizing, coercive efforts

to evoke concrete behaviors that provide a temporary sense of control, safety, or connection. Such coercive behavior erases experiences of helplessness, shame, or vulnerability. Thus, Dr A. could avoid feeling shamed and at risk of humiliation or rejection when his rageful and devaluing tirades evoked in other people the vulnerability and denigration he dreaded to experience himself.

(3) Coercive, non-mentalizing behavior evokes coercive, non-mentalizing responses in others, including treaters. Patients who resort to the active inhibition of mentalizing thus generate self-perpetuating and self-reinforcing impasses (Liddle & Hogue, 2000) or coercive cycles (Bleiberg, 2001) in their interpersonal world. The re-enactment of these impasses in patients' relationships with their treaters dooms the possibility of therapeutic change and leads instead to stalemates, premature terminations, collusion with the patient's dysfunctional behavior, loss of boundaries, or aborted treatment and, at times, to truly catastrophic outcomes, such as suicide.

GOALS AND OBJECTIVES OF MENTALIZATION-FOCUSED TREATMENT

Bateman & Fonagy (1999) describe three distinct stages in the treatment of individuals with personality disorders, each with equally distinct goals. Based on their experience in a partial-hospitalization program, they point out that the first stage aims to achieve the goal of *re-moralization*, a goal that includes resolving the acute crisis and restoring hope. This goal typically can be achieved in one to two months.

The second stage seeks to attain the goal of *remediation*, which includes the resolution of the symptoms of the comorbid Axis I disorders, such as depression, suicidal and para-suicidal behavior, mania or hypo-mania, substance abuse and dependency, anorexia or bingeing and purging. Bateman and Fonagy report that achieving this goal requires 6 to 18 months.

Finally, the third stage of treatment seeks the achievement of the goal of *rehabilitation*, a goal that entails the restoration of the psychological capacities – particularly mentalization – underlying adaptive and healthy patterns of coping, experiencing, and relating. Achieving this goal requires more than 18 months.

The strengths and adaptive capabilities of the patients in the Professionals in Crisis program as reflected in their educational and professional achievements, along with the intensity and total immersion that can be generated in an inpatient milieu, facilitates re-moralization and remediation and *initiates* the process of rehabilitation in a four- to six-week timeframe.

More specifically, these goals are achieved through four objectives: interrupting coercive cycles and addictive or otherwise non-mentalizing patterns that maintain, reinforce, and exacerbate maladjustment; providing pharmacological and psychotherapeutic treatment and psycho-educational interventions targeting specific neuropsychiatric problems; promoting mentalization generally and, in particular, in the interpersonal contexts in which patients inhibit its functioning; and initiating benign cycles based on mentalizing in therapeutic and family relationships that enable individuals who have been previously stuck in their maladjustment and incapable of using treatment to take advantage of treatment and of the healing, nurturing, and support afforded by their attachment networks.

A TREATMENT MODEL FOCUSED ON PROMOTING MENTALIZATION

Focusing on promoting mentalizing provides the Professionals in Crisis program with the conceptual glue that holds together a range of therapeutic interventions in a coherent and integrated treatment model.

A coherent narrative that offers a clear sense of direction and gives meaning to the patients' struggles – and to the inevitable challenges that treatment will engender – is crucial for patients and staff members alike. A particularly compelling aspect of this treatment model is its focus on promoting mentalizing, the capacity to create narrative coherence and cope with adversity and vulnerability.

Staff members are likewise in need of a coherent framework to guide their interventions and to help them manage the coercive pressures and emotional storms they encounter as they become attachment figures to the patient. These therapeutic attachments thus evoke in the patients the very signals of danger to which they are vulnerable in the context of other attachment relationships.

The treatment framework is made explicit in a psycho-educational module on mentalizing that is offered to both patients and staff members (see Haslam-Hopwood and colleagues, Chapter 13). This module uses a lecture, discussion, and practice format to promote understanding of core concepts and practical aspects of treatment. The module discusses motivation and the intentionality and meaning underlying behavior; the trade-offs or therapeutic bargain involved in *not* relying on habitual coping strategies; the components, goals, and objectives of treatment; and the criteria patients can use to identify when they have reached the goals of treatment.

The psycho-educational approach aims to provide an explicit cognitive framework that stresses four principles: the treatment program invites patients to join the treaters in a collaborative relationship designed to address the patients' problems; the ultimate purpose of this collaboration is to promote the capacity to mentalize, a capacity that unfolds in the give-and-take of reciprocal relationships rather than in coercive interactions; the program is based on the premise that mentalizing makes problems amenable to change; and change results from the patient's enhanced ability to make *choices* regarding how to deal with stress, with adversities and life's dilemmas, and with neuropsychiatric vulnerabilities.

The psycho-educational approach makes explicit the therapeutic contract between patients and staff by spelling out the general purpose of treatment as staff members understand it. More concretely, as Gunderson (2000) proposes, the contract refers to an agreement about practical issues, including the anticipated duration of treatment (four to six weeks); the patient's financial obligations; the respective and reciprocal roles of patients and treaters as members of the treatment team; confidentiality; the patient's rights as a voluntary patient; the structure and rules of behavior that patients and staff members are expected to follow, such as the exclusion of drugs or sexual relations; and the requirement that the patient's levels of freedom and responsibility are contingent upon the team's approval.

PROMOTING A THERAPEUTIC ALLIANCE AND A SENSE OF AGENCY

The first step in the treatment process in the Professionals in Crisis program aims at promoting a therapeutic alliance and a sense of agency based on enhanced mentalizing. Fostering the patient's sense of collaboration and agency results from the synergy between group and family interventions all seeking to enhance mentalizing and thereby to strengthen impulse control and to promote awareness of others' mental states.

Enhancing Mentalizing

How does one go about enhancing patients' capacity to mentalize? A critical precondition is an environment where it is safe – and expected – to observe, label, and communicate internal states, including the associated physiological reactions. Thus, the mentalizing perspective links behavior to underlying mental states. Interventions focus on simple mental states, such as conscious beliefs and desires, rather than making explicit links of feelings to dissociated or repressed experiences or to past events. Staff members invite patients to consider current, moment-to-moment changes in their mental states as they occur during clinical rounds with the team, during group sessions with other peers, and during individual encounters – including individual psychotherapy sessions. It is possible, for example, to focus patients' attention on the circumstances that lead to aggression, that is, situations in which they feel misunderstood, blocked, or ignored by others and they are made to feel vulnerable. At the same time, staff members convey the perspective that gaining conscious control over automatic reactions – especially automatic reactions that provide a momentary sense of safety and control – will help them feel more in charge of their own lives and behavior. In this respect, the overall approach pursued in the program is a reversal of the classic psychoanalytic interventions. Psychoanalysis opens paths to the experiences of repudiated affect. In contrast, helping patients who are prone to inhibit mentalizing in the face of threatening internal cues requires that they learn to use their ideational capacity to modulate their emotional experience.

In individual and group interventions, patients are helped to understand which thoughts, interactions, and circumstances – both internal and environmental – result in their feeling certain affective states. Likewise, they receive help in learning to recognize what they say to themselves and the choices they make in terms of ignoring or approaching, communicating or concealing different aspects of their experience. During clinical rounds with the core treatment team, for example, a patient was helped to recognize that when she felt that her psychiatrist was dismissive of her concerns and so rushed that he hardly allowed her to finish her statements, she flew into a rage and thought about leaving the program instead of revealing how hurt and humiliated she felt by the perceived slight. Her choice was to conceal her hurt feelings and avoid her experience of vulnerability. The result of such choices is to put in jeopardy the possibility of her receiving help and to perpetuate the view of others as insensitive and indifferent.

Strengthening Impulse Control and Enhancing Self-regulation

Closely linked to the enhancement of a mentalizing perspective are the efforts to curb the impulsive, automatic, and/or addictive responses triggered by internal or interpersonal cues. A critical perspective conveyed through individual and group interventions – and explicitly discussed in the psycho-educational module – is the appreciation of the adaptive function of impulsive, automatic, and addictive patterns; these behavioral patterns indeed provide relief and a sense of control and safety. The choice to relinquish such patterns is naturally fraught with uncertainty and anxiety, and it is difficult to entertain, particularly for people who have predicated much of their identity and adaptive success on their capacity to selectively disown vulnerability. Staff members help patients articulate their understandable reluctance to give up maladaptive patterns of coping and relating that cause pain while remaining their most effective means of gaining a sense of safety, control, and human connections.

This mentalizing perspective frees patients to examine the price they pay for relying on maladaptive patterns of coping and experiencing as well as coercive modes of relating. These examinations help underscore the therapeutic bargain at the heart of the treatment process: the patient's choice of relinquishing maladaptive, addictive, and coercive patterns of coping and relating – and the illusory sense of control, safety, and connection they derive from them – exposes them to unfamiliar dangers and vulnerabilities. Changing these patterns requires a laborious and painful process of replacing illusory control and coercive relatedness with real mastery and meaningful attachments, a choice that calls for tremendous courage.

An explicit recognition of the patient's dilemma – the choices between patterns and unfamiliar, frightening, but potentially more adaptive responses – can actually exacerbate impulsive, addictive, coercive patterns by increasing the sense of vulnerability that triggers a retreat from mentalizing. In the throes of non-mentalizing functioning, patients require help to manage suicidal, para-suicidal, and other harmful or impulsive behaviors, such as substance abuse or binge eating. It is crucial to appreciate the procedural nature of these addictive or otherwise non-mentalizing patterns, because procedural patterns can be modified only by procedural rather than by verbal-symbolic strategies. Thus patients are assisted in recognizing that they need to first "walk the walk" as implied in a willingness to accept a structure designed to stop impulsive, addictive behavior, and only afterwards "talk the talk" and give narrative coherence and meaning to their life story.

Recognizing the need for procedural strategies to interrupt addictive, procedural patterns resolves an apparent paradox: a treatment program meant to support a sense of agency and self-regulation expects patients to accept the constraints of a structure that bans addictive behaviors and encourages attendance in 12-step support groups. The 12-step model calls for an acceptance of one's helplessness to control addictive patterns as the first step to achieve sobriety and real mastery.

Enhanced impulse and symptom control can be promoted with psycho-educational interventions that help patients understand the procedural nature of eating disordered behavior, addictive patterns, post-traumatic reactions, or overwhelming anxiety – all responses triggered by specific internal states or interpersonal cues. Crisis and relapse-prevention plans help define the triggers of procedural, impulsive, addictive, and coercive patterns and explicate steps patients can take to curb such responses, thereby helping patients retain their capacity to mentalize.

Sharing information about neuropsychiatric vulnerabilities, such as attention deficit/hyperactivity disorder (ADHD) or mood disorder, provides an explanation for some aspects of the disposition to problems in self-control and opens the possibility for planning therapeutic responses to address these vulnerabilities. Such responses include medications, educational remediation, and cognitive approaches to compensate for deficits in attention or organization.

Pharmacotherapy has multiple targets that potentially impair mentalizing: dysregulation of arousal, cognition, affect, and impulse; acute symptoms that emerge during episodes of decompensation and associated longstanding trait vulnerabilities that represent an enduring diathesis to dysfunction; maladaptive personality dimensions, such as affective dysregulation and impulsive behavior (Bleiberg,

2001; Soloff, 1998); and Axis I disorders such as depression, anxiety disorders, ADHD, and mood disorders. By impacting the neurological underpinnings of arousal, cognition, affect, and impulse, pharmacotherapy creates conditions conducive to mentalizing.

Promoting Awareness of Others' Mental States

Through individual and group interventions, patients are encouraged to become aware of the mental states of others. The first aim of these interventions is to help patients appreciate that all may not be as it seems to them, particularly under conditions when they feel vulnerable or threatened. Typically, however, patients actively resist such awareness, as it challenges their habitual patterns of experiencing and relating; thus greater attentiveness to others' mental states exposes patients to feelings they find unbearable.

Awareness of others' mental states is often promoted synergistically with the enhancement of mentalizing. Patients are encouraged to consider what it would be like if they were to report their own experience in a particular interaction and hear the other person's perspective. Individual psychotherapy sessions are particularly conducive to helping patients understand how therapists think about the internal states underlying behavior and how such understanding paves the way for reciprocal relationships – in treatment and beyond – particularly in the face of threatening internal and interpersonal cues. More generally, practicing paying attention to the mental states of staff members and peers facilitates engaging in mentalizing exchanges within patients' families.

The opportunities in treatment to take a playful, humorous, or as-if stance are important steps in promoting mentalizing and the awareness of others' mental states. Play, humor, and pretending require holding in mind simultaneously two realities, the pretend and the actual, in synchrony with a moment-to-moment reading of the other person's state of mind (see Fonagy, Chapter 3). Role-playing offers a way to step back from overwhelming, threatening, or unmanageable interpersonal exchanges and thereby to modulate them.

The ultimate key to setting up benign cycles that promote mentalizing entails aligning the individual's growth in mentalizing capacity with synergistic changes in their family context. The first step in helping families often involves exploring the stressors impinging on family members and the interactive patterns associated with inhibition of mentalizing that trigger coercive patterns of interaction. Reviewing interactions around specific core conflicts in marital or family sessions allows for the planning of new modes of interaction designed to break coercive cycles and promote mentalizing.

Often, the patient and other family members need individual coaching before they can engage in mentalizing interactions involving emotionally loaded or conflictual issues. The coaching is carried out in sessions designed to help family members with "the content and style of what is to be said, prepare for potential reactions by other participants, and solidify a mini-contract that challenges the participants to follow through as planned once the interaction begins" (Liddle & Hogue, 2000, p. 274). The preparatory coaching focuses on enabling family members to appreciate others' points of view and to become clear about their own perspective and motivation, which encourages less extreme and rigid positions. By processing in advance interactions that habitually result in the loss of mentalizing, family members can take a first step toward restoring it.

Dr A., for example, had used individual and group interventions to prepare himself to let his wife know of his desire to seek to repair their badly damaged relationship. After he told her of his desires, she hesitated by perhaps not even a fraction of a second. That momentary hesitation triggered an immediate explosion of rage, suspiciousness, and devaluation. Two weeks of coaching and practicing were needed before he could take the risk of telling his wife that, when she hesitated, he had panicked, not knowing whether she cared about him and their relationship as much as he cared about her.

USING ATTACHMENTS TO MOVE TOWARD INTEGRATION

Meaningful attachments between patients and staff members develop in the context of intensive work designed to help patients mentalize, achieve more effective means of self-regulation, and become aware of others. The stirrings of a growing attachment rekindle hope that help and support can be derived from human connections; yet they also trigger increased anxiety and defensiveness inasmuch as internal states associated with attachment, such as dependency and vulnerability, also signal danger (Allen, 2001; Bleiberg, 2001; Fonagy et al., 2002).

Relationships within the treatment program thus become a crucial arena in which dysfunctional patterns of experiencing, coping, and relating come to life in full force. Yet staff members do not seek to interpret the patient's transference in the classic sense of exploring how specific thoughts, feelings, wishes, fantasies, fears, and conflicts are transferred from important figures in the patient's past to contemporary relationships. Instead, relationships with staff members are central because they provide a relatively controlled route to initiate the development of the capacity to sustain mentalizing in the context of significant attachments.

Perhaps the greatest challenge clinicians face in carrying out this task is their own emotional responses. Staff members grow weary of the repeated alternation between mentalizing and non-mentalizing modes of relatedness. As Gabbard (1995) points out, a common thread in contemporary thinking about countertransference is that the mental contents of the patient are not magically transported from patient to clinician. Rather, argues Gabbard, "interpersonal pressure is applied by specific patient behaviors that evoke specific clinician responses" (p. 477). The coercive nature of the interpersonal pressures applied by these patients stems precisely from the procedural nature of their behavior and communication. Such approaches are not only difficult to resist but also tend to evoke predictable responses in all people, including staff members: the momentary loss of the capacity to mentalize.

Clinicians experience the activation of non-mentalizing modes of functioning in them as an alien force disrupting their sense of self and others. Certain patterns of response reflect efforts to contain this alien internal presence or, alternatively, result from the clinician feeling taken over by coercive pressures to respond unreflectively. Clinicians grow to dread encounters with patients in whose presence they lose key attributes of their personal and professional identities, namely, the capacity to listen empathetically and to respond in a thoughtful, professional, humane, and ethical manner. Instead, clinicians feel fooled by pleas for relatedness that alternate with coercive tyranny. Some patients, bent on evoking helplessness and vulnerability in others, often trigger irritation or rage and a need to demonstrate who is really in charge. Alternatively, when subjected to devaluation, clinicians can become paralyzed and feel as drained, defeated, worthless, and helpless as the patient. Yet the devoted staff members may not have recourse to the protective defensive grandiosity and devaluation available to patients.

Other patients seduce clinicians by attributing to them perfect empathy, extraordinary power, or unique wisdom. Clinicians are vulnerable to experiencing these coercive pressures to become idealized rescuers and healers. The compelling force of such pressures plays a role in the destructive outcome of violations of ethical and professional boundaries.

Patients who threaten suicide or who injure themselves stir up powerful reactions in those who treat them. These patients, such as Ms B., convey the implicit message: "If I die, it will be because of your failure." In response, clinicians struggle with feelings that include not "giving a damn" any more, hate, loss of hope, and the secret – or not so secret – desire for the patient to die.

Although the enactment of the staff's non-mentalizing responses can derail the treatment, anticipating their emergence and processing them as part of the treatment process also opens the path for therapeutic change. Capry (1989) argues that the patient's observation of the clinician's ability to contain, tolerate, and reflect on intense feelings experienced in the therapeutic relationship is mutative in itself. Arguably, clinicians' capacity to mentalize in the face of a barrage of coercive messages and feelings conveys back to the patient that the feelings themselves are potentially manageable. Thus, patients are offered a model of how to break the cycle of coercion and un-reflectiveness, which can be demonstrated when the clinicians follow and discuss with the patient a sequence that includes conducting self-examination and self-supervision (Gabbard & Wilkinson, 1994).

Such self-examination is crucial if clinicians are to avoid urging or cajoling patients into abandoning obviously self-destructive and maladaptive patterns of coping, relating, and experiencing. Acknowledging instead the utter terror patients experience when they enter unexplored and unlived aspects of self–other relatedness is useful in minimizing the tendency to intensify reliance on maladaptive coping strategies. Pointing out the courage required to venture into unfamiliar territory aligns staff with the patients' own thrust toward growth and development. This alignment is generally more effective when clinicians point out the price (in greater anxiety and exposure to unfamiliar vulnerabilities) associated with giving up the mechanisms they have relied on to sustain their identity and sense of security, control, and connection.

Such an emphatic approach can enable patients to examine the price they pay for relying on their maladaptive mechanisms. To reiterate, in individual and group interventions, clinicians can present in more explicit fashion the therapeutic bargain embedded in treatment: relinquishing maladaptive defenses and coercive patterns of relatedness – and the sense of control, safety, and connection they derive from them – for the laborious and oftentimes painful process of seeking to achieve real mastery and meaningful attachments.

Patients deploy strong compensatory mechanisms in response to the offer of a therapeutic bargain. If clinicians and patients can withstand the onslaught of non-mentalizing that often follows, themes of dependence, safety, autonomy, vulnerability, body integrity, envy, and competition, become available for exploration. Intermixed with these problems are the real joy, renewed hope, and genuine pride that result from an increasing capacity to conceive of themselves and others as genuine human beings.

The milestones signaling the end of treatment in the Professionals in Crisis program are as follows: patients give evidence of a capacity to be aware of the implications of their thoughts, feelings, and intentions toward other people while simultaneously retaining an awareness of the other person's point of view; they become able to respond to stress, anxiety, vulnerability, and conflict with coping strategies that do not require the inhibition of mentalization and the deployment of addictive, coercive strategies, but rather involve self-initiated approaches contained in a relapse-prevention plan; and, finally, they demonstrate the reactivation of hope manifested by their capacity to ask for help at moments of anxiety, conflict, or vulnerability.

REFERENCES

Allen, J. (2001). *Traumatic Relationships and Serious Mental Disorders*. Chichester, UK: John Wiley & Sons, Ltd.

Bateman, A. & Fonagy, P. (1999). Effectiveness of partial hospitalization in the treatment of borderline personality disorder: A randomized controlled trial. *American Journal of Psychiatry, 156,* 1563–1569.

Bateman, A. & Fonagy, P. (2003). The development of an attachment-based treatment program for borderline personality disorder. *Bulletin of The Menninger Clinic, 67,* 187–211.

Bleiberg, E. (2001). *Treating Personality Disorders in Children and Adolescents: A Relational Approach.* New York: Guilford.

Capry, D. V. (1989). Tolerating the countertransference: a mutative process. *International Journal of Psycho-analysis, 70,* 287–294.

Flett, G. L. & Hewitt, P. L. (eds). (2002). *Perfectionism: Theory, research, and treatment.* Washington, D.C.: American Psychological Association.

Fonagy, P., Gergely, G., Jurist, E. & Target, M. (2002). *Affect Regulation, Mentalization and the Development of the Self.* New York: Other Press.

Gabbard, G. (1985). The role of compulsiveness in the normal physician. *Journal of the American Medical Association, 254,* 2926–2929.

Gabbard, G. O. (1995). Countertransference: the emerging common ground. *International Journal of Psycho-Analysis, 76,* 475–485.

Gabbard, G. (2005). *The Troubled Physician and the Perils of Perfectionism.* Grand Rounds, Menninger Department of Psychiatry and Behavioral Sciences, Baylor College of Medicine.

Gabbard, G. O. & Wilkinson, S. M. (1994). *Management of Countertransference with Borderline Patients.* Washington, DC: American Psychiatric Press.

Group for the Advancement of Psychiatry. (1973). *The VIP with Psychiatric Impairment.* New York: Scribner.

Gunderson, J. G. (2000). Psychodynamic psychotherapy for borderline personality disorder. In J. G. Gunderson & G. O. Gabbard (eds), *Psychotherapy for Personality Disorders* (pp. 33–64). Washington, DC: American Psychiatric Press.

Katsavdakis, K., Gabbard, G. & Athey, G. (2004). Profiles of impaired health professionals. *Bulletin of The Menninger Clinic, 68,* 60–72.

Liddle, H. A. & Hogue, A. (2000). A family-based, developmental-ecological preventive intervention for high risk adolescents. *Journal of Marital and Family Therapy, 26,* 265–279.

Munich, R. L. (1989). The VIP as patient: syndrome, dynamic and treatment. In A. Tasman, R. E. Hales & A. J. Frances (eds), *American Psychiatric Press Review of Psychiatry* (Vol. 8, pp. 580–593). Washington DC: American Psychiatric Press.

Saari, C. & Johnson, S. R. (1975). Problems in the treatment of VIP clients. *Social Casework, 576,* 599–604.

Soloff, P. H. (1998). Algorithms for pharmacological treatment of personality dimensions: symptom-specific treatments for cognitive-perceptual, affective, and impulsive behavioral dysregulation. *Bulletin of The Menninger Clinic, 62,* 195–214.

Steyn, R. W. (1980). Psychiatric problems of the VIP. *Military Medicine, 145,* 482–483.

Stroudmire, A. & Rhoads, J. M. (1983). When a doctor needs a doctor: special considerations for the physician-patient. *Annals of Internal Medicine, 98,* 654–659.

Weintraub, W. (1964). The VIP Syndrome: A clinical study in hospital psychiatry. *Journal of Nervous and Mental Disease, 138,* 181–193.

13

ENHANCING MENTALIZING THROUGH PSYCHO-EDUCATION

G. Tobias G. Haslam-Hopwood, Jon G. Allen, April Stein,
and Efrain Bleiberg

Psycho-education was developed in the United States in conjunction with efforts to move the concentration of treatment of psychiatric patients out of large-scale facilities and back into the community (Simon, 1997). Initially, psycho-education was designed to help families provide optimal support to patients with schizophrenia (Becker & Thornicroft, 1998); this approach continues to be refined in the treatment of schizophrenia and has proved to be effective in systematic research (Lukens & McFarlane, 2004; McFarlane, Dixon, Lukens & Luckstead, 2003). Concomitantly, psycho-education has been extended to a wide range of disorders beyond schizophrenia, and individual patients as well as their family members have been the recipients (Potter, Williams & Constanzo, 2004). Lukens and McFarlane (2004) provide a judicious critique of a wide range of studies citing studies that demonstrate that psycho-education is efficacious in the treatment of bipolar mood disorder (Colom et al., 2003), depression (Dowrick et al., 2000), post-natal depression (Fristad, Goldberg-Arnold & Gavazzi, 2002), binge eating disorder (Peterson, Mitchell, Nugent, Mussell & Miller, 1998), and in reducing posttraumatic stress disorder (PTSD) and depression in women with a history of partner abuse (Kubany, Hill & Owens, 2003). The utility of psycho-education can be at least partially explained by the idea that providing information and understanding gives all recipients of care the opportunity to move from the traditional role of passively accepting treatment to becoming active agents in the treatment process (Corey, 2000).

Handbook of Mentalization-Based Treatment. Edited by J. G. Allen and P. Fonagy.
© 2006 John Wiley & Sons, Ltd.

The provision of education about psychiatry has been a defining characteristic of The Menninger Clinic since its inception. The reputation of the clinic rests partly on decades of educating a range of professionals, including psychiatrists, psychologists, social workers, nurses, and chaplains. But Karl and Will Menninger did not stop there: through their lecturing and writing, they also targeted the general population to correct misunderstanding and misconceptions about psychiatric illness for the purpose of improving mental health care. Now we call what they were doing "psycho-education." The clinic currently includes psycho-educational groups for patients on a wide range of topics as well as regular two-day workshops for family members that cover the same ground – including education about mentalizing.

In our view, the mentalizing group we describe in this chapter is not on a par with the many other psycho-educational groups in the clinic; rather, the intent of this group is to enable patients to understand and make better use of the rest of the treatment as a whole. Ambitiously, we aspire to promote a cohesive way of thinking about treatment that can be shared by staff members, patients, and their family members alike. In the mentalizing group, we not only explain the concepts that form the basis of treatment but also provide patients with an opportunity to practice the very skills they will employ and refine in the course of treatment more generally. In this sense, the psycho-educational group on mentalizing is a meta-intervention.

This chapter describes the psycho-educational groups for patients that the authors have developed and conducted at the clinic. We present the general process and the essential content of the groups, and we give examples of exercises we designed to enable patients to practice mentalizing in the group. This chapter is necessarily illustrative rather than exhaustive; we strive to convey the spirit of the intervention so that readers might begin experimenting and adapting our methods to their practice.

PSYCHO-EDUCATIONAL PROCESS

We conduct the psycho-educational group on mentalizing in the context of a milieu-based bio-psycho-social approach that places strong emphasis on attachment relationships (see Bleiberg, Chapter 12). In focusing on mentalizing in particular, our primary aim is to teach a skill, not a concept or a theory. We aim to promote mentalizing at both explicit (verbal) and implicit (intuitive) levels (see Allen, Chapter 1); yet, perforce, we teach patients about mentalizing at the explicit level. If we simply provide the theory that underlies the skill, the patient can do little more than describe the theory. Imagine teaching someone to drive a car solely by means of a series of lectures. Thus we interlace lectures about mentalizing with opportunities to practice the skill, receive feedback, and thereby refine the skill. This is no different from teaching many complex skills like driving a car; such skills are taught with a combination of verbal instruction, demonstration, and practice. Moreover, as we continually point out to patients, although we put our minds to mentalizing in the group, the entire treatment program entails practicing these skills. Furthermore, we are keenly aware that the hospital treatment is brief and that patients soon will return to their primary attachment relationships where mentalizing can be most difficult. In interactions, it takes two to mentalize. Thus the treatment includes active family work that provides an opportunity for patients and their family members to practice mentalizing with clinical support. In addition, we strongly encourage family members to attend the psycho-educational workshops, which include consideration of mentalizing. Just as it is for patients, we intend that understanding mentalizing will be empowering for family members in their efforts to become active agents of change.

We conduct the mentalizing psycho-education group in weekly 50-minute sessions. Up to 24 patients attend each group, and members of the staff and trainees attend as well. The group is open-ended, and patients attend throughout their six- to eight-week stay. All patients receive a written description of the course content to orient them (Allen, Bleiberg & Haslam-Hopwood, 2003), and the leaders provide a brief working definition of mentalizing and summarize the purpose of the group for new members at the beginning of each session. Because the focus on mentalizing is pervasive in the treatment, the written material and verbal presentation in the group also orient new patients to the treatment approach as a whole.

We encourage patients to raise questions throughout to clarify their understanding of the concept and to provide counsel regarding the difficulties they are having in their efforts to mentalize on a day-to-day basis. The process of discussion is vital to the group: it fosters the active involvement of the patients, leading to greater learning and retention of the material and to the further development of the ideas being presented; moreover, the discussion itself exemplifies mentalizing insofar as the patients and leaders are thinking about thinking and feelings in the process of the discussion.

DIDACTIC MATERIAL

We group the didactic material into three parts, and we cover each part in two to three sessions to correspond roughly to the typical length of stay. Part I reviews the concept of mentalizing and the developmental conditions that facilitate mentalizing (i.e., secure attachment and optimal emotional arousal). Part II considers how psychiatric disorders and impaired mentalizing exacerbate each other in vicious circles. Part III describes how the various components of treatment are designed to enhance mentalizing capacity.

The Concept of Mentalizing

We immediately let patients know that, although they have never heard the word, they are natural mentalizers and that we will be talking about ideas that they already understand intuitively. We define mentalizing with a few phrases: attending to mental states, keeping mind in mind, and interpreting behavior as based on mental states such as beliefs, wishes, dreams, ambitions, hallucinations, and so forth. We emphasize that mentalizing includes attending to mental states in oneself and others. We often use the example: What would you do if you were in your hometown and you saw a stranger standing at a street corner, map in hand, with furrowed brow and pursed lips, looking down one street then another? Patients quickly state that they would go and ask that individual if he is lost and if he needed directions. We point out that this is mentalizing. The fact that the stranger was lost was not written in a neon sign above his head but could be inferred from observable behaviors. Imagining the stranger's internal state of confusion and frustration is mentalizing in action.

We delineate the scope of mentalizing with a simple diagram (see Figure 13.1). Mentalizing entails awareness of thoughts and feelings in self and others. This diagram helps distinguish mentalizing from related concepts, most notably, empathy. Empathy primarily entails awareness of others' feelings, the lower-right quadrant. Sometimes, however, we use empathy to refer to awareness of others' experience more generally, in which case it encompasses the lower half of the diagram. We then point out that, if we included the idea of empathy for oneself – which we advocate – "empathy" would cover much of the territory of mentalizing.

Figure 13.1 also helps to avoid an overly intellectualized interpretation of mentalizing. We emphasize that, to a large extent, we mentalize about

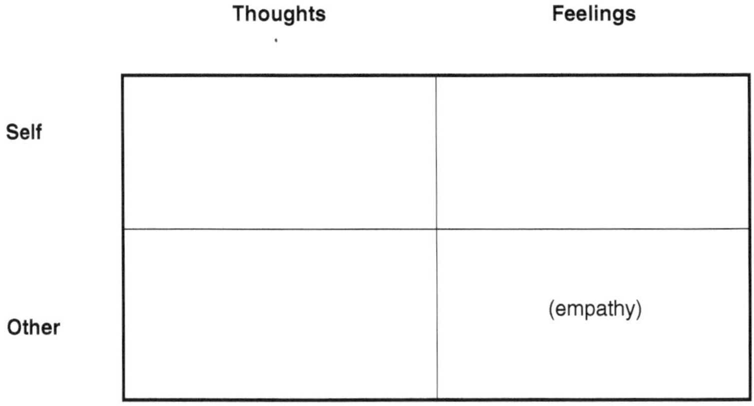

Figure 13.1 The scope of mentalizing

emotion – feelings in others and ourselves. In addition, as we do so, mentalizing is typically infused with emotion. As one of our patients put it, we aspire not only to think clearly but also to *feel clearly*. Also to counter the intellectualized view of mentalizing, we explain the difference between mentalizing implicitly and explicitly. We let patients know that, ideally, mentalizing is an automatic, intuitive, interactive process.

We can teach patients the concept, but we cannot teach them to mentalize – and there is no need to do so, as they already have some capacity. Instead, we can draw their *attention* to the need to mentalize, for example, to be aware of and reflect upon feelings in themselves and others. More generally, we explicitly promote what we call the *mentalizing attitude*: curiosity, inquisitiveness, and imaginativeness. We point out that behavior is most often multiply determined, and that mental states at any one point are likely to be layered and to have conflicting elements. When we mentalize we are open to multiple perspectives. We cannot expect to know the total contents of our own mind, let alone the total content of another person's mind. Thus a feeling of certainty signals a non-mentalizing stance. We have stopped mentalizing when we believe we know *entirely* what is going in our own mind or the mind of another. When we *know*, we cease to be open to new perspectives. Thus mentalizing entails asking questions rather than looking for the answer.

We let patients know that, ideally, we want them to learn to mentalize in the trenches – in the middle of an argument or in the throes of addictive cravings. Yet we recognize that much productive mentalizing occurs after the fact, and we aspire to translate hindsight into foresight. Thus patients can usefully mentalize about past events, such as "What was I thinking just before I relapsed?" Also, they can benefit from mentalizing about the future in an anticipatory way, such as "I wonder how he will feel when I tell him ... "

As we tout the virtues of mentalizing, patients often ask whether one can mentalize too much. Before answering, we have found it important to clarify the question. This question often betrays confusion between mentalizing and ruminating. Obsessive patients tend to think that they are mentalizing when they are thinking about their thoughts. Then we refer back to Figure 13.1 and point out that mental states include both thoughts and feelings. Effective mentalizing would entail awareness of the process of ruminating as well as the feelings of anxiety that fuel the rumination. Mentalizing thus sets the stage for interrupting rumination.

As to whether we can mentalize too much, the simple answer is yes. Many patients, such as those who have been abused, are hyper-vigilant to mental states. In addition, by mentalizing "too much," some patients are referring to mentalizing in a distorted way (e.g., reading too much into others' postures or comments). Mentalizing accurately entails *grounded imagination* (see Allen,

Chapter 1). We also remind patients that there is more to living than mentalizing. We might simply attend to a sunset or "just be" with a partner rather than attending to mental states.

We inform patients that our goal in constructing an effective treatment program is to replicate the optimal developmental conditions that lead to mentalizing. In this regard, we place primary emphasis on two intertwined factors, secure attachment relationships and optimal emotional arousal (see Fonagy, Chapter 3). We explain that the crux of a secure attachment relationship is that the caregiver will be reliably available and will have the child's mind in mind. We emphasize Bowlby (1988) and Fonagy and colleagues' (Fonagy, Gergely, Jurist & Target, 2002) point that the secure base of attachment makes it safe to explore the mind of the self and the other – just what we aim to promote in psychotherapy and treatment more generally as well as in patients' relationships with one another.

To characterize the relation of emotional arousal to mentalizing, we draw the familiar inverted U-shaped curve relating anxiety to performance (Easterbrook, 1959; see Figure 13.2). We begin by stating that, at low levels of arousal, we have no incentive to mentalize. At moderate levels of arousal, such as when an interaction takes an unexpected and problematic turn, we mentalize more actively and explicitly. If arousal becomes excessive, such as when we become enraged or terrified, mentalizing collapses: we move into the automatic fight-or-flight response. We put an evolutionary spin on this point, for example, commenting that when a saber-tooth tiger jumped out of the bushes with its eyes fixed on us it was not to our evolutionary advantage to take time mind-reading the cat's intent. We acknowledge the necessity to be able to switch off mentalizing when protective defenses are needed, but we emphasize that most interpersonal challenges call for mentalizing.

Patients easily relate to this description of moving from the mentalizing to the fight-or-flight mode, for example, commenting, "It was as if my mind went right out of the window." Patients ask how they can get back to mentalizing from the

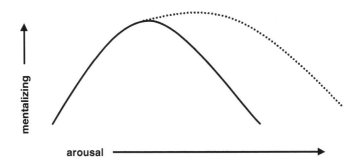

Figure 13.2 Increasing the mentalizing threshold

fight-or-flight response, and we acknowledge what we call the *mentalizing para-dox*: in the midst of intense arousal, you must be aware that you have moved out of the mentalizing mode (i.e., mentalize) in order to be able to mentalize. We resolve this paradox by pointing out that patients can learn from hindsight to be aware of cues that herald a flight from mentalizing; then they can use these cues as prompts to mentalize (e.g., awareness of building irritation with one's spouse can be a prompt to mentalize instead of blaming). Concomitantly, patients can learn to use these cues as stimuli for emotion regulation, for example, by means of self-soothing techniques. Illustratively, a patient described how his spouse's routine request to take the trash out put him into a non-mentalizing mode. In hindsight, he recognized how this innocuous request triggered memories of feel-ing criticized and belittled by his father. He realized that his intense emotional response obscured his awareness of his wife's intent, which in turn prompted an acrimonious interchange when his wife merely wanted the trash removed.

We inform patients that not only do we want them to mentalize in the sense of identifying problematic feelings earlier and coping more effectively but also we want to push the envelope in the sense of enabling them to remain in the men-talizing mode at increasingly high levels of emotional arousal (see Figure 13.2). Contrary to some patients' convictions, we do not deliberately provoke them for this purpose. Yet we do not want to insulate them from naturally occurring stressors and challenges; rather, treatment entails emotional challenges such as family work that provide opportunities to increase stress tolerance and to pro-mote mentalized affectivity – feeling and thinking about feeling simultaneously (Fonagy et al., 2002).

Mentalizing and Psychiatric Disorders

We engage patients in discussing how mentalizing pertains to psychiatric dis-orders by presenting them with a vicious circle: psychiatric disorders impair mentalizing and impaired mentalizing contributes to psychiatric disorders (see Figure 13.3). Recognizing that patients easily feel blamed and defensive when we enter this territory, we invite them to take the lead in the discussion, giving examples of each side of the vicious circle from their experience.

Substance abuse. We begin with the most straightforward and concrete exemplar: how substance abuse impairs mentalizing. Plainly, intoxication clouds think-ing and feeling about everything, including mental states in oneself and others.

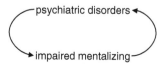

Figure 13.3 Vicious circles in psychiatric disorders

Intoxication induces relatively pervasive mindblindness, and patients easily acknowledge their common obliviousness to the impact of substance abuse on others, especially in their attachment relationships. Some patients also recognize distorted mentalizing, for example, their temporary feelings of omnipotence.

The subtler question: how do mentalizing problems lead to substance abuse? Patients can address this question by identifying triggers; some quickly identify dysphoric feelings; others cite interpersonal difficulties such as arguments with their spouse. In this context, we discuss how mentalizing can be a pathway out of substance abuse: mentalizing promotes emotion regulation and sets the stage for coping in other ways with dysphoric affects. Thus substance abuse provides the clearest example of the need to cultivate mentalized affectivity, as we explain it to patients, the capacity to feel and think about feelings at the same time, the basis of affect tolerance and of the capacity to use feelings as signals for effective coping. We also reiterate the point that mentalizing is the basis of addressing and resolving relationship problems that contribute to substance abuse.

Depression. We approach depression with a similar line of reasoning, beginning by discussing how depression impairs mentalizing. Patients describe a loss of energy and a lack of incentive to mentalize, in effect, "Why bother?" We discuss distortions in mentalizing associated with the notorious negative cognitive bias in depression – the cognitive distortions affect their perceptions and judgments of themselves as well as others. We also discuss how depression is associated with self-absorption and social isolation, putting them out of touch with others' mental states and the impact of their behavior on others.

Distorted mentalizing evident in negative cognitive biases not only stems from depression but also contributes to it in a vicious circle. Projecting their own negative self-concepts onto others is a common example of depressing distortions in mentalizing. In aspiring to cultivate a mentalizing attitude of flexibility, inquisitiveness, and open-mindedness, our discussion counters biases and distortions. Illustratively, some patients recognize that they ignore the positive mental states they experience and, as one patient stated, "cave into the negative and misleading." In addition, we consider how failures to mentalize and distorted mentalizing contribute to conflict in attachment relationships and how conflicts and the ensuing withdrawal and isolation contribute to depression.

During this discussion, knowledgeable patients ask about how mentalizing relates to cognitive-behavioral therapy. We remind patients that mentalizing is not a treatment approach but rather a mental process. We explain that all psychological treatments require mentalizing capacity and have the potential to enhance it. In our view, cognitive behavioral therapy is one particularly effective way of fostering a mentalizing attitude and promoting mentalizing in persons grappling with depression (see Björgvinsson and Hart, Chapter 7).

Anxiety. In discussing anxiety, we refer to the inverted U-shaped graph describing the relationship between arousal and mentalizing (see Figure 13.2). Patients with anxiety disorders describe how their baseline anxiety is so high that it takes little additional arousal to push them over the edge into the non-mentalizing, fight-or-flight mode. We reiterate the potential adaptiveness of this switch but draw patients' attention to the need to recognize – through mentalizing – their individual markers, such as sweating or tingling, signaling that they are reaching their upper limit of their ability to mentalize in the face of emotional arousal. In discussing triggers that escalate anxiety, we emphasize attachment relationships, including discussion of "transference" in the broad sense of past relationship experiences adding emotional fuel to perceptions of current relationships. We encourage patients that gaining insight into attachment triggers through hindsight can foster foresight in mentalizing, that is, anticipating future mental states that might be evoked in particular attachment contexts. We engage patients in practicing mentalizing by having them imagine problematic forthcoming interactions and consider coping strategies they might employ.

We find the concept of mentalizing to be crucial in helping patients understand posttraumatic stress disorder (Allen, 2005). Technical as it may sound, we explain the concept of *psychic equivalence*, namely, equating mental states with reality (see Fonagy, Chapter 3). We use dreaming as an example: the dreamer believes the dream is real. The same is true of full-blown flashbacks, which represent a collapse of mentalizing. We present the challenge of separating past from present as prototypical of mentalizing, that is, recognizing a mental state for what it is, and making the shift from re-experiencing (psychic equivalence) to awareness of remembering (mentalizing).

Personality disorders. In discussing personality disorders, we face a daunting task. The topic often evokes discomfort in clinicians and ire in patients. Many patients have experienced stigma even within the arena of mental health (especially with borderline personality disorder), and they find it difficult not to hear "personality disorder" as having a "bad personality" or being a "bad person." We address these problems forthrightly and reassure patients that personality disorders reflect problematic *aspects* of personality that are most evident in attachment relationships and that persons with personality disorders typically also have many personality strengths. Consistent with our focus on mentalizing, we emphasize the *rigidity* inherent in personality disorders as the main problem, as contrasted to optimal personality functioning which entails sufficient flexibility to adjust responses and behavior to the particular contingencies that a given relationship presents (Yudofsky, 2005). We point out that, given personality rigidity, individuals with personality disorders typically engage in manipulative and coercive behavior, endeavoring to control others to conform to the demands of their personality. Such coercive behavior exemplifies non-mentalizing in the sense that others are not treated as autonomous individuals with their own minds but rather as objects to be manipulated. We draw a contrast between the non-mentalizing efforts to *control* others as objects and the mentalizing stance of aspiring to *influence* others as persons and to be influenced by them – the basis of interpersonal problem solving and the foundation of intimacy in attachment relationships (see Allen, Chapter 1).

We introduce specific personality disorders as exemplifying rigidity in the form of exaggerated personality traits; we emphasize degrees: all traits have adaptive aspects, and the difficulty arises from extremes and rigidity. Paranoia provides a good example, with adaptive prudence and cautiousness at one end, over-generalized suspiciousness in the middle, and frank paranoia at the extreme. Similarly, with dependent personality disorder, we recognize the fundamental adaptiveness of dependency – consistent with our advocacy of secure attachments – but point out the problematic aspects of excessive dependency.

We focus on impaired mentalizing in two personality disorders common in our patient population, narcissistic and borderline personality disorder. With respect to narcissism, we focus on the inability to mentalize the self, evident in defensive distortions in the self-concept as well as lack of awareness that efforts to seek excessive affirmation and validation from others are based on chronic feelings of inadequacy. We also consider the mentalizing distortions entailed by idealization and devaluation of others as well as ways in which narcissism contributes to coercive attempts to obtain admiration and validation coupled with obliviousness to the needs and perspectives of others.

Given its multidimensionality, borderline personality disorder does not lend itself to the exaggerated-trait model of personality disorder, nor does the word "borderline" any longer have a clear referent (i.e., as being between neurosis and psychosis). Thus we emphasize the link to disturbance in attachment relationships, making use of our colleague Helen Stein's colloquialism, *kick-and-cling* relationships. We discuss the intertwining of impaired mentalizing, fear of abandonment, and problems with emotion regulation. We consider the relation between unbearable emotional states and impulsive, self-destructive behavior. Using our colleague Maria Holden's colloquialism, we suggest to patients that, in the throes of intense emotion, they need to learn to push the metaphorical *pause button* by mentalizing rather than impulsively relying on destructive means of self-soothing (Allen, 2001). In the context of borderline personality disorder, the mentalizing challenges are enormous, ranging from greater awareness of abandonment anxiety and the associated self-sabotaging behavior in attachment relationships to the development of the capacity for mentalized affectivity. As we construe it, mentalizing is crucial in setting the stage for putting to use the various emotion-regulation techniques patients with borderline personality disorder learn in other arenas of treatment, such as in dialectical behavior therapy skills training groups (see Lewis, Chapter 8).

To reiterate a theme of this chapter, educating patients about personality disorders engages them in mentalizing. By explaining the dynamics associated with personality disorders, and how these dynamics tend to get expressed in close relationships, we aim to help patients identify their maladaptive patterns and take responsibility and agency for them. We help patients begin to identify the connection between feelings and recurrent conflicts in attachment relationships with the hope that, by recognizing these feelings, they can begin to use them as cues for engaging mentalizing. We encourage patients to engage in a process of backward chaining, that is, to pinpoint the problematic behavior and follow backwards to identify the mental state that led to the behavior. We highlight the need to move from implicit to explicit mentalizing in this context. Patients report catching themselves repeating problematic interactions and saying to themselves, "Here I go again!" They are beginning to push the pause button through mentalizing. We commend the adage "Strike when the iron is cold" (Pine, 1984) – or at least lukewarm – when working on relationship conflicts, on the basis that extreme emotional arousal impairs mentalizing. Thus the psycho-educational arena for mentalizing dovetails with patients' work in individual and group psychotherapy. We hope that, having identified and practiced more adaptive patterns of interaction, patients can move back to more automatic implicit mentalizing.

Mentalizing in Treatment

To reiterate a point we made in the introduction to this chapter, we construe the psycho-educational groups on mentalizing as a meta-intervention in the sense that we are striving to build a therapeutic alliance by explaining to patients how we think about their treatment and how we believe they can best make use of it. We explain that we strive to replicate the developmental conditions that naturally promote mentalizing capacity, focusing particularly on secure attachments and optimal emotional arousal. We maintain that treatment ideally provides sufficient structure to allow for a sense of safety and security while retaining sufficient challenge and stress to push patients to expand their capacity to mentalize in the face of increasingly intense levels of emotional arousal. This discussion sets the stage for describing how the various components of treatment challenge and promote mentalizing, which we explain to patients as follows.

Treatment begins with a comprehensive *assessment*, the goal of which is to clarify the patient's psychiatric disorders and their exacerbating attachment contexts. We draw patients' attention to the fact that the assessment process draws heavily on mentalizing – not only in requiring self-understanding and narrative coherence but also in challenging patients to communicate their understanding, which requires them to keep the assessing clinician's mind in mind. Conversely, this process goes well when the patient has the experience that the clinician has his or her mind in mind. The assessment process exemplifies the spirit of inquisitiveness, for example, as the clinician intervenes, "If I am hearing you correctly what you are telling me is that you were thinking or feeling ... "

Medication might appear to be antithetical to mentalizing; yet we to point out to patients that, paradoxically, medication can be one of our most powerful pro-mentalizing interventions (see Bleiberg, Chapter 12). Mood disturbance, anxiety, and disorganized thinking impair mentalizing capacity; to the extent that medication is effective on all these fronts, medication will enhance mentalizing capacity as well as enabling the patient to make better use of other components of treatment that challenge and facilitate mentalizing.

As we have stated repeatedly, *psycho-education* promotes mentalizing. Not only do we educate patients about core concepts – including mentalizing, agency, and the therapeutic alliance – but also we educate them in depth about a wide range of psychiatric disorders and treatment approaches. Thus patients are learning continually about the influence of psychiatric disorders on their mental states and their relationships as well as about ways of influencing their mental states and relationships for the better.

Individual psychotherapy provides an opportunity for intensive practice in mentalizing. An effective psychotherapeutic relationship is the best analogue of a secure base in attachment that fosters mentalizing. Not only does psychotherapy entail mentalizing in the sense of exploring thoughts, feelings, hopes, wishes, dreams, and the like, but also psychotherapy provides the opportunity to experience and learn from failures in mentalizing, such as occur in transference enactments. Thus patients learn about conditions that promote mentalizing as well as about feelings and conflicts that impede it. With the help of the therapist, they learn how to mentalize in the face of conflicts and thereby to resolve conflicts – a skill we hope will generalize to other relationships.

Group psychotherapy offers one of the richest – and most demanding – mentalizing experiences in treatment. Like individual psychotherapy, group psychotherapy provides an opportunity to experience successes and failures in mentalizing, and group psychotherapy places a premium on remaining flexible and inquisitive, in effect, keeping the mind online in the face of emotional challenge. Group psychotherapy offers opportunities beyond individual psychotherapy to practice exploring the minds of others and to observe how others' mental states are affected by interpersonal interactions. Patients offer each other forthright feedback about mentalizing failures with comments such as "I don't think you are hearing me correctly." Patients also have the opportunity to clarify mental states with comments such as "Let me tell you what I meant when I said ... "

The treatment *milieu* provides ubiquitous informal opportunities for patients to wrestle with mentalizing challenges in innumerable interpersonal interactions and relationships. Interpersonal conflicts occur naturally in the milieu, and many patients explicitly recognize the need to mentalize in addressing and resolving these conflicts. As in individual and group psychotherapy, these interactions can provide opportunities to mentalize in relatively secure as well as in emotionally charged interpersonal contexts.

The Menninger Clinic employs a team approach that includes twice weekly *clinical rounds* with the patient as a central member of the core team (Munich, 2000). These 15-minute group rounds allow the entire team to address concerns that arise throughout the course of treatment. Often rounds are intense, partly due to time pressure and partly due to feelings evoked by being evaluated by a group of persons in authority. The interpersonal and emotional pressures provide a difficult mentalizing challenge. Indeed, we have dubbed clinical rounds a "mentalizing extravaganza" for a number of reasons: there are typically five or six individuals in the room at any one time; each individual has a different perspective; and there are multiple and sometimes conflicting agendas. The challenge for all members – clinicians as well as the patient – is keeping all other minds in mind with the goal of working toward some form of consensus.

We construe *marital and family therapy* as "mentalizing in the trenches," that is, in the crucible of attachment relationships. These relationships characteristically provoke the most glaring impairments in mentalizing; yet effective mentalizing is most crucial in these relationships. As most patients attest, feelings never run so high as when they are with their "nearest and dearest." These intense feelings can escalate rapidly in family situations, resulting in more heat than light. The inclusion of a marital or couples therapy process provides critical opportunities to identify failures in mentalizing in the presence of a therapist who can provide help, both by modeling mentalizing and by providing guidance to patients and their family members that afford the opportunity to practice. In a sense, all of treatment is a training ground for what will ultimately be of paramount importance: mentalizing in these attachment relationships.

EXPERIENTIAL EXERCISES

As just discussed, all of treatment affords opportunities to mentalize. Yet we are experimenting with supplementing the didactic material and group discussions with experiential exercises. These exercises demonstrate mentalizing in action and pinpoint patients' attention on the process. We practice what we preach: attend to mental states! Thus the exercises not only clarify what we mean by mentalizing but also give patients the opportunity to practice while receiving direct feedback during the course of the group. The following illustrates some of the exercises that we are currently using; the number and variety of such exercises is limited only by imagination (see also Fearon and colleagues, Chapter 10).

Tell a Story

This exercise uses images from an evocatively unstructured projective device known as the Object Relations Technique (Phillipson, 1955; Shaw, 2002). Each stimulus depicts shadowy figures engaged in ambiguous interactions. Patients write down a brief story about what might be happening in the picture, including the thoughts and feelings of the characters. Then patients share their stories, the essential elements of which are written on a large blackboard. The leaders highlight individual differences through the wide variations in the stories told. This discussion brings into bold relief the multiplicity of perspectives on mental states in ambiguous situations, which we extrapolate to real interpersonal interactions. In this context we reiterate the value of an inquisitive attitude as opposed to the non-mentalizing stance of certainty in interpreting interpersonal situations.

Next we engage patients in interpreting selected stories. Again, this process illustrates quite different interpretations of the same story. Notably, patients provide interpretations that differ in depth, typically dependent on how well they know the storyteller. Finally, the storyteller is asked to reflect on the varying interpretations, leading into discussions of the multiply determined nature of mental states and associated actions. We end the discussion by reflecting on the multi-layered nature of mental states and the proposition that mentalizing is more about asking questions and less about finding definitive answers.

Finding the Metaphor

A patient in the educational group proposed that we exploit the imaginative and playful facet of mentalizing by conveying mental states through metaphors. This exercise entails mentalizing at two levels: first, in generating the metaphors; second, in engaging group members in speculating about the feelings their peers' metaphors represent which, in turn, can be confirmed and disconfirmed by the person who generated the metaphor. The exercise invariably generates a wealth of metaphors from the commonplace (e.g., "stormy weather") to the unique (e.g., "bubbles in a jar with no lid"). The exercise also reveals individual differences as different participants read different meanings into the metaphors, partly as a result of their own projections. Some examples of metaphors will illustrate: "gray and red," symbolizing a patient's argument with her treatment team, after which she felt numb then enraged; and "the drain in a roomful of energy," symbolizing the patient's sense that he was not as alive and energized as others and that his depression drained the energy out of them. Another patient characterized his treatment thus: the medicine was his "armor" and the therapies his "weapons." Other metaphors include "two earthmovers doing battle," "a volcano exploding in the aftermath of a hurricane," and "a rampaging thunderstorm." We also ask for metaphors for hope, which have included "a sliver of sunlight coming in between the window shade and the window sill," "a yellow rose growing in the sand," and "an expanse of ocean with no obstacles."

Welcome to My Mind

Patients are asked to write up a list of facts that describe themselves, including their name, age, date of birth, schools they have attended, occupation, parents' occupations, spouse, and family members' names and occupations, pets, and the like. The list need not be exhaustive but rather illustrative in drawing attention to facts they typically use to describe themselves in social situations. Next patients are asked to describe themselves *without* any such facts with the intent of thinking about themselves in terms of mental states, including personality traits along with thoughts, feelings, wishes, fantasies, and so forth. This exercise shifts the focus from external to internal factors, and discussion often centers on what appears to be missing from the list.

Illustratively, Julie, a 25-year-old woman, was admitted for evaluation and treatment of longstanding difficulties in interpersonal relationships and problems "sticking to anything." She reported a long history of depression and anxiety and stated, "Everyone has given up on me because I am such a bitch," adding, "I've even given up on myself." Julie attended the mentalizing group with the hope that she would begin to understand the reasons for her feelings and actions as well as the impact of her behavior on herself and others in her world. Consistent with her reaction to most other groups, Julie initially scoffed at the syllabus, stating, "I've been through all this before – what good can talking about this stuff do for me?" Despite her derogatory attitude, however, she quickly became involved in this exercise; she listed her "credentials" while also minimizing her ability to "do anything right." When asked to describe herself without these facts, however, Julie's attitude entirely changed. She was the first group member to volunteer to describe her attributes: "bitchy, angry, frustrated, hard to like, but really a baby, needy, dependent, scared, fragile, spoiled, a real mess – I need help!" Through her self-description, she and other members of the group (including staff members) began recognizing her conflict: she longed for closeness and comfort but acknowledged that her fear and vulnerability led her to drive people away by being pushy. The group discussed how their view of her shifted and recognized their difficulty in mentalizing her, that is, seeing her more vulnerable side. This process allowed Julie to be more real in the group and to become more curious about what drove her. We used this opportunity to emphasize how the *recognition of conflict* is a sure sign of effective mentalizing.

Just the Facts

In this exercise patients are asked to think of a meaningful recent interaction and to write down a description of that interaction using only the objective facts – no mental states. Patients read their description and group members infer the mental states of the individuals involved. In turn, the patient in the situation validates or invalidates the inferences as well as considering new points of view. As in other exercises, the discussion highlights the varying levels and complexities of mental states as well as the challenges in being an accurate mind reader.

Illustratively, Amy, a 35-year-old professional woman, stated these facts to the group: "I went into clinical rounds to talk to my team about taking a pass to go shopping, and they told me I couldn't go." Group members first inferred that Amy's primary feeling was one of anger. They hypothesized that she might feel angry in the context of feeling let down and disappointed. One member suggested that the anger might also be a way of covering up feeling rather humiliated inasmuch as she – an adult professional – was being told that she could not go out to a shopping mall. Another group member took the conversation into the arena of control by suggesting that Amy's anger might also be a reaction to feeling vulnerable and impotent. After further discussion, Amy was asked to give feedback to the group. She stated that the group feedback she had received was accurate, but there was another important feeling that she had come to recognize only in the course of this discussion: she was also relieved that the team had declined her request. Although she had been making excellent progress, she was still feeling somewhat unsteady. She was pleased not only that her team had recognized this unsteadiness but also that they were willing risk her ire and disappointment in telling her of their concerns.

Looking to the Future

An extension of the Just the Facts exercise, this exercise focuses on a future interaction. Patients are asked to write down the facts of an interaction that they anticipate in the near future. Group members read their factual description, and the subsequent discussion focuses on anticipating possible mental states that the various individuals in the interaction might experience. The intent of this experience is to provide patients with examples of how *anticipatory mentalizing* can be helpful in preparing for challenging interactions.

Illustratively, Steven, a 47-year-old physician, had been admitted for treatment of depression and addiction to Valium that he had been self-prescribing. Steven told the group that he was planning to telephone his medical practice partner to inform her about his substance abuse problems. Initially, the group anticipated that his partner might be angry at Steven for self-prescribing, but the focus quickly shifted to the possibility that her anger might reflect significant concern for Steven's well being and health. The group also supposed that Steven would be anxious about making this call, fearing his partner's anger. Alternatively, another group member suggested that Steven might be eager to make the call inasmuch as it would bring his problem out in the open. A group member who knew him quite well anticipated that Steven would be ashamed, inasmuch as he had always placed such a high priority on being strong and perfect. Another member speculated that Steven might feel a sense of accomplishment in being able to throw off the mantle of perfection by admitting his faults and asking his partner for help. Steven reported that the whole discussion was helpful, because he had felt stuck in shame, and the dialogue opened his mind to a wide range of feelings such that he could approach the call with an open mind and greater curiosity.

Role-Play

In this exercise patients role-play a difficult interaction they recently had with someone, for example, a family member. After some discussion, the patient switches roles with the partner and takes the place of the family member. The ensuing discussion considers the patient's new perspective on the family member's mental states.

Illustratively, Greg, a 21-year-old patient, volunteered a recent discussion he had had with his father in which he told his father about his plans to return to college following the completion of his hospital stay. Greg reported that his father quickly became intensely angry, telling him that his plans were "hair-brained" and "evidence of how little you have done in treatment." After the initial role-playing, the group immediately focused on how scared the father appeared to be, speculating that his anger was covering up his fear that Greg might relapse into depression at college. After switching roles, Greg stated that he felt a keen sense of empathy for his father, especially in light of the impact his suicide attempt had on his father. He reported that he wanted to call his father again to give him more details about his discharge plans and to ask his father about his concerns. He reported that this new perspective allowed him to see that his father was not simply trying to control him but rather that his father likely shared his own fears about life beyond the hospital.

EFFECTIVENESS

We have not conducted a formal investigation of the effectiveness of this psycho-educational program inasmuch as it is an integral part of the treatment design; its unique contribution is difficult to gauge, because it is intermingled with a multiplicity of interventions also intended to promote mentalizing. Thus we are limited to anecdotal clinical observations. Most concretely, patients begin to talk with each other and with clinicians in terms of "mentalizing." We routinely overhear patient conversations including statements such as "I don't think you are mentalizing me correctly" or "I am having trouble mentalizing with so and so." Plainly, we have succeeded in drawing patients' attention to what we consider a crucial skill. Apparently, patients are becoming more aware of their difficulty mentalizing and therefore of when they are headed for dangerous interpersonal territory.

Conducting treatment within a therapeutic milieu allows patients to have a significant impact on the outcome of each other's treatment. Patients spend more time with one another than they do with clinicians; thus they are in an optimal position to support the treatment goals of the whole team. Patients are more likely to see problems within one another as they occur in the moment, and providing them with a common language allows them to help one another in critical moments. Thus we are encouraged to hear that patients are talking about mentalizing in their daily interactions.

We believe that giving patients a common language to use with us clinicians enhances the therapeutic alliance – a common factor in positive treatment outcomes. Patients rightly perceive that we respect their intelligence. They feel empowered in being able to talk to their treaters about the difficulties they are having with the concept and their practice of mentalizing. Identifying these difficulties promotes collaboration on specific treatment goals, thereby allowing for a finer focus on what needs to be achieved through the treatment process. Thus we are encouraged when we hear from patients' individual psychotherapists (who work in other treatment programs) that patients are using the concept of mentalizing constructively in their therapy.

We group leaders have become clear about another significant outcome: conducting these psycho-educational groups has dramatically refined our understanding of mentalizing and its complexities. Patients' feedback about how they understand and misunderstand the concept has provided much fertile ground for discussion, leading to an evolution of the concept and the process of teaching the concept to patients. Thus the group provides a mentalizing challenge to the leaders as well as the patients, and we have become keenly aware of the role of our own mentalizing capacities in the effectiveness of treatment. Ironically, educating patients about mentalizing requires an exceptionally high level of mentalizing, always a work in progress.

REFERENCES

Allen, J. G. (2001). *Traumatic Relationships and Serious Mental Disorders*. Chichester, UK: John Wiley & Sons, Ltd.

Allen, J. G. (2005). *Coping with Trauma: Hope through Understanding* (2nd edn). Washington, DC: American Psychiatric Publishing.

Allen, J. G., Bleiberg, E. & Haslam-Hopwood, G. T. G. (2003). *Mentalizing as a Compass for Treatment*. Houston, TX: The Menninger Clinic.

Becker, T. & Thornicroft, G. (1998). Community care and management of schizophrenia. *Current Opinion in Psychiatry, 11*, 49–54.

Colom, F., Vieta, E., Martinez-Aran, A., Reinares, M., Goikolea, J. M. & Benabarre, A. (2003). A randomized trial on the efficacy of group psychoeducation in the prophylaxis of recurrences in bipolar patients whose disease is in remission. *Archives of General Psychiatry, 60,* 402–407.

Corey, G. (2000). *Theory and Practice of Group Counseling* (5th edn). Stamford, CT: Brooks/Cole.

Dowrick, C., Dunn, G., Ayuso-Mateos, J. L., Dalgard, O. S., Page, H. & Lehtinen, V. (2000). Problem solving treatment and group psychoeducation for depression: multicentre randomized controlled trial. Outcomes of Depression International Network Group. *British Medical Journal, 321,* 1450–1454.

Easterbrook, J. A. (1959). The effect of emotion on cue utilization and the organization of behavior. *Psychological Review, 66,* 183–207.

Fonagy, P., Gergely, G., Jurist, E. & Target, M. (2002). *Affect Regulation, Mentalization, and the Development of the Self.* New York, NY: Other Press.

Frager, D. C., Coyne, L., Lyle, J., Coulter, P. L., Graham, P., Sargent, J., et al. (1999). Which treatments help? The patient's perspective. *Bulletin of The Menninger Clinic, 63,* 388–400.

Fristad, M. A., Goldberg-Arnold, J. S. & Gavazzi, S. M. (2002). Multifamily psychoeducation groups for families of children with bipolar disorder. *Bipolar Disorders, 4,* 254–262.

Kubany, E. S., Hill, E. E. & Owens, J. A. (2003). Cognitive trauma therapy for battered women with PTSD: preliminary findings. *Journal of Traumatic Stress, 16,* 81–91.

Lukens, E. P. & McFarlane, W. R. (2004). Psychoeducation as evidence based practice: considerations for practice, research and policy. *Brief Treatment and Crisis Intervention, 4,* 205–225.

McFarlane, W. R., Dixon, L., Lukens, E. P. & Luckstead, A. (2003). Family psychoeducation and schizophrenia: a review of the literature. *Journal of Marital and Family Therapy, 29,* 223–245.

Munich, R. L. (2000). Leadership and restructured roles: the evolving inpatient treatment team. *Bulletin of The Menninger Clinic, 64,* 482–493.

Peterson, C. B., Mitchell, J. E., Engboom, S., Nugent, S., Mussell, M. P. & Miller, J. P. (1998). Group cognitive behavioral treatment of binge eating disorder: a comparison of therapist led versus self-help formats. *International Journal of Eating Disorders, 24,* 125–136.

Phillipson, H. (1955). The object relations technique (plates and manual). London: Taristock Press.

Pine, F. (1984). The interpretive moment: variations on classical themes. *Bulletin of The Menninger Clinic, 48,* 54–71.

Potter, M. L., Williams, R. B. & Constanzo, R. (2004). Using nursing theory and structured psychoeducational curriculum with inpatient groups. *Journal of the American Psychiatric Nurses Association, 10,* 122–128.

Shaw, M. (2002). The object relations technique: assessing the individual. Manhasset, New York: ORT Institute, See also www.ortinstitute.org.

Simpson, I. (2002). Inpatient group work for patients with psychosis. *Nursing Times, 98,* 33–35.

Yudofsky, S. C. (2005). *Fatal Flaws: Navigating Destructive Relationships with People with Disorders of Personality and Character.* Washington, DC: American Psychiatric Publishing.

PART V

PREVENTION

14

MINDING THE BABY: A MENTALIZATION-BASED PARENTING PROGRAM

Lois S. Sadler, Arietta Slade, and Linda C. Mayes

Minding the Baby (MTB) is an interdisciplinary, collaborative, community-based home visiting program serving high-risk first-time parents living in the inner city. For young women living in urban poverty, the transition to parenthood poses a daunting challenge, as they must learn to care for their children against the backdrop of disadvantage, social isolation, and threats to physical and emotional survival. Often, they come to motherhood with their own histories of trauma, abandonment, and loss. The goal of MTB is to enhance the physical health, mental health, and development of infants and their mothers, and to develop sustaining and healthy attachments between mothers, children, and extended families (Slade et al., 2006; Slade, Sadler & Mayes, 2005).

In its emphasis on the development of healthy and sustaining mother–child relationships, MTB is in many respects similar in focus and emphasis to a range of successful home visiting programs in the United States and other developed countries, and indeed shares a variety of techniques with well established home visiting and infant mental health models (Olds, Hill, Robinson, Song & Little, 2000). We emphasize in this chapter, however, our specific focus on the development of parental reflective functioning (RF) or mentalization, and on helping parents keep their babies "in mind" physically, emotionally, and developmentally (Slade, 2002). For reasons we will describe below, we see the emphasis on the development of parental reflective capacities as crucial to promoting healthy attachment relationships as well as a range of physical, social, and emotional

Handbook of Mentalization-Based Treatment. Edited by J. G. Allen and P. Fonagy.
© 2006 John Wiley & Sons, Ltd.

developments in the mother, child, and other family members. We considered MTB as a mentalization-based treatment (Bateman & Fonagy, 2004; Fonagy & Target, 2005) from its inception, aimed particularly at the development of *reflective parenting*. We see this approach as particularly suited to the needs of high-risk parents.

We will first briefly review the background and guiding principles of MTB. The remainder of the chapter will be devoted to describing the specific conceptual and technical aspects of our reflective parenting approach. We will close with a brief review of our first wave of research findings and with directions for future research.

BACKGROUND

The two home visiting models that have been most rigorously evaluated are the nurse home visitation (NHV) model pioneered by David Olds, Harriet Kitzman, and their colleagues (Olds, 2002; Olds et al., 2000) and the infant–parent psychotherapy or mental health model pioneered by Selma Fraiberg (Fraiberg, 1980), and elaborated by Alicia Lieberman, Jeree Pawl, Christopher Heinicke, and their colleagues (Heinicke et al., 1999, 2000, Heinicke, Fineman, Ponce & Guthrie, 2001; Lieberman, Silverman & Pawl, 1999; Lieberman & Zeanah, 1999; Seligman, 1994).

MTB was born out of the attempt to bring these two models together; we aspired to provide high quality nursing care to developing families, while at the same time providing a depth of mental health and infant mental health care not previously offered in traditional NHV programs. Existing programs have tended to focus either on the physical health of the baby and coping resources of the mother or upon the emotional health of the mother–child dyad and the quality of the attachment relationship. While nursing models include attention to relationship building, this is not their primary focus, and most pediatric or public health nurses are not extensively trained in mental health. Indeed, it is often the case that mental health issues overwhelm public health nurses who are usually not adequately trained to handle them; at the same time, the nursing dimension has been critical to families' willingness to allow home visitors into their homes. Thus we developed MTB with the notion that a range of services to enhance physical health, mental health, parenting, and child development would be delivered by a nursing/mental health team.

PROGRAM OVERVIEW

In the MTB program, master's trained clinicians, including a clinical social worker (CSW) and a pediatric nurse practitioner (PNP), provide in-home interventions beginning in pregnancy and lasting until the child's second birthday.

During the prenatal phase of the intervention, MTB clinicians attempt to establish a relationship with the mother and other family members, to assess health and psychological functioning in the mother, and to make the baby and impending parenthood more real and presumably less overwhelming for the mothers.

After the birth of the baby and throughout the first year, MTB clinicians visit with participating families on a weekly basis, supporting the mother and modeling appropriate care giving. The PNP teaches each mother about basic infant care as well as about the child's growing skills in cognitive and language development, motor abilities, and social-emotional growth. The CSW provides information about social services and parenting, and continues to provide direct mental health interventions as needed. By providing the mothers with the necessary tools – both mental and physical – MTB clinicians enable the mothers to be better parents and to continue to grow as young adults. PNP and CSW visits are alternated weekly, beginning in pregnancy, and then move to an every-other-week schedule in the second year of the intervention. At the child's first birthday, we hold a "transition" visit with both home visitors, mother, and child. Home visitors bring small token gifts for mother and child, and they discuss the family's progress over the first 15 months of the intervention. Goals are set for the second year, both for the mother and her own life and her growing relationship with her child, as well as for the child's health and development.

During the second year, the focus of developmental and childrearing discussions changes to the content around toddler issues, behavior, feeding, discipline, and planning for toilet training, all of which reflect the emerging individuation in the child; discussion also considers the feelings of competition, sadness, or sometimes anger that are stirred up in mothers in response to their more demanding child. Ongoing attention is given to physical health issues for mother (particularly contraceptive care) and child, and to the emotional health of the mother and child. At the child's second birthday there is a "graduation" visit with both home visitors, mother, child, and any family members invited by the mother. At this visit a small photo album is given to the mother as a remembrance of the work and progress during the program, and final goals and goodbyes are accomplished. Phone contact is available after graduation. Mothers often find it reassuring to check in with the home visitors after graduation, for this allows them a gradual way of letting go and assuming more complete responsibility for childrearing, while still feeling the clinicians' support and guidance.

The plan for the content and progression of visits is organized and developed in an intervention manual (Slade et al., 2004) but also remains flexible and is adjusted depending upon a range of factors: the mother's or the baby's needs (e.g., perinatal psychosis in mother, premature twins, etc.), or crises that the family might be experiencing that day (e.g., impending loss of housing). Even when there are crises, each event is considered from the vantage point of its impact upon the mother's and the baby's needs and feelings: "How would hearing this argument you've been having with your boyfriend make the baby feel? How has she behaved since the argument?" The clinicians use a variety of published supplemental curricula and teaching materials that have been previously developed and tested for similar populations of families (see Slade et al., 2004).

Guiding Principles

MTB is based upon a series of guiding principles. While space does not permit us to explicate them fully here, a brief summary follows (see also Slade et al., 2005, in press).

(1) The intervention is based in and driven by theory, in this case attachment and social ecology theory generally, and mentalization theory in particular (Fonagy et al., 2002).
(2) MTB is based upon an interdisciplinary team approach, with services provided by both an advanced practice nurse practitioner and a licensed CSW. "Interdisciplinary" in this context refers to the effort to provide services in a truly integrated way.
(3) MTB services are provided by master's level clinicians, whose training presumably puts them in a better position to manage and assess the complex clinical issues involved in working with highly disadvantaged and traumatized populations.
(4) The intensity of home-based services must match the level of complexity and need in high-risk families.
(5) The development of RF, as well as a range of health and mental health outcomes, occurs within the context of a relationship. Because the relationship between the mother and home visitor – and indeed the family and home visitor – is crucial to change along a range of dimensions, understanding and developing such relationships is crucial to every single aspect of our work.
(6) Successful interventions must be embedded in a system of community health care. Programs that are not adequately linked to the range of services provided by local health providers and other community agencies risk becoming as isolated and disenfranchised as the populations they serve.
(7) All these assumptions, and the interventions that flow from them, require rigorous and ongoing evaluation. Thus from the start we have embedded our intervention within a program of research, which we will describe below.

MTB: A Mentalization-Based Parenting Program

MTB is grounded in attachment and social ecology theories; however, it is also aimed specifically at the development of parental RF or mentalization. Mentalizing (Fonagy, Gergely, Jurist & Target, 2002) refers to the capacity to envision mental states in the self or the other, and mentalizing capacity is operationalized in measures of RF. Fonagy and his colleagues first addressed the import of mentalization for the development of a range of social relationships within the context of attachment theory over 10 years ago (Fonagy et al., 1995). In a broad-ranging series of papers published since then, Fonagy and his colleagues (2002) have extended these initial formulations in a number of ways, establishing the importance of the mentalizing capacity for a range of clinical, biosocial, neuropsychological, and developmental outcomes (see Fonagy, Chapter 3).

Inherent in all of Fonagy's work is the notion that the mother's capacity to keep her child in mind makes it possible for him to discover his own mind; in other words, the mother's mentalizing capacity plays a crucial role in the development of mentalizing capacities in the child. In recent research, we tested this assumption directly by evaluating *parental RF* (Slade, 2005), namely, *a mother's capacity to make sense of her own and her child's mental states*. In a series of research studies, we found that a mother's mentalizing capacity – *as it pertains specifically to her relationship with her child* – predicts secure attachment organization in the child (Slade, Grienenberger, Bernbach, Levy & Locker, 2005), and it is negatively correlated with hostile, intrusive, or withdrawn caregiving behaviors (Grienenberger, Slade & Kelly, 2005). And, while RF is generally lower in a high-risk population of inner-city mothers, the effects of poverty and trauma on RF are greatly exacerbated by maternal drug use, with drug using mothers scoring the lowest on RF in a cohort of high-risk mothers (Truman, Levy, Mayes & Slade, 2002).

In view of the theory and evidence described by Fonagy, Gergely, Jurist and Target (2002), as well as the findings of our own research, we felt strongly that targeting the development of parental mentalizing capacities would be central to any successful intervention. That is, while one of our general aims was to enhance the attachment relationship between mother and child, we felt that focusing on the development of mentalizing capacities in mothers provided a crucial means to help them become more regulating, sensitive, and autonomy promoting. Virtually all the mothers we serve are at high risk for the development of relationship disturbances, given their histories of trauma, mental illness, and the deleterious effects of chronic poverty; hence the emphasis on the development of mentalizing capacities seemed especially crucial. Fonagy and his colleagues have repeatedly suggested that reflective capacities serve a range of protective functions in relation to trauma (Fonagy et al., 1995, 2002).

It is important to note that the development of maternal mentalizing is likely one of the outcomes of all successful relationship-based interventions; in particular, it is likely that the mother's developing ability to separate her experience of the child from her own projections and distorted affects is a specific outcome of the development of reflective capacities. Mentalization provides the *mechanism* whereby both representations and behavior are changed. A parent high in RF is able to see her child – even as a young infant – as having needs, desires, and intentions that are different from her own. This is not to say that she feels *separate* from her child; indeed, RF appears related in a number of ways to the development of affectively vital, positive, and coherent representations of the child. Rather, she sees herself as intimately connected to and therefore able to contain and regulate this child who is at once a part of her and uniquely separate. Parents who are low in RF are vulnerable to developing distorted and pathological representations of their children and of attributing malevolent and otherwise distorted intentions to them, whereas more developed reflective capacities appear to preclude the elaboration and reification of such disrupted representations. At the highest levels of RF, mothers are not only well able to regulate their children but also can see them as complex, intentional beings whose mental states emerge in dynamic relation to those of their caregivers.

MTB: The Development of the Reflective Stance

MTB is based on the notion that the development of reflective capacities is crucial to a mother's developing a facilitating and secure relationship with her child. Thus, one of our primary aims in working with the mothers in our study is to help them develop a *reflective stance*, that is, to be able to envision mental states in themselves and in their children. This stance begins with the ability to identify basic mental states, namely, *thoughts, feelings, desires, intentions, and beliefs* in the self and others. From the ability to identify mental states emerges the capacity to think about and imagine them in a variety of ways, that is, to mentalize.

We think of this process as having four stages: the development of a therapeutic relationship, the provision of concrete services, the development of the capacity to acknowledge and tolerate mental states, and the move toward mentalization. The starting point is the establishment of a therapeutic relationship. At first, this relationship is defined primarily by the provision of concrete services and by a benign, accepting, and supportive presence. Only after the relationship has been well established, and the mothers feel assured in real ways about our availability and consistency, can we begin to work with them around first acknowledging and then reflecting about mental states. At these later stages, the *in vivo* work with mother and baby allows myriad opportunities for home visitors to bring alive aspects of a reflective stance.

In the sections that follow, we describe each of these components in greater detail, and we specify some of the techniques that we have developed or borrowed from other home visiting models that help mothers (and families) make meaning of mental states. Home visitors receive extensive training in attachment and mentalization theory. It is important to note in this context that the development of reflective capacities is only one aspect of the work that we do; some of our techniques are targeted to develop mentalization specifically, whereas other things that we do may or may not have an indirect impact on mentalizing.

Thus, how home visitors engage mothers in the moment emerges out of their understanding of the construct and their recognition of the precursors and signs of RF. This allows them to creatively synthesize their theoretical knowledge on the one hand and their understanding of the mother and baby on the other.

The Development of the Relationship

The ability to contemplate one's internal experience, and that of the other, evolves within the context of a safe and containing relationship. Ideally, this process happens first in infancy, when the child begins to experience herself as an intentional being, held in mind by her caregiver as feeling, desiring, and believing (Fonagy et al., 1995). Few, if any, of the mothers in our study had sustaining and secure relationships with their own mothers or other caregivers. For the most part, their primary relationships had been disrupted by violence, abandonment, and other sorts of profound betrayals (Slade et al., 2005). Many of our mothers have struggled with depression and anxiety; some have struggled with more severe forms of mental illness, including psychosis and posttraumatic stress disorder. As Fonagy and his colleagues have noted, for individuals whose memories, thoughts, and feelings are intense and overwhelming, and whose experience of others has been fraught with fear and malevolent intent, the contemplation of minds can be very fraught (Fonagy et al., 2002), resulting in failures in the development of mentalizing capacities. Indeed, most of our mothers began the study with very low levels of RF, and they often found keeping themselves or another "in mind" very frightening and disruptive.

From the beginning, home visitors provide mothers with a comprehensive web of care (Lieberman, 2003) that includes attention to their (and the baby's) physical health and emotional health; this array of concrete services is of utmost value and importance to young women who are often at a loss when it comes to taking care of themselves and obtaining basic medical and social services. Above and beyond concrete services, however, is the less tangible experience of being known, accepted, and affirmed by the home visitors. As has been documented again and again by clinicians working within relationship-based models (Fraiberg, 1980; Lieberman, 2003; Lieberman & Pawl, 1993), the provision of a secure base is intrinsic to any successful intervention program. The experience of being heard by a caring, containing adult who does not force her opinions upon the mother, is not judging or critical, and who is able to hold the mother's chaotic and painful history in mind without becoming dysregulated and fragmented, is profoundly healing. Equally crucial is the clinician's *affirmation* and praise for the mother's successes in taking care of herself and her baby. The therapeutic aspect of this relationship extends beyond its power to help the mother begin to experience others as trustworthy and reliable; it also serves as a template for the kind of relationship we hope she will have with her child (and that we try to have with the child as he or she develops).

The home visitors allow the mother to discover her own feelings and capacities without placing rigid constraints on her autonomy; at the same time they create boundaries that are containing and allow her to feel safe. They move slowly and respectfully, perhaps meeting away from the home in the library or a coffee shop until the mother is comfortable opening her home to the clinicians, conducting interviews, and gathering material at a rate that is comfortable for the mother. Because few mothers have had experiences with health clinicians that are positive, ongoing, or consistent, it often takes a while for families and mothers to realize that the MTB home visitors are accessible and reliable; if they are called, they will follow up with returned calls and questions answered. It may also take a while for families to understand that home visitors will not give up on the family with missed appointments and will stay engaged and gradually teach them about the structure and mutual rules for visits (e.g., calling to cancel or writing down visit times/days on a calendar) while the relationship is strengthening and growing.

From the start, the clinicians treat mothers as *mentalizing beings* whose internal experiences are tolerable, meaningful, and comprehensible; they *model* the reflective stance, beginning with the basic assumption that the mothers' behavior and emotional dispositions make sense and can be understood. It is important to emphasize that we are not *teaching* RF. While mothers learn many different kinds of things from the home visitors, they are not taught to mentalize in any kind of formal, didactic way. Mentalization arises out of the relationship; while it is modeled by home visitors all the time, and while mothers' efforts to make sense of themselves and their children are scaffolded by home visitors in myriad ways, this is an interpersonal and not a didactic process. The mothers experience themselves as *meaningful* in the eyes of the home visitors; the experience of being held in mind as a coherent, intentional person who is trying to do her best allows mothers to start experiencing themselves and in the baby in the same way.

The Provision of Concrete Services

As described above, home visitors deliver an array of concrete services to mothers; this begins from the first day of the program. It is hard to emphasize sufficiently how deprived many of our mothers are, and how desperately they need to be connected with health, social service, educational, and other supports. They need help remembering medical visits, getting to medical visits, and obtaining medicines; they also need help with housing, benefits, schooling, food, and the like. Home visitors offer mothers tangible evidence of their support and concern: they carry a bag of handouts, books, videos, and toys; and sometimes when necessary they bring diapers and fresh food. They bring the necessary forms to sign up for housing and welfare benefits, and they sit with mothers while they fill them out. They accompany mothers to agency visits, standing in line beside them for hours. They tackle the administrative phone calls that can be so onerous, slowly turning the job over to mothers. They teach the mother to attend to the body in a variety of ways: helping her prepare nutritious meals for herself and her baby, reduce her own stress through yoga stretches and relaxation, and help her baby relax through massage. Home visitors try to leave behind something of themselves after each visit: a list they've written together with the mother of simple goals for the week, a rubber duck for the baby, a handout on stress reduction – evidence that they have been there and will return. This extraordinary level of need can be very hard to grasp, and the experience provides an immediate and painful lesson for home visitors on the broad and deep impacts of urban poverty.

The link between concrete services and the development of mentalization may seem obscure but, like the establishment of a therapeutic relationship, the link is a crucial aspect of the mothers' slowly starting to identify themselves and the baby as having bodily and psychological needs that can be described and met. Psychoanalysts, beginning with Winnicott and later Stern, have described the path to affect regulation and self-containment as beginning with the child's having his basic needs met (Winnicott, 1965) and attuned to (Stern, 1985) within the context of his primary relationship. The mother's capacity to *meet the infant's gesture* (Winnicott, 1965), namely, treat his needs as real and *meaningful*, is what ultimately makes self-experience feel real and interpersonally meaningful *to the child*. For many of our mothers, self-experience has remained murky, uncharted territory, largely because they have had few experiences of being truly known by their primary caregivers. Thus the home visitors' initial and continuing recognition of mothers' basic needs begins to help them experience these needs as real, and – even more important – to recognize that they can develop the tools to get them met and attended to. The kind of diffuse neediness that is often intrinsic to persons immersed in chronic poverty is thus transformed into organized care seeking and problem solving.

The Capacity to Acknowledge and Tolerate Mental States

The development of the therapeutic relationship and the provision of concrete services are necessary prerequisites for any mentalizing work, and they provide the context for the next two steps in the process: the development of the capacity to acknowledge and tolerate mental states, and the emergence of mentalization. The acknowledgement of mental states is a first and crucial step in the development of the mentalizing.

For the most part, the mothers in our project show very little evidence of RF or mentalizing capacities. They rely upon a physical stance; that is, they describe their own and others' experience in terms of concrete actions and physical properties ("He's a bad seed," "My mother's just a pig"). Many of our mothers begin the project with very few words for their most basic emotional experiences. When asked, for instance, how they felt when they found out they were pregnant, most mothers answer in diffuse, non-specific ways. Common responses such as "crazy," "shocked," and "weird" convey the general experience of being overwhelmed and confused by strong emotion (Patterson, Slade & Sadler, 2005). They have little appreciation of the relationship between thoughts, feelings, and actions, and they tend to be quite impulsive and inflexible in their understanding. They often have little sense of the shape or potential meaning of their own life history, particularly as it pertains to their experience in relationships.

Thus, one of the first things home visitors have in mind is to help mothers begin to identify their most basic feelings and needs. To this end, home visitors label feelings all the time (Fonagy & Target, 2005). In addition, providing an array of services and meeting needs mothers don't realize they have is a first step in helping them begin to identify their own internal experience. So are the discussions of health concerns, nutrition, housing, education, childcare, and the like that form the basic structure of early home visits. By keeping in mind the mother's needs and concerns, and by beginning to meet them, clinicians are helping mothers bring them to the fore and articulate them for the first time. In essence, concrete needs are the vehicle whereby the mother begins to express more complex internal desires and fears.

Once these feelings begin to be articulated (or in some cases, enacted), the home visitors can set about helping the mother cope with them. As an example, many mothers have a great deal of anxiety about labor and delivery, anxiety that often stems from fears of losing control and of being restrained. These anxieties are especially marked in women who have experienced sexual or physical abuse. Under such circumstances, the nurse practitioner works with the mother to develop a labor plan (Seng, 2002; Simkin, 1992), and together they walk through every potential step in the labor process. The nurse practitioner helps the mother to think through the decisions she'll be asked to make as labor progresses and to anticipate her reactions to being physically vulnerable and potentially restrained. For many women, developing a labor plan provided a crucial opportunity to put their feelings into words and to consider ways to master and contain the potentially traumatizing aspects of labor. This is but one example of the move from concrete need to feeling to a coping strategy that is at the heart of our model: identify a feeling and then develop a means of regulating and containing it.

While one of the primary goals of our intervention is to help the mother hold the baby in mind, the work always begins with the mother finding the words for her own internal experience, and for her own life history. Only then can she begin to tolerate and regulate her baby's experience. Understanding that the baby *has* feelings and desires is an achievement for most of our mothers. Indeed, many begin the project with very little sense of what a real baby will be like. Some have idealized expectations, and some have none at all; a very few (typically those who had cared for younger siblings or extended family members) can actually envision what it will be like to care for an infant. The work of the home visitors in these situations is to begin slowly to make the baby real for the mother. Again, we do this first via concrete preparation and planning; for instance, we help the mother set up the baby's bed and sleeping area, or we help her imagine how she will balance her return to school with caregiving. Simple creative activities such as making something for the baby – a poem, a blanket, or a painting – offer a slightly different form of concrete preparation, one that often brings positive and hopeful feelings to the fore.

Once the baby is born, home visitors use a number of other techniques to help mothers see their babies as feeling and intentional beings. This begins, for instance, with simple and ongoing attention to infants' states: crying, active alert, quiet alert, drowsy, and sleeping. Simple techniques like speaking for the baby (Carter, Osofsky & Hann, 1991) and imitating the baby provide a direct way of teaching the mother that the baby has feelings, expectations, needs, and desires, just as they do, and that these can be understood by becoming attentive and responsive to their cues. This experience also helps them adjust their own expectations and interactions to the baby's readiness for engagement and learning. It is our hope that such techniques will ultimately allow mothers to sit with, observe, and tolerate the baby's state themselves.

Such exercises offer ideal opportunities for *foreshadowing*, that is, beginning to think through and rehearse with the mother the next stages in the child's and her own development. These rehearsals, which take place all the time during home visits, are in effect little mentalization exercises: "You're going to be feeling this and that when you deliver." "Your baby is going to want to get up and walk when she's in the playpen." Thus the home visitor provides a scaffold for the mother's developing capacity first to recognize and then to envision mental states.

The emergence of mentalization. Once mothers can begin to label and tolerate thoughts and feelings, mentalizing becomes increasingly possible. The key components of a reflective stance are described by Fonagy and his colleagues (Fonagy, Target, Steele & Steele, 1998) as an awareness of the nature of mental states, the capacity to tease out mental states underlying behavior, and recognizing developmental aspects of mental states. As mothers begin to be able to observe and tolerate their own feelings, as well as observe and tolerate their babies' feelings, we hope to see manifestations of each of these components begin to emerge.

An awareness of the nature of mental states. Mental states have both normative and idiosyncratic properties; for instance, a child will naturally be sad at being separated from mother but also may have reactions and feelings that cannot readily be understood. In this way, mental states are can be both predictable and opaque. Once mothers begin to recognize feelings and other internal experiences in themselves and in their children, they can begin to play with mental states.

Dialogues with home visitors provide an ideal opportunity to do this. "Maybe he's feeling a little out of sorts today because he just had his shots." "Maybe you're feeling a little overwhelmed at going back to school so soon after the baby's birth." In other words, mental states make sense and can be understood. Sometimes this playful thinking takes a little work or guessing on the part of the mother, but the discovery then becomes part of the process. We often see that mothers' willingness to be curious about their children's internal experience will lead to much more productive and pleasurable interactions. For instance, one mother found her daughter's insistence on being in the kitchen while she was cooking very annoying. Once she recognized her daughter's wish to be *with* her and *like* her, however, she gave her daughter her own "cooking" materials. This gave the child much pleasure and led to many playful, loving exchanges between them.

The capacity to tease out mental states underlying behavior. Gradually, mothers begin to understand that their own and their child's behavior can be understood in terms of mental states. Thus, for instance, the child's clinging in anticipation of separation is understood as evidence of his *wish* to have his mother stay. The child is no longer understood concretely in terms of his behavior, but as an intentional being who expresses his feelings through behavior. The capacity to read behavior in terms of underlying intention also depends upon one's ability to read mental states accurately. The more accurately a parent reads a child's mental state, for instance, the more she will be able to respond sensitively to his behavior. Mothers often misread their child's intention; Fonagy and Target (2005) refer to this as *pseudomentalizing* (see also Fearon and colleagues, Chapter 10). One mother, for instance, began to tease her child when he cried after catching his finger in the door. "You're a faker!" she exclaimed, mocking him. The home visitor gently spoke for the baby: "Ooh, that hurt. You're kinda' scared and want Mommy to make it feel better." Thus, she was first trying to help mother *accurately* perceive the child's intention. Then, once mother began to see the child's distress, the home visitor could guide her toward comforting the child. By reframing the baby's intention for the mother, home visitors can correct derailed interactions.

Finally, the *recognition of the developmental aspects of mental states*: mental states change over time and in relation to each other. Unless they are un-modulated, most mental states diminish over time; mental states also have other dynamic properties, such that they are mutually influenced by other mental states and behaviors. The realization that mental states are not concrete entities, but rather fluid and changing dynamic states, can be enormously helpful to mothers: the baby's distress will lessen, her own anxiety will pass, and she can regulate something which had overwhelmed her in the past. This kind of understanding grows out of the ongoing conversation she is having with the home visitors about internal experience. Comments like "See how much longer he's able to wait for the bottle today" and "See how much less worried you are about getting him calmed down" serve to continuously underline the changing nature of internal experience.

Techniques

There are three aspects of the stance that home visitors take that aid in the development of mentalizing. First, they are always wondering about the mother's internal state, about the baby's, and about the meaning and intention underlying behavior. Thus, in their wondering, they become the voice for mother's and others' internal experience. Second, they are always asking the mother to wonder what she might be feeling and what the child might be feeling. In this way, home visitors engage the mother in wondering herself, engaging her in the act of mentalizing on an ongoing basis: "What do you suppose he's feeling now?" "Why do you think he might be waking up in the middle of the night all of a sudden?" Third, by modeling a reflective stance, and encouraging the mother to take a reflective stance, home visitors are also modeling taking a moment to pause and contemplate (Fonagy & Target, 2005), a crucial step in the regulation of affect and behavior.

Language is one way to bring internal experience alive for the mothers. Another is providing concrete reminders of the processes underscored in the home visits; handouts, videotapes, books, supplies, and other tangible materials support the process of contemplation and reflection. Another particularly powerful tool is the review of previously videotaped interactions between mother and child. Mothers and babies are videotaped at four months in face-to-face interaction with their babies, and a copy is made for the mother to keep at home. These tapes are then reviewed with the social worker at clinically appropriate intervals. The sessions in which the mother and clinician observe the videotape provide ideal opportunities for the social worker to speak for the baby; even more important, they allow the mother to begin to think about the baby's intention at some remove. She can look at the tape, and – given the support of the home visitor – actively begin to contemplate what the baby might have been feeling and what she might have been feeling. It is also in this context that the mother can begin to think about changes in the baby's intentions over time, and she can see very directly the relationship between her own mental state and the baby's behavior. This very powerful tool offers an *in vivo* opportunity to mentalize, outside the immediate pressures of the baby's demands and the mother's own emotional (and presumably physiological) reactions.

Play, which is something that many mothers find quite difficult in the beginning, provides another kind of opportunity for mentalizing. By definition, the state a mother enters into when she plays (and that the child enters into when he plays) is one in which feelings, ideas, fantasies, and wishes are treated as experiences that can be played with in an unthreatening way. That is, they can be envisioned, or mentalized. They are not *real*, but rather experiences to be reversed, laughed over, exaggerated, or enacted, but always within the context of play. Home visitors often help mothers engage in face-to-face play in the earliest months of their infants' lives; these simple games are often some of the earliest ways that mothers can take on the child's emotional and physical experience and play with it. As children get older, mothers are encouraged to get down on the floor and play with the children directly and, as they get even older, to participate in pretend and other forms of imaginary play. All these simple games help mothers to envision mental states in the child, and they create an experience in which the child is held by the mother in an unthreatening and intimate way.

It has been our experience and interpretation of the home visiting program literature that none of the key elements of the MTB program are effective as a stand-alone approach to working with at-risk families; however, when all the elements and strategies are implemented in an integral system of preventive care for young first-time families, we are learning that this program can be a very powerful experience in their lives. The trusting and consistent relationship (or secure base) provided by clinicians becomes the conduit for the information imparted as well as for the reflective parenting strategies modeled for parents. Mothers report that their experience of being held in mind by the home visitors is an extremely positive experience. They report feeling respected by accessible clinicians who provide useful information as well as helpful approaches to raising their children. They come to think of the home visitors as part of the family who want to help them become competent and more independent young adults as well as nurturing parents. One young mother said of the MTB home visitors, "They help you to *help you*," "They always asked for your input and they were accessible, like they always returned your phone calls," and finally, "They have concern for you the parent as well as your baby ... I was clueless ... I have this baby, now what do I do? Minding the Baby helps you develop a plan for raising your child and for your own goals in life."

Regarding the reflective parenting process, one mother stated, "When you are aware about yourself, it's easier to be aware of your child." Another comment referred to how the home visitors helped one mother stop and think when interacting with her daughter, "They changed my framework of thinking about my daughter. They helped me to think things out ... and to think about her personality when I talk to her."

EARLY RESEARCH FINDINGS

These qualitative impressions have been supported by our initial research findings. Since the program's inception, the team has been very encouraged by its impact on maternal and child health. While still involved in an ongoing evaluation of the program, the MTB team has seen several key improvements in parenting and family skills. During the first phase of feasibility testing, we evaluated the effects of the intervention on a small cohort of mothers, and we developed a clinical intervention manual. Our results indicate that MTB has had a significant impact on the health, welfare, and quality of life of the first cohort of mother–infant dyads and their families enrolled in the program.

The experimental longitudinal two-group study is ongoing and includes a sample of multi-ethnic and socio-economically disadvantaged first-time mothers between the ages of 14 and 25 (and their infants) who live in an urban community and are recruited through prenatal groups at a community health center. Both study groups receive standard prenatal, postpartum, and pediatric primary care at the community health center. The intervention group also receives the manualized MTB program as previously described. Maternal variables (demographics, depression, mastery, RF, and maternal life course outcomes) and child outcome variables (health and attachment classification) are followed over time (pregnancy, 12 months, and 24 months) as well as compared between the two groups.

We are following both groups (31 intervention and 10 control) of mothers (and infants) with 66% of Latina, 23% African American, and 11% diverse ethnic backgrounds and with a mean age of 20.5 years. Marital status includes 13% married, 60% cohabiting, and 27% single with no involvement from the infant's father. Mothers' backgrounds include much early trauma (41% sexual abuse, 38% physical abuse, and 27% with posttraumatic symptoms), and family and partner relationships reflecting poverty, violence (25% with domestic violence and 55% with drug/alcohol abuse in the family), and mental health concerns. At baseline, 55% of the mothers reported a previous history of depression; 60% scored in the mild-to-moderate range of depressive symptoms, and 65% reported low mastery scores.

In the intervention group, by 15 to 18 months we see families with positive relationships with both home visitors, mothers returning to school and work, no mothers with rapid subsequent pregnancies or sexually transmitted infections, and many with stabilized relationships with partners or termination of destructive relationships. Preliminary findings reveal that infant health outcomes include high breastfeeding rates (73% at birth; 40% at 3 months), all children are up to date with immunizations; there are no reports to the Department of Children and Families (DCF), and there are no cases of asthma or dental caries. Maternal RF scores are low at baseline (3.15 ± 0.92) and inversely correlated with posttraumatic stress symptoms ($r = -0.43$). Parental RF (Parent Development Interview) at 24 months appears improved from baseline, and preliminary review of infant attachment (Strange Situation Procedure) at 12 to 18 months indicates only 8% of the sample show the most insecure (disorganized) pattern of attachment.

SUMMARY

Ongoing study will help evaluate changes over time and the contrasts between groups. We believe that our preliminary positive findings may be associated with relationship building with home-visitor clinicians; modeling of reflective parenting approaches; close follow-up that conveys importance of their health and caring concern of home visitors; regular safety checks/teaching in households; environmental work with potential allergens; encouragement of breastfeeding and no second-hand smoke exposure; and pediatric anticipatory guidance reinforced and made to come alive in the home and family. The mental health and social outcomes may be associated with the tenacious follow-up of social needs, problems, and care referrals; orienting mothers to the agencies and approaches needed for necessary social and health services; coaching families through the difficult systems and institutions needed for help; in-home therapy for mothers; and much work around issues of domestic violence and safety.

Preliminary findings suggest that this intensive relationship-based home visiting program may be crucial to helping high-risk families for whom significant attachment and relationship disruption preclude response to other less intensive interventions. Ongoing evaluation of the program will continue to inform us about the effectiveness and the many potential benefits of this preventive model with young families.

ACKNOWLEDGEMENTS

This work was supported by grants from the Irving B. Harris Foundation, the Anne E. Casey Foundation, NIH/NINR (P30NR08999), and NIH/NICHD (R21HD04869-01A1). The work grew out of collaboration among the Yale Child Study Center, the Yale School of Nursing, and the Fair Haven Community Health Center. We wish to thank members of our clinical and research teams, including Cheryl deDios-Kenn, Denise Webb, Michelle Patterson, Nancy Close, Patricia Miller, Serena Cherry, Tracey Fender, and Alex Meier-Tomkins. We would also like to thank Jean Adnopoz, the Director of Family Support Services at the Yale Child Study Center, as well as Janice Ezepchick, both of who were instrumental in beginning the program. Finally, we wish to thank the administration and staff at Fair Haven Community Health Center, particularly Katrina Clark, Kate Mitcheom, Karen Klein, and Laurel Shader, who helped develop the program and have provided MTB with a clinical home.

REFERENCES

Bateman, A. W. & Fonagy, P. (2004). *Psychotherapy for Borderline Personality Disorders: Mentalization Based Treatment*. Oxford, England: Oxford University Press.

Carter, S., Osofsky, J. & Hann, D. (1991). Speaking for the baby: a therapeutic intervention with adolescent mothers and their infants. *Infant Mental Health Journal, 12,* 291–301.

Fonagy, P. & Target, M. (2005). *Short-Term Mentalization and Relational Therapy (SMART), for Families of Children with Emotional or Conduct Problems.* Paper presented at the Yale Child Study Center, New Haven, CT, 15 March 2005.

Fonagy, P., Gergely, G., Jurist, E. & Target, M. (eds). (2002). *Affect Regulation, Mentalization, and the Development of the Self.* New York: Other Press.

Fonagy, P., Steele, H., Steele, M., Leigh, T., Kennedy, R., Mattoon, G., et al. (1995). Attachment, the reflective self, and borderline states: the predictive specificity of the Adult Attachment Interview and pathological emotional development. In S. Goldberg, R. Muir & J. Kerr (eds), *Attachment Theory: Social, Developmental, and Clinical Perspectives* (pp. 233–278). New York: Analytic Press.

Fonagy, P., Target, M., Steele, H. & Steele, M. (1998). *Reflective Functioning Manual, Version 5.0, for Application to Adult Attachment Interviews.* London: University College London.

Fraiberg, S. (Ed.). (1980). *Clinical Studies in Infant Mental Health.* New York: Harcourt Brace.

Grienenberger, J., Slade, A. & Kelly, K. (2005). Maternal reflective functioning, mother-infant affective communication, and infant attachment: exploring the link between mental states and observed caregiving behavior in the intergenerational transmission of attachment. *Attachment and Human Development.*

Heinicke, C., Fineman, N. R., Ponce, V. A. & Guthrie, D. (2001). Relation based intervention with at-risk mothers: outcomes in the second year of life. *Infant Mental Health Journal, 22,* 431–462.

Heinicke, C., Fineman, N., Ruth, G., Recchia, L., Guthrie, D. & Rodning, C. (1999). Relationship-based intervention with at-risk first time mothers: outcome in the first year of life. *Infant Mental Health Journal, 20,* 349–374.

Heinicke, C., Goorsky, M., Moscov, S., Dudley, K., Gordon, J., Schneider, C., et al. (2000). Relationship based interventions with at-risk mothers: variations in process and outcome. *Infant Mental Health Journal, 21,* 133–155.

Lieberman, A. F. (2003). *Starting Early: Prenatal and Infant Intervention.* Paper presented at Irving B. Harris Festschrift, Chicago, IL, 12 May 2003.

Lieberman, A., Silverman, R. & Pawl, J. (1999). Infant-parent psychotherapy: core concepts and current approaches. In C. H. Zeanah (ed.), *Handbook of Infant Mental Health* (pp. 472–485). New York: Guilford Press.

Lieberman, A. F. & Pawl, J. H. (1993). Infant-Parent Psychotherapy. In C. H. Zeanah (ed.), *Handbook of Infant Mental Health* (pp. 427–442). New York: Guilford.

Lieberman, A. F. & Zeanah, C. (1999). Contributions of attachment theory to infant-parent psychotherapy and other interventions with young children. In J. Cassidy & P. Shaver (eds), *Handbook of Attachment* (pp. 555–574). New York: Guilford Press.

Olds, D. (2002). Prenatal and infancy home visiting by nurses: from randomized trials to community replication. *Prevention Science, 3,* 153–172.

Olds, D., Hill, P., Robinson, J., Song, N. & Little, C. (2000). Update on home visiting for pregnant women and parents of young children. *Current Problems in Pediatrics, 30,* 109–141.

Patterson, M., Slade, A. & Sadler, L. S. (2005). *Maternal Representations and Reflective Functioning among High-Risk Young Women during Pregnancy: Associations with Trauma Symptoms.* Paper presented at the Biennial Meetings of the Society for Research in Child Development, Atlanta, GA, 8 April 2005.

Seligman, S. (1994). Applying psychoanalysis in an unconventional context: adapting infant-parent psychotherapy to a changing population. *Psychoanalytic Study of the Child, 49,* 481–500.

Seng, J. (2002). A conceptual framework for research on lifetime violence, post traumatic stress and childbearing. *Journal of Midwifery and Women's Health*, *47*, 337–361.

Simkin, P. (1992). Overcoming the legacy of childhood sexual abuse: the role of caregivers and childbirth educators. *Birth*, *19*, 224–225.

Slade, A. (2002). Keeping the baby in mind: a critical factor in perinatal mental health. *Zero to Three*, *22*, 10–16.

Slade, A. (2005). Parental reflective functioning. *Attachment and Human Development*, *7*, 269–281.

Slade, A., Grienenberger, J., Bernbach, E., Levy, D. & Locker, A. (2005). Maternal reflective functioning, attachment, and the transmission gap: a preliminary study. *Attachment and Human Development*, *7*, 283–298.

Slade, A., Sadler, L., Currier, J., Webb, D., Dedios-Kenn, C., Mayes, L., et al. (2004). *Minding the Baby: A Manual*. New Haven, CT: Yale Child Study Center.

Slade, A., Sadler, L. S., de Dios-Kenn, C., Webb, D., Ezepchick, J. & Mayes, L. C. (2006). Minding the Baby: a reflective parenting program. *Psychoanalytic Study of the Child*, *60*, 74–100.

Slade, A., Sadler, L. S. & Mayes, L. (2005). Minding the Baby: enhancing parental reflective functioning in a nursing/mental health home visiting program. In L. Berlin, Y. Ziv, L. Amaya-Jackson & M. Greenberg (eds), *Enhancing Early Attachments*. New York: Guilford Publications.

Stern, D. (1985). *The Interpersonal World of the Infant*. New York: Basic Books.

Truman, S., Levy, D., Mayes, L. & Slade, A. (2002). *Reflective Functioning as Mediator between Drug Use, Parenting Stress, and Child Behavior*. Paper presented at meetings of the College of Drug Dependence. Quebec City, Quebec: College of Drug Dependence.

Winnicott, D. W. (1965). *Maturational Processes and the Facilitating Environment*. Madison, WI: International Universities Press.

15

TRANSFORMING VIOLENT SOCIAL SYSTEMS INTO NON-VIOLENT MENTALIZING SYSTEMS: AN EXPERIMENT IN SCHOOLS[1]

Stuart W. Twemlow and Peter Fonagy

In this chapter we will contrast a mentalization-based approach to school bullying and violence with a social-systems approach to the same problem and then attempt a synthesis of the two (Twemlow, 2000). We will then summarize the findings of a test of these ideas in a randomized-controlled trial involving several schools and over 3,000 children. More specifically, our goal was to see if the serious contemporary problem of bullying and interpersonal violence in schools could be approached with a focus on the relationships between the members of the social system as a whole, rather than the more traditional strategy seen in prevention studies, that of identifying disturbed and at-risk children and separating them from the social system for special attention.

A PROBLEM CHILD AS A SYMPTOM OF A PATHOLOGICAL SOCIAL SYSTEM

We begin with a vignette composed of details culled from several stories of everyday teaching disruptions by two middle-school teachers who have been teaching for many years in a mid-western school, in a low-income area in a

[1] This chapter is based on an article published in The Bulletin Menninger Clinic (2005, 69(4), pp 281–303). Reproduced by permission of Guilford Press.

Handbook of Mentalization-Based Treatment. Edited by J. G. Allen and P. Fonagy.
© 2006 John Wiley & Sons, Ltd.

mid-sized city. The school has close to 2,000 students and security guards guard its entryways. Violence is not uncommon in this school, including serious violence resulting in injury. The teachers are divided into teams, each with a team leader, including one of the authors of this vignette. Each team is tasked with coordinating efforts to maintain a peaceful and productive classroom learning environment and curriculum.

The school climate is tense; teachers report often feeling frightened for their safety and desperate for support from the administration due to ongoing harassment from parents and children. They often do not feel they have the necessary social skills and psychological knowledge to cope with the children, many of whom they see as seriously disturbed; they frequently request that the children be separated from their peer groups into special classrooms or referred for treatment.

The student at the center of our vignette, whom we shall call "Billy," a slightly overweight, round-faced 11-year-old, enters the classroom on a Monday morning, rushes to his desk, sits down with a loud commotion and yells out, "I hate Mondays. School is such a waste of time!" The teacher, whom we shall call "Ms Jones," is allowing students to make up missing assignments during that particular class period. Billy has quite a few late language arts assignments to do. Billy makes it quite clear to Ms Jones that language arts is the subject he hates the most and that he knows very well that he will not complete these assignments before the end of the period. On the basis of similar experiences, Ms Jones knows that he plans to misbehave so as to cause conflict and avoid doing any work.

Initially, Ms Jones tries to ignore Billy's initial comments and behavior. She thinks to herself, "Here we go again," thus confirming her frustrations not only with Billy but also with his mother, whom she felt was encouraging Billy's disruptive behavior and constantly finding ways to criticize the school. Ms Jones has become very frustrated with the situation, one that seems to be escalating. She dreads the period that she has him because she knows that the help she requires is not available.

Billy's outburst is the culmination of many days of avoiding his work in numerous classes. When Ms Jones mentions that she will call his mother, Billy becomes rude and indignant, adding that he couldn't care less because his mother thinks the school is "stupid" anyway. Billy's comments only add to the mounting frustration that Ms Jones feels about this particular school year, which in her view has seen a marked increase in complaints by displeased parents. She feels that the students realize they have the upper hand and can passively aggressively manipulate their teachers because of their parents' or guardians' lack of faith in the public school system.

It seems to Ms Jones that Billy has realized that he can get away with these daily disruptions because his mother, who is a single parent, allows it and is constantly threatening the school. When Ms Jones has previously attempted to contact Billy's mother, she has been treated with such disrespect that she now refuses to speak to the mother. All communication must go through the principal.

Every time Ms Jones intervenes in an attempt to deter Billy's outbursts, his behavior worsens. She asks him to sit down and keep quiet so that the other students may do their work without distraction. With increasing emphasis, she tells him to "Stop making that noise!" to no avail. Finally, raising her voice she exclaims, "Billy, just sit down! *Now!* And I *mean* it!" The escalation in behavior that results from these failed interventions causes constant disruption to the class, leaving the remainder of the students unattended during various parts of the class period.

Unfortunately, when Ms Jones finally refers Billy to the principal, he is basically "babysat" for the remainder of that period and is then sent to his next class. Ms Jones feels that the principal refrains from more severe punishment in fear of reprisals to the school board by Billy's mother.

Ms Jones notes that Billy has had a history of difficulty with his peers since elementary school. He did not play cooperatively in elementary school and had trouble sharing playground equipment at recess. He seems always to have wanted to control and dominate the mode of play. In pickup basketball, he would pout if he were not elected captain of the team; he would make constant appeals to others, especially to male teachers, to take his side.

By middle school, Billy's bullying behavior made him feared and unpopular. He made an effort to associate with the popular peer group, but he lacked the necessary social skills to carry off his role as a "cool, popular kid." His attempts to affiliate with the popular group did not give him the attention he seemed to need. He tried to ally himself with the leader of the popular clique, as a sort of bodyguard, a role that was not always appreciated or appropriate. His classroom and peer relationship problems dominated his life and, of course, led to a significant drop in his school grades.

Commentary from a Mentalization Perspective

From Ms Jones' standpoint, Billy appears to be a boy who, through cunning manipulation of his mother and even the principal, achieves mafia-like protection from the system and an almost unlimited license to disrupt and bully teachers and students alike. While she is cognizant of his social failings, Ms Jones has no genuine understanding of the reasons for Billy's misbehavior. Her model of Billy's actions is based on the assumption that Billy, like herself, is an average mentalizer. Paradoxically, average mentalizers often find themselves in difficulty because they assume that those around them have the same capacity as they do. A super-mentalizer might identify Billy's problems with mentalizing, and someone with below average mentalizing capacities might also interact well with Billy because he would not have the expectation of mentalizing on Billy's part. Ms Jones, however, assumes that Billy depicts with reasonable accuracy the beliefs and desires of those around him and has a developmentally adequate sense of his own psyche. Thus it seems clear to her that his behavior must be purposeful – aimed, for example, at avoiding work that he does not enjoy.

Ms Jones does not blame Billy. She feels that the fault lies with Billy's mother, who communicates her attitude that the appropriate response to feeling bad in relation to the school is to attack it. The problem is a trans-generational one in Ms Jones' eyes. The mother's lack of respect for the school becomes manifested in the child's behavior by a process of identification, although perhaps she does not think of it as such. In any case, she anticipates disrespect from Billy's mother, who is feared even by the principal. Ms Jones feels helpless as her attempts to calm Billy or rebuke him generate the apparently paradoxical consequence of escalating the violence of his outbursts. In her attempt to find an explanation for Billy's behavior, to contextualize his acts, Ms Jones gropes towards exploring Billy's experiences of having been rejected by his peers. She sees his bullying as a solution he has found to achieve esteem, notwithstanding his brutishness and poor social skills. She sees a positively accelerating curve of bad behavior feeding into poor performance in class and further violence to protect Billy's basically flawed self-esteem.

Now let us take a second look at this scene, without some of the assumptions entailed by Ms Jones' view of Billy as a basically rational person whose behavior could be understood in terms of putative beliefs and desires. Ms Jones does this spontaneously, intuitively and by and large not even consciously. Ms Jones feels confident that she can divine the beliefs that rational agent Billy ought to have, given his actions, his apparent goals, and the context in which these occur. She even ventures to identify the desires underlying Billy's behavior, including his wish to avoid work. Basically, as Dennett (1987) identified, she predicts that rational agent Billy will act to further his goals (to avoid any work) in the light of his belief that there are no substantial negative consequences to force alternative choices of action. Her model of Billy's behavior seems to us reasonably accurate. It certainly appears to predict quite effectively what Billy goes on to do (i.e., create further mayhem).

Beliefs are representations of reality. There are no absolutes about beliefs in relation to particular experiences. Mentalizing is by definition inexact. The mind is opaque. We have to share internal experiences with others to make them meaningful. Ms Jones does not know that Billy is disrupting the class with the sole purpose of avoiding work, supported by the belief that he can get away with it.

Recognizing the inherent uncertainty of mental states offers us remarkable freedom to speculate about the nature of actions, to consider alternative perspectives, and to find an infinite variety of meanings behind behavior. Sadly, emotional arousal, the kind of arousal which Billy's behavior creates in Ms Jones, restricts our capacity to mentalize, to find this richness and variety; instead, it forces us to be as economical as possible with our models of behavior and wherever possible to revert to stereotypical fixed patterns of conceptualization (see also Björgvinsson and Hart, Chapter 7). Feeling the weight of the responsibility for the entire class, Ms Jones does not give Billy the benefit of the doubt. She really does not know that Billy's exclamation, "I hate Mondays," is truly borne of his desire to create turmoil motivated by his wish to avoid unpleasant work. Thus, Ms Jones does not know that Billy's mother screamed at him before he left home, to get out of the house, to go to school, to leave her alone, adding for good measure, that she thought Billy was "a waste of time." Billy's provocative (aggressive) behavior driven by his emotional arousal, and the anxiety this gave rise to in Ms Jones in relation to her responsibilities to the other students in the class, prevented Ms Jones from exploring possible alternative wishes behind Billy's behavior. She did not conceive of any alternatives to exploitation and manipulation; moreover, it never occurred to her to ask him what the matter was, why he felt so terribly frustrated that morning. Her reaction was to inhibit mentalizing, to simplify matters and assume immediately that the past was repeating in the present. "Here we go again," she said to herself, without thinking of the specific instance. Billy gives only the faintest of indications of the nature of the turmoil he feels. When threatened with his mother's involvement, he expresses little apparent concern. He knows that for his mother the school is a convenient place to park Billy and that her overriding concern is not that he should have an education but rather that he should not be at home under her feet.

Little wonder then that Ms Jones' interaction was unsuccessful. Her interventions of trying to reason with Billy are aimed at a rational agent. She attempts to reason with him, trying to show him the effect he is having on the class. But this strategy assumes that Billy can distinguish between his feelings and those of the rest of the class members. That kind of self-regulation is quite simply beyond Billy's capability at this point. He experiences the rebuke as an assault from yet another hostile mind, which simply confirms his need to shut off, to make a noise, to disrupt, and to protect himself from what is unbearably painful. Perhaps if it were easier to think about Billy, either Ms Jones or the principal might have considered Billy's past difficulty in getting on with his peers in this context. Billy clearly lacks the capacity to be attuned to his peers. He seems out of touch with them and reacts to them in ways that they find disturbing. When he was anxious or eager to please, Billy had trouble in reading his peers' thoughts or feelings. He would then repeatedly do the wrong thing, making him an object of ridicule. He inadequately defends against this state – which all of us find almost unbearable – by asserting himself physically, creating a position for himself through the exertion of physical power, coercion, and sometimes cruelty. No one notices that these instances of cruelty are almost invariably linked to moments when he feels profoundly threatened by those around him. No one notices precisely because the kind of teleological physicalistic way he has resorted to control the minds of those around him, to subjugate them, is precisely the state that precludes the possibility of mentalizing. Billy has created a system around him that increasingly responds solely to physical threats rather than reason.

How can we help Billy? Or Ms Jones, in her struggle with him? It would be impractical to try and explain the intricate communication patterns we have outlined above. It would have been folly to ask Ms Jones to consider even a tiny proportion of these elaborations. She is far too busy having to cope with an entire class. If she were to engage with Billy's putative mental states in this kind of detail, she would undoubtedly have had to completely sacrifice her educational duties in favor of psychology. Would Billy benefit from therapy? Experience shows that boys like Billy respond poorly to such efforts, however skilled they may be. If Billy were younger, perhaps there would be more hope of helping his mother to relate more positively to him. After all she is no monster. The economic and social pressures on her as a single parent partly explain her criticism and negativity towards her oppositional child. But Billy at 11 is working to weaken the attachment to his mother. Moreover, it is not in the family context that Billy is experienced as a problem. We believe that disrupting the vicious cycle that Billy finds himself in is best undertaken in Billy's school, in fact, in Billy's class. Furthermore, given Billy's sensitivity to humiliation, the intervention might best not directly concern Billy at all but rather the whole class.

We may seem to be using a sledgehammer to crack a nut to advocate modifying the behavior of the class rather than imposing individual consequences on Billy. Yet if we take a broader view we can see that it is not just Billy but all those interacting with him who have difficulty in considering thoughts and feelings. The problems may originate in Billy but Ms Jones – normally a sensitive and caring person – finds herself reacting to Billy by shouting and bullying. Her reactions, in turn, paralyze the other children to a point where there is little expectation on anyone's part that thinking about what is going on could achieve more than imposing physical consequences. What is needed in this scenario is a pause button: Ms Jones would stop the class immediately after Billy started creating a commotion and mark some space for reflection on what was happening. She would ask other children to comment on what they thought was going on with Billy, to mentalize his behavior and thus create an experience for Billy that he was being thought about. Billy's classmates suddenly would have ceased to be passive bystanders observing a student bullying a teacher only to be exposed to the same kind of bullying a few moments later. Rather than being spectators enjoying the opportunity of not having to think, they would be drawn in to consider actively what the motivations for shortcutting meaningful interpersonal interaction through physical control might be. What could Billy be trying to achieve? Is it because he hates language arts? Or is it because he was feeling bad from before? One student might observe that Billy looked very upset even before the class started. Another might volunteer that he also sometimes felt like disrupting the class when he wanted to avoid work. Having thus been mentalized, Billy might chime in that, unlike this student, today he felt like doing language arts. Ms Jones could then quickly take advantage of the shift in the prevailing winds, alter course, and continue to sail the class through the choppy waters of its assignments.

Commentary from a Social-System Power-Dynamics Perspective

The social-systems perspective makes certain assumptions about the way social systems operate. Of particular importance in this application is the way in which Billy immediately forces everybody's attention to his problems by coercive misery, provocation, and contempt: *School is a waste of time and you won't do anything 'til you deal with my problems!* Unwittingly, Ms Jones has been dragged into the role of victim as Billy adopts the victimizer role. Billy likely has learned this pattern by observing aggressiveness in the home. Power has achieved primitive control objectives for him, modeled by his parents and other family members. Ms Jones is at the end of her rope with Billy and his mother, and she demonstrates the incapacitating power of the victim's role by her impoverished and uncreative thoughts to herself – the "here we go again" feeling, which creates a feeling of being defeated from the outset. Arousal of the sympathetic nervous system is signaled through the activation of the fight–flight hormones, creating a victim mindset that is highly focused, narrow, uncreative, and perseverative. Thus Ms Jones has perhaps unwittingly fallen into the power dynamic of victim, which renders her even less able to respond in a constructive way to Billy's problems. Billy, although he may be crying out for help, also has unwittingly adopted a position of power that is facilitated and even enhanced by the submissiveness of the surrounding bystander system that cannot cope with him.

Research has shown that, in serious aggression, submission encourages a controlling grandiose response by projective identification of disavowed self-representations into the victimizer (Twemlow, 1995a, 1995b). Thus the victimizer becomes locked in a hateful "dance," which decreases the capacity to think and increases the tendency to stereotype the other, all in an ambience that is not conducive to creative and constructive compromises. This school has literally run out of ideas about Billy!

From this perspective, Billy's fundamental problem is a systemic one. He is a pawn in a much larger social game, a game that involves his ever-changing role as bully and victim in the interchange with his social group, both of his teachers and of his peers. The victimized response of the authority system, especially the teachers who have to deal with him directly, and the audience of bystanders who occupy a variety of different roles, unwittingly aggravate the victimization. This process enhances Billy's ability to control the system by his help-rejecting complaining (victim role) and his carping aggressiveness (bully role), thus reducing the probability that learning can occur for anybody in the school. If Billy's problems are to be contained, and he is to become part of a creative and peaceful school-learning environment, these pathological roles must be addressed.

The energy or power of the system that positions Billy in the dominating role arises from the failure to deal with the power dynamic that keeps it going. This perspective depicts the bystander in a less obvious role, which we believe nonetheless to be the key to normalizing the system. Bystanders, all of whom feel disempowered by the combined force of Billy and his mother, include all school personnel – administration, parents, teachers, volunteers, support staff, and security personnel – as well as the students. Billy has heard that his mother feels that the school is stupid, so the mother has created here a *folie à deux*; she has become, like Billy, engaged in a power struggle with the school, attempting to control it to do her will. In the position of the victim, Ms Jones is over-whelmed and discouraged, and she is now going to the principal for help, since she most likely has realized that her rage and helplessness is a reactive concrete repetition of Billy's role as victim. Thus the talion principle reigns in this middle school, with an accompanying mindset that tends to stereotype and oversimplify human relationships. Billy becomes an intolerable monster. People have become dehumanized part objects rather than whole individuals, and the problem esca-lates. In spite of a detailed assessment of Billy and the knowledge that his family has problems, this information does not seem to help because the staff stereo-types Billy through a narrow, perseverative, and uncreative mindset aggravated by stress.

Billy's history suggests opportunities for successful interventions. Billy has always had problems in his relationships with his peers. The natural tendency of children at this age is to form peer groups (Espelage & Swearer, 2003), often with tightly structured codes of conduct that require reflection and subtlety to negotiate, a very difficult task for Billy. Frequently he uses his large size to achieve what he could not with more sophisticated social influence. Satisfying social relationships become submerged under the more power-centered, non-reflective ones. Potentially healthy self-criticism takes the form of victimized depression and suicidal thoughts. Active playfulness becomes coercive triumph, with the power dynamics enacted in struggles between Billy and his peers into an us-versus-them philosophy.

The individual-within-the-group medical approach to this problem will not solve it. Traditionally, Billy would be assessed and then placed in a behavior disor-der classroom and referred for psychiatric care. Instead, we propose that the bystanding community, the crucible within which this violent mindset develops, must be addressed for any lasting solution to emerge.

In summary, all persons in Billy's life have at different times adopted the roles of bully, victim, and bystander – even from one classroom period to another. The social-systems power-dynamics perspective construes this as a dissociating process; the victim is dissociated from the school community as "not us" by the bully on behalf of the bystanding community. In this instance Billy is the bully in terms of overt behavior, but he is also the victim of a group process: the community bystander role can be described as an abdicating one. The abdicating bystander projects blame for problem children onto others – often those in the school system, such as teachers, administrators, and school security personnel. From this vantage point any intervention in the school setting must focus on the transformation of the bystander into a committed community member.

A successful intervention should promote recognition within the large school group of the dissociated elements represented by the victim, Billy, as a part of each of the participants of the group, a part about which they are anxious. The intervention might lead to the recognition of this dissociating process, represented by Billy in his bullying role, as a defensive action for which the bystanders are in part responsible. This dissociating process is a largely unconscious effort to deal with the anxiety felt by all in response to a dysfunctional, coercive, and disconnected social system. Any remedy for this state of affairs requires a clear conceptualization of the group's task from a perspective that does not permit scapegoating, empowers bystanders into a helpful altruistic role, and does not overemphasize the importance of therapeutic efforts with the victim or victimizer. The symptom is not merely a problem to solve, but rather a dysfunctional solution or adaptation, which obscures a larger and more painful and meaningful problem. The helpful bystander role is a critical catalyst in converting Billy's school into a peaceful, mentalizing school-learning environment. In this sense bystanding can be defined as an active role with a variety of manifestations, in which an individual or group indirectly and repeatedly participates in a victimization process as a member of the social system. The victim–victimizer–bystander roles are not useful when considered as separate entities. Bystanding can either facilitate or ameliorate the victimization, and the bystander is propelled into the role by the dialectical interaction with the victim and victimizer. Bullying is thus defined as a triadic rather than dyadic process (Twemlow, Fonagy & Sacco, 2004).

MENTALIZING SCHOOL COMMUNITIES WITH BALANCED POWER DYNAMICS: A MODERN SYNTHESIS

From a psychobiological perspective, we assume that mentalizing and its loosely coupled counterpart, attachment, create a social environment that is incompatible with interpersonally aggressive, violent behavior (Fonagy, 2003). In general, social systems that are incompatible with violence are mentalizing social systems, because individuals are, from an evolutionary point of view, incapable of exercising interpersonal aggression in a context in which they successfully mentalize their victim's distress. When a social system becomes coercive, as in Billy's school, the players in the social game share a common characteristic. They all have lost their individuality in favor of a social role, which they will be forced to adopt by group pressure. That social role fosters social stereotypes, along with perseverative robotic group behavior that fails to recognize and mentalize the individual-in-the-group, as evidenced, for example, in the fighting behavior of the military or in cultist religious groups. The unique individual presence of the other is negated by the requirements of a stereotyped social role. Theoretically, a social system may need to engage in violence to protect itself and to provide food. Such a system still retains a mentalizing component, because the killing necessary is in the service of the dyad and the social system as a whole, and not merely a reflection of the idiosyncratic interpersonal problems of the individual predator bent on forcing others to comply with his or her non-mentalizing mindset.

Billy and Ms Jones have been sucked into the roles of victimizer and victim, respectively. Neither can be considered solely responsible for their position, nor can their responsibility simply be assigned to a faceless social organization. To do so would lead us down a non-productive path of blaming the system itself without regard to the individuals within it. It is, however, the persons within the organization who paradoxically adopt a position where they prefer to employ stereotypes rather than seeing the full complexity of individuals. Klein (1940) proposed that the natural development of psychic maturity evolves from the depressive position, which arises in depressive anxieties associated with having to see an individual not as a part object but as a whole person, complete with defects and strengths. The difference between a violent and a non-violent community must then be the degree to which the implicit social conventions are structured to encourage all participants to be aware of the mental states of others of that group and to take these into account when forming rules and regulations and procedures for the system. The rules must embody the perspective of mentalization.

The complexities of mentalizing and the sense of self that emerges from this process are reflected in several conceptual difficulties in understanding how an individual is both part of a social system and at the same time an individual in that system, with his or her own will and sense of separateness. As interpersonalist and relational theories hold, the person feels defined by the social system, and his or her sense of reality is rooted in that reality being shared by others. We know that the world outside is real ultimately because others respond to us in ways that are consistent with our reactions.

The extraordinary impact of social responses on the developing individual is illustrated by experiments with six-month-old infants using the still-face paradigm (Weinberg & Tronick, 1996). In such research, an infant is interacting with his mother and, by instruction, she freezes her face for a minute or so during their interaction. After a few seconds of the mother not reacting, the infant tends to go into a state of despair. The infant recovers after normal interaction is resumed. The catastrophic effect on the infant is not just due to the loss of the caregiving object. Subsequent research with children of the same age has demonstrated that, even if the person who freezes their interaction with the infant is a total stranger, the effect is sufficiently stressful that, a year later at age 18 months, the child avoids the picture of that stranger. The still-face paradigm is not unique to the mother–child relationship but merely an example of the failure of the others to validate the infant's experience of the world outside. The mirroring, understanding, and attuned social world is essential to us in early development, not just to ensure that we acquire a sense of who we are as Kohut (1984) and others have suggested, but also so that the child can develop an accurate appreciation of a shared external world. From this mentalizing perspective, the personal consensus between two people may be seen as creating an external (social) reality. When power dynamics influence that social reality, either through individual psychopathology or a social system that is disintegrating over using coercion and punishment, then victim, victimizer, and bystander mindsets are created in members of the system, who then function in the robotic roles created by the non-mentalizing social system. In contrast, a mentalizing interaction between individuals in the system allows the individual to be both an individual and a member of the social system.

Is it possible to create a mentalizing social system with balanced power dynamics? In 1993 we began an experiment in schools designed to test that hypothesis. The first seven years of the study involved piloting and refining interventions, and the results of these efforts are reported in detail elsewhere (Twemlow et al., 2001a; Twemlow, Fonagy & Sacco, 2001b). The inciting incident was the attempted rape of a second-grade girl by several second-grade boys in a school with the highest out-of-school suspension rate in the school district and the poorest academic performance on standardized achievement tests. After this first phase, in which the school did very well, a randomized control trial was conducted involving nine elementary (K-5) schools and over 3,600 students.

THE PEACEFUL SCHOOLS PROJECT: A MENTALIZING SOCIAL SYSTEM

Our approach encouraged the creation of a philosophy rather than a program (Twemlow, Fonagy & Sacco, 2005a, 2005b). We encouraged the reflective component of mentalizing by involving participants in the process rather than merely following a dehumanized research protocol. Understanding how the system works from the mentalizing power-dynamics perspective allows the individual teachers and students to develop innovative ways for creating that social climate in the school. The components of the program philosophy included several elements.

Positive Climate Campaigns

The positive climate campaigns use counselor-led discussions, posters, magnets, bookmarks, and other devices to encourage a shift in language and thinking of all students and personnel in the school (e.g., a magnet lists nine ways to handle bullies; a poster lists how to recognize anger and how to handle it). These language tools help identify and resolve problems that develop when coercive power dynamics dominate the school environment. For example, children help each other resolve issues without adult participation. Such effects are observed as they share playground equipment peacefully and do not push and jostle in the lunch line. Positive climate campaigns repeatedly underscore for both students and teachers the dynamic that takes place between bully, victim, and bystander. This climate creates a context in which no participant can experience the situation without awareness of the mental state of the other and, indeed, without self-awareness.

Rarely is the best way of achieving this climate to draw attention to the bully. Instead, the focus should be on the relationship between bully, victim, and bystander, which implicitly creates a demand on the child, the teacher, and other staff members to consider this interpersonal situation from a mentalizing perspective. It would be counterproductive to force students and teachers to explicitly describe the mental states of the participants. This might induce pseudo-mentalization, where mentalizing terms are used but the connection to the reality of the experience has been lost.

Classroom Management (Discipline Plan)

This approach assists teachers' efforts at discipline by focusing on correcting root problems instead of punishing and criticizing behaviors. A behavior problem in a single child is conceptualized as a problem for the whole class who participate in bully, victim, or bystander roles. Scapegoating is reduced and insight into the meaning of the behavior becomes paramount. From this new perspective, a child's disruptive behavior is seen as an attempt to locate a valid social role within the group. At the point of disruption, the teacher would stop teaching and assign bully, victim, and bystander roles during class discussion – the bully being the child, the victim being the teacher, and the bystanders being the rest of the class members, who may have laughed at the teacher's response to the disruptive student. If such a child repeatedly offends, the class would collectively fill out a *power-struggle referral alert*. That is, every student would participate in determining and defining the bullying, victim, and bystander behavior according to a standardized form. At a later point the children involved (and sometimes even the parents of the child) would be seen by the school counselor or social worker for a further understanding of the event. Punishment would not be invoked except as a last resort when the disciplinary infractions were serious enough to require intervention by the school principal.

The child with a propensity to act violently is encouraged by this approach to develop a mental representation of his experiences and adapt to it in a non-persecutory way. The essential component of this approach is that children do not experience themselves as having been punished, which would inhibit rather than facilitate mentalizing. Thus, the environment becomes conducive to thinking within the context of a counseling relationship that encourages mentalizing. When a child is sent to the principal, the anxiety created by the system begins to inhibit any capacity to mentalize. This is so to the extent that principals are defensive owing to school board and parental harassment, and their capacity to mentalize is inhibited accordingly. Thus an encounter between a child and a principal in such a setting paradoxically cannot involve any reflecting from a mentalizing perspective. The pattern we advocate encourages the child to think about the perspective of others, including his or her parents as well as teachers and principals.

Peer and Adult Mentorship

Mentorship approaches are attempts to mirror outside the classroom what the classroom management plan does in the classroom. These approaches aim to involve everyone in the school system in understanding the violent interaction, and to see if there is a way to resolve the problem collaboratively and without blame. Male mentors seem particularly helpful on the playground where much childhood aggression comes out. The most effective male mentors are rather relaxed, non-competitive older men of any race; many are retired and have children and grandchildren of their own. One particularly skilled mentor cleverly used magic tricks to distract children. He would make himself a buffer; for example, "Why don't you go first on the jungle gym and I will try and catch each of you?" Thus the fight became a game, with him as the referee.

Looking at mentoring from a mentalizing perspective requires the point of view of the "third" (Ogden, 1992). The mentor allows each party within the conflict to see from the mentor's perspective. It takes the problem out of a coercive dyad and brings in a third through which each person can perceive the other. The mentalizing action of the mentor and his magic trick creates a transitional space by this distraction; the participants – the bully, the victim, and the bystander – start thinking about a third thing, with a spontaneity essential for mentalizing.

In a mentalizing peer group, Billy's abortive attempts to identify with his peer group by becoming a bodyguard to the leader would allow the group to see him as a real person and to identify with his loneliness and social isolation. His peers would also be able to perceive his bodyguard role not simply as a wish to appear powerful but instead as showing his desire to make social contact. Billy would feel increasingly recognized and able to relinquish his dependence on the enforcer role. Instead, his self-esteem would be maintained by mentalizing.

The Gentle Warrior Physical Education Program

This approach satisfies the physical education requirements in most school systems, using a combination of role-playing, relaxation, and defensive martial arts techniques. The approach helps children protect themselves and others with non-aggressive physical and cognitive strategies, thereby providing students with alternatives to fighting. Combined with classroom discussion, learning ways to physically defend oneself when being grabbed, pushed, or shoved teaches personal self-control as well as respect and helpfulness towards others. These confidence-building skills support an essential component of the capacity to mentalize by allowing children to feel confident enough and safe enough to be able to think. If a child is too frightened, the capacity to think is paralyzed, and the victim mindset is adopted. A child experiencing an emergency mode of thinking is presented with simple-minded choices, such as running away or submitting. At the level of brain functioning there is an inhibition of the prefrontal cortex in favor of the posterior parts of the brain and the sub-cortex that facilitates the fight–flight reaction (Frith & Frith, 2003; Frith & Wolpert, 2004; see also Fonagy, Chapter 3). Yet the fight-or-flight reaction is incompatible with mentalizing. A safe environment from a mentalizing perspective has to be one in which children experience a situation that they can cope with (Twemlow, Fonagy & Sacco, 2002).

Reflection Time

Adler (1958) pointed out that a natural social group has no right to exclude any member or, conversely, that every member of the group has a right to belong. From his point of view, narcissistic injury represented by bully, victim, and some bystander reactions are attempts by the child to regain entry into a social group and to be accepted by that social group. Although teachers may see the Peaceful Schools Program as training the child, the real aim is that the teachers actively become involved in mentalizing the child via the process of training. The serious problem of teachers who bully and are bullied by students and parents (Twemlow, Fonagy, Sacco & Brethour, in press; Twemlow & Fonagy, 2005) is one example of how important the mentalizing teacher becomes to this process. Hence the system through its members becomes more psychologically aware; eventually, the rules, regulations, and policies of the system will embody mentalizing principles.

Reflection time is one such method to encourage mentalizing in teachers and students. During this period of 10 minutes or so at the end of each day, the classroom engages in a discussion of the day's activities from the point of view of bully, victim, and bystander behavior. After discussing this behavior, they make a decision about whether to display a banner outside the classroom indicating that the class has had a good day. Teachers note that the children are rather critical of themselves and do not put the banner up as much as teachers might. Thus mentalizing children are capable of being self-critical without a drop in self-esteem. The reflection time is a way of consolidating the day's activities and allowing the child and teacher to take a systems view of what is going on. In many ways the subject of the reflection matters less than that the reflection is taking place. If a system cannot be thought about in this way, then no mental representation of it can be created. We are not advocating mentalizing for its own sake; the important thing is that it makes the system more peaceful.

RESULTS OF THE PEACEFUL SCHOOLS PROJECT

The complex structured methodology and analytic strategy for this project is described in detail elsewhere (Fonagy, Twemlow, Vernberg, Sacco & Little, 2005; Fonagy et al., 2005). In brief, three interventions were compared: a traditional school psychiatric consultation, an intervention based on a mentalizing and power-dynamics systems approach as described in the body of this chapter, and a treatment-as-usual condition in which schools had been promised whichever was the more successful of the other two interventions in return for collecting data. The study was a cluster-level randomized-controlled trial with stratified restricted allocation. Efficacy was assessed after two years of active intervention and effectiveness after one year of minimal input maintenance intervention.

Nine elementary schools with 1,345 third- to fifth-graders provided data for the trial, which was conducted in a medium-size mid-western city. Approximately 3,600 children were exposed to the interventions. The outcomes of the interventions were measured with peer and self-reports of bullying and victimization, peer reports of aggressive and helpful bystanding, self-reports of empathy towards victims of bullying, self-reports of belief that aggression is legitimate, and classroom behavioral observation of disruptive and off-task behavior.

Compared to the other two conditions, results indicated that the experimental intervention showed a decrease in peer-reported victimization, aggression, and aggressive bystanding compared to control schools. The intervention group also showed less of the usual decline in empathy for victims expected as children grow older compared to psychiatric consultation and control conditions. Peaceful Schools also produced a significant decrease in off-task behavior and disruptive classroom behavior, whereas behavioral change was not observed in the psychiatric consultation and control schools. The findings of reduced victimization aggression and aggressive bystanding were maintained in the follow-up year.

We concluded that this program philosophy was effective in reducing children's experiences of aggressiveness and victimization. One strength of the study lay in its extraordinarily careful and detailed evaluation. The program showed that children became more involved in helping to reduce aggressiveness as suggested by the increasing engagement of Peaceful Schools children in non-aggressive and helpful bystanding behaviors. A helpful bystander was defined as an individual or peer group assisting children being bullied to handle bullying and to create a social climate that discouraged bullying without using force to do so. Such children help each other resist individual victimization by bullies, in part by mentalizing a victim. This awareness allows children, teachers, and other staff members to take action to normalize power dynamics in the social system as a whole.

The Peaceful Schools intervention seems to reduce the natural tendency for children to harden their attitude to victimization over time as other studies have shown (Vernberg, Jacobs, Twemlow, Sacco & Fonagy, submitted). In related work Gamm and colleagues (2005) found that greater teacher adherence to the Peaceful Schools philosophy was related to greater student empathy, defined as a student's awareness of a negative effect of victimization on other students over time. Students whose teachers reported greater adherence to the mentalizing principles were viewed by peers to show less aggressive bystanding (i.e., encouraging bullying without active physical participation) than students whose teachers reported poorer adherence. Over the second and third years of the program, helpful bystanding was significantly related to the adherence of teachers to the main elements of the program and awareness of it usefulness, with children in high-adherence classrooms showing more helpful behavior over time than other students.

Concluding Comments

In this chapter we have synthesized a theoretical and philosophical perspective on mentalizing and power dynamics as a type of attachment pattern between individuals that is essential to how social systems operate. We have outlined a set of steps to create mentalizing schools that have a sophisticated developmental focus on the individual needs of the members as reflected in the conduct of the system as a whole. Although this approach merits additional experimental and empirical verification, the chapter reports a successful test of these hypotheses in a randomized-controlled trial in a series of elementary schools. In a nutshell, the intervention showed that such a program could work and produce a significant lasting result.

The larger question of whether a community can reflect the mentalizing power-dynamics perspective in the way it organizes itself remains unanswered. We believe that for communities to reflect the high quality of life demanded by citizens in an open democracy, such changes in how the system as a whole operates must occur.

ACKNOWLEDGEMENTS

We thank Megan and Brad Culver, who provided the case vignette and discussed with us their rewarding but stressful experiences teaching in United States public schools. This research was supported by Foundation grants to Child and Family Program, Menninger Department of Psychiatry and Behavioral Sciences at the Baylor College Medicine, Houston, TX.

REFERENCES

Adler, A. (1958). *What Life Should Mean to You*. New York: Putnam Capricorn Books.
Dennett, D. (1987). *The Intentional Stance*. Cambridge, MA: MIT Press.
Espelage, D. & Swearer, S. (2003). Research on school bullying and victimization: What have we learned and where do we go from here? *School Psychology Review, 32*, 365–383.
Fonagy, P. (2003). Towards a developmental understanding of violence. *British Journal of Psychiatry, 183*, 190–192.
Fonagy, P., Twemlow, S., Vernberg, E., Mize, J., Dill, E., Little, T., et al. (2005). A randomized controlled trial of a child-focused psychiatric consultation and a school systems-focused intervention to reduce aggression, submitted for publication.
Fonagy, P., Twemlow, S., Vernberg, E., Sacco, F. & Little, T. (2005). Creating a Peaceful School Learning Environment: The Impact of an Anti-Bullying Program on Educational Attainment in Elementary Schools. *Medical Science Monitor, 11*, 317–325.
Frith, C. D. & Wolpert, D. M. (2004). *The Neuroscience of Social Interaction: Decoding, Imitating and Influencing the Actions of Others*. Oxford, England: Oxford University Press.
Frith, U. & Frith, C. D. (2003). Development and neurophysiology of mentalizing. *Philosophical Transactions of the Royal Society of London B, Biological Sciences, 358*, 459–473.
Gamm, B. K., Vernberg, E., Twemlow, S. W., Dill, E. J. & Fonagy, P. (2005). Teacher Adherence and Child Outcome in a School Violence Prevention Program, submitted for publication.
Klein, M. (1940). Mourning and its relation to manic depressive states. *Love Guilt and Reparation and Other Works 1921–1945* (pp. 344–369). Delacorte Press/Seymour Lawrence, 1975.
Kohut, H. (1984). In A. Goldberg (ed.), *How Does Analysis Cure?* Chicago, IL: Chicago University.
Ogden, T. (1992). The dialectically constituted/decentered subject of analysis II: the contributions of Klein and Winnicott. *International Journal of Psychoanalysis, 73*, 613–626.
Twemlow, S. W. (1995a). The psychoanalytical foundations of a dialectical approach to the victim/victimizer relationship. *Journal American Academy of Psychoanalysis, 23*, 543–558.
Twemlow, S. W. (1995b). Traumatic object relations configurations seen in victim/victimizer relationships. *Journal American Academy of Psychoanalysis, 23*, 559–575.

Twemlow, S. W. (2000), The roots of violence: converging psychoanalytic explanatory models for power struggles and violence in school. *Psychoanalytic Quarterly, 69,* 741–785.

Twemlow, S. W. & Fonagy P. (2005). A note on teachers who bully students in schools with differing levels of behavioral problems. *American Journal of Psychiatry, 162,* 2387–2389.

Twemlow, S. W., Fonagy, P., Sacco, F. C., Gies, M., Evans, R. & Ewbank, R. (2001a). Creating a peaceful school learning environment: a controlled study of an elementary school intervention to reduce violence. *American Journal of Psychiatry, 158,* 808–810.

Twemlow, S. W., Fonagy, P. & Sacco, F. C. (2001b). An innovative psychodynamically influenced intervention to reduce school violence. *Journal of the American Academy of Child and Adolescent Psychiatry, 40,* 377–379.

Twemlow, S. W., Fonagy, P. & Sacco, F. (2002). Feeling safe in school. *Smith College Studies in Social Work, 72,* 303–326.

Twemlow, S., Fonagy, P. & Sacco, F. (2004). The role of the bystander in the social architecture of bullying and violence in schools and communities. *Annals of New York Academy of Sciences, 1036,* 215–232.

Twemlow, S., Fonagy, P. & Sacco, F. C. (2005a). A developmental approach to mentalizing communities: I. A model for social change. *Bulletin of The Menninger Clinic, 69,* 265–281.

Twemlow, S., Fonagy, P. & Sacco, F. C. (2005b). A developmental approach to mentalizing communities: II. The Peaceful Schools project. *Bulletin of The Menninger Clinic, 69,* 282–304.

Twemlow, S., Fonagy, P., Sacco, F. & Brethour, J. (in press). Teachers who bully students: a hidden trauma. *International Journal of Social Psychiatry.*

Vernberg, E., Jacobs, A., Twemlow, S., Sacco, F. & Fonagy, P. (Submitted). Assessing bystander beliefs and aggression related attitudes as predictors of aggression and victimization in childhood and adolescence.

Weinberg, K. M. & Tronick, E. Z. (1996). Infant affective reactions to the resumption of maternal interaction after the still-face. *Child Development, 67,* 905–914.

16

DOES MENTALIZING PROMOTE RESILIENCE?

Helen Stein

Why do some people bounce back from painful experience, apparently against all odds? This phenomenon, resilience, has inspired myths, memoirs, and a large body of research. This chapter begins with a review of resilience and associated concepts from the developmental psychopathology literature. Mechanisms of resilient adaptation are not well elucidated, and mentalizing will be explored in this light. An extended case example will follow, based on research conducted at The Menninger Clinic designed specifically to address the relationship between resilience and mentalizing. By taking an idiographic approach, I illustrate how resilience, mentalizing, and associated constructs can be applied to enrich clinical understanding.

RESILIENCE

Early resilience researchers, searching for an explanation of why some children do well and others do not, focused on individual qualities, suggesting that resilience is the capacity for successful adaptation in circumstances normally associated with psychological dysfunction (Stein, Fonagy, Ferguson & Wisman, 2000a). This view has led to a blame-the-victim attitude toward those with poor outcomes (Luthar & Zelazo, 2003) and an underestimation of the influences of the family and the larger community. More recently, resilience has been studied as a *dynamic process* that unfolds over time in the context of multiple environmental influences including family, school, peers, and community, resulting

Handbook of Mentalization-Based Treatment. Edited by J. G. Allen and P. Fonagy.
© 2006 John Wiley & Sons, Ltd.

in the organization and integration of experience in functionally adaptive and developmentally appropriate ways.

Some have taken a broader eco-systemic view, noting that systems beyond the community – including the physical environment, social class, biology, ethnicity, spirituality, poverty, racism, and social policy – interact with each other and the child, family, and community (Waller, 2001). Changes in any of these systems can signal changes in an individual's ability to adapt at different points in development. Simple good or bad luck can have a crucial impact as well; consider victims and survivors of 9–11 or the many natural disasters of 2005.

Resilience implies exposure to risk factors (adversities) and protective factors (beneficial resources) leading to developmentally appropriate (and thus resilient) outcomes. Some investigators have focused on particular risk factors such as parental mental illness or divorce; others have taken a broader view, studying children living in poverty or violent communities, or creating indices of multiple risk factors. Even factors such as parental mental illness affect children through a variety of pathways, including the generation of stressful life events, patterns of coping with those events, and their impact on the acuity of the parent's illness. Although there is consensus about a range of factors that confer risk, outcome can reflect the sheer *quantity* of risk factors (Fergusson & Horwood, 2003; Sameroff, Gutman & Peck, 2003). In a study of the impact of cumulative risk factors in early and middle childhood on adolescent behavior, a linear model rather than a threshold model best accounted for outcome, suggesting that there is no tipping point beyond which resilience is impossible (Appleyard, Egeland, Van Dulmen & Sroufe, 2005).

Protective factors have been less clearly defined than risk factors. Individual traits (e.g., cognitive competence, even temperament, and capacity for self-regulation); family factors (e.g., warm relationship with parents, secure attachment, and reasonable discipline and structure); and community factors (e.g., good schools, health care and social services, community safety, pro-social peers, and constructive activities) have been linked to better outcomes. Differences in terminology remain. Rutter (1985) initially defined protective factors as requiring a statistical interaction, thus principally benefiting children at risk. Fergusson and Horwood (2003) have noted the importance, in addition, of *compensatory* processes that serve as resources for all children, regardless of their exposure to adversity; these are also known as *promotive* factors (Sameroff et al., 2003) and *resource* factors (Hammen, 2003). Finally, some protective factors also function as outcomes; for example, secure attachment can be seen as a protective factor or as a measure of positive outcome in studies of resilience in early childhood.

Because resilience cannot be assessed directly, investigators select developmentally appropriate, conceptually relevant measures, using cut-off points or cumulative indices to distinguish between resilient and non-resilient functioning.

Examples include measures of academic adaptation (e.g., achievement, school retention, or quality of peer relationships); individual wellbeing (e.g., self-esteem, efficacy, temperament, and capacity to self-regulate); improved family dynamics (e.g., attachment or parental warmth and consistency); and psychopathology (most commonly, internalizing and externalizing symptoms). The sources for these judgments include self-report; teacher, parent, and peer report; school records; and, less commonly, interviews. It is important to consider multiple domains, preferably from multiple informants, because resilience is rarely evident across all domains, especially in high-risk situations such as maltreatment (Bolger & Patterson, 2003).

In 1987, Michael Rutter, a pre-eminent resilience researcher, urged his colleagues to:

> focus on protective mechanisms and processes. That is, we need to ask why and how some individuals manage to maintain high self-esteem and self-efficacy in spite of facing the same adversities that lead other people to give up and lose hope. How is it that some people have confidants to whom they can turn? What has happened to enable them to have social supports that they can use effectively at moments of crisis? Is it chance, the spin of the roulette wheel of life, or did prior circumstances, occurrences, or actions serve to bring about this desirable state of affairs? The search is not for broadly defined protective factors but, rather, for the developmental and situational mechanisms involved in protective processes. (p. 317)

Rutter specifically suggested looking at mechanisms that reduce risk impact, inhibit negative chain reactions, establish self-esteem and self-efficacy, and open new opportunities – processes that typically operate at key turning points in persons' lives. Luthar (2006) notes that the field has made scant response to Rutter's challenge.

PROTECTIVE RELATIONSHIPS AND MENTALIZING

The most obvious place to begin the search for mechanisms of resilience is the family. Several lines of evidence support the view that resilient outcomes are the product of the quality of relationships in a child's life, particularly relationships with primary caregivers. Consistently, across numerous studies, secure attachment, warm and sensitive parenting, and appropriate discipline appear to protect children growing up in adverse circumstances. Children with at least one good relationship are more likely to expect and seek nurturance from others (Luthar, 2006; Conger, Cui, Bryant & Elder, 2000). Interventions targeting parent–child relationships have had positive behavioral outcomes, for example, in the context of divorce and bereavement (Sandler, Wolchik, Davis, Haine & Ayers, 2003), low-income families (Heinicke, Rineman, Ponce & Guthrie, 2001), and maltreatment (Toth, Maughan, Manly, Spagnola & Cicchetti, 2002).

While good care protects, numerous studies link early and enduring maltreatment by primary caregivers to poor outcomes, including failure to manage the developmental tasks of childhood and problematic functioning in cognitive, emotional, social, and even physical realms. Maltreatment impacts the development of intrapsychic capacities as well, including children's expectations of how others will see them and relate to them, sense of self, pattern of attachment, and ability to regulate emotion. These capacities ordinarily help children establish constructive relationships with peers and adults inside and outside the family.

Close ameliorative relationships with individuals other than parents at various points in the lifespan can promote resilience (Luthar, 2006). Sources of positive relationships include siblings, peers, extended family members, foster parents, teachers, mentors, and marital partners. Such relationships are especially crucial when the family is the source of pervasive negative experiences (Rutter, 1999). Reciprocal close friendships may enhance self-esteem for maltreated children (Bolger & Patterson, 2003). Children mentored by Big Brothers or Big Sisters were less likely to skip school; relationships with parents and self-reported academic functioning improved relative to controls (Rhodes, Grossman & Resch, 2000; Grossman & Rhodes, 2002). The number of improvements was directly related to *duration* of the mentoring relationship (Grossman & Rhodes, 2002). The Study of Adult Development at Harvard followed individuals from their twenties into their eighties (Vaillant, 2002). Growing up in "loveless" family environments conveyed risk for mental illness, distrust, inflexibility, and isolation throughout life, but some individuals managed to find support and solace from individuals other than parents, even beyond childhood.

What is it exactly about secure attachment and positive relationships that helps children rise above adversity? Do warm relationships and secure attachments trigger a set of processes or capabilities that can then be used to avoid adversity when possible and cope with it when inevitable? The capacity that Fonagy and colleagues call mentalizing, the ability to conceive of one's own mind and the minds of others, normally becomes activated through early secure relationships (see Fonagy, Chapter 3). Because it permits flexible thinking about one's own and others' mental states, mentalizing can, in theory, protect self-esteem, advance self-efficacy, and aid in making informed judgments about risk in interpersonal situations. In the absence of early secure attachments, mentalizing can be developed in close relationships at any point in the life cycle, including therapeutic relationships. This fact alone makes mentalizing noteworthy to clinicians.

Mentalizing is not a hard-wired capacity. If a parent responds empathically to her three-month-old infant's cries of distress, several processes ensue. The infant is soothed by the parent's intervention, in part because the parent has distracted the infant from the intensity of her distress. The infant's distress is down-regulated, and her mental state changes. She begins to sense and take pleasure in her own agency: her actions have elicited a much-needed response from her parent. And the infant sees in her parent's expression an accurate depiction of her own distress as well as the parent's view of this distress ("You're wet and I'll change you. You'll feel better in a minute. I love you, honey."). With repeated episodes, she begins to internalize the parent's empathy. This apparently simple sequence of action and response thus motivates selective attention, self-regulation, sense of agency, internal representation of mental states, and the first stages of seeing self and others in terms of mental states. As the infant develops, secure attachment figures increasingly and appropriately verbalize the mental states of the child and other family members, at the moment or in reflection. This helps the child link mental state concepts with her own and others' internal experience. Parents and children play, exploring the nature of inner and outer reality in a setting where mental state changes can be expressed freely. In this atmosphere, the child is frequently in a state of calm, able to take in information about the complex social relationships around her. She learns to explore mental states in her mind through reflection rather than through physical action.

Not surprisingly, a great deal of evidence links secure attachment with mentalizing capacities in children and with parental use of mental state terms (Bateman & Fonagy, 2004; Fonagy, Chapter 3). In contrast, maltreated children typically show mentalizing deficits in childhood concomitant with a tendency to shift quickly into states of high emotional arousal. Adults with a history of maltreatment also exhibit mentalizing deficits (Fonagy et al., 2006). Adults with a history of maltreatment and low mentalizing abilities are at high risk for borderline personality disorder (Fonagy et al., 1996) and for negative and distorting perceptions of their toddlers (Schecter, 2003). On the other hand, mentalizing confers protection: mothers with a history of deprivation who acquire a mentalizing stance are likely to have secure infants of their own (Fonagy, Steele, Steele, Higgitt & Target, 1994).

How might mentalizing promote resilience? In clinical terms, we might imagine a kind of intrapsychic filtering system that is put into place through early secure relationships. This system would allow children to endure and metabolize some kinds of painful experiences without their taking an incalculable toll on self-concept or expectations of others. Mentalizing might promote recognition of requests for, or acceptance of, support when it is offered in a reliable and appropriate form. This system might also keep alive realistic hope, alternatives to be put into action as new resources and contexts permit. Thus, the capacity to mentalize may provide at-risk persons with a capacity that opens a range of possibilities for understanding past adversities, judging the motives and feelings of others in the present, and detecting realistic alternatives for the future.

Next I present a case example to examine the role of mentalizing as a mechanism of resilience. Although Alan was not exposed to extreme maltreatment, he experienced many challenges. By presenting his case rather than a set of group results, I hope to allow the reader to follow Alan's developmental process, noting turning points and possible intervening processes, including mentalizing, that could account for his resilient course.

ALAN[1]

Method

Alan was a participant in a research study on resilience, The Long-term Effects of the Quality of Parenting on Adult and Adolescent Functioning, carried out at the Child and Family Center of The Menninger Clinic between 1995 and 2003.[2] He, along with other participants, completed a lengthy set of structured clinical interviews about childhood (George, Kaplan & Main, 1985; Bifulco, Brown, Neubauer, Moran & Harris, 1994; Stein, Allen, Allen, Koontz & Wisman, 2000b), past and current psychiatric illness (First, Spitzer, Gibbon & Williams, 1996), and current functioning (Hill & Stein, 2002). He also completed a demographics interview and a questionnaire to screen for personality disorder (First, Gibbon, Spitzer & Williams, 1997). (For more complete information on methods, see Stein et al., 2000a.)

To supplement Alan's own account, interview data were pooled with information from his childhood medical chart, which was established when he attended a preschool day-treatment center during 10 months following his fifth birthday. These data included monthly teacher summaries of his classroom behavior, therapist accounts of mother guidance sessions, and his mother's responses to a detailed developmental history questionnaire. In the description that follows, I will review his early history before age six, mainly culled from these sources. This will be followed by a description of risk factors elicited from the Childhood Experiences of Care and Abuse and additional risk factors that emerged in the interviews. The Revised Adult Personality Functioning Assessment was the source of information about Alan's current functioning. I will also discuss Alan's current psychiatric diagnoses. Alan's ability to mentalize was measured by two tests. In the Reading the Mind with the Eyes test (Baron-Cohen, Joliffe, Mortimore & Robertson, 1997), he was presented with a set of photographs of different facial expressions, showing only the eyes and forehead of the model. He was asked to choose from two descriptors the one that best captured the mental state in the photograph. Recognition of expressions is considered prototypical of implicit mentalizing (Bateman & Fonagy, 2004). His Adult Attachment Interview was rated using the Reflective Function Scale (Fonagy, Target, Steele & Steele, 1998). This scale codes evidence of awareness of the nature of mental states, explicit efforts to explain mental states underlying behavior, recognition

---

[1] To protect Alan's confidentiality, names and other identifying details have been disguised.

[2] This research project was supported by the endowment of The Menninger Clinic, the William Randolph Hearst Foundation, and the O'Shaughnessy Foundation.

of developmental aspects of mental states, and indications of awareness of mental states in the interviewer.

Alan, a large, handsome, well-dressed African-American man, was interviewed at our research center. Friendly and confident, he described his history with coherence and ease. Interviews regarding his childhood were conducted by the author; diagnostic interviews and interviews on current functioning were conducted by Kristine Wheat, a research team member.

Early History

Alan is the second of three sons born to Joe and Angela Banks. Mark was born 13 months before and Darren three years after Alan. The family lived in Lincoln, the city of Angela's birth, and the boys grew up surrounded by her extended family, sharing weekly meals with their maternal grandparents and celebrating large family reunions each summer. Like Alan, Angela was a middle child. She felt sandwiched between her brothers, the child without special privileges who was assigned the most work in the household. When she got her first paying job as a teenager, her parents demanded rent. Joe was raised in an African-American Catholic community in a large city; Angela converted when they married. From second grade on, Alan attended a Catholic school in Lincoln where he was the only African-American child in his grade.

All of Angela's pregnancies were unplanned. Depression and frequent arguments with Joe about finances marked her pregnancy with Alan. They made decent wages, she as a paraprofessional in the school system and he as a supervisor in the public works department, but Joe did not manage money well. Angela did not see Alan for 36 hours after the apparently normal delivery, even though she was planning to breast-feed. Fearful that something was wrong with him, she later learned that the baby nursery had been understaffed. She noticed a problem with his legs but stated, "I covered him up and don't recall thinking about it again." A severe leg deformity was diagnosed when he was six months old; at 11 months he was seen by an orthopedist. Alan had begun to walk at 10 months despite his handicap, much to the surprise of this doctor. The orthopedist prescribed corrective boots and warned that he might have to learn to walk again. When Angela brought him home in his new boots and placed him on the floor, he cried for an hour. Then he got up and walked.

At two-and-a-half years of age, Alan was chased by a dog. Just as he was recovering from that incident, he began wearing full-leg braces and was now unable to bend at the knee. It was hard for him to sit on the toilet, and he was afraid that he would soil the braces. Chased again by a dog a few months later, he was saved by the owner who restrained the dog just as he was about to bite Alan. A neighbor told Angela that a teenager had goaded the dog to attack Alan. Alan now refused to go out of the house. In his interviews, Alan misremembered the details, believing that his mother had rescued him. He also recalled a repetitive nightmare

> where somebody was chasing me. And I was running near the creek and sooner or later I ran into a fence. And I couldn't climb the fence, and I fell down to my knees and started crying, and this person had a knife, and right when he started to take the knife to cut my foot, I woke up, you know.

Alan began attending nursery school at age three. During this difficult year, his mother gave birth to Darren, and his maternal grandfather died. Angela did not think that Alan was bothered by his grandfather's death. Sleep difficulties were legion. He refused to nap at nursery school, crawled in with his parents at night, and napped at home only with his father. He wet his bed up to five times a night and often woke up screaming that his leg hurt (presumably from the recurrent nightmare). He picked at the walls of the rooms in the house, making holes until his mother forbade it.

Angela brought Alan to the therapeutic preschool when he was five because of his animal phobia, bowel movements in his pants several times a week, and aggression. The staff saw him as anxious, fearful, and angry. With little provocation, he would have a meltdown, screaming and crying, kicking, hitting, and jumping up and down. When his teachers attempted a preventive interpretation about his fears, he would refuse to admit to any of them. After an outburst, he could sometimes talk about his concerns. On the other hand, he was friendly to peers and adults and enjoyed playing with other children. Initially a caretaker, he became a leader as the school year progressed. Intellectually precocious and serious about learning, his emotional development lagged about three years behind his chronological age.

Alan was very sensitive to uncertainties at home. Although his leg braces were removed during the fall of his preschool year, he lived with the possibility that he would have to resume wearing them (in fact, he didn't). He told his teacher that he felt that no one understood him. Sensitive to any perception of inequality, he was especially competitive with his brother, Mark, and couldn't understand why he wouldn't catch up to Mark's abilities and privileges. His terror of dogs had generalized to all animals, even stuffed ones, and he expressed a fear of death and of being alone.

Angela regularly attended mother guidance sessions with the preschool director who initially observed how depressed and overwhelmed she seemed. Dedicated to advancing her sons' intellectual and social development, Angela was now juggling 12 hours of college courses with her sons' schedules (each was attending a different school). Joe worked nights. Angela, who blamed herself for problems in the marriage, was reluctant to request his help; it was also not clear that he was willing to share responsibilities.

With difficulty, Angela revealed her own past and current phobias. She worried that her boys would absorb her fears even without seeing them demonstrated. She felt alone against the world, unable to act. This concern was especially poignant with Alan. She believed that she was supposed to talk him out of his feelings or make him feel good, and she was exhausted by his continual questions. In the language of mentalizing, she had no sense of agency and felt responsible for changing her son's states of mind rather than acknowledging and thereby modulating them. The director read Angela's own mental states accurately. She suggested ways for Angela to help Alan identify his feelings rather than change them (thereby mentalizing him). She encouraged Angela to involve Alan in joint problem solving, thereby helping him to feel like an agent. Responding to the director's suggestion that she ask for help with childcare from her family in the late afternoons when she was most exhausted, Angela made a wise choice. Her grandmother, "Grandma Ella," became their childcare provider after school, an arrangement that continued for many years.

As the year progressed, Alan's toilet habits improved and Angela felt more comfortable with him. At the end of the school year, the preschool staff recommended that Alan go on to kindergarten with the support of individual therapy. Angela brought him to the clinic where she and Joe attended couples counseling, and he began to attend a psychotherapy group.

Risk Factors

Alan reported some parental discord. He thought his parents argued perhaps every other week. He recalled no tension but noted that his mother had told him that Joe refused to communicate with her, leading to their divorce when Alan was six or seven. Angela, however, told the preschool director that she and Joe had three to four verbal fights a week. After the divorce, the boys were protective when Angela was dating. Alan recalled an incident when three little boys with baseball bats threatened one of her boyfriends. At another time, the police came, but Alan isn't sure what events preceded their arrival.

Alan also reported some physical abuse. Mother and father "whupped" him a couple of times a month from ages six to 12. He thought it started around the time of the divorce but according to Angela's account in the medical chart she was spanking before he was five. Joe spanked with his hand or a belt; Angela used a switch or a belt. According to Alan, the whippings left welts. Alan stated that his mother was angry, not enraged, and "knew when to stop." He noted that there was never a time when they had to be taken to the hospital or couldn't sit down after a spanking. He felt that she was basically fair, and such whippings were the community standard.

Alan reported a period of physical neglect. During his sophomore and junior years of high school, Alan and his brothers lived with their father while Angela was struggling with depression and trying to complete her master's degree in special education. Sometimes the boys ate hot dogs for all three meals. Alan wonders whether they really liked hot dogs or whether the larder was otherwise bare. Frequently, the utilities were turned off, sometimes for as long as a two-week pay cycle. They burned candles at night, used the toilet at a nearby emergency room, and showered at school. Alan remembers sleeping in one bed with his brothers to keep warm when their father was sleeping comfortably across town with his girlfriend. Alan used money earned at an after-school job to have a phone installed and pay the bill. Joe often borrowed $20 from Alan but usually paid him back. We considered this to be moderate physical neglect: While Joe ostensibly had the financial resources to pay the bills, he often did not, and he gave himself preferential treatment over his sons.

Although our study focused primarily on maltreatment as sources of risk, Alan's narrative revealed other risk factors, including his previously mentioned handicap. He suffered two important losses during childhood. His grandfather died when Alan was three. According to chart notes, he was still questioning his mother about grandfather's death two years later. When Angela finally got to the bottom of his concerns, he revealed that he couldn't understand how his grandfather could get to heaven if he was buried underground. When he was 12, Grandma Ella died. Alan was again confused, this time because the cause of her death was "a cut on her finger." He recalls sitting in the funeral home with Mark's arm around him, saying over and over, "I hate death." His hatred of death dogged him until his twenties, when his religious faith facilitated greater understanding and acceptance.

Alan mentioned Angela's struggles with depression when he was 15 and she was briefly hospitalized. According to chart notes, Angela reported being depressed during her pregnancy with Alan, and she appeared to be depressed when he began preschool. Alan recalls his mother crying frequently, talking about how hard it was to raise three boys alone. He didn't take this as rejection but rather as her wish for Joe to appreciate her struggles. When Alan was a junior in high school, Joe, then 43, was treated for colon cancer. The next year he had a recurrence. He died when Alan was 20.

Racism, first in the form of name-calling by other children in elementary school, was a common and disturbing experience. Even his best friend, Ted Leary, used a racial epithet. In high school, racism surfaced around dating. He and a close friend, a white girl, went everywhere together, even to the movies. But her parents refused to let her "date" him. He met Marnie in his junior year, and they dated until graduation. She was the only girl "who had the guts to tell her mother that she was dating me."

Angela struggled financially. After the divorce Joe provided no child support. Alan remembers getting "fancy cereal" and real eggs on special occasions. He feels ashamed that they received food stamps and public assistance, and that an unknown benefactress contributed to their private school tuition.

Protective Factors

In our study, we considered the following protective factors, queried by the Childhood Experiences of Care and Abuse interview: relationships that were protective "enough," childhood competence in academic and non-academic areas, and mastery, that is, the ability to solve problems effectively and to solicit help constructively. The following paragraphs focus on the protective nature of Alan's close relationships, noting their connection to mastery and competence.

Alan's mother was strict and demanding, but also loving and comforting. She set the rules, maintained mealtimes and bedtimes, and expected the boys to share the work of the household. Once when Alan left for school alone, thinking his brothers would cause him to be late, she ran after him and took him out of class to warn him that it wasn't safe to walk alone. Angela was a willing audience for the boys' skits and musical performances at home and at school. She made sure that they had regular medical and dental care. Joe and relatives on both sides of the family were strongly opposed to correcting Alan's leg deformity, but she insisted.

Both parents listened carefully, mentalizing Alan's tales of conflict, deciding if he was at fault or if he had been treated unfairly. In the former case, he was punished. In the latter, they never hesitated to call a parent, teacher, or principal to defend him. His capacity to mentalize was probably strengthened by how well they heard him. After returning from scout camp at age 12, he felt that his mother's assignment of chores was unfair and told her that he wanted to move in with his father. She called Joe, who modified his bachelor existence so that Alan could live there for a year.

He sought comfort from his mother in most realms. When other children called him names

> [s]he would just explain that you're going to come up against these kind of people in the world and you can either react negatively to it or know when to just turn and walk away, or be bigger than they are. She didn't let them attack me – the person. I can remember sitting on the couch with her arm around me and just her letting me know it's okay. And, just explaining how the world works, you know.

Some teachers suggested to Alan in his sophomore year that he ask a senior girl, also a friend, to the prom because she didn't have a date. His mother ran interference for him, calling the girl's parents to be sure Alan's invitation would be well-received. He went to her with questions about sex, not to Joe. In his distress, Angela was always there to "put those big old arms around me," to rock him even in adolescence, helping him to regulate his emotions.

Angela encouraged respect and politeness, especially to adults. When transported by other children's parents, he always offered gas money. He now considers that this was a way for him to disarm racists. Despite his experiences with racism, he found people to care about him in his neighborhood, at school, at church, in his sports leagues. Doubtless, the social skills modeled and taught by both parents helped him develop social competence and handle racist encounters with a sense of agency.

Angela was almost but not quite perfect. When Alan got his first paying job as a sophomore, she complained that she had to transport him. He reminded her of her parents' reaction when she got her first job.

Alan's father was very well-known and respected in the community. People still stop Alan to reminisce about Joe. He knew how to take care of himself and avoid risks as a black man in a predominantly white community. From Alan's perspective, Joe never felt second class to anyone. He has a clear memory of his father taking him out in a field for an entire day when he was 11, and helping him master the skills involved in football. Football became his sport, and he proceeded to win recognition and awards for his abilities. Joe wasn't as available as Alan would have liked after the divorce, and Alan was sorry to miss out on father–son events. As Alan matured, he began to see Joe as a mentor who respected his right to make his own decisions and actively encouraged him to be the best person he could be.

Joe was a negative role model because of his inability to provide for his family. At Joe's funeral, many priests and ministers described him as "a giant of a man":

> And I was sitting next to my grandfather, my dad's dad. And he had this blank expression on his face, because these guys were not talking about my dad. They were talking about some image that overall he wasn't, you know. I just feel like my dad made some mistakes. He did the best he could but he wasn't a giant, he wasn't superman. And I can remember thinking and grabbing my grandpa by the hand and walking out of the funeral because they weren't talking about my dad.

Alan has fond memories of spending his afternoons at Grandma Ella's apartment throughout elementary school. She taught the boys to sew and they made plastic-covered book bags. Most important, during her lifetime, she fostered a sense of identity and family pride – a cultural secure base.

> She was kind of the matriarch of the family. Growing up, we always had family reunions, big family reunions, and we could always count on Grandma Ella making her peach cobbler. You know, when she died, that was one less reason to celebrate. And over time as the older members have passed away, the reunion has just kind of slid down to the point that, really, now, none of us knucklehead young kids take the time to put it together … Death didn't really bring the family closer together; it kind of crumbled the foundation of the family. I don't have the history. That's

what we lost. We lost part of the family tree, the history that could tie everybody together ... what I see now is what, just as a black person in general, I feel like it's kind of hard to know your roots because they were just torn ... Then when your elders in your family start dying – Boom! – you just lost probably 70 years of your family history.

Alan met his current best friend, Ted Leary, in third grade, and they played together, stuck up for each other, and confided about everything except racism. He also developed a close relationship with Ted's father. Mr. Leary was available to Alan when his own father wasn't and, according to Alan, treated him like a son. Alan was adept at making and keeping friends. In high school, he was a major player in the most prestigious clique. An average student – he says that he never pushed himself academically – he "got back on track" when the mother of a good friend encouraged him to improve his grades so that he could go to college. In his junior and senior years he made As and Bs. Thus Alan had a range of exceptionally protective relationships, and his needs were met by the many members of his social world.

Adulthood Functioning

When we met Alan as an adult, he was living with his wife of 15 years, Suzanne, in a house out in the country. They had been college sweethearts. After he proposed, she became pregnant, and they married. At the time of our interview, Suzanne was pregnant with their fifth child and in business breeding and training golden retrievers at home. Alan was very involved in church and his children's school and sports activities. The account below describes his functioning at work, as a marriage partner, and as a friend over the five years before the interview.

After college, Alan worked for a company that provided services to the state and other large-scale employers. He began as a clerk and advanced until he was negotiating contracts with CEOs and the governor, and he was managing accounts receivable for his company. He did not have supervisory authority over his two assistants. He often found it easier to do a task himself rather than ask an irritable, if competent, assistant. Because he had worked his way up, he knew the content of others' jobs and felt he was respectful of them. His performance reviews were always excellent. He was not assertive about his own complaints. He twice applied for a managerial position and was turned down. In the first instance, he felt that the process was unfair but didn't tell his supervisor. The second time, he realized that he needed to leave the company.

A year before we met Alan, he had been recruited by a national company that wanted a visible minority presence. He had gone through seven months of training and passed certification exams, had set up his own office and hired staff, and was now struggling "to get my numbers up." He likes making his own hours and hiring his own staff. He tells them, "If we like each other, that's gravy but we're here to get a job done." The pressures are great and the hours demanding, limiting his time with his family. Racism has reared its ugly head:

I have had customers who left my business just because of my race. They haven't even had a chance to meet me. So to me that's a person going out of their way to give me a hard time. Because most people meet me like me. So, but again, I think that it's their deal, I don't have anything to do with it.

Although Suzanne is Native American and he is African-American, they have much in common. They were raised Catholic, their parents divorced, their fathers worked for the city, and their mothers struggle with depression. Unlike their siblings, they have stayed in Lincoln and look after older family members. Early in their relationship, they agreed to refrain from name-calling when fighting. Alan thinks it's hard enough to resolve what you are fighting about, so why add an extra burden? He and Suzanne enjoy gardening and bird-watching together, and being with their children. They confide in depth about each other's families, finances, and childrearing, and support each other in dealing with ageing family members. Sometimes Alan feels under-appreciated – after all, he doesn't run around or drink. "But it's not about whether she appreciates me or not, it's about me doing what I'm supposed to do."

Three years ago they were not intimate for 10 months. "We still loved each other but we didn't like each other." Alan had taken out a loan to start a business without telling (or mentalizing) Suzanne, hoping to surprise her with a *fait accompli*. She was furious not to have been included in his decision-making, and he ultimately recognized that she was right. Now they fight weekly, usually because he has forgotten to let her know about his schedule. He likes to talk things through at the time of the fight, and she prefers to wait a while. His recognition of this difference suggests awareness of mental states. They sometimes express their anger in action as well, by sleeping on the couch.

Until Suzanne began to stay home and raise dogs two years ago, household responsibilities were evenly divided, and not long ago when she had an evening job, he helped with cooking, cleaning, and laundry every night. At this point, she does the shopping, cooking, cleaning, and bill paying, partly because she has a certain way she wants things done. He helps her with cleaning up after dinner and makes all the repairs. Because they have so many meetings, he wants to help her more in the evenings, something he reflected upon during his interview. They try to set aside time after the children are in bed as their special time together. The house is usually clean and in order, they eat on time, and clean clothes are available. They buy what they need and sacrifice where they have to, never accumulating any serious debt.

Alan has two very close friends: Ted, who now lives 30 miles away, and Ben. He and Ted see or talk to each other about five times a month, communicating by phone, e-mail, or in person. After all three attended a church event where men were encouraged to get together and to be accountable to one another, they established "Dad's night," a bi-weekly get-together where they talk "men talk" and discuss their kids. Alan tells Ben and Ted about his marital problems and his job stress. He and Ben see each other more frequently because they live in the same community. They attend church meetings and Sunday prayer group each week, help each other with practical things like construction projects, and fish together.

Alan remains in touch with two college friends. He sees James every couple of months for an athletic event. Ron has just moved back to Lincoln from New York. Alan visited him there a few times. He feels excited that they are becoming closer again. Alan recently met Doug through their daughters' soccer team. Unlike Alan's other friends, he's quite a bit older and very opinionated. But they have learned to rely on each other. Doug "would loan you $10 in a minute"; he helps with practical things until the job is done. Doug took over Alan's coaching job when he started his new business venture. We considered Alan to be an exceptional friend.

Psychiatric Disorder and Mentalizing Capacity

Alan did not meet criteria for any psychiatric disorder. "Down" feelings last minutes rather than days, and he easily distracts himself, evidencing the capacity to self-regulate through selective attention. Unlike the vast majority of our participants, Alan has no history of alcohol or drug abuse, even during his college years. He endorsed some narcissistic traits: he likes to be admired, dresses in a way that attracts attention, likes to spend time with people who are influential, and expects others to do what he asks without question because of who he is. We saw these traits as manifestations of healthy narcissism. His physical health is excellent.

Alan's scores on the Eyes test and on the Reflective Function Scale were both above the mean for our sample, indicating that he has better than average mentalizing skills.

DISCUSSION

How important was mentalizing in helping Alan cope with adversity? What is the evidence for its relationship to his developmental path and current functioning? Our account of his development suggests that he did not have a secure early attachment with his mother. Angela found it hard to hold Alan's mind in her mind during his infancy and preschool years. Her own depression, fears, and lack of support limited her ability to tolerate his distress and accept his vulnerabilities.

She found his persistent questions (e.g., about his grandfather's death) irritating, and she felt obligated to transform his distress to happiness. It was not surprising that Alan felt misunderstood, afraid, and angry.

Alan's enrollment in the therapeutic nursery was a significant turning point. The director mentalized Angela, realizing how alone and overwhelmed she felt. With her direction, Angela was able to tolerate Alan's feelings and help him articulate them. By taking his questions seriously, she began to focus on and learn about what was going on in his mind. As Alan developed, Angela's role as comforter was crucially important. By holding and rocking him, she helped him regulate his distress so that he could think with her about alternatives. His capacity to self-regulate may explain his impulse control in adolescence. He has been drunk only once, and he chose to postpone sexual intercourse until college.

Angela responded to Alan's racist encounters by mentalizing, conveying her understanding of how this felt to him. She explained how the world worked but expressed her view that he could be bigger and walk away. She protected him when she could, presented options and advice about how to handle himself, and expressed confidence that he would ultimately be okay. She did not minimize or deny racism's impact on his daily life. Alan commented that she helped him feel that he, the person, wasn't the problem. He now speaks about racism in mentalistic terms. He interprets his friend Ted's name-calling in elementary school as a "dig," rather than reflecting malignant intent. He notes with indignation the hypocrisy of his white female friends and their parents, in contrast to his girlfriend with "guts." With conscious effort, he now separates the racist mental states that he encounters in his business from the man he is.

Alan was surrounded by a community of people who cared enough: Angela and Joe, who collaborated as parents more easily after than before their divorce, his extended family, particularly his great-grandmother, friends' parents, and teachers. While many children would have felt isolated and alienated as one of a tiny minority at church and at school, he found it a challenge to relate to people from diverse races and religions. Politeness is a social skill, not an aspect of mentalizing. In Alan's case, however, politeness was linked with awareness of how other minds are likely to perceive one's actions, and with a sense of agency. His behavior apparently changed the way other people regarded him and other African-Americans. The links between his efforts to be heard and appreciated and the responses of adults around him conferred efficacy and self-esteem, qualities that support resilience (Rutter, 1987) and develop in tandem with mentalizing.

As a mentalizing adult, Alan has created a complex web of secure attachments and a range of relationships, including intimacy with his wife and best friends, collaboration with Doug, easy-going interaction with neighbors and church members, and institutional attachments to church and work. Keeping close to a secure base is very important to Alan. As a result, perhaps, he is a cautious planner in contrast to his brothers who have left Lincoln. Unplanned events tend to fit in with his larger plan or are the impetus for a proactive plan. Not getting a promotion prompted his leaving the security of his company job for a business of his own. Mentalizing is not the crux of planning but, in order to make workable plans, the kinds of cognitive operations involved in mentalizing are very helpful – considering and playing with alternatives, forecasting their impact on self and others, and being able to think flexibly.

While his capacity to mentalize is evident in his relationships, Alan also shares an account of his miscalculations of the workings of others' minds. His 10 months of distance with Suzanne had its origin in his failure to consider her wish to be involved in an important family decision. Their conflicts involve his failures to communicate his schedule, currently a product of the demands of his new business. But he also knows that they fight differently, and he used the interview process to reflect on increasing his share of household responsibilities.

The coherence of Alan's narrative also testifies to his mentalizing abilities. He came with a clearly stated agenda, to show us that children growing up poor and African-American in a single-parent family can become successful adults. Nonetheless, his account of his early years, consonant with his medical chart, illustrates his awareness of his interviewers' agenda. He provided a missing piece, conveying the details of the repetitive childhood nightmare that woke him repeatedly. Like many healthy adults, he minimized his hardships, making light of the impact and frequency of his mother's depressions and dismissing the welts left by whippings as innocuous. He remembered his beloved mother being his rescuer from the vicious dog. Perhaps his lack of recall of the extent of his parents' conflicts has helped him protect his relationships with them. Yet, at the same time, he presents most of those close to him as complex individuals who made mistakes but, enough of the time, took his own mind into consideration.

Mentalizing hardly accounts for all aspects of Alan's successful adaptation. While Angela's ability to mentalize him improved when he was five, many other changes occurred simultaneously. His leg braces came off, removing a major obstacle to his sense of physical safety, independent functioning (including toileting), and healthy expression of aggression. A year or two later, family conflicts diminished with his parents' divorce. Although, in an earlier section of the chapter I discouraged thinking of resilience as the product of individual traits, Alan's constitution and temperament made an obvious contribution. His physical endowment at 10 months propelled him to walk despite his handicap, and then to relearn to walk. A day of football practice with his father at 11 put him on a trajectory as an athlete that won him awards, recognition, and a college scholarship. Despite his frequent meltdowns at the therapeutic preschool, teachers and peers responded to his outgoing personality, sensitivity, and intellectual curiosity. Now his commanding physical presence, his choice of clothes, and his extroverted yet sensitive manner demands attention and earns liking and respect from anyone who gets to know him.

Alan also has been sustained by strong values and a moral center, factors molded and strongly reinforced by his religious beliefs. He states that he does what is right because it is right. The intergenerational connectedness in Angela's family and Joe's lapses helped solidify Alan's own sense of commitment and loyalty to family. Both parents had a strong work ethic, and Alan has been a hard worker from the moment of his first step. A desire for fair treatment remains an important value, probably fueled by competition with his brothers, his own experiences of handicap and racism, and his mother's efforts to provide fairly for her sons.

CONCLUSION

This chapter began by reviewing the research literature on resilience, including risk and protective factors and developmentally appropriate outcomes. Mentalizing was explored as a key mechanism of resilience. Likely to flourish in the context of secure attachment and playful interaction and wither in an atmosphere of maltreatment, the capacity to mentalize develops in tandem with self-regulation and attentional control. Mentalizing individuals have alternative ways of conceiving of their own and other minds, are able to reflect on their own mental states, make clear judgments about others' mental states, and avoid impulsive choices. They are better prepared for resilient adaptation in the face of adversity.

The case example described Alan and his family's efforts to cope with adversities including physical handicap, marital conflict and divorce, poverty, racism, mental and physical illness, and loss, along with some maltreatment. After a shaky beginning, Alan's mother discovered a way to listen to and comfort her son, validating his hard realities, protecting him when she could, and expressing confidence in his ability to endure. Alan has found his way, struggling to mentalize at times in his marriage, but using it to understand his mistakes, to contend with racism, and to succeed with a wide range of constructive relationships.

The stated purpose of this chapter is to provide clinicians with concepts that enrich clinical understanding. This leads me to a cautious conclusion. In contrast to other resilient individuals included in the Menninger research project, Alan has met age-appropriate cultural expectations and functions optimally across many domains. Persons like Alan, however, do not frequent our consulting rooms. Although many of our research participants have not met conventional expectations, a number have made ingenuous life choices, finding niches in the world that work for them. As clinicians, we need to look beyond cultural expectations and understand and support our patients' adaptations in the context of their histories and their current strengths and vulnerabilities.

REFERENCES

Appleyard, K., Egeland, B., van Dulmen, M. H. M. & Sroufe, L. A. (2005). When more is not better: the role of cumulative risk in child behavior outcomes. *Journal of Child Psychology and Psychiatry, and Allied Disciplines, 46,* 235–245.

Baron-Cohen, S., Joliffe, T., Mortimore, C. & Robertson, M. (1997). Another advanced test of theory of mind: evidence from very high functioning adults with autism or Asperger syndrome. *Journal of Child Psychology and Psychiatry, and Allied Disciplines, 38,* 813–822.

Bateman, A. & Fonagy, P. (2004). *Psychotherapy for Borderline Personality Disorder.* Oxford, England: Oxford University Press.

Bifulco, A., Brown, G. W., Neubauer, A., Moran, P. M. & Harris, T. O. (1994). *Childhood Experiences of Care and Abuse (CECA) Training Manual.* London: Royal Holloway, University of London.

Bolger, K. E. & Patterson, C. J. (2003). Sequelae of child maltreatment: vulnerability and resilience. In S. S. Luthar (ed.), *Resilience and Vulnerability: Adaptation in the Context of Childhood Adversities* (pp. 156–181). Cambridge, England: Cambridge University Press.

Conger, R. D., Cui, M., Bryant, C. M. & Elder, G. H. (2000). Competence in early adult romantic relationships: a developmental perspective on family influences. *Journal of Personality and Social Psychology, 79,* 224–237.

Fergusson, D. & Horwood, L. J. (2003). Resilience to childhood adversity: results of a 21-year study. In S. S. Luthar (ed.), *Resilience and Vulnerability: Adaptation in the Context of Childhood Adversities* (pp. 130–155). Cambridge, England: Cambridge University Press.

First, M. B., Gibbon, M., Spitzer, R. L. & Williams, J. W. (1997). *Structured Clinical Interview for DSM-IV Personality Disorders (SCID-II) Questionnaire.* Washington, DC: American Psychiatric Publishing.

First, M. B., Spitzer, R. L., Gibbon, M. & Williams, J. B. W. (1996). *Structured Clinical Interview for DSM-IV Axis I Disorders, SCID-I, Clinician Version (SCID-CV).* Washington, DC: American Psychiatric Press.

Fonagy, P., Leigh, T., Steele, M., Steele, H., Kennedy, R., Mattoon, G., et al. (1996). The relation of attachment status, psychiatric classification, and response to psychotherapy. *Journal of Consulting and Clinical Psychology, 64,* 22–31.

Fonagy, P., Steele, M., Steele, H., Higgitt, A. & Target, M. (1994). Theory and practice of resilience. *Child Psychology and Psychiatry, 35,* 231–257.

Fonagy, P., Stein, H., Allen, J. G., Allen, D., Chen, C. F. & Vrouva, I. (2006). The relationship of childhood and adolescent adversity to impairment of mentalizing capacity and psychological disorder Unpublished manuscript. University College London, London, UK.

Fonagy, P., Target, M., Steele, M. & Steele, H. (1998). *Reflective-Functioning Manual, Version 5.0, for Application to Adult Attachment Interviews.* London: University College London.

George, C., Kaplan, N. & Main, M. (1985). *The Berkeley Adult Attachment Interview,* Unpublished protocol. Berkeley, CA: Department of Psychology, University of California.

Grossman, J. B. & Rhodes, J. E. (2002). The test of time: predictors and effects of duration of in youth mentoring relationships. *American Journal of Community Psychiatry, 30,* 199–219.

Hammen, C. (2003). Risk and protective factors for children of depressed parents. In S. S. Luthar (ed.), *Resilience and Vulnerability: Adaptation in the Context of Childhood Adversities* (pp. 50–75). Cambridge, England: Cambridge University Press.

Heinicke, C. M., Rineman, N. R., Ponce, V. A. & Guthrie, D. (2001). Relation-based intervention with at-risk mothers: outcome in the second year of life. *Infant Mental Health Journal, 22*, 431–462.

Hill, J. & Stein, H. (2002). *Revised Adult Personality Functioning Assessment* (Tech. Rep. No. 02–0052). Topeka, KS: The Menninger Clinic, Research Department.

Luthar, S. S. & Zelazo, L. B. (2003). Research on resilience: an integrative review. In S. S. Luthar (ed.), *Resilience and Vulnerability: Adaptation in the Context of Childhood Adversities* (pp. 510–549). Cambridge, England: Cambridge University Press.

Luthar, S. S. (2006). Historical overview of childhood resilience: central features. In D. Cicchetti & D. J. Cohen (eds), *Developmental Psychopathology: Risk, Disorder, and Adaptation* (2nd edn). (pp 739–795) New York: John Wiley & Sons, Inc.

Rhodes, J. E., Grossman, J. B. & Resch, N. L. (2000). Agents of change: pathways through which mentoring relationships influence adolescents' academic adjustment. *Child Development, 21*, 1662–1671.

Rutter, M. (1985). Resilience in the face of adversity: protective factors and resistance to psychiatric disorder. *British Journal of Psychiatry, 147*, 598–611.

Rutter, M. (1987). Psychosocial resilience and protective mechanisms. *American Journal of Orthopsychiatry, 57*, 316–331.

Rutter, M. (1999). Resilience concepts and findings: implications for family therapy. *Journal of Family Psychotherapy, 21*, 119–144.

Sameroff, A., Gutman, L. M. & Peck, S. C. (2003). Adaptation among youth facing multiple risks: prospective research findings. In S. S. Luthar (ed.), *Resilience and Vulnerability: Adaptation in the Context of Childhood Adversities* (pp. 364–391). Cambridge, England: Cambridge University Press.

Sandler, I., Wolchik, S., Davis, C., Haine, R. & Ayers, T. (2003). Correlational and experimental study of resilience in children of divorce and parentally bereaved children. In S. S. Luthar (ed.), *Resilience and Vulnerability: Adaptation in the Context of Childhood Adversities* (pp. 213–242). Cambridge, England: Cambridge University Press.

Schecter, D. S. (2003). Intergenerational communication of maternal violent trauma: understanding the interplay of reflective functioning and posttraumatic psychopathology. In S. W. Coates, J. L. Rosenthal & D. S. Schecter (eds), *September 11 Trauma and Human Bonds* (pp. 115–142). Hillsdale, NJ, Analytic Press.

Stein, H., Allen, D., Allen, J. G., Koontz, A. D. & Wisman, M. (2000b). *Supplementary Manual for Scoring Bifulco's Childhood Experience of Care and Abuse Interview (M-CECA): Version 2.0.* Topeka, KS: The Menninger Clinic Research Department.

Stein, H., Fonagy, P., Ferguson, K. S. & Wisman, M. (2000a). Lives through time: an ideographic approach to the study of resilience. *Bulletin of The Menninger Clinic, 64*, 281–305.

Toth, S. L., Maughan, A., Manly, J. T., Spagnola, M. & Cicchetti, D. (2002). The relative efficacy of two interventions in altering maltreated preschool children's representational models: implications for attachment theory. *Development and Psychopathology, 14*, 877–908.

Vaillant, G. (2002). *Aging Well.* Boston, MA: Little, Brown and Company.

Waller, M. A. (2001). Resilience in ecosystemic context: evolution of the concept. *American Journal of Orthopsychiatry, 71*, 290–297.

EPILOGUE
THINKING ABOUT MENTALIZATION

Robert Michels

It is surprising when those who are advancing a new therapeutic strategy announce in the first paragraph of their introduction that it is the "least novel" approach imaginable and that they "claim no innovation." Yet whatever modesty may be involved, this assertion is central to the concept of mentalization, and to its role in therapy as presented by Allen and Fonagy. They have taken a virtually universal elemental human capacity, indeed one that is at the core of our definition of being human, and made it the object of careful study. It is central to normal psychological functioning, disturbed in a number of pathological conditions, importantly shaped by early experience with primary caretakers, potentially modified by later experience in critical relationships (such as with therapists, almost regardless of the therapist's theoretical beliefs or preferred methods) and therefore offers an important new perspective on psychological functioning, early development, psychopathology and psychotherapy.

What is mentalization? Is it a familiar notion or a new one? To what does it call our attention and from what might it distract us? What is its significance in treatment, and does it make any difference if the therapist has it in mind? With what patients and in what treatments is it likely to be helpful? Finally, what are the possible dangers, the cautions we should exercise regarding its impact on our thinking and on our therapeutic work? This collection of studies of mentalization-based treatments invites our consideration of all of these questions.

DEFINITION

Holmes quotes Bateman and Fonagy's 2004 definition: "the mental process by which an individual implicitly and explicitly interprets the actions of himself and

Handbook of Mentalization-Based Treatment. Edited by J. G. Allen and P. Fonagy.
© 2006 John Wiley & Sons, Ltd.

others as meaningful on the basis of intentional mental states such as personal desires, needs, feelings, beliefs and reasons." Allen condenses this to "attending to states of mind in oneself and others," and admires Fonagy's even terser "holding mind in mind." Allen and Fonagy think of it as a skill (they call it a "dynamic skill," but Bateman and Fonagy make clear that by "dynamic" they don't mean psycho-dynamic – that is, determined by mental forces in conflict, but rather as developing in a relationship context and vulnerable to environmental deficiencies).

Some features of these definitions merit our attention:

(1) Mentalization is mental – not neurobiological or social. As with other mental phenomena, we may be interested in neurobiological correlates, or social context, or developmental origins, or evolutionary adaptive value, and this volume speculates about each of these, but the phenomenon itself is mental.

(2) Mentalization is a process, skill, or capacity – not a wish, desire, motive, etc. It refers to the way the mind works, an abstract psychological concept, not to the contents of subjective experience the things we all have in mind. Allen and Fonagy thought about mentalizing while writing this book, and I have thought about it while reading it and writing this epilogue, but patients don't think about it (even while doing it) and, at least until now, neither have therapists.

(3) Mentalization may be explicit (conscious, verbal) or implicit (pre-conscious). This distinction is mentioned, but not emphasized in these papers. To me it seems crucial. Mentalization is normally implicit – most humans employ the capacity constantly but rarely if ever think about it explicitly. It is acquired as infants interact with caretakers in dyads, neither member of which has ever heard of mentalizing. When all goes well – like respiration, digestion or circulation – there is no need to think about it (indeed, thinking about it may even interfere with it). Allen, Fonagy and others argue that, when all hasn't gone well, the capacity fails to develop or its development is impaired, and that treatment may correct this deficit. However the deficit is in implicit mentalization, while treatments aimed at mentalization for the most part seem to emphasize explicit mentalization. Allen suggests (p. 10) that a "gradual process of representational re-description from implicit to explicit which takes place over the course of development – and over the course of psychotherapy." Is this the resumption of a development that was derailed because of failures in early relationships, or the learning of a replacement (explicit mentalization) for a normal capacity that for some reason has been aborted (implicit mentalization)? Bateman and Fonagy (p. 191) warn about "quasi-mentalizing in which the patient takes on the explanations without question and makes them his own." The question is whether the capacity for explicit mentalization developed in psychotherapy is a step toward the development of a capacity for implicit mentalization, the core human characteristic that has been impaired, or a kind of "quasi-mentalization" which

appears to be explicit mentalization but is more usefully understood as a transference enactment, an attempt to please or placate a therapist by pretending "humanoid" behavior, or more likely, when it is one and when it is the other.

(4) Mentalization refers both to oneself and to others. This seems fundamental to me, almost suggesting two distinct capacities, but again is not emphasized in these papers. Do they develop simultaneously or in sequence? Are there pathological conditions in which the major impairment is in one or the other? Are there treatment strategies that focus on one or the other?

(5) What are "intentional mental states?" Do they include unconscious as well as conscious mentation? How do they relate to the unconscious motives, wishes or drives so central to psychoanalytic theory and technique? How do they relate to feelings and desires that originate in the body, and for which others are "objects" in the pre-object relations meaning of necessary for gratification? Does "mentalization" as a concept presume object relations or interpersonal models of development, psychopathology and treatment? Does it distract from the traditional psychoanalytic concern with unconscious mental life, and particularly unconscious dynamic forces – wishes, fears and their derivatives?

Thus we have a rich concept, one that leads us to reconsider some of the core issues of psychoanalytic thinking – mentalism, explicit and implicit psychological functioning, self and other, and the content of mental life, both conscious and unconscious.

PSYCHOPATHOLOGY AND PSYCHOTHERAPY

The capacity for mentalization develops early in life. The original focus of psychoanalytic theory and therapy was not on such capacities, but rather on the contents of mental life – the wishes, fears, thoughts, emotions, fantasies, and conflicts that are experienced by patients, reported to therapists, and particularly when unconscious, central to the psychoanalytic understanding of psychopathology. The major emphasis of this early psychoanalytic thinking was on a period later than that in which the capacity for mentalization is believed to crystallize, one that was originally labeled the Oedipal period. Of course there is no contradiction between, on the one hand, an interest in mentalization and the first few years of life, and, on the other, an interest in the mental themes of the Oedipal period. Other psychoanalytic theories such as object relations or separation-individuation have focused on early or pre-Oedipal stages. However they have emphasized mental contents, subjective experience rather than psychological capacities.

Turning to psychopathology, earlier periods of development and disturbances of psychological capacity are usually associated with more serious psychopathology – autism, severe character disorders or borderline conditions rather than classical neuroses and less severe personality disorders. They are also associated with treatments designed to facilitate the development of absent or impaired psychic structure, rather than treatments that aim to expand awareness of unconscious themes and facilitate more adaptive patterns of conflict resolution. Mentalization therapies endeavor to facilitate the development of capacities that we presume the patient has failed to acquire – they are akin to treating dyslexia or doing physical therapy with a person who has cerebral palsy; they have important educational components and try to facilitate adaptation to deficits. Traditional psychoanalytic therapies employ interpretation to help the patient recognize and integrate wishes and fears that have been outside of awareness, but that have remained part of the patient's mental life. The integration that results may be new, but the components are not, and the treatment is more akin to debriding a wound or physical therapy for a patient recovering from a traumatic injury. It facilitates resolution of interferences or obstacles to optimal functioning, with the assumption that the capacity for such functioning has been present all along.

For patients who do not have major problems with mentalization, focusing on it would seem to have little therapeutic rationale. For patients who do have such problems, the traditional interpretive foci of dynamic psychotherapy would seem to offer little therapeutic leverage unless the deficit in mentalization is attended to first. A two-phase treatment in which the facilitation of mentalization is followed by an interpretive exploration of psychological conflicts also seems plausible, just as pharmacological approaches or non-interpretive soothing, holding or containing strategies have been suggested as preparatory to interpretive approaches. Just as with these other combined treatment strategies, there is a question of possible interference of one approach by the other. Can mentalization approaches interfere with dynamic psychotherapy? Does the deficit assumption lead to the avoidance of the exploration of unconscious conflict? How do we decide when mentalization is an optimal strategy as opposed to offering a transference–counter-transference collusion that fails to deal with the conflictual origins of a secondary inhibition?

The answers to these questions will require studies that have not yet been attempted. Fonagy, in other contexts, has asked, "What works for whom?" That is the question here. In general the demonstration that a well intentioned treatment helps a group of people tells us little unless we can specify what kind of people it helps and how the effects of this treatment compare with those of other well intentioned treatments. Mentalization-based therapies are well intentioned and have an interesting rationale. They have clearly earned the opportunity to be compared to other treatments with various groups of patients so that we can establish their appropriate role. On the basis of theory, we would predict that they are most appropriate for more impaired patients, those with disturbances of early relationships, apparent problems in mentalizing, and poor responses to more traditional therapies, and perhaps those without prominent focal symptoms or "Axis I" psychopathology.

THE MENTALIZING COMMUNITY

The theme of mentalization and its relation to the community or institutions that conduct the therapy is an important and welcome contribution of this volume. There are papers on mentalization therapies, on mentalization and other therapies, on training residents in mentalization, and on psycho-educational (rather than psychotherapeutic) approaches. Furthermore, the many papers from the Menninger institution together suggest a therapeutic culture in which mentalization has become an integrating symbol.

The papers on mentalization and traditional therapies tend to define mentalization in positive terms – as an inherent good, the more the better – rather than as a psychological capacity which like other capacities can be used pathologically as well as adaptively and which can be hyper-trophic as well as underdeveloped. This positive definition tends to sidestep the therapist's dilemma of when a mentalistic focus might not be a good idea as well as the potential risks of quasi-mentalization, a collaboration between patient and therapist to pretend mentalization without the real thing. In addition, these papers focus on explicit mentalization, seemingly with little concern for how this translates into the more normal implicit capacity. We are all familiar with the humorous portrayal of the psychotherapy patient who is preoccupied with his own and others' psycho-dynamics, oblivious to the way in which others respond. One can envision a person, or community, in which explicit preoccupation with quasi-mentalization leads to a similar phenomenon, but this is not discussed. Their general theme of the discussion of other therapies is that they have, each in their own way, been promoting mentalization all along and that the new theory provides a plausible description of a mechanism of action for the traditional therapy, along with suggestions for potential enhancement of its efficacy.

This calls to mind one of the important characteristics of new theories of psychotherapy. In general they are presented with arguments for the scientific validity of their underlying hypotheses and for the potential value of the specific interventions that they suggest – mentalization would be an example. However theories have other important although indirect effects as well. They are important to therapists who "believe" in them, affecting their allegiance, interests and attitudes, and supporting a positive outlook that may then be transmitted to patients. "Mentalization" has the characteristics of a good psychotherapy theory. It suggests a domain of inquiry in the clinical process – early childhood; it has powerful face-validity and it supports a therapeutic dialogue that is relatively jargon-free and conducted in the language of everyday experience – the kind of dialogue preferred by most experienced therapists. It also provides a bridge to empirical scientific inquiry – a powerful reassurance for contemporary therapists. Note that this does not mean that the therapy itself has been tested empirically, although there have been some early steps in that direction, nor even that the developmental hypothesis on which it is based has undergone critical tests, but rather that the conceptual model is derived from empirical research rather than clinical intuition.

These papers make clear that The Menninger Clinic has become a mentalization culture, that the training of residents in mentalization techniques involves the supervisor mentalizing with the resident, and that mentalization has become a central theme in the treatment of a wide variety of patients in a wide variety of settings. The nature of the theory, the method of training, and its incorporation into the culture of the institution all promote a powerful positive although indirect effect of the theory on the therapists who have embraced it. Its scientific status further enhances that effect.

MENTALIZATION AND POSITIVE PSYCHOLOGY

The book closes with a series of papers that view mentalization as a positive adaptive capacity, and in doing so shift from a medical model of pathology and therapy to an educational or public health perspective, with the hope for a method for preventing social disorder and for encouraging optimal childrearing. In many ways this highlights an essential characteristic of all mentalization-based therapies. They are designed to replace a missing or facilitate the improvement of a flawed essential "natural" capacity, not to treat a disorder. Metaphorically they are more akin to vitamins than to antibiotics – everyone needs them, most get an adequate supply in the normal course of development; for those who don't supplements may be essential, and although in rare cases overdoses may lead to harm, generally supplements do little damage. Finally there is little risk in combining them with other therapies, with the possible exception of those therapies that work by artificially interfering with the involved natural mechanism – anti-metabolites in the case of vitamins, and possibly some versions of psychoanalysis in the case of mentalization.

Developing and enhancing vital natural capacities is certainly a worthwhile goal, and interventions that achieve this may be of immense value with a variety of populations. The research designs that demonstrate the effectiveness of such interventions may be different, and perhaps more demanding, than those involved in evaluating treatments for specific disorders.

CONCLUSION

In summary, mentalization is a powerful theory that postulates an important psychological capacity, perhaps the most fundamental one that distinguishes humans from other animals. These papers offer a conceptual model of its development in the context of primary relationships, the potential for failures and derailment of that development, the role that this might play in the origins of psychopathology and possibilities for therapeutic interventions. A number of traditional treatments are reconsidered from the perspective of their relationship to mentalization, and several new mentalization-based treatments are described. In addition, the picture of a therapeutic culture that treats a variety of patients in a variety of settings, and that trains new therapists, all with mentalization as a prominent theme emerges. Finally, mentalization is considered as an adaptive skill relevant to positive mental health – education and prevention rather than pathology and treatment. Throughout, we are aware of a powerful and potentially transforming new paradigm, one that emphasizes psychological capacity rather than mental content, with the patient as learning to interpret rather than himself being the object of interpretation, and that promises the continuing production of important new knowledge. The importance of systematic empirical research in generating new ideas, in developing treatments, and in assessing their efficacy is emphasized throughout.

INDEX

Made in the USA
Lexington, KY
08 February 2019